THE CLAY SANSKRIT LIBRARY

FOUNDED BY JOHN & JENNIFER CLAY

GENERAL EDITOR

Sheldon Pollock

EDITED BY

Isabelle Onians

www.claysanskritlibrary.com

www.nyupress.org

Artwork by Robert Beer.
Typeset in Adobe Garamond Pro at 10.25 : 12.3+pt.
XML-development by Stuart Brown.
Editorial input from Dániel Balogh, Ridi Faruque,
Chris Gibbons, Tomoyuki Kono & Eszter Somogyi.
Printed and bound in Great Britain by
T.J. International, Cornwall, on acid-free paper.

BHAṬṬI'S POEM: THE DEATH OF RĀVAṆA

by BHAṬṬI

TRANSLATED BY

Oliver Fallon

NEW YORK UNIVERSITY PRESS

JJC FOUNDATION

2009

First Edition 2009

The Clay Sanskrit Library is co-published by
New York University Press
and the JJC Foundation.

Further information about this volume
and the rest of the Clay Sanskrit Library
is available at the end of this book
and on the following websites:
www.claysanskritlibrary.com
www.nyupress.org

ISBN-13: 978-0-8147-2778-2 (cloth : alk. paper)
ISBN-10: 0-8147-2778-6 (cloth : alk. paper)

Library of Congress Cataloging-in-Publication Data
Bhaṭṭi.
[Bhaṭṭikāvya. English & Sanskrit]
Bhatti's poem : the death of Ravana / by Bhatti ;
translated by Oliver Fallon. -- 1st ed.
p. cm.
In English and Sanskrit (romanized) on facing pages;
includes translation from Sanskrit.
Includes bibliographical references.
ISBN-13: 978-0-8147-2778-2 (cl : alk. paper)
ISBN-10: 0-8147-2778-6 (cl : alk. paper)
I. Fallon, Oliver. II. Title.
PK3791.B562B513 2009
891.2'1--dc22
2008048540

CONTENTS

CSL CONVENTIONS

Sanskrit Alphabetical Order

Vowels: *a ā i ī u ū ṛ ṝ ḷ ḹ e ai o au ṃ ḥ*
Gutturals: *k kh g gh ṅ*
Palatals: *c ch j jh ñ*
Retroflex: *ṭ ṭh ḍ ḍh ṇ*
Dentals: *t th d dh n*
Labials: *p ph b bh m*
Semivowels: *y r l v*
Spirants: *ś ṣ s h*

Guide to Sanskrit Pronunciation

a b*u*t
ā, â f*a*ther
i s*i*t
ī, î f*ee*
u p*u*t
ū, û b*oo*
ṛ vocalic *r*, American p*ur*dy or English p*re*tty
ṝ lengthened *ṛ*
ḷ vocalic *l*, ab*le*
e, ê, ē m*a*de, esp. in Welsh pronunciation
ai b*i*te
o, ô, ō r*o*pe, esp. Welsh pronunciation; Italian s*o*lo
au s*ou*nd
ṃ *anusvāra* nasalizes the preceding vowel
ḥ *visarga*, a voiceless aspiration (resembling the English *h*), or like Scottish lo*ch*, or an aspiration with a faint echoing of the last element of the preceding vowel so that *taiḥ* is pronounced *taih^{i}*
k lu*ck*
kh blo*ckh*ead
g *g*o
gh bi*gh*ead
ṅ a*n*ger
c *ch*ill
ch mat*chh*ead
j *j*og
jh aspirated *j*, he*dgeh*og
ñ ca*ny*on
ṭ retroflex *t*, *t*ry (with the tip of tongue turned up to touch the hard palate)
ṭh same as the preceding but aspirated
ḍ retroflex *d* (with the tip

	of tongue turned up to touch the hard palate)	*b*	*b*efore
		bh	a*bh*orrent
ḍh	same as the preceding but aspirated	*m*	*m*ind
		y	*y*es
ṇ	retroflex *n* (with the tip of tongue turned up to touch the hard palate)	*r*	trilled, resembling the Italian pronunciation of *r*
		l	*l*inger
t	French *t*out	*v*	*w*ord
th	ten*t h*ook	*ś*	*sh*ore
d	*d*inner	*ṣ*	retroflex *sh* (with the tip of the tongue turned up to touch the hard palate)
dh	guil*dh*all		
n	*n*ow		
p	*p*ill	*s*	hi*ss*
ph	u*ph*eaval	*h*	*h*ood

CSL Punctuation of English

The acute accent on Sanskrit words when they occur outside of the Sanskrit text itself, marks stress, e.g., Ramáyana. It is not part of traditional Sanskrit orthography, transliteration, or transcription, but we supply it here to guide readers in the pronunciation of these unfamiliar words. Since no Sanskrit word is accented on the last syllable it is not necessary to accent disyllables, e.g., Rama.

The second CSL innovation designed to assist the reader in the pronunciation of lengthy unfamiliar words is to insert an unobtrusive middle dot between semantic word breaks in compound names (provided the word break does not fall on a vowel resulting from the fusion of two vowels), e.g., Maha·bhárata, but Ramáyana (not Rama·áyana). Our dot echoes the punctuating middle dot (·) found in the oldest surviving samples of written Indic, the Ashokan inscriptions of the third century BCE.

The deep layering of Sanskrit narrative has also dictated that we use quotation marks only to announce the beginning and end of every direct speech, and not at the beginning of every paragraph.

CSL Punctuation of Sanskrit

The Sanskrit text is also punctuated, in accordance with the punctuation of the English translation. In mid-verse, the punctuation will not alter the sandhi or the scansion. Proper names are capitalized. Most Sanskrit meters have four "feet" (*pāda*); where possible we print the common *śloka* meter on two lines. In the Sanskrit text, we use French *Guillemets* (e.g., *«kva saṃcicīrṣuḥ?»*) instead of English quotation marks (e.g., "Where are you off to?") to avoid confusion with the apostrophes used for vowel elision in sandhi.

SANDHI

Sanskrit presents the learner with a challenge: *sandhi* (euphonic combination). Sandhi means that when two words are joined in connected speech or writing (which in Sanskrit reflects speech), the last letter (or even letters) of the first word often changes; compare the way we pronounce "the" in "the beginning" and "the end."

In Sanskrit the first letter of the second word may also change; and if both the last letter of the first word and the first letter of the second are vowels, they may fuse. This has a parallel in English: a nasal consonant is inserted between two vowels that would otherwise coalesce: "a pear" and "an apple." Sanskrit vowel fusion may produce ambiguity.

The charts on the following pages give the full sandhi system.

Fortunately it is not necessary to know these changes in order to start reading Sanskrit. All that is important to know is the form of the second word without sandhi (pre-sandhi), so that it can be recognized or looked up in a dictionary. Therefore we are printing Sanskrit with a system of punctuation that will indicate, unambiguously, the original form of the second word, i.e., the form without sandhi. Such sandhi mostly concerns the fusion of two vowels.

In Sanskrit, vowels may be short or long and are written differently accordingly. We follow the general convention that a vowel with no mark above it is short. Other books mark a long vowel either with a bar called a macron (*ā*) or with a circumflex (*â*). Our system uses the

VOWEL SANDHI

Initial vowels:	Final vowels: a	ā	i	ī	u	ū	ṛ	e	ai	o	au
a	' â	" â	y a	y a	v a	v a	r a	e '	ā a	o '	āv a
ā	' ā	" ā	y ā	y ā	v ā	v ā	r ā	a ā	ā ā	a ā	āv ā
i	' ê	" ê	' î	" î	v i	v i	r i	a i	ā i	a i	āv i
ī	' ē	" ē	' ī	" ī	v ī	v ī	r ī	a ī	ā ī	a ī	āv ī
u	' ô	" ô	y u	y u	' û	" û	r u	a u	ā u	a u	āv u
ū	' ō	" ō	y ū	y ū	' ū	" ū	r ū	a ū	ā ū	a ū	āv ū
ṛ	a' r	a" r	y ṛ	y ṛ	v ṛ	v ṛ	' ṝ	a ṛ	ā ṛ	a ṛ	āv ṛ
e	' âi	" âi	y e	y e	v e	v e	r e	a e	ā e	a e	āv e
ai	' āi	" āi	y ai	y ai	v ai	v ai	r ai	a ai	ā ai	a ai	āv ai
o	' âu	" âu	y o	y o	v o	v o	r o	a o	ā o	a o	āv o
au	' āu	" āu	y au	y au	v au	v au	r au	a au	ā au	a au	āv au

CONSONANT SANDHI

Permitted finals: k	ṭ	t	p	ṅ	n	m	*(Except āḥ/aḥ)* ḥ/r	āḥ	aḥ	*Initial letters:*
k	ṭ	t	p	ṅ	n	ṃ	ḥ	āḥ	aḥ	k/kh
g	ḍ	d	b	ṅ	n	ṃ	r	ā	o	g/gh
k	ṭ	c	p	ṅ	ṃś	ṃ	ś	āś	aś	c/ch
g	ḍ	j	b	ṅ	ñ	ṃ	r	ā	o	j/jh
k	ṭ	ṭ	p	ṅ	ṃṣ	ṃ	ṣ	āṣ	aṣ	ṭ/ṭh
g	ḍ	ḍ	b	ṅ	ṇ	ṃ	r	ā	o	ḍ/ḍh
k	ṭ	t	p	ṅ	ṃs	ṃ	s	ās	as	t/th
g	ḍ	d	b	ṅ	n	ṃ	r	ā	o	d/dh
k	ṭ	t	p	ṅ	n	ṃ	ḥ	āḥ	aḥ	p/ph
g	ḍ	d	b	ṅ	n	ṃ	r	ā	o	b/bh
ṅ	ṇ	n	m	ṅ	n	ṃ	r	ā	o	*nasals* (n/m)
g	ḍ	d	b	ṅ	n	ṃ	r	ā	o	y/v
g	ḍ	d	b	ṅ	n	ṃ	*zero*[1]	ā	o	r
g	ḍ	l	b	ṅ	l̃[2]	ṃ	r	ā	o	l
k	ṭ	c ch	p	ṅ	ñ ś/ch	ṃ	ḥ	āḥ	aḥ	ś
k	ṭ	t	p	ṅ	n	ṃ	ḥ	āḥ	aḥ	ṣ/s
gg h	ḍḍ h	dd h	bb h	ṅ	n	ṃ	r	ā	o	h
g	ḍ	d	b	ṅ/ṅṅ[3]	n/nn[3]	m	r	ā	a[4]	*vowels*
k	ṭ	t	p	ṅ	n	m	ḥ	āḥ	aḥ	*zero*

[1]ḥ or r disappears, and if a/i/u precedes, this lengthens to ā/ī/ū. [2]e.g. tān+lokān=tāĩ lokān.
[3]The doubling occurs if the preceding vowel is short. [4]Except: aḥ+a=o '.

macron, except that for initial vowels in sandhi we use a circumflex to indicate that originally the vowel was short, or the shorter of two possibilities (*e* rather than *ai*, *o* rather than *au*).

When we print initial *â*,	before sandhi that vowel was *a*
î or *ê*,	*i*
û or *ô*,	*u*
âi,	*e*
âu,	*o*
ā,	*ā*
ī,	*ī*
ū,	*ū*
ē,	*ī*
ō,	*ū*
ai,	*ai*
āu,	*au*
’, before sandhi there was a vowel *a*	

When a final short vowel (*a*, *i*, or *u*) has merged into a following vowel, we print ’ at the end of the word, and when a final long vowel (*ā*, *ī*, or *ū*) has merged into a following vowel we print ” at the end of the word. The vast majority of these cases will concern a final *a* or *ā*. See, for instance, the following examples:

What before sandhi was	is represented as
atra asti	*atr’ âsti*
atra āste	*atr’ āste*
kanyā asti	*kany” âsti*
kanyā āste	*kany” āste*
atra iti	*atr’ êti*
kanyā iti	*kany” êti*
kanyā īpsitā	*kany” ēpsitā*

Finally, three other points concerning the initial letter of the second word:

(1) A word that before sandhi begins with *ṛ* (vowel), after sandhi begins with *r* followed by a consonant: *yatha” rtu* represents pre-sandhi *yathā ṛtu*.

(2) When before sandhi the previous word ends in *t* and the following word begins with *ś*, after sandhi the last letter of the previous word is *c*

and the following word begins with *ch*: *syāc chāstravit* represents pre-sandhi *syāt śāstravit*.

(3) Where a word begins with *h* and the previous word ends with a double consonant, this is our simplified spelling to show the pre-sandhi form: *tad hasati* is commonly written as *tad dhasati*, but we write *tadd hasati* so that the original initial letter is obvious.

COMPOUNDS

We also punctuate the division of compounds (*samāsa*), simply by inserting a thin vertical line between words. There are words where the decision whether to regard them as compounds is arbitrary. Our principle has been to try to guide readers to the correct dictionary entries.

Exemplar of CSL Style

Where the Devanagari script reads:

कुम्भस्थली रक्षतु वो विकीर्णसिन्धूररेणुर्द्विरदाननस्य ।
प्रशान्तये विघ्नतमश्छटानां निष्ठ्यूतबालातपपल्लवेव ॥

Others would print:

kumbhasthalī rakṣatu vo vikīrṇasindūrareṇur dviradānanasya /
praśāntaye vighnatamaśchaṭānāṃ niṣṭhyūtabālātapapallaveva //

We print:

kumbha|sthalī rakṣatu vo vikīrṇa|sindūra|reṇur dvirad'|ānanasya
praśāntaye vighna|tamaś|chaṭānāṃ niṣṭhyūta|bāl'|ātapa|pallav" êva.

And in English:

May Ganésha's domed forehead protect you! Streaked with vermilion dust, it seems to be emitting the spreading rays of the rising sun to pacify the teeming darkness of obstructions.

("Nava·sáhasanka and the Serpent Princess" 1.3)

Wordplay

Classical Sanskrit literature can abound in puns (*śleṣa*). Such paronomasia, or wordplay, is raised to a high art; rarely is it a *cliché*. Multiple meanings merge (*śliṣyanti*) into a single word or phrase. Most common are pairs of meanings, but as many as ten separate meanings are attested. To mark the parallel senses in the English, as well as the punning original in the Sanskrit, we use a *slanted* font (different from *italic*) and a triple colon (⁝) to separate the alternatives. E.g.

> yuktaṃ Kādambarīṃ śrutvā kavayo maunam āśritāḥ
> *Bāṇa/dhvanāv* an|adhyāyo bhavat' îti smṛtir yataḥ.
>
> It is right that poets should fall silent upon hearing the Kadámbari, for the sacred law rules that recitation must be suspended when *the sound of an arrow* ⁝ *the poetry of Bana* is heard.
>
> (Soméshvara·deva's "Moonlight of Glory" I.15)

For Margit, my *gurvī*, with love, and
thank you for a very special night out.

ACKNOWLEDGMENTS

Firstly thank you to Somdev Vasudeva who originally suggested I take on this text. “What the one with all those aorists?” “Yes.” “Oh, I might quite enjoy that.” But at the time I had no idea what a delight it would be to get into its layers of intertextuality and its commentaries and traditions and its sheer exuberance of poetry and learning: Bhatti is now my deep friend.

It happened that this project was completed under very challenging circumstances, the kind where you learn who your true friends are, and both Isabelle Onians and Chris Gibbons turned out to be such. Stuart Brown and Tomoyuki Kono were also patiently unstinting in their technical assistance.

In the aftermath of such an effort no translator could wish for a better proof-reader, more than that, a truly sympathetic, intelligent and intuitive eye: Dániel Balogh. Venetia Ansell also read carefully with a real sensitivity for the nuance of Sanskrit vocabulary and many parts of the translation were improved at her suggestion. No thanks suffices for my wife and children and my parents and siblings and Ann for their acceptance of the situation and their support where it was not deserved: we can cruise insouciantly through the vicissitudes of life while those who love us just have to look on in baffled anxiety.

All those who wrote and visited are friends for life, whatever happens: Helen Rattray; Julia and Luke Middleton; Aleksandra Nijemcevic; Dave, Joe and Rachel Winter; Nick Howard; Christine Hazell; Kate and Vernon Gardiner; Stephanie and all the Guideras; John, Paul and Bernard

Fallon; George Cselko; Patrick Wyatt; David Boddy; David and Miriam Stollar; David Mendez da Costa; Kevin Gould; Simon Smith; Greg Thompson; Colin Peters. If I have forgotten anyone, please forgive me, I have not the letters to hand.

Colin Morris, Deborah Youens and Laurie Harpburn know how to help people in spite of the system, and I thank them for their good company and understanding.

Last but not least, the "bruvverin" of the 'Ville and Standford Hill: Raj, Chris, Mandeep, Kevin, Holmes, Keith, Fred, Tim, Nick and many others *en passant*, for companionship and good humor.

INTRODUCTION

"BHATTI'S POEM" (*Bhaṭṭikāvya*) is one of the boldest experiments in classical literature. In the formal genre of "great poem" (*mahākāvya*) it incorprates two of the most powerful Sanskrit traditions, the "Ramáyana" and Pánini's grammar, and several other minor themes. In this one rich mix of science and art, Bhatti created both a poetic retelling of the adventures of Rama and a compendium of examples of grammar, metrics, the Prakrit language and rhetoric. As literature, his composition stands comparison with the best of Sanskrit poetry, in particular cantos 1, 2 and 10. "Bhatti's Poem" provides a comprehensive exemplification of Sanskrit grammar in use and a good introduction to the science (*śāstra*) of poetics or rhetoric (*alaṃkāra*, lit. ornament). It also gives a taster of the Prakrit language (a major component in every Sanskrit drama) in an easily accessible form. Finally it tells the compelling story of Prince Rama in simple elegant Sanskrit: this is the "Ramáyana" faithfully retold.

The learned Indian curriculum in late classical times had at its heart a system of grammatical study and linguistic analysis. The core text for this study was the notoriously difficult "Eight Books" (*Aṣṭādhyāyī*) of Pánini, the *sine qua non* of learning composed in the fourth century BCE, and arguably the most remarkable and indeed foundational text in the history of linguistics. Not only is the "Eight Books" a description of a language unmatched in totality for any language until the nineteenth century, but it is also presented in the most compact form possible through the use of an elaborate and sophisticated metalanguage, again unknown anywhere else in linguistics before modern times. This grammar of Pánini had been the object of intense study for the ten centuries prior to the composition of "Bhatti's Poem." It was plainly Bhatti's purpose to provide a study aid to Pánini's text by using the examples already provided in the existing grammatical commentaries in the context of the gripping and morally improving story of the "Ramáyana." To the dry bones of this grammar Bhatti has given juicy flesh in his poem. The same could be said for poetics, prosody and Prakrit. The intention of the author was to teach these advanced sciences through a relatively easy and pleasant medium but not so easy as to provide the reader with no opportunity to extend his learning. In his own words:

> *This composition is like a lamp to those who perceive the meaning of words and like a hand mirror for a blind man to those without grammar. This poem which is to be understood by means of a commentary, is a joy to those sufficiently learned: through my fondness for the scholar I have here slighted the dullard.*
>
> ("Bhatti's Poem" 22.33–34)

The traditional story given to account for the technical or shastric nature of the poem goes that Bhatti's class on grammar was one day disturbed by an elephant ambling between him and his pupils. This bestial interruption necessitated an interdiction of study for a year as prescribed by the solemn law books. To ensure that no vital study time was lost our poem was composed as a means of teaching grammar without resorting to an actual grammatical text.

All that we can reliably know of Bhatti himself is what he tells us at the end of the book:

> *I composed this poem in Válabhi which is protected by Naréndra, son of Shri·dhara, hence may the fame of that king increase, since the king causes joy among his subjects.*
> ("Bhatti's Poem" 22.35)

Even this eulogy is unreliable since variant readings of the verse show that his patron may instead have been Shri Dhara·sena. Either way, the composition of the poem is placed at about 600 CE.

In form the "Bhatti's Poem" is a "great poem" (*mahā-kāvya*). It fits well within the definition of this genre given later by Dandin in his "Mirror of Poetry" (*Kāvyādarśa*):

> *It springs from a historical incident or is otherwise based on some fact; it turns upon the fruition of the four-fold ends and its hero is clever and noble;*
>
> *By descriptions of cities, oceans, mountains, seasons and risings of the moon or the sun; through sportings in garden or water, and festivities of drinking and love;*
>
> *Through sentiments-of-love-in-separation and through marriages, by descriptions of the birth-and-rise of princes, and likewise through state-counsel, embassy, advance, battle, and the hero's triumph;*
>
> *Embellished; not too condensed, and pervaded all through with poetic sentiments and emotions; with cantos none too lengthy and having agreeable meters and well-formed joints,*
>
> *And in each case furnished with an ending in a different meter—such a poem possessing good figures-of-speech*

wins the people's heart and endures longer than even a kalpa.[1] (*Kāvyādarśa* 1.15–19, trans. BELVALKAR)

Its subject matter is the life of a single hero, both a member of the warrior caste and a god. Each canto has a uniform meter and there is one canto (canto 10) deploying a variety of meters. The end of each canto suggests the topic for the next. The main sentiment or *rasa* of the poem is "heroic" (*vīrya*). The poem through its form and subject matter is conducive to the attainment of the four aims of human life (*puruṣārthas*): "righteousness" (*dharma*), "wealth and power" (*artha*), "pleasure" (*kāma*) and "spiritual liberation" (*mokṣa*). "Bhatti's Poem" contains descriptions of cities, the ocean, mountains, seasons, the rising and setting of the sun and moon, and the sports of love and sex. Five such poems are traditionally enumerated in addition to which our work is sometimes named the sixth. The five are the "Lineage of Raghu" (*Raghuvaṃśa*) and the "Birth of Kumára" (*Kumārasambhava*) of Kali·dasa, the "Slaying of Shishu·pala" (*Śiśupālavadha*) of Magha, "Árjuna and the Mountain Man" (*Kirātārjunīya*) of Bháravi and the "Adventures of the Prince of Níshadha" (*Naiṣadhacarita*) of Shri Harsha. The multitude of manuscripts found in libraries demonstrates the popularity of the *Bhaṭṭikāvya* and the thirteen extant and eight further attested commentaries instantiate its importance to the tradition (NARANG 1969).

How does "Bhatti's Poem" illustrate Páninian grammar? This is done in three distinct sections.

From the end of canto 5 up to the end of canto 9 the verses exemplify in sequence long series of aphorisms (*sūtras*) from the "Eight Books" of Pánini. These aphorisms are short coded rules, almost algebraic in form. As an example, consider Pánini's rule 6.1.77: *iko yaṇ aci*. This translates as "When followed by any vowel, the vowels *i, u, ṛ* and *ḷ* in any length are respectively replaced by the semivowels *y, v, r* and *l*." This is quite a mouthful of translation for five syllables of Sanskrit. How does Pánini do it? To start with, the three words of the rule in their uninflected form are *ik*, *yaṇ* and *ac* which are a type of acronym for their respective series of letters: the simple vowels *i, ī, u, ū, ṛ, ṝ, ḷ*; the semivowels *y, v, r, l*; and all the vowels *a, ā, i, ī, u, ū, ṛ, ṝ, ḷ, e, o, ai, au*. The cases are used to indicate the operation which is to take place: the genitive of *ik* indicates "in place of *ik*;" the locative of *ac* indicates "when *ac* follows" and *yaṇ* in the nominative indicates "there should be a *yaṇ*" or "*yaṇ* is the replacement." Pánini gives metarules to explain the formation and use of these acronyms and the special uses of the cases within the rules. It is thus a rule for the simple sandhi which would occur for example between the words *iti* and *evam*, smoothing the juncture between their vowels into *ity evam*. This is but a tiny taster of the economy, intricacy, beauty and intellectual power of the "Eight Books," surely one of the greatest wonders and perhaps the supreme intellectual achievement of the ancient world. It is to the layman a treasure chest whose key is locked deep inside itself. However, the reader does not have to be familiar with this system to enjoy the *Bhaṭṭikāvya*. By using the references to the "Eight Books" given at the end of this volume, the reader may refer to the rules as he reads and become familiar with them in advance of reading each verse. The examples used in "Bhatti's Poem" are not included in the actual aphorisms of the "Eight Books" themselves but are ones given by later commentators to facilitate discussion. The most widely used traditional examples are included in the two editions of the "Eight Books" cited in the bibliography.

The table below shows how "Bhatti's Poem" is structured as a pedagogic text.

Verse	Rule (*Sūtra*)	Topic Illustrated
The Illustration of Diverse Rules (*Prakīrṇa*)		
1.1–5.96	Miscellaneous rules	
The Illustration of Particular Topics (*Adhikāra*)		
5.97–100	Pā. 3.2.17–23	The affix *Ṭa*
5.104–6.4	Pā. 3.1.35–41	The suffix *ām* in the periphrastic perfect
6.8–10	Pā. 1.4.51	Double accusatives
6.16–34	Pā. 3.1.43–66	Aorists using *sĪC* substitutes for the affix *CLI*
6.35–39	Pā. 3.1.78	The affix *ŚnaM* for the present tense system of class 7 verbs
6.46–67	Pā. 3.1.96–132	The future passive participles or gerundives and related forms formed from the *kṛtya* affixes *tavya*, *tavyaT*, *anīyaR*, *yaT*, *Kyap*, and *ṆyaT*
6.71–86	Pā. 3.1.133–150	Words formed with *nirupapada kṛt* affixes *ṆvuL*, *tṛC*, *Lyu*, *ṆinI*, *aC*, *Ka*, *Śa*, *Ṇa*, *ṢvuN*, *thakaN*, *ṆyuṬ* and *vuN*
6.87–93	Pā. 3.2.1–15	Words formed with *sopapada kṛt* affixes *aṆ*, *Ka*, *ṬaK*, *aC*
6.94–111	Pā. 3.2.28–50	Words formed with affixes *KHaŚ* and *KhaC*
6.112–143	Pā. 3.2.51–116	Words formed with *kṛt* affixes

7.1–25	Pā. 3.2.134–175	*kṛt* (*tācchīlaka*) affixes *tṛN*, *iṣṇuC*, *Ksnu*, *Knu*, *GHinUṆ*, *vuÑ*, *yuC*, *ukaÑ*, *ṢākaN*, *inI*, *luC*, *KmaraC*, *GhuraC*, *KuraC*, *KvaraP*, *ūka*, *ra*, *u*, *najIṄ*, *āru*, *Kru*, *KlukaN*, *varaC* and *KvIP*
7.28–34	Pā. 3.3.1–21	*niradhikāra kṛt* affixes
7.34–85	Pā. 3.3.18–128	The affix *GhaÑ*
7.91–107	Pā. 1.2.1–26	*Ṅit-Kit*
8.1–69	Pā. 1.3.12–93	*Ātmanepada* affixes
8.70–84	Pā. 1.4.24–54	The use of cases under the *adhikāra* '*kārake*'
8.85–93	Pā. 1.4.83–98	*Karmapravacanīya*
8.94–130	Pā. 2.3.1–73	*Vibhakti*
9.8–11	Pā. 7.2.1–7	The suffix *sIC* and *vṛddhi* of the *parasmaipada* aorist
9.12–22	Pā. 7.2.8–30	The prohibition of *iṬ*
9.23–57	Pā. 7.2.35–78	The use of *iṬ*
9.58–66	Pā. 8.3.34–48	*visarga* sandhi in compounds
9.67–91	Pā. 8.3.55–118	Retroflexion of *s*
9.92–109	Pā. 8.4.1–39	Retroflexion of *n*
	Aesthetics (*Prasanna*)	
10.1–22		Figures of sound, *śabdālaṃkāra*
10.23–75		Figures of sense, *arthālaṃkāra*
11		Sweetness, *mādhurya guṇa*
12		Intensity of Expression, *bhāvikatva*
13		Simultaneous Prakrit and Sanskrit, *bhāṣāsama*
	Finite Verb Forms (*Tiṅanta*)	
14		The perfect tense
15		The aorist tense
16		The simple future
17		The imperfect tense
18		The present tense

19	The optative mood
20	The imperative mood
21	The conditional mood
22	The periphrastic future

In the first section of the poem, the "Diverse Rules Section" (*Prakīrṇa Khaṇḍa*), where the intention appears to be the illustration of miscellaneous rules, it is not obvious how to determine which specific rule if any is intended to be exemplified in any particular verse. Hundreds of rules could in theory be applicable. The commentators assist somewhat where they cite those rules which they think to be worth quoting in that context. The other guide is the Sanskrit language itself: it is likely that the most unusual or aberrant forms would have been exemplified. The frequent coincidence of these two heuristic principles is also helpful. Where the word in the verse is also given as an example in the grammatical texts then we can be almost certain about the topic. Such rules have not been mentioned in the notes unless reference to the grammatical text in question appears to be most useful for understanding the form of the word in the verse.

I would conjecture that within this section of "Diverse Rules" those verses which were intended to illustrate the grammar would be those without figures of speech or at least with very simple figures. That supposition would be consistent with the lack of ornament in some sections of the poem and would also explain why there is such a marked distinction between Bhatti's high style in canto 1 and much of 2 and his plainer style in much of the rest of the poem. It may be that "Bhatti's Poem" was first intended to be a typical courtly epic or "high *kāvya*" and that the idea of creating this new genre of educational poem (*śāstra/kāvya*) evolved as the poem was being composed. This is supported by the progression in styles from highly ornate poetry in the first two cantos, through unadorned verse with no apparent systematic exemplification of grammar, the so-called "Diverse Rules Section" (*Prakīrṇa Khaṇḍa*), to the second major section from near the end of canto 5 until the end of canto 9: "Particular Topics Section" (*Adhikāra Khaṇḍa*) in which the verses exemplify in sequence long series of rules from the "Eight Books." Here again poetry is subjugated to the pedagogic purpose of exemplification: the meter is the humble *anuṣṭubh* or *śloka* and there are few figures of speech to decorate the tale. This change of meter from the longer 44 syllable *upajāti* for the first three cantos to the shorter and simpler 32 syllable *anuṣṭubh* for the next six may also be indicative of a gradually evolving intention.

A detailed study of the examples given in the *Bhaṭṭikāvya* compared with those of the earlier "Great Commentary" (*Mahābhāṣya*) of Patánjali and later works such as the "Kashi Commentary" (*Kāśikā*) and "Moonlight on the Tradition" (*Siddhāntakaumudī*) still needs to be done. It would be of particular interest to see to what extent examples of usage may have been introduced into the grammatical tradition by "Bhatti's Poem." Might the poem itself then have become an authority on usage?

The figures of speech are illustrated in canto 10. This section of the poem has been the most studied in modern times. It constitutes an important text in its own right in the history of Sanskrit poetics. That said, its importance lies in its raising far more questions than it answers.

Chronologically it stands between the "Science of Theater" (*Nāṭyaśāstra*) as the earliest surviving text on Sanskrit poetics and the first great systematic treatments of the subject in the "Mirror of Poetry" (*Kāvyādarśa*) of Dandin (660–680 CE) and the "Ornament of Poetry" (*Kāvyālaṃkāra*) of Bhámaha (700 CE). Tantalizingly, we have the examples only and not the explanations or contemporary commentaries. A major problem of Sanskrit poetics is the lack of agreement on any system of nomenclature for the figures. The figures are given names in some manuscripts of the *Bhaṭṭikāvya* but this is no proof that these were the names that Bhatti knew. The fact that this naming of figures is quite different to that of the writers on poetics suggests that they might well predate them. If this is the case then in these we have the fragmentary residua of a missing link in the tradition of poetics *alaṃkāra*. It is most likely that Bhatti based his treatment of the figures of speech on a text now lost. Other questions about this canto present themselves. Why is there only one example of alliteration (*anuprāsa*)? Was this figure not fully elaborated until Dandin? Why do those verses said to exhibit the figure "illuminator" (*dīpaka*) in the manuscripts show nothing of the sort according to later theorists? Given that many of the verses contain more than one figure, does this mean that they were not intended to be a systematic illustration of figures but rather a collection of verses showing diverse poetic traits? Since the order of the names given in the manuscripts corresponds to the order of figures treated by Dandin, did Dandin base his own work on this order or were the names applied retrospectively to "Bhatti's Poem" in an attempt to match it up to later systems? That "Bhatti's

Poem" canto 10 is a major work on Sanskrit poetics is amply demonstrated by SÖHNEN (1995) in her examination of "doubling" (*yamaka*) of 10.2–22 showing that the treatment of this figure in Dandin's "Mirror of Poetry" and Bhámaha's "Ornament of Poetry" is influenced by "Bhatti's Poem."

Cantos 11 and 12 are held to display respectively the quality (*guṇa*) of "sweetness" (*mādhurya*) and the sentiment (*rasa*) of "intensity of expression" (*bhāvikatva*). The texts describing these qualities post-date Bhatti so again we cannot be sure that what he intended to illustrate is what happens to be described by later authors. Assuming that Bhatti did intend to show these qualities, their precise characteristics described in his source text would be best discovered from careful analysis of the language of his own work rather than from the pronouncements of later writers on poetics.

Canto 13 is written in what is called "like the vernacular" (*bhāṣāsama*), that is, it can be read in two languages simultaneously: Prakrit and Sanskrit. The Prakrit used here is of course no real vernacular but a literary version almost as highly codified as Sanskrit. Because of this Prakrit's similarity to Sanskrit it can be read in that elevated language by someone with no knowledge of Prakrit. With minor exceptions the vocabulary and grammar used are common to both languages. Where the grammar is not common the differences are disguised by sandhi. As many of the Prakrit terminations originate in Sanskrit forms generalized to their most common forms in sandhi, this is not impossible. As an example, the nominative singular of substantives in *-a* in Sanskrit is *-aḥ* and in Prakrit it is *-o*. In verse 13.2 we have three nominative singulars in *-a*: *bhīmaḥ*, *rasaḥ* and *samaḥ*. In Prakrit they would be *bhīmo*, *raso* and *samo*. Because the following words all begin with voiced consonants, in Sanskrit sandhi the ending *-aḥ* is in all these cases changed to *-o*, thus making the form indistinguishable from the Prakrit. Where the Sanskrit termination is undisguisably altered in Prakrit as for example with the instrumental plural *-bhiḥ* which becomes *-hi*, these terminations are concealed within compounds. It is for this reason that long compounds are so extensively used in this canto. The reader will also notice a lack of finite verb forms. It is more common for participle forms to be the same in the two languages. On occasion the commentators need a deal of learning and ingenuity to explain how forms are defensible in both languages. For instance in verse 13.3 the Sanskrit *sabhā* "hall" would normally become *sahā* in Prakrit by the rule *khaghathadhabhāṃ haḥ*, "*h* is the replacement for *kh*, *gh*, *th*, *dh* and *bh*" (*Prākṛtaprakāśa* 2.27). Malli·natha defends the retention of *sabhā* in Prakrit by saying that there is the continued operation (*anuvṛtti*) of *prāyaḥ*, "generally," from an earlier rule. With the exception of verse 13.7 which is irregular and verses 13.26–28 which are in the *upajāti* meter, the entire canto is composed in the *āryāgīti* meter which is the older lyric meter most commonly used for Prakrit texts.

Cantos 14 through to the end at canto 22 are each written in a particular tense or mood. Given that this is a rather broad restriction it is surprising that Bhatti does not indulge in more ornamentation in these verses. He does include many obscurer roots here but in other respects his language is simple and uncluttered.

The influence of "Bhatti's Poem" has extended beyond the geographical bounds of the Indian Subcontinent to Java where it became the source text for the Old-Javanese "Ramáyana" which is the oldest surviving example of classical Javanese epic poetry (*Kakawin*, from *kāvya*). The Javanese "Ramáyana" follows "Bhatti's Poem" closely as far as canto 12, sometimes to the extent of directly translating a verse, but begins to diverge thereafter. It would seem that the form of "Bhatti's Poem" as a "great poem" (*mahākāvya*) was important to the Javanese author as many of his additions make more complete the conformity of the Old-Javanese "Ramáyana" to the genre as described by Dandin, indicating that his "Mirror of Poetry" or its precursor as followed by Bhatti was also available to him (HOOYKAAS 1958). Moreover HOOYKAAS has also shown that the Old-Javanese "Ramáyana" uses "doubling" (*yamaka*) under Bhatti's influence.

The *Bhaṭṭikāvya* also has "The Death of Rávana" (*Rāvaṇa-vadha*) as an alternative title. It is improbable that this was the original title as Rávana's death is only one short episode in the whole poem. It may have acquired this title to distinguish it from other works concerning themselves with the deeds of Rama.

Our poem is the earliest example of an "instructional poem" (*śāstra/kāvya*). That is not a treatise written in verse but an imaginative piece of literature which is also intended to be instructive in specific subjects. To modern tastes this creates an unpardonable artificiality in the composition. To the critics of late classical times in India technical virtuosity was much admired. Much of the *Bhaṭṭikāvya*'s popular success could also be ascribed to the fact that it must have been useful as a textbook. As modern readers we have to let go our acquired aesthetic sensibilities, put ourselves into the mindset of seventh-century India and enjoy this poem on its own terms as the masterpiece it is.

The Sanskrit Text

The edition used for this translation is that of JOSHI AND SARMA (1914). Typographical emendations and emendations on philological grounds are given in the notes at the end of the book.

Note

1 *itihāsa|kath"|ôdbhūtam, itarad vā sad|āśrayam,*
catur|varga|phal'|āyattaṃ, catur|udātta|nāyakam,
nagar'|ârṇava|śaila'|rtu|candr'|ârk'|ôdaya|varṇanaiḥ,
udyāna|salila|krīḍā|madhu|pāna|rat'|ôtsavaiḥ,
vipralambhair vivāhaiś ca, kumār'|ôdaya|varṇanaiḥ,
mantra|dūta|prayāṇ'|āji|nāyak'|âbhyudayair api
alaṃ|kṛtam, a|saṃkṣiptaṃ, rasa|bhāva|nirantaram,
sargair an|ativistīrṇaiḥ, śravya|vṛttaiḥ su|saṃdhibhiḥ,
sarvatra bhinna|vṛttāntair upetaṃ, loka|rañjanam
kāvyaṃ kalp'|ântara|sthāyi jāyate sad|alaṃkṛti.

Bibliography

MODERN WORKS

Rev. ANDERSON, P. 1850. "Some Account of the Bhatti Kavya." *Journal of the Bombay Branch of the Royal Asiatic Society*. Vol 3, no. 13.

APTE, VAMAN SIVARAM. 1957–59. *The Practical Sanskrit-English Dictionary*. 3 vols., Poona: Prasad Prakashan.

GEROW, EDWIN. 1971. *A Glossary of Indian Figures of Speech*. The Hague: Mouton.

———. 1977. *A History of Indian Literature: Vol. V, fasc. 3. Indian Poetics*. Wiesbaden: Otto Harassowitz.

HENRY, PATRICIA B. 2001. "The Poetics of the Old Javanese Rāmāyaṇa: A Comparison with the Sanskrit Bhaṭṭikāvya." Presented at the International Rāmayaṇa Conference, Northern Illinois University, DeKalb, IL. September 21–23, 2001.

HOOYKAAS, C. 1957. "On Some Arthālaṃkāras in the Baṭṭikāvya X." *Bulletin of the School of Oriental and African Studies*. Vol. 20, no. 3, Studies in Honour of Sir Ralph Turner, Director of the School of Oriental and African Studies, 1937–57.

———. 1958. *The Old Javanese Rāmāyaṇa, an Exemplary Kakawin as to Form and Content*. Amsterdam.

KANE, P.V. 1971. *History of Sanskrit Poetics*. Delhi: Motilal Banarsidass.

KEITH, A.B. 1928. *A History of Sanskrit literature*. Oxford: Clarendon Press.

MONIER WILLIAMS, MONIER. 1899. *A Sanskrit-English Dictionary.* Oxford: Clarendon Press.

NARANG, SAYTA PAL. 1969. *Bhaṭṭikāvya, A Study.* Delhi: Motilal Banarsidass.

———. 2003. *An Analysis of the Prākṛta of Bhāśā-sama of the Bhaṭṭikāvya (Canto XII)*. In: *Prof. Mahapatra G.N., Vanijyotih: Felicitation Volume*, Utkal University, Bhuvaneshwar.

SÖHNEN, RENATE. 1995. "On the Concept and Presentation of 'yamaka' in Early Indian Poetic Theory." *Bulletin of the School of Oriental and African Studies.* Vol. 58, no. 3, pp. 495–520.

Sudyaka, Lidia. 2002. *What Does the Bhaṭṭi-kāvya teach?* In: *Essays in Indian Philosophy, Religion and Literature.* Piotr Balcerowicz and Marek Mejor (eds.), Warsaw.

Whitney, W.D. 1885. *The Roots, Verb Forms and Primary Derivatives of the Sanskrit Language*. New Haven.

———. 1924. *Sanskrit Grammar*. 5th ed., Leipzig.

EDITIONS AND TRANSLATIONS OF BHAṬṬIKĀVYA

Brough, J. 1951. *Selections from Classical Sanskrit Literature, with English Translation and Notes*. London: Luzac.

———. "JB N/4 Notes on the Bhattikavya undated: 1 bundle (1) and 1 vol (2) English and Sanskrit, JB N/4/1 Draft transcription and translation of cantos 1–2, 10, 15 and 22, incomplete, JB N/4/2 Notes on cantos 1–2." University of Cambridge, Faculty of Oriental Studies, Archive Collections.

Joshi, V.N.S. and Sarma, S.V. 1914. *The Bhaṭṭikāvya of Bhaṭṭi with the Commentary of Jayamaṅgala*. Bombay: Nirnaya Sagar Press.

Karandikar, M.S. & Karandikar S. 1982 *Bhaṭṭikāvyam, Edited with an English Translation.* Delhi: Motilal Barnasidass.

Leonardi, G.G. 1972. *Bhaṭṭikāvyam, Translation and Notes*. Leiden: E.J. Brill.

Shastri, Shri Shesharaj Sharma. Undated. *Bhaṭṭikāvyam, Edited with the Candrakala-Vidyotini Sanskrit-Hindi Commentary*. 3 vols. Haridas Sanskrit Series no. 136. Varanasi: Chowkhambha Sanskrit Series Office.

Trivedi, K.P. 1898. *The Bhaṭṭikāvya or Rāvaṇavadha composed by Śri Bhaṭṭi with the Commentary of Mallinātha with critical and explanatory notes*. 2 vols. Bombay Sanskrit Series no. 56. Bombay.

Turner, R.L. "JB B/12 Translation of the Bhattikavya, undated, 2 vols. JB B/12/1 Translation of cantos 6–14, Annotated by Brough; JB B/12/2 Translation of cantos 15–17." University of Cambridge, Faculty of Oriental Studies, Archive Collections.

OTHER SANSKRIT TEXTS

Agnipurāṇa. Kale, G.B. 1957. *Agnipurāṇa*. Ānanadasrama Sanskrit Series, 41. Poona: Anandasrama.

Arthaśāstra. Kangle, R.P. 1965–72. *The Kauṭilīya Arthaśāstra*. 3 Parts. Bombay: University of Bombay.

Aṣṭādhyāyī of Pāṇini. [Pā] Sharma, R.N. 1987–2003. *The Aṣṭādhyāyī of Pāṇini*. 6 vols. Delhi: Munshiram Manoharlal. Vasu, S.C. 1891–98. *The Aṣṭādhyāyī of Pāṇini, edited and translated into English*. 2 vols. Allahabad: The Panini Office.

Dhātupāṭha of Pāṇini. See *Aṣṭādhyāyī* for editions.

Jātakamālā of Āryaśūra. Kern, H. 1891. *The Jātaka-Mālā*. Harvard Oriental Series vol. 1. Boston: Harvard University Press.

Kāvyādarśa of Daṇḍin. Boehtlingk, O. 1890. *Dandin's Poetic (Kāvyādarśa)*. Leipzig: Verlag von H. Haessel.

Kāvyādarśa of Daṇḍin. Belvalkar, S.K. 1924. *Kāvyādarśa of Daṇḍin. Sanskrit Text and English Translation*. Poona: Oriental Book-supplying Agency.

Kāvyālaṃkāra of Bhāmaha. Tatacharya Siromani, D.T. 1934. ed., *Bhāmaha, Kāvyālaṃkāra, with Udyāna Vṛtti*, Tiruvadi: Srinivasa Press.

Kāvyālaṅkāra of Rudraṭa. Durgaprasad and Panasikar. 1887. *Rudraṭa's Kāvyālaṅkāra*. Vidyabhavana Rashtrabhasha Granthamala 136. Bombay: Kavyamala.

Kāvyālaṅkārasārasaṅgraha of Udbhaṭa. Banhatti, N.D. 1925. *Udbhaṭa's Kāvyālaṅkārasārasaṅgraha*. Poona: Bhandarkar Oriental Research Institute.

Kāvyālaṅkāravṛtti of Vāmana. Cappeller, C. 1875. *Vāmana: Lehrbuch der Poetic (Kāvyālaṅkāravṛtti)*. Jena.

Kāvyaprakāśa of Mammaṭa. Dhundhiraja Shastri. 1951. *Mammaṭa: Kāvyaprakāśa; with the commentary of Hariśaṅkaraśarman*. Kashi Sanskrit Series 49. Benares.

Mahābhārata. Critically edited by V.S. Sukthankar et al. 1927–66. 19 vols. Poona: Bhandarkar Oriental Research Institute.

Manusmṛti. OLIVELLE, PATRICK, 2005. *Manu's Code of Law: a critical edition and translation of the Mānava-Dharmaśāstra*. Oxford University Press.

Nāṭyaśāstra of Bharata. RAMAKRISHNA KAVI, M. 1926–34. *Nāṭyaśāstra; with the Commentary of Abhinavagupta*. 4 vols. Gaekward Oriental Series, 36, 68. Baroda.

Raghuvaṃśa of Kālidāsa. GOODALL, DOMINIC and ISAACSON, HARUNAGA, 2003. *The Raghupañcikā of Vallabhadeva, being the earliest commentary on the Raghuvaṃśa of Kālidāsa, Critical Edition with Introduction and Notes*, Volume 1. Groningen : Egbert Forsten. GOODALL, DOMINIC and ISAACSON, HARUNAGA, forthcoming. *Raghu's Lineage*. Two volumes. New York: New York University Press (Clay Sanskrit Library).

Rāmāyaṇa of Vālmīki. GOLDMAN, R. et al. 1984–. *The Rāmāyaṇa of Vālmīki.* 7 vols. Princeton: Princeton University Press. GOLDMAN, R. *et al*. 2005–. *Ramáyana*. Books One to Five. New York: New York University Press (Clay Sanskrit Library).

Ṛgveda. VAN NOOTEN, BAREND A. and HOLLAND, GARY B. 1994. *Rig Veda: a Metrically Restored Text*. Harvard University Press.

Siddhāntakaumudī of Bhaṭṭojī Dīkṣita. VASU, S.C. 1904. *Siddhanta Kaumudi of Bhattoji Dikshita, edited and translated into English*. 2 vols. Allahabad: The Panini Office.

Śiśupālavadha of Māgha. DURGAPRASADA. 2000. *Śiśupālavadha of Magha*. Varanasi: Chowkhamba Sanskrit Series Office, K.S.S. no. 77. DUNDAS, PAUL, forthcoming. *The Slaying of Shishu·pala*. New York: New York University Press (Clay Sanskrit Library).

Abbreviations

WORKS AND AUTHORS

Ag. = *Agnipurāṇa*
GEROW = GEROW (1971), "A Glossary of Indian Figures of Speech"
Jay. = commentary of Jayamaṅgala
KB = *Kāvyālaṃkāra* of Bhāmaha
KD = *Kāvyādarśa* of Daṇḍin
KM = *Kāvyaprakāśa* of Mammaṭa
KR = *Kāvyālaṅkāra* of Rudraṭa
KU = *Kāvyālaṅkārasārasaṅgraha* of Udbhaṭa
KV = *Kāvyālaṅkāravṛtti* of Vāmana
Mall. = commentary of Mallinātha
MW = MONIER WILLIAMS, "A Sanskrit-English Dictionary."
Nāṭ. = *Nāṭyaśāstra*
Pā. = *Aṣṭādhyāyī* of Pāṇini
WR = WHITNEY (1885), "The Roots, Verb Forms and Primary Derivatives of the Sanskrit Language"

GRAMMAR

Ā. = *Ātmanepada* (middle)
acc. = accusative
aor. = aorist
caus. = causative
cond. = conditional
conj. = conjugation
desid. = desiderative
du. = dual
fem. = feminine
fut. = future
imp. = imperative
impf. = imperfect
inst. = instrumental
intens. = intensive
loc. = locative
masc. = masculine
nom. = nominative
P. = *Parasmaipada* (active)
pass. = passive
perf. = perfective
pl. = plural
pres. = present
pt. = participle
s. = singular

BHATTI'S POEM
THE DEATH OF RÁVANA

CANTO 1
THE BIRTH OF RAMA

1.1 Abhūn nṛpo vibudha|sakhaḥ paraṃ|tapaḥ
śrut'|ânvito Daśaratha ity udāhṛtaḥ,
guṇair varaṃ bhuvana|hita|cchalena yaṃ
sanātanaḥ pitaram upāgamat svayam.

so 'dhyaiṣṭa vedāṃs, tri|daśān ayaṣṭa,
pitṝn apārīt, samamaṃsta bandhūn,
vyajeṣṭa ṣaḍ|vargam, araṃsta nītau,
sa|mūla|ghātaṃ* nyavadhīd arīṃś ca.

vasūni toyaṃ ghanavad vyakārīt,
sah' āsanaṃ Gotrabhid" âdhyavātsīt,
na Tryambakād anyam upāsthit' âsau,
yaśāṃsi sarv'|êṣu|bhṛtāṃ nirāsthat.

puṇyo mahā|brahma|samūha|juṣṭaḥ,
saṃtarpaṇo nāka|sadāṃ, vareṇyaḥ,
jajvāla loka|sthitaye sa rājā
yath" âdhvare vahnir abhipraṇītaḥ.

1.5 sa puṇya|kīrtiḥ Śatamanyu|kalpo
Mahendra|loka|pratimāṃ samṛddhyā
adhyāsta sarva'|rtu|sukhām Ayodhyām
adhyāsitāṃ brahmabhir iddha|bodhaiḥ.

nirmāṇa|dakṣasya samīhiteṣu
sīm" êva Padmāsana|kauśalasya
ūrdhva|sphurad|ratna|gabhastibhir yā
sthit" âvahasy' êva puraṃ Maghonaḥ.

THERE WAS A king, friend to the wise, a torment to 1.1
his enemies, endowed with sacred knowledge, Dasha·ratha by name, whom, being the best by his virtues, the eternal chose as his own father on the pretext of benefiting the world.

He recited the Vedas, he sacrificed to the gods, he sated his ancestors, he honored his kinsmen, he conquered the six inner foes,* he delighted in good government and he killed his enemies, cutting them down at the root.

He dispensed wealth as a cloud does water, he sat together with Indra the stockade breaker on his throne, he worshipped no other god than the three eyed Shiva, he eclipsed the reputations of all other archers.

Virtuous, delighting in gatherings of great brahmins, a restorative to the gods, the most excellent, that king blazed in order to sustain the world like fire brought to the sacrifice.

He whose virtue was his glory, like Indra of hundredfold 1.5
wrath, dwelt in Ayódhya, lovely in all seasons, comparable to the world of the great lord Indra in its abundance, the home of brahmins of burning intellect.

At the very pinnacle of dexterity in creation of things undertaken by the cleverness of the lotus-throned Brahma, Ayódhya with the rays of its jewels shining upwards stood as if mocking the city of Indra.

sad|ratna|muktā|phala|vajra|bhāñji
vicitra|dhātūni sa|kānanāni
strībhir yutāny apsarasām iv' âughair
Meroḥ śirāṃs' îva gṛhāṇi yasyām.

antar|niviṣṭ'|ôjjvala|ratna|bhāso
gav'|âkṣa|jālair abhiniṣpatantyaḥ
Himādri|ṭaṅkād iva bhānti yasyāṃ
Gaṅg"|âmbu|pāta|pratimā gṛhebhyaḥ.

dharmyāsu kām'|ârtha|yaśas|karīṣu
matāsu loke *'dhigatāsu kāle*
vidyāsu vidvān iva so 'bhireme
patnīṣu rājā tisṛṣ' ûttamāsu.

1.10 putrīyatā tena var'|âṅganābhir
ānāyi vidvān kratuṣu kriyāvān
vipaktrima|jñāna|gatir manasvī
mānyo muniḥ svāṃ puram Ṛṣyaśṛṅgaḥ.

aihiṣṭa taṃ kārayituṃ kṛt'|ātmā
kratuṃ nṛpaḥ putra|phalaṃ mun'|îndram.
jñāt'|āśayas tasya tato vyatānīt
sa karmaṭhaḥ karma sut'|ânubandham.

rakṣāṃsi vedīṃ parito nirāsthad,
aṅgāny ayākṣīd abhitaḥ pradhānam,
śeṣāṇy ahauṣīt suta|saṃpade ca
varaṃ vareṇyo nṛpater amārgīt.

Its houses were like the peaks of Mount Meru furnished with fine jewels, pearls and diamonds, full of colorful minerals and golden ores, thronged with women like streams of *ápsaras*es.

The rays from the shining inlaid jewels flying out through the latticed windows of the houses shone like the cascades of the Ganges from the slopes of the Himálaya.

The king took delight in his three perfect wives, like a scholar delighting in his studies:* they were *righteous : virtuous*, conducive to pleasure, profit and reputation, esteemed popularly and *acquired at the proper time : approached sexually at the right time.**

Because he desired a son the king, using the most beauti- 1.10
ful women, lured to his own city the wise and esteemed sage Rishya·shringa,* who was learned and skilled in sacrifice and the resort of perfected knowledge.

The self-controlled king wished that best of sages to perform a sacrifice to produce a son. That expert in sacrifice, who knew the disposition of his mind, then carried out a rite productive of sons.

The best of sages drove away the demons surrounding the altar, performed the auxiliary rites relating to the main sacrifice, poured the remaining offerings for the acquisition of a son and prepared the way for the king's boon.

niṣṭhāṃ gate dattrima|sabhya|toṣe
vihitrime karmaṇi, rāja|patnyaḥ
prāśur hut'|ôcchiṣṭam udāra|vaṃśyās
tisraḥ prasotuṃ caturaḥ su|putrān.

Kausalyay" âsāvi sukhena Rāmaḥ
prāk, Kekayīto Bharatas tato 'bhūt,
prāsoṣṭa Śatrughnam udāra|ceṣṭam
ekā Sumitrā saha Lakṣmaṇena.

1.15 ārcīd dvi|jātīn param'|ârtha|vindān
udejayān bhūta|gaṇān nyaṣedhīt,
vidvān upāneṣṭa ca tān sva|kāle
yatir Vaśiṣṭho yamināṃ variṣṭhaḥ.

vedo 'ṅgavāṃs tair akhilo 'dhyagāyi*
śastrāṇy upāyaṃsata jitvarāṇi.
te bhinna|vṛttīny api mānasāni
samaṃ janānāṃ guṇino' dhyavātsuḥ.

tato 'bhyagād Gādhi|sutaḥ kṣit'|îndraṃ
rakṣobhir abhyāhata|karma|vṛttiḥ,
Rāmaṃ varītuṃ parirakṣaṇ'|ârthaṃ.
rāj" ārjihat taṃ madhu|parka|pāṇiḥ.

«aiṣīḥ punar|janma|jayāya yat tvaṃ,
rūp'|ādi|bodhān nyavṛtac ca yat te,
tattvāny abuddhāḥ pratanūni yena,
dhyānaṃ» nṛpas «tac chivam» ity avādīt.

When the rite, which had satisfied the court because of the gifts, had been properly completed, the three queens of the best lineages ate the remnant offerings in order to give birth to four excellent sons.

First Rama was born easily from Kausálya, then Bharata was born of Kékayi and finally Sumítra gave birth to Shatrúghna of noble conduct and also Lákshmana.

Vashíshtha, striving, best of the strivers, honored the twice- 1.15
born who were seeking the supreme truth, made the swarms of ghosts tremble and being wise initiated them at the proper time.

They learned the entire Veda and its subsidiary sciences and took up victory-giving weapons. Those exemplars settled themselves equally into the peoples' hearts in all their variety.

Then Vishva·mitra, the descendant of Gadhi, his course of sacrifices obstructed by demons, approached the lord of the earth in order to turn to Rama for protection. The king, honey offering in hand, honored him.

The king said: "You sought an auspicious meditation in order to overcome rebirth, which turned you away from the perception of material forms, and by which you have understood the very subtle essences."

ākhyan munis «tasya śivaṃ samādher,
vighnanti rakṣāṃsi vane kratūṃś ca.
tāni dviṣad|vīrya|nirākariṣṇus
tṛṇedhu Rāmaḥ saha Lakṣmaṇena.»

1.20 sa śuśruvāṃs tad|vacanaṃ mumoha
rāj" â|sahiṣṇuḥ suta|viprayogam.
ahaṃyun" âtha kṣiti|paḥ śubhaṃyur*
ūce vacas tāpasa|kuñjareṇa:

«mayā tvam āpthāḥ śaraṇaṃ bhayeṣu:
vayaṃ tvay" âpy āpsmahi dharma|vṛddhyai.
kṣatraṃ dvijatvaṃ ca paraspar'|ârthaṃ.
śaṅkāṃ kṛthā mā: prahiṇusva sūnum.

ghāniṣyate tena mahān vipakṣaḥ,
sthāyiṣyate yena raṇe purastāt.
mā māṃ, mah"|ātman, paribhūr: a|yogye
na mad|vidho nyasyati bhāram agryam.»

«krudhyan kulaṃ dhakṣyati vipra|vahnir,
yāsyan sutas tapsyati māṃ sa|manyum.»
itthaṃ nṛpaḥ pūrvam avāluloce,
tato 'nujajñe gamanaṃ sutasya.

āśīrbhir abhyarcya muniḥ kṣit'|îndraṃ
prītaḥ pratasthe punar āśramāya.
taṃ pṛṣṭhataḥ praṣṭham iyāya namro,
hiṃsr'|êṣu|dīpt'|āpta|dhanuḥ, kumāraḥ.

The sage declared: "That contemplation is auspicious but demons are obstructing the forest rites. Let Rama and Lákshmana who are used to distaining the valor of their enemies crush them."

When the king, unable to bear separation from his son, had 1.20
heard his words he was stupefied. Then that proud foremost ascetic said to the splendid king:

"I have come to you as a refuge from dangers; you too have come to us for the increase of *dharma*. The warrior and priestly castes are mutually supportive. Do not fear; send your son.

Placed in the forefront of the battle, he will kill a great adversary. Do not disregard me, O great-souled one: one such as I would not place an unbearable burden on one who is unfit."

"As an angry fire this brahmin will consume my clan; whereas my son who is about to leave will burn me as I grieve," the king first considered thus, then he sanctioned the departure of his son.

The delighted sage, honoring the lord of the earth with blessings, set out again for his hermitage. The humble prince, his bow gleaming with cruel arrows, followed after the departing sage.

1.25 prayāsyataḥ puṇya|vanāya jiṣṇo
Rāmasya rociṣṇu|mukhasya, dhṛṣṇuḥ
traimāturaḥ kṛtsna|jit'|âstra|śastraḥ
sadhryaṅ rataḥ śreyasi Lakṣmaṇo 'bhūt.

iṣu|mati Raghu|siṃhe dandaśūkāñ jighāṃsau
dhanur aribhir a|sahyaṃ muṣṭi|pīḍaṃ dadhāne
vrajati, pura|taruṇyo baddha|citr'|âṅgulitre
katham api guru|śokān mā rudan māṅgalikyaḥ.

atha jagadur a|nīcair āśiṣas tasya viprās;
tumula|kala|ninādaṃ tūryam ājaghnur anye;
abhimata|phala|śaṃsī cāru pusphora bāhus
taruṣu cukuvur uccaiḥ pakṣiṇaś c' ânukūlāḥ.

As he reveled in the good of the victorious and bright- 1.25
countenanced Rama just setting out for the holy forest, bold Lákshmana of three mothers,* who had completely mastered missiles and weapons, went along with him.

Whilst Rama, lion of the line of Raghu, was setting out with his arrows, intent on killing mordacious demons, bearing a bow unbearable to his enemies clutched in his fist, his colorful finger guard strapped on, the young girls of the city most auspiciously somehow managed not to weep with heavy grief.

Then the priests loudly uttered blessings for him; others struck a drum of sound loud and sweet; his arm throbbed agreeably promising the desired fruit and the birds in the trees sang loudly in accord.

CANTO 2
MARRIAGE TO SITA

2.1 VANAS|PATĪNĀṂ sarasāṃ nadīnāṃ
tejasvināṃ kānti|bhṛtāṃ diśāṃ ca
niryāya tasyāḥ sa puraḥ samantāc
chriyaṃ dadhānāṃ śaradaṃ dadarśa.

taraṅga|saṅgāc capalaiḥ palāśair
jvālā|śriyaṃ s'|âtiśayāṃ dadhanti
sa|dhūma|dīpt'|âgni|rucīni rejus
tāmr'|ôtpalāny ākula|ṣaṭpadāni.

bimb'|āgatais tīra|vanaiḥ samṛddhiṃ
nijāṃ viloky' âpahṛtāṃ payobhiḥ
kūlāni *s'|āmarṣatay*" êva tenuḥ
saroja|lakṣmīṃ sthala|padma|*hāsaiḥ*.

niśā|tuṣārair nayan'|âmbu|kalpaiḥ,
patr'|ânta|paryāgalad|accha|binduḥ,
upārurod' êva nadat|pataṅgaḥ
kumudvatīṃ tīra|tarur din'|ādau.

2.5 vanāni toyāni ca netra|kalpaiḥ
puṣpaiḥ saro|jaiś ca nilīna|bhṛṅgaiḥ
paras|parāṃ vismayavanti lakṣmīm
ālokayāṃ cakrur iv' ādareṇa.

prabhāta|vāt'|āhati|kampit'|ākṛtiḥ
kumudvatī|reṇu|piśaṅga|vigraham
nirāsa bhṛṅgaṃ kupit" êva padminī:
na māninī saṃsahate 'nya|saṅgamam.

THEN AS HE went out of the city he saw all around him the fall setting out the glory of the trees, lakes, rivers, luminaries and the bright horizons. 2.1

The red lotuses displayed an extraordinary flame-like beauty, their petals were atremble with the lapping waves, with their crowds of bees they shone, their light like fire from a smoking lamp.

As they saw their own flourishing imitated by the waters in which the bankside groves were reflected, the banks as if *emulous : ireful* increased the beauty of the water lotuses with the *whiteness : mockery* of their land lotuses.

With its tears of night dew as clear drops trickling to the tips of its leaves, a bank-side tree with its bees droning in it seemed to lament the lotus at daybreak.*

The trees with their eye-like blossom and the waters with their lotuses to which the black bees resort, also eye-like, both in astonishment, gazed avidly upon each others' beauty. 2.5

The day lotus, her form trembling in the morning breeze as if angered at the black bee for wearing a smear of night lotus pollen, banishes him: for a proud woman cannot bear for her lover to consort with another.

datt'|âvadhānaṃ madhu|lehi|gītau
praśānta|ceṣṭaṃ hariṇaṃ jighāṃsuḥ,
ākarṇayann utsuka|haṃsa|nādān,
lakṣye samādhiṃ na dadhe mṛgāvit.

girer nitambe marutā vibhinnaṃ
toy'|âvaśeṣeṇa him'|ābham abhram
sarin|mukh'|âbhyuccayam ādadhānaṃ
śail'|âdhipasy' ânucakāra lakṣmīm.

garjan hariḥ s'|âmbhasi śaila|kuñje
pratidhvanīn ātma|kṛtān niśamya,
kramaṃ babandha kramituṃ sa|kopaḥ
pratarkayann anya|mṛg'|êndra|nādān.

2.10 adṛkṣat' âmbhāṃsi nav'|ôtpalāni,
rutāni c' âśroṣata ṣaṭ|padānām,
āghrāyi vān* gandha|vahaḥ su|gandhas*
ten' âravinda|vyatiṣaṅgavāṃś ca.

lat"|ânupātaṃ* kusumāny agṛhṇāt
sa, nady|avaskandam upāspṛśac ca,
kutūhalāc, cāru|śil"|ôpaveśaṃ
Kākutstha īṣat smayamāna āsta.

tigm'|âṃśu|raśmi|cchuritāny a|dūrāt
prāñci prabhāte salilāny apaśyat
gabhasti|dhārābhir iva drutāni
tejāṃsi bhānor bhuvi saṃbhṛtāni.

As he sought to kill a deer as it stood still and gave its attention to the song of a honey-licking bee, the huntsman, hearing the calls of the restless geese,* was unable to concentrate on his target.

A snowlike cloud, broken up by the wind on the ridge of a mountain and swelling the mouths of the rivers with the remainder of its water, emulated the beauty of the king of mountains.

A roaring lion in his watery mountain goyle, hearing his self-made echoes, thinking them the echoes of some other king of beasts, was bound in his anger to take a stance.

Rama saw the waters with their new lotuses, he heard the 2.10
six-footed bees humming and he smelt the lotus-entangled scent-bearing breeze blowing fragrantly.

Rama eagerly went to each creeper and gathered blossom, as he stooped to each stream he sipped the water and as he reached each attractive stone he sat with a slight smile.

Nearby in the east at dawn he saw the waters inlaid with the gleams of the sun as if the luster of the sun had been dissolved by streams of rays and collected on the earth.*

dig|vyāpinīr locana|lobhanīyā
mṛj"|ânvayāḥ *sneham* iva sravantīḥ
ṛjv|āyatāḥ śasya|viśeṣa|paṅktīs
tutoṣa paśyan vitṛṇ'|ântarālāḥ.

viyoga|duḥkh'|ânubhav'|ân|abhijñaiḥ
kāle nṛp'|âṃśaṃ vihitaṃ dadadbhiḥ
āhārya|śobhā|rahitair a|māyair
aikṣiṣṭa pumbhiḥ pracitān sa goṣṭhān.

2.15 strī|bhūṣaṇaṃ ceṣṭitam a|pragalbhaṃ
cārūṇy a|vakrāṇy api vīkṣitāni
ṛjūṃś ca viśvāsa|kṛtaḥ svabhāvān
gop'|âṅganānāṃ mumude vilokya.

vivṛtta|pārśvaṃ rucir'|âṅga|hāraṃ
samudvahac|cāru|nitamba|ramyam
āmandra|mantha|dhvani|datta|tālaṃ
gop'|âṅganā|nṛtyam anandayat tam.

vicitram uccaiḥ plavamānam ārāt*
kutūhalaṃ trasnu tatāna tasya
megh'|âtyay'|ôpātta|van'|ôpaśobhaṃ
kadambakaṃ vātam|ajaṃ mṛgāṇām.

sit'|âravinda|pracayeṣu līnāḥ
saṃsakta|pheṇeṣu ca saikateṣu
kund'|âvadātāḥ kala|haṃsa|mālāḥ
pratīyire śrotra|sukhair ninādaiḥ.

He delighted to see the straight long rows of corn with their grassless interstices reaching to the horizons, beautiful to behold and pure, as if oozing their *oil : love.*

He saw cowfolds collected together by guileless men, whose beauty was unembellished, who were innocent of the experience of separation's sorrow and who paid their ordained tax to the king on time.*

He rejoiced to see that ornament of women: the modest 2.15
manner of the cowherd girls whose glances were charming though not coquettish, and whose natures were honest and confiding.

The dance of the cowherd girls, its beat provided by the deep sound of churning, delighted him as they twisted their flanks and made their charming gestures, cute as they lifted their pretty buttocks.*

Revealed as the clouds passed, a timid herd of spotted deer drew his curiosity from afar, swift as the wind, jumping high, the ornament of the forest.

Skeins of geese white as jasmine, lying among the clumps of white lotuses and on the foam-strewn sandbars were distinguishable only by their ear-pleasing calls.*

na taj jalaṃ, yan na su|cāru|paṅkajaṃ;
na paṅkajaṃ tad, yad a|līna|ṣaṭpadam;
na ṣaṭpado 'sau, na juguñja yaḥ kalaṃ;
na guñjitaṃ tan, na jahāra yan manaḥ.

2.20 taṃ yāyajūkāḥ saha bhikṣu|mukhyais
tapaḥ|kṛśāḥ śānty|uda|kumbha|hastāḥ,
yāyāvarāḥ puṣpa|phalena c' ânye
prāṇarcur arcyā jagad|arcanīyam.

vidyām ath' âinaṃ vijayāṃ jayāṃ ca
rakṣo|gaṇaṃ kṣipnum a|vikṣat'|ātmā
adhyāpipad Gādhi|suto yathāvan
nighātayiṣyan yudhi yātu|dhānān.

āyodhane sthāyukam astra|jātam
a|mogham abhyarṇa|mah"|āhavāya
dadau vadhāya kṣaṇadā|carāṇāṃ
tasmai muniḥ śreyasi jāgarūkaḥ.

taṃ vipra|darśaṃ kṛta|ghāta|yatnā
yāntaṃ vane rātri|carī ḍuḍhauke,
jighāṃsu|vedaṃ dhṛta|bhāsur'|âstras
tāṃ Tāḍak"|ākhyāṃ nijaghāna Rāmaḥ.

ath' āluloke huta|dhūma|ketu|
śikh"|âñjana|snigdha|samṛddha|śākham
tapo|vanaṃ prādhyayan'|âbhibhūta|
samuccarac|cāru|patatri|śiñjam.

2.25 kṣudrān na jakṣur hariṇān mṛg'|êndrā;
viśaśvase pakṣi|gaṇaiḥ samantāt;
nannamyamānāḥ phala|ditsay" êva
cakāśire tatra latā vilolāḥ.

There was no water that had no brilliantly beautiful lotuses; there was no lotus but it had a six-footed bee hidden inside; there was no bee that did not hum a soft note; there was no note that did not steal his heart.

Those venerable men along with the foremost mendicants 2.20
and others emaciated by their austerities and constantly engaged in sacrifice, always wandering with pots of holy water in hand, worshipped Rama worthy of the whole world's respect with flowers and fruit.

Then Vishva·mitra, who wished to kill fiends in war, of unwounded soul, the son of Gadhi, instructed him properly in the magical sciences of Victory and Conquest for the destruction of the demon host.

The sage, intent upon the good, gave him a collection of weapons which would endure in battle and not fail in order to kill the demons in the great war looming.

A night-wandering demoness who strove to kill brahmins whenever she saw them stalked him while he was traveling in the forest. As Rama held his radiant weapons he slew that demoness named Tádaka in the knowledge that she wished to kill him.

Then he saw the hermits' grove, where the full branches were smeared with the soot from the flames of sacrificial fires and where the sweet co-mingling songs of birds were outdone by the sound of Vedic chanting.

Lions did not eat the little deer; the flocks of birds all around 2.25
were trustful and the tremulous vines shone as they bowed very low, as if wishing to offer fruit.

apūpujan viṣṭara*|pādya|mālyair
ātithya|niṣṇā vana|vāsi|mukhyāḥ.
pratyagrahīṣṭāṃ madhu|parka|miśraṃ
tāv āsan'|ādi kṣiti|pāla|putrau.

«daity'|âbhibhūtasya yuvām avoḍhaṃ*
magnasya dorbhir bhuvanasya bhāram.
havīṃṣi saṃpraty api rakṣataṃ,» tau
tapo|dhanair ittham abhāṣiṣātām.

tān pratyavādīd atha Rāghavo 'pi,
«yath"|ēpsitaṃ prastuta karma dharmyam.
tapo|marudbhir bhavatāṃ śar'|âgniḥ
saṃdhukṣyatāṃ no 'ri|samindhaneṣu.»

pratuṣṭuvuḥ karma tataḥ praklptais
te yajñiyair* dravya|gaṇair yathāvat.
dakṣiṇya*|diṣṭaṃ kṛtam ārtvijīnais
tad yātu|dhānaiś cicite prasarpat.

2.30 āpiṅga|rūkṣ'|ōrdhva|śirasya*|bālaiḥ
śirāla*|jaṅghair giri|kūṭa|daghnaiḥ*
tataḥ kṣap"|âṭaiḥ pṛthu|piṅgal'|âkṣaiḥ
khaṃ prāvṛṣeṇyair* iva c' ānaśe 'bdaiḥ.

adhijya|cāpaḥ sthira|bāhu|muṣṭir
udañcit'|âkṣo 'ñcita|dakṣiṇ'|ôruḥ,
tān Lakṣmaṇaḥ sannata|vāma|jaṅgho
jaghāna śuddh'|êṣur a|manda|karṣī.

The foremost of the forest dwellers, adepts in hospitality, honored them with couches, foot water and flowers. The two princes accepted seats and other things along with the honey-offering.

The ascetics addressed them thus: "You have borne with your arms the burden of the world sunk down, overcome with demons. You should now also protect the sacrificial offering."

Then Rama replied to them: "Begin the holy rite as you desire. May the winds of your austerities make the fire of my arrows bright amongst the kindling of our enemies."

Then with the sacrificial equipment properly prepared they commenced the rite. Worthy of the ritual gift, they performed it as ordained by the sages. The demons observed it as it proceeded.

Then the sky as if with monsoon clouds was filled with 2.30
demons with reddish rough hair growing upwards on their heads, with sinewy shanks, and as high as mountain peaks.

His bow strung, his arms and fists steady, his eyes raised up, his right leg bent, his left knee crooked, Lákshmana drew back hard with his pure arrows and killed them.

Gādheya|diṣṭaṃ virasaṃ rasantaṃ
Rāmo 'pi māyā|caṇam astra|cuñcuḥ*
sthāsnuṃ raṇe smera|mukho jagāda
Mārīcam uccair vacanaṃ mah"|ârtham.

«ātmaṃ|bharis* tvaṃ piśitair narāṇāṃ
phale|grahīn haṃsi vanas|patīnām.
śauvastikatvaṃ vibhavā na yeṣāṃ
vrajanti, teṣāṃ dayase na kasmāt.»

«admo dvijān, deva|yajīn nihanmaḥ,
kurmaḥ puraṃ preta|nar'|âdhivāsam,
dharmo hy ayaṃ Dāśarathe nijo no,
n' âiv' âdhyakāriṣmahi veda|vṛtte.»

2.35 «dharmo 'sti satyaṃ tava rākṣas' âyam,
anyo vyatiste* tu mam' âpi dharmaḥ,
brahma|dviṣas te praṇihanmi* yena,
rājanya|vṛttir dhṛta|kārmuk'|êṣuḥ.»

itthaṃ|pravādaṃ yudhi saṃprahāraṃ
pracakratū Rāma|niśā|vihārau,
tṛṇāya matvā* Raghunandano 'tha,
bāṇena rakṣaḥ pradhanān nirāsthat.

jagmuḥ prasādaṃ dvija|mānasāni,
dyaur varṣukā* puṣpa|cayaṃ babhūva,
nirvyājam ijyā vavṛte, vacaś ca
bhūyo babhāṣe muninā kumāraḥ.

Rama, renowned for his arrows, with a smiling face spoke loud words of great significance to Marícha who was notorious for his magic, enduring in battle and who, when pointed out by Vishva·mitra, was screaming horribly.

"You nourish yourself with the flesh of men, you harm those who glean fruit from the trees. Why do you not pity those whose wealth will not last until tomorrow?"

"We eat the twiceborn, we slay those who sacrifice to the gods, we make the city an abode of the dead, for this is our own *dharma*, O son of Dasha·ratha. We have not been authorized to perform Vedic rites."

"This may well be your true *dharma*, demon, but I have 2.35
another superior duty by which I, following the way of the warrior and holding bow and arrow, will kill you the brahmin-hater."

Riposting thus, Rama and the night-wandering demon began to fight in a battle. Then the delight of Raghu considering him mere grass removed the fiend from the fight with a single arrow.

The hearts of the twiceborn became serene, the sky began to rain heaps of flowers, sacrifice proceeded without obstacle and the prince exchanged more words with the sage.

«mahīyyamānā* bhavat" âtimātraṃ
sur'|âdhvare ghasmara*|jitvareṇa
divo 'pi Vajrāyudha|bhūṣaṇāyā
hriṇīyate vīravatī na bhūmiḥ.

Balir babandhe, jala|dhir mamanthe,
jahre 'mṛtaṃ, daitya|kulaṃ vijigye,
kalp'|ânta|duḥsthā vasudhā tath" ōhe
yen' âiṣa bhāro 'tigurur na tasya.»

2.40 iti bruvāṇo madhuraṃ hitaṃ ca
tam āñjihan Maithila|yajña|bhūmim,
Rāmaṃ muniḥ prīta|manā makh'|ânte,
yaśāṃsi rājñāṃ nijighṛkṣayiṣyan.*

«itaḥ* sma Mitrā|Varuṇau kim etau?
kim aśvinau soma|rasaṃ pipāsū?»
janaṃ samastaṃ Janak'|āśrama|sthaṃ
rūpeṇa tāv aujihatāṃ nṛ|siṃhau.

ajigrahat taṃ Janako dhanus tad
yen' ārdidad daitya|puraḥ* Pinākī,
jijñāsamāno balam asya bāhvor.
hasann abhāṅkṣīd Raghunandanas tat.

tato nadī|ṣṇān pathikān giri|jñān
āhvāyakān bhūmi|pater Ayodhyām
ditsuḥ sutāṃ yodha|harais turaṅgair
vyasarjayan Maithila|martya|mukhyaḥ.

"In overcoming the gluttonous demons you honor the earth beyond measure in the sacrifice to the gods. It is now possessed of warriors and is not ashamed even before heaven whose ornament is the lightning-weaponed Indra.

This burden is not too heavy for one who bound the demon Bali, who churned the ocean, who seized the nectar of immortality, who conquered the demon race and who bore up the earth in peril at the end of an eon."*

Speaking thus sweetly and for his benefit the sage, whose 2.40
heart was glad at the conclusion of the sacrifice, incited
Rama to seek to overpower the fame of the other kings and
sent him to the sacrificial enclosure of the king of Míthila.

On account of their beauty, those two lion-like men made all those resident in Jánaka's hermitage wonder, "Have Mitra and Váruna come? Are these the Ashvins seeking to drink the *soma* juice?"

Jánaka wanting to know the strength of his arms made him take up that bow with which Shiva had destroyed the cities of the demons. The scion of Raghu snapped it with a smile.

Then because he sought to bestow his daughter, the foremost among the mortals of Míthila sent guides who knew the rivers and the mountains on war-horses to Ayódhya as messengers for the king.

kṣipraṃ tato 'dhvanya|turaṅga|yāyī
yaviṣṭhavad vṛddhatamo 'pi rājā
ākhyāyakebhyaḥ śruta|sūnu|vṛttir
a|glāna|yāno Mithilām agacchat.

2.45 vṛndiṣṭham ārcīd vasudh"|âdhipānāṃ
taṃ preṣṭham etaṃ guruvad gariṣṭham
sadṛṅ|mahāntaṃ sukṛt'|âdhivāsaṃ
baṃhiṣṭha|kīrtir* yaśasā variṣṭham.

«tri|varga|pārīṇam* asau bhavantam
adhyāsayann āsanam ekam Indraḥ
viveka|dṛśvatvam* agāt* surāṇāṃ,»
taṃ Maithilo vākyam idaṃ babhāṣe.

hiraṇmayī* sāla|lat" êva jaṅgamā,
cyutā divaḥ sthāsnur iv' â|cira|prabhā
śaśāṅka|kānter adhidevat"|ākṛtiḥ
sutā dade tasya sutāya Maithilī.

labdhāṃ tato viśva|janīna*|vṛttis
tām ātmanīnām udavoḍha* Rāmaḥ,
sad|ratna|muktā|phala|bharma|śobhāṃ
saṃbaṃhayantīm Raghu|vargya*|lakṣmīm.

suprātam āsādita|saṃmadaṃ tad
vandārubhiḥ saṃstutam abhy|Ayodhyam
aśvīya|rājanyaka|hāstik'|āḍhyam
agāt sa|rājaṃ balam adhvanīnam.

Then when he heard the news of his son from the messengers the king riding post-horses quickly like the youngest of men though very old, went without fatigue to Míthila.

Similar to him, Jánaka of abundant fame honored Dasha· 2.45
ratha most excellent of the rulers of the earth and like a teacher in his great importance, the great abode of merit and the greatest in renown.

Jánaka said to him, "By seating you who are on the verge of achieving the three aims of human life on the throne, Indra has of all the gods become the one who has seen reason."

Jánaka gave his daughter, the Princess of Míthila, who moved like a golden vine on a tree, like a continuous lightning flash fallen from heaven, in form the divinity of moonlight, to Dasha·ratha's son.

Then Rama, whose conduct benefited all, married the girl he had won, she who was most suited to him, splendid with ornaments of fine jewels, pearls, and gold, and who established firmly the glory of the house of Raghu.

In the beautiful dawn the delighted army, praised by the bards, replete with horse, infantry and elephants, proceeded on its way towards Ayódhya with the king.

2.50 viśaṅkaṭo vakṣasi bāṇa|pāṇiḥ
sampanna|tāla|dvayasaḥ purastāt
bhīṣmo dhanuṣmān upa|jānv|aratnir
aiti sma Rāmaḥ pathi Jāmadagnyaḥ.

uccair asau Rāghavam āhvat' «êdaṃ
dhanuḥ sa|bāṇaṃ kuru, m" âtiyāsīḥ.»
parākrama|jñaḥ priya|santatis taṃ
namraḥ kṣit'|îndro 'nuninīṣur ūce:

«anekaśo nirjita|rājakas tvaṃ,
pitṝn atārpsīr nṛpa|rakta|toyaiḥ,
saṃkṣipya* saṃrambham a|sad|vipakṣaṃ.
k" āsth" ârbhake 'smiṃs tava, Rāma, Rāme?»

ajīgaṇad* Dāśarathaṃ na vākyaṃ
yadā sa darpeṇa, tadā kumāraḥ
dhanur vyakārkṣīd guru|bāṇa|garbhaṃ,
lokān alāvīd vijitāṃś ca tasya.

jite nṛp'|ârau, sumanī|bhavanti
śabdāyamānāny a|śanair a|śaṅkam
vṛddhasya rājño 'numate balāni
jagāhire 'n|eka|mukhāni mārgān.

2.55 atha puru|java|yogān nedayad* dūra|saṃsthaṃ
davayad atirayeṇa prāptam urvī|vibhāgam,
klama|rahitam a|cetan nīrajī|kārita|kṣmāṃ
balam upahita|śobhāṃ tūrṇam āyād Ayodhyām.

On the road, Rama Jámadagnya,* broad of chest, arrows 2.50
in hand, as tall as a palm tree, fearsome, bearing a bow, his
forearms reaching to his knees, came before them.

He loudly challenged Rama: "Fix an arrow to this bow of yours. Go no further." Because he knew his power and held his own son dear, the king of the earth bowed down and, wishing to conciliate him, said:

"You have slain innumerable kings and you have placated your ancestors with water in the form of the blood of those kings: restrain your unchallengeable anger. What concern have you with this youth Rama, O Rama?"

When he in his pride did not heed Dasha·ratha's son's words, the prince drew back the bow pregnant with a heavy arrow and excised those worlds which he had won.*

When the enemy of the kings had been conquered the troops were delighted in their hearts and cheered loudly. They plunged down the roads in many directions with the permission of the old king with speed and confidence.

Then as it drew near to far off places with great speed and as 2.55
it very quickly became distant to regions of the earth that it
had already reached, the army without fatigue and without
concern soon reached Ayódhya which had been exquisitely
decorated and whose ground had been cleared of dust.

CANTO 3
THE EXILE OF RAMA

3.1 Vadhena saṃkhye piśit'|âśanānāṃ
kṣatr'|ântakasy' âbhibhavena c' âiva
āḍhyaṃ|bhaviṣṇur yaśasā kumāraḥ
priyaṃ|bhaviṣṇur na sa yasya n' āsīt.

tataḥ sucetī|kṛta|paura|bhṛtyo
«rājye 'bhiṣekṣye sutam» ity a|nīcaiḥ
āghoṣayan bhūmi|patiḥ samastaṃ
bhūyo 'pi lokaṃ sumanī|cakāra.

ādikṣad ādīpta|kṛśānu|kalpaṃ
siṃh'|āsanaṃ tasya sa|pāda|pīṭham,
santapta|cāmīkara|valgu|vajraṃ
vibhāga|vinyasta|mah"|ârgha|ratnam.

prāsthāpayat pūga|kṛtān sva|poṣaṃ
puṣṭān prayatnād, dṛḍha|gātra|bandhān,
sa|bharma|kumbhān, puruṣān
samantāt pat|kāṣiṇas tīrtha|jal'|ârtham āśu.

3.5 ukṣāṃ pracakrur* nagarasya mārgān,
dhvajān babandhur, mumucuḥ kha|dhūpān,
diśaś ca puṣpaiś cakarur vicitrair
artheṣu rājñā nipuṇā niyuktāḥ.

mātā|mah'|āvāsam upeyivāṃsaṃ
mohād a|pṛṣṭvā Bharataṃ tadānīm
tat Kekayī soḍhum a|śaknuvānā,
vavāra Rāmasya vana|prayāṇam.

By killing the flesh-eaters and defeating the killers of warriors in battle the prince became rich in fame and dear to all. 3.1

Then the king who had already so delighted the hearts of his citizens and dependents had it loudly proclaimed: "I will anoint my son as king" and once again gladdened the hearts of his whole people.

He ordered a lion's throne for him and a footstool in form like blazing fire, with gorgeous diamonds in molten gold and its sections inlaid with gems of great price.

To get water from the holy fords he quickly sent men out on foot in all directions. They were formed into groups and were carefully supported by his own wealth, their bodies were of firm constitution and they bore golden pots.

The king employed specialists in these matters to have the streets of the city sprinkled, to put up banners, burn incense, and strew the quarters with multifarious flowers. 3.5

Because of her foolishness Kékayi did not consult Bharata who was at that time absent at his maternal grandfather's house. She was unable to bear it and sought Rama's forest exile.

karṇe|japair āhita|rājya|lobhā
strainena nītā vikṛtiṃ laghimnā,
Rāma|pravāse vyamṛśan na doṣaṃ
jan'|âpavādaṃ sa|nar'|êndra|mṛtyum.

vasūni deśāṃś ca nivartayiṣyan
Rāmaṃ nṛpaḥ saṃgiramāṇa eva
tay" âvajajñe, Bharat'|âbhiṣeko
viṣāda|śaṅkuś ca matau nicakhne.

tataḥ pravivrājayiṣuḥ kumāram
ādikṣad asy' âbhigamaṃ vanāya
Saumitri|Sīt"|ânucarasya rājā
Sumantra|netreṇa rathena śocan.

3.10 ke cin ninindur nṛpam a|praśāntaṃ,
vicukruśuḥ ke cana s'|âsram uccaiḥ,
ūcus tath" ânye Bharatasya māyāṃ,
«dhik Kekayīm» ity aparo jagāda.

«gato vanaṃ śvo bhavit" êti Rāmaḥ»
śokena dehe janat" âtimātram,
dhīrās tu tatra cyuta|manyavo 'nye
dadhuḥ kumār'|ânugame manāṃsi.

prasthāsyamānāv upaseduṣas tau
śośucyamānān idam ūcatus tān
«kiṃ śocat' êh' âbhyudaye bat' âsmān
niyoga|lābhena pituḥ kṛt'|ârthān?

Her greed for the kingdom was engendered by those whispering in her ear and she was led to perversity by her feminine lack of gravitas. She did not consider the matter of Rama's exile to be an evil though it brought the censure of the people and the death of the king.

The king hoped to prevent Rama's departure and promised her wealth and lands. She scorned him and the coronation of Bharata was a nail of despair implanted in his heart.

Then the wailing king cooperated with the prince's departure and ordered his departure to the forest accompanied by Lákshmana and Sita in a chariot with Sumántra as driver.

Some blamed the unhappy king, some cried loudly and 3.10
tearfully, others spoke of the delusion of Bharata and one even said "Damned be Kékayi."

Tomorrow Rama will have gone to the forest!" So grief burned the people excessively, but some were firm of mind and setting aside their grief, fixed their hearts upon following the princes.

As they were about to set out the two princes said this to those who had approached grieving intensely: "Why in this dawn do you lament for us who have gained a great objective through our father's commission?

asṛṣṭa yo, yaś ca bhayeṣv arakṣīd,
yaḥ sarvad" âsmān apuṣat sva|poṣam,
mah"|ôpakārasya kim asti tasya
tucchena yānena vanasya mokṣaḥ?

vidyut|praṇāśaṃ sa varaṃ pranaṣṭo,
yad v" ōrdhva|śoṣaṃ tṛṇavad viśuṣkaḥ,
arthe durāpe kim uta pravāse
na śāsane 'vāsthita yo gurūṇām?

3.15 paurā, nivartadhvam» iti nyagādīt,
«tātasya śok'|âpanudā bhaveta.
mā darśat' ânyaṃ Bharataṃ ca matto.»
«nivartay' êty āha rathaṃ» sma sūtam.

jñātv" êṅgitair gatvaratāṃ janānām,
ekāṃ śayitvā rajanīṃ sa|pauraḥ
rakṣan vane|vāsa|kṛtād bhayāt tān
prātaś chalen' âpajagāma Rāmaḥ.

asrākṣur asraṃ, karuṇaṃ ruvanto,
muhur muhur nyaśvasiṣuḥ kav'|ôṣṇam*
«hā Rāma, hā kaṣṭam» iti bruvantaḥ
parāṅ|mukhais te nyavṛtan manobhiḥ.

sūto 'pi Gaṅgā|salilaiḥ pavitvā
sah'|âśvam ātmānam an|alpa|manyuḥ,
sa|Sītayo Rāghavayor adhīyan
śvasan kaduṣṇaṃ puram āviveśa.

Can a trifling journey to the forest free us from our debt for the great assistance of our father who begat us, protected us from dangers and always nourished us with his own abundance?

It would be better for a man to be destroyed by lightning or to be withered standing like a blade of grass were he not to abide by the orders of his elders in a difficult matter, so what then of a mere sojourn?

Return, O citizens," he declared, "Remove my father's grief. 3.15
Do not look upon Bharata as other than me." He then told his driver to turn the chariot.

Rama knew by their movements that the people intended to go with him and slept one night among them protecting them from the dangers of the jungle wildlife and departed early by stealth.

They shed tears and crying pitifully they sighed warmly again and again saying, "O Rama, oh alas!" and then turned back with reluctant hearts.

Even the charioteer with no small sorrow purified himself and his horses in the waters of the Ganges and thinking of the two scions of Raghu together with Sita, sighed warmly as he re-entered the city.

pratīya sā pūr dadṛśe janena
dyaur bhānu|śīt'|âṃśu|vinā|kṛt" êva,
rājanya|nakṣatra|samanvit" âpi,
śok'|ândhakāra|kṣata|sarva|ceṣṭā.

3.20 vilokya Rāmeṇa vinā Sumantram
acyoṣṭa sattvān nṛ|patiś cyut'|āśaḥ
madhūni n' āiṣīd vyalipan na gandhair,
mano|rame na vyavasiṣṭa vastre.

āsiṣṭa n' âikatra śucā, vyaraṃsīt
kṛt'|â|kṛtebhyaḥ kṣiti|pāla|bhāgbhyaḥ.
sa candan'|ôśīra|mṛṇāla|digdhaḥ
śok'|âgnin" âgād dyu|nivāsa|bhūyam.

vicukruśur bhūmi|pater mahiṣyaḥ,
keśāl̄ luluñcuḥ, sva|vapūṃṣi jaghnuḥ,
vibhūṣaṇāny unmumucuḥ, kṣamāyām
petur, babhañjur valayāni c' âiva.

tāḥ sāntvayantī Bharata|pratīkṣā
taṃ bandhutā nyakṣipad āśu taile.
dūtāṃś ca rāj'|ātmajam āninīṣūn
prāsthāpayan mantri|matena yūnaḥ.

«supto nabhastaḥ patitaṃ nirīkṣāṃ
cakre vivasvantam adhaḥ sphurantam,»
ākhyad vasan mātṛ|kule sakhibhyaḥ
paśyan pramādaṃ Bharato 'pi rājñaḥ.

To the returning people that city though full of constellations of warriors seemed like the sky deprived of the sun and moon, all activity impaired by the darkness of grief.

When the king saw Sumántra without Rama he lost his 3.20
hope and lost his self command. He did not want sweet drinks, he did not anoint himself with perfumes and he did not put on his fine vestments.

He could not sit in one place for grief, he abandoned unfinished the duties that are the part of the king. On account of the fire of grief he went anointed with sandal, vetiver and lotus root to the world of the denizens of heaven.

The queens of the earth's lord cried out, tore their hair, struck their own bodies, pulled off their ornaments, fell to the earth and broke their bangles.

The family consoling the queens and out of respect for Bharata quickly embalmed him. With the approval of the ministers they sent young messengers eager to bring the king's son.

Bharata was staying with his mother's family. He saw the calamity of the king and said to his friends, "While asleep I saw the sun fallen from the sky lie quivering below."

3.25 aśiśravann ātyayikaṃ tam etya
dūtā yad" ârthaṃ prayiyāsayantaḥ,
āṃhiṣṭa jāt'|âñjihiṣas tad" âsāv
utkaṇṭhamāno Bharato gurūṇām.

bandhūn aśaṅkiṣṭa samākulatvād
āseduṣaḥ sneha|vaśād apāyam:
gomāyu|sāraṅga|gaṇāś ca samyaṅ
n' âyāsiṣur, bhīmam arāsiṣuś ca.

sa proṣivān etya puraṃ pravekṣyan
śuśrāva ghoṣaṃ na jan'|âugha|janyam,
ākarṇayām āsa na veda|nādān,
na c' ôpalebhe vaṇijāṃ paṇ'|āyān.

cakrandur uccair nṛ|patiṃ sametya
taṃ mātaro 'bhyarṇam upāgat'|âsrāḥ,
purohit'|âmātya|mukhāś ca yodhā
vivṛddha|manyu|pratipūrṇa|manyāḥ.

didṛkṣamāṇaḥ paritaḥ sa|Sītaṃ
Rāmaṃ yadā n' āikṣata Lakṣmaṇaṃ ca,
rorudyamānaḥ sa tad" âbhyapṛcchad,
yathāvad ākhyann atha vṛttam asmai.

3.30 ābaddha|bhīma|bhru|kuṭī|vibhaṅgaḥ
śeśvīyamān'|âruṇa|raudra|netraḥ,
uccair upālabdha sa Kekayīṃ ca,
śoke muhuś c' â|virataṃ nyamāṅkṣīt.

When the messengers intent upon their object came to him 3.25
without delay they did not tell him. Once he had decided
to go, Bharata set out longing for his elders.

Perplexed by his being overcome by affection, he feared that his relatives were about to meet with some calamity; packs of jackals and herds of deer passed inauspiciously and howled terribly.

He, after sojourning abroad, about to enter the city on his return, did not hear the cacophony made by the crowds of people, did not hear the Vedic chanting, or the hawking of the merchants.

His mothers joined him when he was near. With streaming tears they loudly lamented the king, as did the soldiers led by the priests and ministers, their throats full with swelling grief.

When he looked around to see Rama with Sita and Lákshmana and did not see them, he asked about them weeping bitterly. Then they told him what had happened just as it was.

With his fierce brows bound into a furrow, his red raging 3.30
eyes so swollen, he loudly reproached Kékayi and plunged
instantly into uninterrupted grief.

«nṛp'|ātmajau cikliśatuḥ sa|Sītau,
mamāra rājā, vidhavā bhavatyaḥ,
śocyā vayaṃ, bhūr a|nṛpā: laghutvaṃ
Kekayy|upajñaṃ bata bahv|an|artham.

n' âitan mataṃ matkam» iti bruvāṇaḥ
sahasraśo 'sau śapathān aśapyat.
udvāśyamānaḥ pitaraṃ sa|Rāmaṃ
luṭhyan sa|śoko bhuvi rorudāvān.

taṃ susthayantaḥ sacivā nar'|êndraṃ
didhakṣayantaḥ samudūhur ārāt
anty'|āhutiṃ hāvayituṃ sa|viprāś
cicīṣayanto 'dhvara|pātra|jātam.

udakṣipan paṭṭa|dukūla|ketūn,
avādayan veṇu|mṛdaṅga|kāṃsyam,
kambūṃś ca tārān adhaman samantāt,
tath" ānayan kuṅkuma|candanāni.

3.35 śrotr'|âkṣi|nāsā|vadanaṃ sa|rukmaṃ
kṛtv" âjine prāk|śirasaṃ nidhāya,
sañcitya pātrāṇi yathā|vidhānam
ṛtvig juhāva jvalitaṃ cit"|âgnim.

kṛteṣu piṇḍ'|ôdaka|sañcayeṣu,
hitv" âbhiṣekaṃ prakṛtaṃ prajābhiḥ
pratyāninīṣur vinayena Rāmaṃ
prāyād araṇyaṃ Bharataḥ sa|pauraḥ.

śīghrāyamāṇaiḥ kakubho 'śnuvānair
janair a|panthānam upetya sṛptaiḥ
śokād a|bhūṣair api bhūś cakāsāṃ
cakāra nāg'|êndra|rath'|âśva|miśraiḥ.

"The two princes and Sita have suffered, the king is dead, you ladies are widows, we are pitiful, the earth is without a king: alas how shallow Kékayi is discovered to be and how disastrous that shallowness!"

"This was not my plan," he said and cursed a thousand times. Pleading for his father and Rama and rolling on the ground in grief he wept bitterly.

The ministers and the brahmins cared well for him and induced him to want to cremate the body of the king. They had it taken nearby so that he would wish to collect the sacrificial vessels to perform the final oblation.

As they put up banners of silk cloth, they sounded flutes, drums and gongs, they blew loud conches all around and so also they brought saffron and sandal.

After placing gold on its ears, eyes, nose and mouth and 3.35
placing the corpse facing east on the skin of a blackbuck and arranging the utensils according to rule, the priest sacrificed into the blazing pyre.

When the offerings of food and water were made and the collecting of the bones was done, Bharata set aside the installation ceremony proposed by his subjects and went to the forest with the citizens with the intention of restoring Rama with all propriety.

Though for grief they were without ornaments, the earth shone with the people mingled with great elephants and horses, moving quickly, filling the horizons, continuing over pathless tracts.

uccikyire puṣpa|phalaṃ vanāni,
  sasnuḥ pitṝn pipriyur āpagāsu,
āreṭur itvā pulināny a|śaṅkaṃ,
  chāyāṃ samāśritya viśaśramuś ca.

saṃprāpya tīraṃ Tamas"|âpagāyā
  Gaṅg"|âmbu|samparka|viśuddhi|bhājaḥ,
vigāhituṃ Yāmunam ambu puṇyaṃ
  yayur niruddha|śrama|vṛttayas te.

3.40 īyur Bharadvāja|muner niketaṃ
  yasmin viśaśrāma sametya Rāmaḥ.
cyut'|âśanāyāḥ* phalavad|vibhūtyā
  vyāsyann udanyāṃ śiśiraiḥ payobhiḥ.

vācaṃ|yamān sthaṇḍila|śāyinaś ca
  yuyukṣamāṇān a|niśaṃ mumukṣūn
adhyāpayantaṃ vinayāt praṇemuḥ
  pad|gā Bharadvāja|muniṃ sa|śiṣyaṃ.

ātithyam ebhyaḥ pari|nirvivapsoḥ*
  kalpa|drumā yoga|balena pheluḥ,
dhāma|prathimno mradim'|ânvitāni
  vāsāṃsi ca drāghimavanty udūhuḥ.

ājñāṃ pratīṣur, vinayād upāsthur,
  jaguḥ sa|rāgaṃ, nanṛtuḥ sa|hāvam,
sa|vibhramaṃ nemur udāram ūcus
  Tilottam"|ādyā vanitāś ca tasmin.

They gathered flowers and fruit in the woods, they bathed themselves and propitiated their ancestors in the rivers and coming to the sandy banks without fear they chattered and upon finding shade they rested.

They reached the bank of the Támasa river, which partook of holiness through its confluence with the waters of the Ganges, and without feeling tired they went on to bathe in the holy waters of the Yámuna.

They went to the house of the sage Bharad·vaja where Rama 3.40
had reposed on meeting him. The abundance of fruiting plants drove away their hunger and they slaked their thirst with the cool waters.

Going on foot out of respect they bowed to the sage Bharad·vaja and his students, as he taught those who controlled their speech, who slept on sacrificial ground, who sought only to practice yoga and who constantly desired liberation.

When the sage great in radiance sought to give them hospitality the wish-granting trees fruited through the force of his yoga and bore raiment lengthy and soft.

And Tilóttama and the other nymphs accepted his command, served modestly, sang melodiously, danced captivatingly, bowed gracefully and spoke nobly.

vastr'|ânna|pānaṃ śayanaṃ ca nānā
kṛtv" âvakāśe ruci|saṃprakḷptam,
tān prītimān āha munis tataḥ sma
«nivadhvam ādhvaṃ pibat' âtta śedhvam.»

3.45 te bhuktavantaḥ su|sukhaṃ vasitvā
vāsāṃsy uṣitvā rajanīṃ prabhāte
drutaṃ samadhvā ratha|vāji|nāgair
Mandākinīṃ ramya|vanāṃ samīyuḥ.

vaikhānasebhyaḥ śruta|Rāma|vārttās
tato viśiñjāna|patatri|saṅgham
abhraṃ|lih'|âgraṃ ravi|mārga|bhaṅgam
ānaṃhire 'driṃ prati Citrakūṭam.

dṛṣṭv" ōrṇuvānān kakubho bal'|âughān,
vitatya śārṅgaṃ, kavacaṃ pinahya,
tasthau sisaṃgrāmayiṣuḥ śit'|êṣuḥ
Saumitrir, akṣi|bhruvam ujjihānaḥ.

śukl'|ôttar'|āsaṅga|bhṛto, viśastrān,
pādaiḥ śanair, āpatataḥ pramanyūn,
auhiṣṭa tān vīta|viruddha|buddhīn
vivandiṣūn Dāśarathiḥ sva|vargyān.

sa|mūla|kāṣaṃ cakaṣū rudanto
Rām'|ântikaṃ bṛṃhita|manyu|vegāḥ
āvedayantaḥ kṣiti|pālam uccaiḥ|
kāraṃ mṛtaṃ Rāma|viyoga|śokāt.

Ensuring clothes, food, drink and bedding were arranged beautifully in various locations, the delighted sage then said to them, "Dress, sit, drink, eat and sleep."

They ate with great delight, putting on the clothes and stay- 3.45
ing the night, and at first light they were on the road with chariots, horses and elephants towards the Mandákini river and its pleasant groves.

When they heard news of Rama from the anchorites, they set out for the Chitra·kuta mountain with its flocks of calling birds and its cloud-licking peaks which broke the course of the sun.

Seeing a mass of troops surrounding the peaks Lákshmana yearning for battle strung his bow and fastened on his armor and stood with his sharp arrows, raising his eyes and brows.

As they approached wearing white outer garments, weaponless, with quiet steps, the grief-stricken son of Dasha·ratha realized them to be his own people without hostile intent, seeking to honor him.

They writhed weeping and rubbing themselves into the rooty ground. The force of their grief increased as they came near to Rama and they declared loudly that because of the anguish from Rama's separation the king had died.

3.50 ciraṃ ruditvā karuṇaṃ sa|śabdaṃ
gotr'|âbhidhāyaṃ saritaṃ sametya
madhye|jalād Rāghava|Lakṣmaṇābhyāṃ
prattaṃ* jalaṃ dvy|añjalam antike 'pām.

«araṇya|yāne sukare pitā mā
prāyuṅkta, rājye bata duṣ|kare tvām,
mā gāḥ śucaṃ vīra, bharaṃ vah' âmum»
ābhāṣi Rāmeṇa vacaḥ kanīyān.

«kṛtī śrutī vṛddha|mateṣu dhīmāṃs
tvaṃ paitṛkaṃ ced vacanaṃ na kuryāḥ,
vicchidyamāne 'pi kule parasya
puṃsaḥ kathaṃ syād iha putra|kāmyā?

asmākam uktaṃ bahu manyase ced,
yad' īśiṣe tvaṃ na mayi sthite ca,
jihreṣy a|tiṣṭhan yadi tāta|vākye,
jahīhi śaṅkāṃ, vraja, śādhi pṛthvīm.»

«vṛddh'|āurasāṃ rājya|dhurāṃ pravoḍhuṃ
kathaṃ kanīyān aham utsaheya?
mā māṃ prayukthāḥ kula|kīrti|lope»
prāha sma Rāmaṃ Bharato 'pi dharmyam.

3.55 «ūrjasvalaṃ hasti|turaṅgam etad,
amūni ratnāni ca rāja|bhāñji,
rājanyakaṃ c' âitad ahaṃ kṣit'|îndras
tvayi sthite syām iti śāntam etat.»

After weeping piteously and loudly for a long time Rama 3.50
and Lákshmana came to the river and offered a handful of water from the midst of its waters on the shore while declaring his name.

Rama spoke these words to his younger brother: "Father appointed me to the easy duty of exile in the forest and you alas to the hard task of kingship. Do not grieve, hero. Carry your burden.

If you who are wise and who practice and are learned in the ancient precepts would not carry out your father's command then how could any other man here wish for a son, even if his family were being destroyed?

If you value my words well and if you will not rule while I stay here, if you are ashamed at not abiding by our father's command, then give up your doubt, return and rule the earth."

Bharata justly replied to Rama, "How am I as the younger able to bear the burden of kingship proper to my elder brother? Do not order me to destroy the reputation of our family.

This force of elephants and horses and these jewels fit for 3.55
kings and this swathe of soldiers and the idea that I might be king while you live—this must stop."

iti nigaditavantaṃ Rāghavas taṃ jagāda
«vraja Bharata! gṛhītvā pāduke tvaṃ madīye,
cyuta|nikhila|viśaṅkaḥ, pūjyamāno jan'|âughaiḥ,
sakala|bhuvana|rājyaṃ kāray' âsman|matena.»

As he was speaking, Rama said to him: “Return, Bharata! Take my sandals and with all doubt gone, being worshipped by the people, ensure the whole earth is governed under my authority.”

CANTO 4
THE REJECTION OF SHURPA·NAKHA

4.1 Nivṛtte Bharate dhīmān
Atre Rāmas tapo|vanam
prapede, pūjitas tasmin
Daṇḍak'|âraṇyam īyivān.

aṭāṭyamāno 'raṇyānīṃ sa|Sītaḥ saha|Lakṣmaṇaḥ
balād bubhukṣuṇ" ôtkṣipya jahre bhīmena rakṣasā.

avāk|śirasam ut|pādaṃ
Kṛtānten' âpi dur|damam
bhaṅktvā bhujau Virādh'|ākhyaṃ
taṃ tau bhuvi nicakhnatuḥ.

āṃhiṣātāṃ Raghu|vyāghrau Śarabhaṅg'|āśramaṃ tataḥ
adhyāsitaṃ śriyā brāhmyā śaraṇyaṃ śaraṇ'|âiṣiṇām.

4.5 puro Rāmasya juhavāṃ cakāra jvalane vapuḥ
Śarabhaṅgaḥ pradiśy' ārāt Sutīkṣṇa|muni|ketanam.

«yūyaṃ samaiṣyath' êty asminn āsiṣmahi vayaṃ vane.
dṛṣṭāḥ stha, svasti vo, yāmaḥ sva|puṇya|vijitāṃ gatim.»

tasmin kṛśānusād bhūte* Sutīkṣṇa|muni|sannidhau
uvāsa parṇa|śālāyāṃ bhramann a|niśam āśramān.

vaneṣu vāsateyeṣu nivasan parṇa|saṃstaraḥ,
śayy"|ôtthāyaṃ mṛgān vidhyann, ātitheyo vicakrame.

WHEN BHARATA had turned back, wise Rama went to Atri's hermitage, was honored there and then went on to the Dándaka forest. 4.1

While Rama, Sita and Lákshmana were roaming about the wilderness, a fierce hungry demon took them up by force and carried them off.

They broke the arms of that demon called Virádha whom even the god of death found difficult to subdue and they buried him in the ground head down and feet up.

Then Raghu's two tigers went to the hermitage of Shara·bhanga which was saturated with holy radiance, an asylum for those who sought refuge.

Shara·bhanga pointed out the abode of the sage Sutíkshna 4.5
nearby and then in front of Rama he sacrificed his own body in the fire.

He said, "We expected that you would come so we stayed in this forest. Now that we have seen you—a blessing be upon you—we are going to the place we have won by our merit."

When Shara·bhanga had been burned to a cinder, Rama dwelt in a leaf hut in the forest near to the sage Sutíkshna and constantly visited the hermitages.

The hospitable Rama lived in the sheltering forest on a bed of leaves, and got up from his bed to roam in search of game.

Ṛg|Yajuṣam adhīyānān Sāmānyāṃś ca samarcayan
bubhuje devasāt kṛtvā* śūlyam ukhyaṃ ca homavān.

4.10 vasānas tantraka|nibhe
sarv'|âṅgīṇe taru|tvacau,
kāṇḍīraḥ, khāḍgakaḥ, śārṅgī,
rakṣan viprāṃs, tanutravān,

hitv" āśitaṃ|gavīnāni, phalair yeṣv āśitaṃ|bhavam,
teṣv asau dandaśūk'|ârir vaneśv ānabhra nirbhayaḥ.

vrātīna|vyāla|dīpr'|âstraḥ, sutvanaḥ paripūjayan
parṣadvalān, mahā|brahmair āṭa naikaṭik'|āśramān.

pare|dyavy adya pūrve|dyur anye|dyuś c' âpi cintayan
vṛddhi|kṣayau mun'|îndrāṇāṃ priyaṃ|bhāvukatām agāt.

ā tiṣṭhad|gu japan sandhyāṃ
prakrāntām āyatī|gavam,
prātastarāṃ patatribhyaḥ
prabuddhaḥ praṇaman ravim.

4.15 dadṛśe parṇa|śālāyāṃ rākṣasy" âbhīkay" âtha saḥ,
bhāry"|ōḍhaṃ tam avajñāya tasthe Saumitraye 'sakau.

dadhānā valibhaṃ madhyaṃ karṇa|jāha|vilocanā,
vāk|tvacen' âtisarveṇa candra|lekh" êva pakṣatau.

Honoring those learned in the Rig and Yajur Vedas and those skilled in chanting the Saman, Rama performed his rites and ate after he had offered his roast and stewed meats to the gods.

Dressing himself in tree bark which covered his whole body 4.10
like cloth fresh from the loom, bearing arrows, a sword, a bow, wearing armor, protecting the priests,

Leaving the pastures fit only for cows to graze, that enemy of malignant demons fearlessly wandered in the forests where there was satiety of fruit.

With his shining weapons raised against those who were vicious towards itinerant ascetics and honoring the *soma*-drinkers and their retinues, he wandered with the great brahmins among the neighboring ashrams.

By taking thought for their gains and losses tomorrow, today, yesterday and on any other day he became beloved of the great sages.

He chanted in the evening from the return of the cows until the end of milking; he woke earlier than the birds and bowed to the sun.

A lustful demoness saw him in his hut but disregarded him, 4.15
a married man, and set herself at Lákshmana.

She had a waist with pretty folds and eyes extending to the tips of her ears, her voice and skin surpassed all and she was like the sliver of the moon on the first day of the month.

supād, dvirada|nās'|ōrūr, mṛdu|pāṇi|tal'|âṅguliḥ,
prathimānaṃ dadhānena jaghanena ghanena sā,

un|nasaṃ dadhatī vaktraṃ śuddha|dal lola|kuṇḍalam,
kurvāṇā paśyataḥ śaṃyūn sragviṇī suhas'|ānanā,

prāpya cañcūryamāṇ" âsau patīyantī Raghūttamam
anukā prārthayāṃ cakre priyā|kartuṃ priyaṃ|vadā.

4.20 «Saumitre, mām upāyaṃsthāḥ
kamrām icchur vaśaṃ|vadām
tvad|bhogīnāṃ saha|carīm
a|śaṅkaḥ puruṣ'|āyuṣam.»

tām uvāca sa «gauṣṭhīne vane strī|puṃsa|bhīṣaṇe
a|sūryaṃ|paśya|rūpā tvaṃ kim a|bhīrur arāryase.

mānuṣān abhilaṣyantī rociṣṇur divya|dharmiṇī
tvam apsarāyamāṇ" êha sva|tantrā katham añcasi?

ugraṃ|paśy'|ākule 'raṇye śālīnatva|vivarjitā
kāmuka|prārthanā|paṭvī pativatnī kathaṃ na vā?

Rāghavaṃ parṇa|śālāyām icch' ânurahasaṃ patim,
yaḥ svāmī mama kāntāvān aupakarṇika|locanaḥ,

4.25 vapuś cāndanikaṃ yasya, kārṇaveṣṭakikaṃ mukham,
saṃgrāme sarva|karmīṇau pāṇī yasy' āupajānukau,

She had beautiful feet, thighs tapered like the trunk of an elephant, elegant fingers and palms on her hands, and buttocks firm and well developed,

She had a face bearing a well-formed nose, white teeth and dangling earrings, she wore a garland and with her smiling visage she delighted those who saw her.

She slunk about seeking a consort, and when she found Lákshmana, the lustful sweet-spoken girl wooed him to make herself attractive.

“O son of Sumítra, you are willing and resolute. You should 4.20
take me, desirous, submissive and compliant to your wishes as I am, for the length of your human life.”

He said to her, “In this forest which used to be cow pasture but now terrifies men and women both, why do you whose fair body has never seen the sun* wander about so fearless?

How do you come to be wandering here, lusting after men, shining, divinely endowed, behaving like an *ápsaras* and master of yourself?

How comes it that in this forest filled with savage beasts, you who are entirely without shyness and who are skilled at soliciting lovers are without a husband?

If you want a husband seek out Rama, my master, who is sitting alone in his leaf hut, who has a wife and whose eyes reach to his ears,

His body is anointed with sandal, his face is framed by his 4.25
earrings, his hands are fitted to all acts of war and reach down to his knees,

baddho durbala|raks"|ârtham
  asir yen' āupanīvikaḥ,*
yaś cāpam āśmana|prakhyaṃ
  s'|êṣuṃ dhatte 'nya|durvaham.

jetā yajña|druhāṃ saṃkhye dharma|santāna|sūr vane
prāpya dāra|gavānāṃ yaṃ munīnām a|bhayaṃ sadā.»

tato vāvṛtyamān" âsau Rāma|śālāṃ nyavikṣata,
«mām upāyaṃsta Rām'» êti vadantī s'|ādaraṃ vacaḥ.

«a|strīko 'sāv, ahaṃ strīmān, sa puṣyatitarāṃ tava
patir» ity abravīd Rāmas. «tam eva vraja, mā mucaḥ.»

4.30 Lakṣmaṇaṃ sā vṛṣasyantī
  mah"|ôkṣaṃ gaur iv' āgamat
Manmath'|āyudha|sampāta|
  vyathyamāna|matiḥ punaḥ.

tasyāḥ sāsadyamānāyā lolūyāvān Raghūttamaḥ
asiṃ kaukṣeyam udyamya, cakār' âpanasaṃ mukham.

«ahaṃ Śūrpaṇakhā nāmnā nūnaṃ n' ājñāyiṣi tvayā,
daṇḍo 'yaṃ kṣetriyo yena mayy apāt'» îti s" âbravīt.

paryaśāpsīd divi|ṣṭh" âsau
  saṃdarśya bhaya|daṃ vapuḥ
apisphavac ca bandhūnāṃ
  ninaṅkṣur vikramaṃ muhuḥ.

Khara|Dūṣaṇayor bhrātroḥ paryadeviṣṭa sā puraḥ,
vijigrāhayiṣū Rāmaṃ Daṇḍak'|âraṇya|vāsinoḥ.

He binds a sword to his girdle to protect the weak, and he holds a rock-like bow and arrows which others can hardly lift.

The sages and their wives and kine will never fear now they have found that victor in the battle with the sacrifice wreckers, who also promotes the eternal religion."

Then making her choice she entered Rama's hut saying eagerly "Rama, marry me!"

"He is without a wife; I am married. He will be a more fulfilling husband for you," said Rama. "Go to him and do not leave him."

She lusted after Lákshmana and came at him again like a 4.30
cow to a large bull, her mind unbalanced by the flight of Love's arrows.

As she sat splaying herself, Rama drew his sheathed sword ready to slash and rendered her face noseless.

"I am Shurpa·nakha who you have surely not recognized. You have inflicted a punishment without remedy on me," she said.

Hovering in the air and showing her fearsome form she reviled him, and seeking destruction she again and again vaunted the prowess of her kinsmen.

She wept before her brothers Khara and Dúshana who dwelt in the Dándaka forest, seeking to make them fight Rama.

4.35 «kṛte saubhāgineyasya Bharatasya vivāsitau
pitrā daurbhāgineyau yau, paśyataṃ ceṣṭitaṃ tayoḥ.

mama Rāvaṇa|nāthāyā
bhaginyā yuvayoḥ punaḥ
ayaṃ tāpasakād dhvaṃsaḥ:
kṣamadhvaṃ, yadi vaḥ kṣamam!

a|saṃskṛtrima|saṃvyānāv an|uptrima|phal'|āśinau
a|bhṛtrima|parīvārau paryabhūtāṃ tath" âpi mām.»

«śvaḥ|śreyasam avāpt" âsi»
bhrātṛbhyāṃ pratyabhāṇi sā,
«prāṇivas tava mān'|ârthaṃ,
vraj' āśvasihi, mā rudaḥ.

jakṣimo 'n|aparādhe 'pi
narān naktaṃ|divaṃ vayam,
kutastyaṃ bhīru, yat tebhyo
druhyadbhyo 'pi kṣamāmahe?»

4.40 tau caturdaśa|sāhasra|balau niryayatus tataḥ
pāraśvadhika|dhānuṣka|śāktika|prāsik'|ânvitau.

atha sampatato bhīmān
viśikhai Rāma|Lakṣmaṇau
bahu|mūrdhno dvi|mūrdhāṃś ca
tri|mūrdhāṃś c' âhatāṃ mṛdhe.

tair vṛkṇa|rugṇa|sambhugna|
kṣuṇṇa|bhinna|vipannakaiḥ,
nimagn'|ôdvigna|saṃhrīṇaiḥ
papre dīnaiś ca medinī.

"Look how those two sons of an unfavored wife have behaved, they who have been exiled by their father for the sake of the son of a favored wife. 4.35

My lord is Rávana and I am also your sister. I have been ruined by a petty hermit: tolerate it if you can!

Even though they are not well adorned, they are without upper garments, they live on wild fruit and are without hired retinue, they have insulted me."

"You will have satisfaction tomorrow," said her brothers to her, "We breathe only for your honor. Go, take heart and do not cry.

We eat men night and day even when no wrong has been done to us. Why should you fear that we would tolerate anyone who is hostile to you also?"

Then they advanced with a force of fourteen thousand axe- 4.40
men, bowmen, spear carriers and missile bearers.

In the battle Rama and Lákshmana struck with arrows at the streaming horrors, multi-headed, two-headed and triple-headed.

They filled the earth: those who were cut down, injured, broken, pulverized, dismembered, slain and fallen; the dejected, the terrified and the ashamed.

ke cid vepathum āsedur,
anye davathum uttamam,
sa|raktaṃ vamathuṃ ke cid,
bhrājathuṃ na ca ke cana.

mṛgayum iva mṛgo 'tha dakṣiṇermā,
diśam iva dāhavatīṃ marāv udanyan,
Raghu|tanayam upāyayau tri|mūrdho,
viśa|bhṛd iv' ôgra|mukhaṃ patatri|rājam.

4.45 śita|viśikha|nikṛtta kṛtsna|vaktraḥ,
kṣiti|bhṛd iva kṣiti|kampa|kīrṇa|śṛṅgaḥ
bhayam upanidadhe sa rākṣasānām
akhila|kula|kṣaya|pūrva|liṅga|tulyaḥ.

Some sat down trembling, others were in extreme pain, some vomited blood. None were glorious.

As a deer wounded on its flank comes upon the hunter, as a thirsty man in a desert comes upon a place on fire, as a snake comes upon the king of birds of fierce visage, so the triple-headed demon approached Rama.

With all his heads sliced off by sharp arrows, like a moun- 4.45
tain with its peaks toppled by an earthquake he sowed fear among the demons, as if presaging the destruction of the entire race.

CANTO 5
THE ABDUCTION OF SITA

5.1 NIRĀKARIṢṆŪ VARTIṢṆŪ vardhiṣṇū* parato raṇam
utpatiṣṇū sahiṣṇū ca ceratuḥ Khara|Dūṣaṇau.*

tau khaḍga|musala|prāsa|cakra|bāṇa|gadā|karau
akārṣṭām āyudha|cchāyaṃ* rajaḥ|saṃtamase raṇe.

atha tīkṣṇ'|āyasair bāṇair
adhi|marma Raghūttamau
vyādhaṃ vyādham a|mūḍhau tau
Yamasāc cakratur* dviṣau.

hata|bandhur jagām' âsau tataḥ Śūrpaṇakhā vanāt
pāre|samudraṃ Laṅkāyāṃ vasantaṃ Rāvaṇaṃ gatim.*

5.5 saṃprāpya rākṣasa|sabhaṃ* cakranda krodha|vihvalā,
nāma|grāham arodīt sā bhrātarau Rāvaṇ'|ântike.

«Daṇḍakān adhyavāttāṃ yau
vīra, rakṣaḥ|prakāṇḍakau
nṛbhyāṃ saṃkhye 'kṛṣātāṃ tau
sa|bhṛtyau bhūmi|vardhanau.

vigrahas tava Śakreṇa Bṛhaspati|purodhasā
sārdhaṃ Kumāra|senānyā, śūnyaś c' âs' îti ko nayaḥ?

yady ahaṃ nātha n' āyāsyaṃ
vi|nāsā hata|bāndhavā,
n' ājñāsyas tvam idaṃ sarvaṃ
pramādyaṃś cāra|durbalaḥ.

kariṣyamāṇaṃ vijñeyaṃ kāryaṃ, kiṃ nu kṛtaṃ paraiḥ?
apakāre kṛte 'py a|jño vijigīṣur na vā bhavān?

Khara and Dúshana roamed around the battle being obstructive, slaying, inflating themselves, leaping around and surviving. 5.1

With their swords, crushers, darts, discuses, arrows and clubs in hand they drew the shadow of their weapons over the dust-covered battle.

Then with sharp steel arrows the two best of Raghu's line, unconfused, made over to Yama their two enemies as they pierced their vital organs again and again.

Then when her kinsmen had been slain Shurpa·nakha went from the forest to her refuge Rávana who dwelt in Lanka on the far side of the ocean.

She reached the demons' hall and shrieked, wild with anger, 5.5
and grasping for their names she wept for her brothers in the presence of Rávana.

"O hero, those two most excellent of demons who dwelt in the Dándaka region, along with their followers, were in battle ploughed in to fatten the earth by two men.

You had a war with Indra whose priest was Brihas·pati and whose general was Kumára and now you are nothing: how can that follow?

If I, O Lord, had not arrived noseless and with my brothers slain, heedless and deficient in spies as you are you would not have known all this.

One should know what one's enemies are about to do, how much more what they have done? Even when a wrong has been committed you remain ignorant; how comes it that you do not wish for victory?

5.10 vṛtas tvaṃ pātre|samitaiḥ
khaṭv"|ārūḍhaḥ* pramādavān
pāna|śauṇḍaḥ śriyaṃ netā
n' âtyantīnatvam unmanāḥ.

adhvareṣv agnicitvatsu somasutvata āśramān
attuṃ mah"|êndriyaṃ bhāgam eti Duścyavano 'dhunā.

āmikṣīyaṃ dadhi|kṣīraṃ puroḍāśyaṃ tath" auṣadham
havir haiyaṃ|gavīnaṃ ca n' âpy upaghnanti rākṣasāḥ.

yuva|jānir, dhanuṣ|pāṇir bhūmi|ṣṭhaḥ, kha|vicāriṇaḥ
Rāmo yajña|druho hanti kāla|kalpa|śilīmukhaḥ.

māṃsāny oṣṭh'|âvalopyāni sādhanīyāni devatāḥ
aśnanti. Rāmād rakṣāṃsi bibhyaty aśnuvate diśaḥ.*

5.15 kuru buddhiṃ kuś'|âgriyām. anukāmīnatāṃ* tyaja.
lakṣmīṃ paramparīṇāṃ* tvaṃ putrapautrīṇatāṃ naya.

sahāyavanta udyuktā bahavo nipuṇāś ca yām
śriyam āśāsate, lolāṃ tāṃ haste|kṛtya mā śvasīḥ

lakṣmīḥ* puṃ|yogam āśaṃsuḥ kulaṭ" êva kutūhalāt.
antike 'pi sthitā patyuś, chalen' ânyaṃ nirīkṣate.

You are surrounded by parasites, you love the pleasures of 5.10
the bed, you are heedless, drunken, unbalanced in mind and you will not keep your glory for long.

To eat the portion proper to the great lord at sacrifices performed by those who keep the sacrificial fire, Indra, who cannot be toppled, now goes to ashrams where they press the *soma*.

The demons do not even take the milk and curds for the *amíksha* offering, the rice and herbs for the sacrificial cakes or the offering of ghee prepared from yesterday's milking.

Rama has a young wife, he holds a sword in his hand, he stands on the ground, yet he kills the enemies of the sacrifice with his death-like arrows even as they travel through the air.

The gods eat meat so fit for sacrifice that it can be torn off merely by the lips. The demons, fearing Rama, eat the empty horizons.

Make your mind as sharp as a tip of *kusha* grass. Leave 5.15
off following your own desires. Thus make your inherited wealth available to your sons and grandsons.

Many who have allies, who are well prepared and skilled wish for that fickle fortune. If it comes to your hand, do not trust it.

Fortune like a wanton woman is always seeking to conjoin with men out of curiosity. Though she stands beside her husband, on a pretext she casts her glance at another.

yoṣid|vṛndārikā tasya dayitā haṃsa|gāminī
dūrvā|kāṇḍam iva śyāmā nyagrodha|parimaṇḍalā.

n' āsyaṃ paśyati yas tasyā,
nimste danta|cchadaṃ na vā,
saṃśṛṇoti na c' ôktāni,
mithy" âsau nihit'|êndriyaḥ.

5.20 sāro 'sāv indriy'|ârthānāṃ,
yasy' âsau tasya nandathuḥ.
talpe kānt"|ântaraiḥ sārdhaṃ
manye 'haṃ dhiṅ nimajjathum.

na taṃ paśyāmi, yasy' âsau bhaven n' ôdejayā mateḥ.
trailokyen' âpi vindas tvaṃ tāṃ krītvā sukṛtī bhava.

n' âiv' Êndrāṇī, na Rudrāṇī, na Mānavī na Rohiṇī,
Varuṇānī na, n' Âgnāyī tasyāḥ sīmantinī samā.»

pratyūce rākṣas'|êndras tām «āśvasihi, bibheṣi kim?
tyaja naktaṃ|cari kṣobhaṃ vācāṭe Rāvaṇo hy aham!

mām upāsta didṛkṣāvān yāṣṭīka|vyāhato Hariḥ,
ājñā|lābh'|ônmukho dūrāt kākṣeṇ' ân|ādar'|ēkṣitaḥ.

5.25 virugṇ'|ôdagra|dhār"|âgraḥ kuliśo mama vakṣasi
a|bhinnaṃ śata|dh" ātmānaṃ manyate balinaṃ balī.

kṛtvā Laṅkā|drum'|ālānam aham Airāvataṃ gajam
bandhane 'n|upayogitvān nataṃ tṛṇavad atyajam.

His wife with her goose-like gait is like a goddess amongst women, slender like a stalk of *darbha* grass and curved like a banyan tree.

He has been endowed with senses in vain who cannot see her or kiss her lips or listen to her talk.

She is the essence of the objects of sense, he who has her 5.20
has happiness. I think it a disgrace to bed other women.

I have not met the person whose mind she would not shake. You should do well to find her and buy her even at the cost of the three worlds.

No woman, not even the wife of Indra, of Rudra, of Manu, of Soma, of Váruna or of Agni is her equal."

The lord of the demons replied to her, "Take heart, why are you afraid? Let go of your worry, O demoness, for I, O prattler, am Rávana.

Indra waited upon me, wishing to see me, and was repulsed by my doorkeeper. When noticed scornfully with a glance from afar, he was eager to receive my commands.

His powerful thunderbolt, the tip of whose blade 5.25
snapped against my chest, considered itself mighty that it was not shattered into a hundred pieces.

I tied the Airávata elephant* to a tree in Lanka. Because in captivity he was unworthy of me I left him bent over like a blade of grass.

āho|puruṣikāṃ paśya
mama: sad|ratna|kāntibhiḥ
dhvast'|ândhakāre 'pi pure,
pūrṇ'|êndoḥ sannidhiḥ sadā.

hṛta|ratnaś cyut'|ôdyogo rakṣobhyaḥ kara|do divi
Pūtakratāyīm abhyeti sa|trapaḥ kiṃ na Gotrabhit?

a|tulya|mahasā sārdhaṃ Rāmeṇa mama vigrahaḥ
trapā|karas, tath" âpy eṣa yatiṣye tad|vinigrahe.»

5.30 utpatya khaṃ Daśagrīvo mano|yāyī, śit'|âstra|bhṛt,
samudra|savidh'|āvāsaṃ Mārīcaṃ prati cakrame.

sampatya tat|sa|nīḍe 'sau taṃ vṛttāntam aśiśravat.
trasnun" âtha śrut'|ârthena ten' âgādi Daśānanaḥ:

«antardhatsva Raghu|vyāghrāt
tasmāt tvaṃ rākṣas'|ēśvara,
yo raṇe dur|upasthāno
hasta|rodhaṃ dadhad dhanuḥ.

bhavantaṃ Kārtavīryo yo hīna|sandhim acīkarat,
jigāya tasya hantāraṃ sa Rāmaḥ sārvalaukikam.

yam'|āsya|dṛśvarī tasya Tāḍakā vetti vikramam
śūraṃ|manyo raṇāc c' âhaṃ nirastaḥ siṃha|nardinā.

5.35 na tvaṃ ten' ânvabhāviṣṭhā, n' ânvabhāvi tvay" âpy asau,
anubhūto mayā c' âsau, tena c' ânvabhaviṣy aham.

See how I can boast of my power: even though the brilliance of my jewels has removed darkness from the city, the full moon is always present.

Indra himself in heaven has been robbed of his jewels, he is bereft of enterprise, he renders tribute to the demons and is ashamed to approach his own wife.

My quarrel with Rama whose greatness is not equal to mine is a source of shame. Nevertheless, I will strive to subdue him."

Ten-headed Rávana flew up into the air swift as thought, 5.30
and bearing sharp arrows made his way to Marícha who dwelt near the ocean.

When he reached his presence he told him the news. Then timidly, Marícha, who had heard the matter, spoke to Rávana:

"O lord of demons, you should hide yourself from this tiger of Raghu who cannot be approached in battle and who holds a bow clenched in his hand.

Rama vanquished the world-famous killer of Karta·virya* who deprived your honor of peace.

The demoness Tádaka knew his prowess as she looked death in the face, and I who prided myself on valor was driven from the field by him as he roared like a lion.

He has not encountered you and you have not encountered 5.35
him but I have encountered him and he has encountered me.

adhyaṅ śastra|bhṛtāṃ Rāmo:
  nyañcas taṃ prāpya mad|vidhāḥ.
sa kanyā|śulkam abhanaṅ
  Mithilāyāṃ makhe dhanuḥ.

saṃvittaḥ saha|yudhvānau tac|chaktiṃ Khara|Dūṣaṇau,
yajvānaś ca sa|sutvāno, yān agopīn makheṣu saḥ.

sukha|jātaḥ surā|pīto nṛ|jagdho mālya|dhārayaḥ
adhi|Laṅkaṃ striyo dīvya, m" ārabdhā bali|vigraham.»

taṃ bhītaṃ|kāram* ākruśya Rāvaṇaḥ pratyabhāṣata
«yāta|yāmaṃ vijitavān sa Rāmaṃ yadi, kiṃ tataḥ?

5.40 aghāni Tāḍakā tena lajjā|bhaya|vibhūṣaṇā.
strī|jane yadi tac chlāghyaṃ, dhig lokaṃ kṣudra|mānasam.

yad gehe|nardinam asau śarair bhīrum abhāyayat
ku|brahma|yajñake Rāmo bhavantaṃ, pauruṣaṃ na tat.

cira|kāl'|ôṣitaṃ jīrṇaṃ kīṭa|niṣkuṣitaṃ dhanuḥ
kiṃ citraṃ yadi Rāmeṇa bhagnaṃ kṣatriyak'|ântike!

vana|tāpasake vīrau vipakṣe galit'|ādarau
kiṃ citraṃ yadi s'|âvajñau mamratuḥ Khara|Dūṣaṇau?

tvaṃ ca bhīruḥ su|durbuddhe! nityaṃ śaraṇa|kāmyasi,
guṇāṃś c' âpahnuṣe 'smākaṃ, stauṣi śatrūṃś ca naḥ sadā.

Among the bearers of arms Rama is the best; when those such as I meet him we are humble. At the contest at Míthila he broke the bow whose prize was the girl Sita.

Khara and Dúshana and their troops knew well of his power, and the sacrificers and the *soma* pressers whom he protected at the sacrifices knew it too.

You have become happy drinking wine, eating humans and wearing garlands. Play with your women in Lanka, do not begin a war against this powerful man."

Rávana, screaming at him for being a coward, answered him, "So what if he has defeated Párashu·rama who has run his course?

He killed Tádaka whose ornaments were modesty and timid- 5.40
ity. If that act against a female is praiseworthy then fie on the mean-hearted world.

When at the sacrifice of some wretched brahmins Rama with his arrows inspired fear in you who roar only in your own home, that was not manliness.

How wonderful that a bow lain up for a long time, worn out, riddled by worms should be broken by Rama in the presence of some princelings!

What wonder that Khara and Dúshana were killed for their contempt, two heroes who had no respect for their little forest hermit opponent.

You are a coward, you imbecile! You are always looking for a refuge, you deny our virtues and you always praise our enemies.

5.45 śīrṣa|cchedyam ato 'haṃ tvā karomi kṣiti|vardhanam,
kārayiṣyāmi vā kṛtyaṃ vijighṛkṣur van'|âukasau.»

tam udyata|niśāt'|âsiṃ pratyuvāca jijīviṣuḥ
Mārīco 'nunayaṃs trāsād «abhyamitryo* bhavāmi te.

«harāmi Rāma|Saumitrī mṛgo bhūtvā mṛga|dyuvau,
udyogam abhyamitrīṇo* yath"|êṣṭaṃ tvaṃ ca saṃtanu.»

tataś citrīyamāṇo 'sau hema|ratna|mayo mṛgaḥ
yathā|mukhīnaḥ* Sītāyāḥ pupluve bahu lobhayan.

ten' âdudyūṣayad Rāmaṃ mṛgeṇa mṛga|locanā
Maithilī vipul'|ôraskaṃ prāvuvūrṣur mṛg'|âjinam.

5.50 yoga|kṣema|karaṃ kṛtvā Sītāyā Lakṣmaṇaṃ tataḥ
mṛgasy' ânupadī Rāmo jagāma gaja|vikramaḥ.

sthāyaṃ sthāyaṃ kva cid yāntaṃ
  krāntvā krāntvā sthitaṃ kva cit,
vīkṣamāṇo mṛgaṃ Rāmaś
  citra|vṛttiṃ visiṣmiye.

ciraṃ kliśitvā marmā|vid* Rāmo vilubhita|plavam
śabdāyamānam avyātsīt bhaya|daṃ kṣaṇadā|caram.

śrutvā visphūrjathu|prakhyaṃ ninādaṃ paridevinī,
matvā kaṣṭa|śritaṃ Rāmaṃ, Saumitriṃ gantum aijihat.

You deserve decapitation and hence I will either add you 5.45
to the soil of the earth, or in my desire to seize those forest
dwellers, I will force you to do your duty."

Marícha wished to live and out of fear conciliated him who had his sharpened sword upraised. He replied: "I will become your vanguard.

Rama and Lákshmana delight in game. Becoming a deer I shall lure them away and you as the attacker may accomplish your purpose as you wish."

Then to their astonishment he became a deer made of gold and jewels. Serving as a mirror for Sita and greatly exciting her desire, he dashed to and fro.

Wishing to wear its skin, the doe-eyed Sita induced the broad-chested Rama to want to chase the deer.

Rama, who had the strength of an elephant, left Lákshmana 5.50
to ensure Sita's well being and went in pursuit of the deer.

As it stopped here and there, then went on and bounded about, then stood still, Rama watched the deer with its wonderful antics and was amazed.

After harrying it for a long time, Rama pierced its vital organs. He wounded the fearsome nightstalker as it leaped about wildly, screaming.

Hearing a cry like thunder and thinking with lament that Rama was in trouble, Sita was eager for Lákshmana to go to him.

«eṣa prāvṛṣij'|âmbhoda|nādī bhrātā virauti te,
jñāteyaṃ kuru Saumitre: bhayāt trāyasva Rāghavam.»

5.55 «Rāma|saṃghuṣitaṃ n' âitan, mṛgasy' âiva vivañciṣoḥ
Rāma|svanita|saṅkāśaḥ svāna» ity avadat sa tām.

«āpyāna|skandha|kaṇṭh'|âṃsaṃ
  ruṣitaṃ sahituṃ raṇe
prorṇuvantaṃ diśo bāṇaiḥ
  Kākutsthaṃ bhīru, kaḥ kṣamaḥ?

dehaṃ bibhrakṣur astr'|âgnau mṛgaḥ prāṇair didevisan
jyā|ghṛṣṭa|kaṭhin'|âṅguṣṭhaṃ Rāmam āyān mumūrṣayā.

śatrūn bhīṣayamāṇaṃ taṃ Rāmaṃ vismāpayeta kaḥ?
mā sma bhaiṣīs, tvay" âdy' âiva kṛt'|ârtho drakṣyate patiḥ.»

«yāyās tvam iti kāmo me, gantum utsahase na ca,
icchuḥ kāmayituṃ tvaṃ mām» ity asau jagade tayā.

5.60 mṛṣodyaṃ* pravadantīṃ tāṃ satya|vadyo Raghūttamaḥ
niragāt: «śatru|hastaṃ tvaṃ yāsyas'» îti śapan vaśī.

gate tasmin, jala|śuciḥ, śuddha|dan, Rāvaṇaḥ śikhī,
jañjapūko,* 'kṣa|mālāvān, dhārayo mṛd|alābunaḥ,*

kamaṇḍalu|kapālena, śirasā ca mṛjāvatā,
saṃvastrya lākṣike, vastre mātrāḥ saṃbhāṇḍya, daṇḍavān,*

"That was your brother shouting with a cry like a monsoon cloud. Lákshmana, do your kindred duty: protect Rama from danger."

"That sound was not made by Rama, it was the call of the 5.55
deer wishing to deceive by sounding like Rama," said he to her.

"O timid one, who can stand up to Rama with his stout back, shoulders and neck, when he is roused in battle and veiling the skies with arrows?

The deer, with a wish to die, seeking to roast its body in the fire of his arrows, wanting to gamble with its very life breath, has approached Rama whose bowstring-rubbed thumb is toughened.

Who could confound Rama who terrifies his enemies? Do not fear, this very day you will see your husband successful."

She said to him, "My wish is that you should go and you cannot bear to go. You want to make love to me."

The truthful scion of Raghu cursed Sita for speaking falsely: 5.60
"You are heading into the grasp of your enemy!" and departed still in control of himself.

When he had gone, Rávana, purified with water, with white teeth, tonsured, continuously muttering prayers, wearing a string of aksha beads, bearing a cup of clay,

With a gourd for an alms bowl, with his head clean, wearing two lac-dyed garments, holding his goods together in a cloth, bearing a staff,

adhīyann ātma|vid|vidyāṃ, dhārayan maskari|vratam,
vadan bahv|aṅguli|sphoṭaṃ, bhrū|kṣepaṃ ca vilokayan,

saṃdidarśayiṣuḥ sāma, nijuhnūṣuḥ kṣapāṭatām,
caṃkramāvān, samāgatya Sītām ūce «sukhā bhava.

5.65 sāyantanīṃ tithi|praṇyaḥ paṅkajānāṃ divātanīm
kāntiṃ kāntyā sadātanyā hrepayantī śuci|smitā.

kā tvam ekākinī bhīru, niranvaya|jane vane?
kṣudhyanto 'py aghasan vyālās tvām a|pālāṃ kathaṃ na vā?

hṛdayaṃ|gama|mūrtis tvaṃ
subhagaṃ|bhāvukaṃ vanam
kurvāṇā bhīmam apy etad
vad' âbhyaiḥ kena hetunā?

sukṛtaṃ priya|kārī* tvaṃ kaṃ rahasy* upatiṣṭhase?
puṇya|kṛc cāṭu|kāras te kiṅkaraḥ surateṣu kaḥ?

pari pary udadhe,* rūpam ā|dyu|lokāc ca durlabham
bhāvatkaṃ dṛṣṭavatsv etad asmāsv adhi su|jīvitam.

5.70 āpīta|madhukā bhṛṅgaiḥ su|div" êv' âravindinī
sat|parimala|lakṣmīkā n' â|puṃsk" âs' îti me matiḥ.

mithy" âiva Śrīḥ Śriyaṃ|manyā,
Śrīman|manyo mṛṣā Hariḥ,
sākṣāt|kṛty' âbhimanye 'haṃ
tvāṃ harantīṃ śriyaṃ Śriyaḥ

Reciting the wisdom of the knowers of the self, pretending to a mendicant's vow, speaking with frequent movements of his fingers and raising his eyebrows as he looked,

Wishing to display tranquility, seeking to hide his fiendish nature, wandering about, he approached Sita and said, "Be happy.

With its constant beauty your bright smile puts to shame 5.65
the evening beauty of the moon and the daytime beauty of the lotuses.

Who are you, here all alone in this unpeopled forest, O timid one? How is it that the ravenous beasts do not eat you while you are not protected?

You have a beauty which goes straight to the heart. Tell me why you have come to this forest, which though terrible you make a source of good fortune?

Who has done such good that one as delightful as you waits upon him in private? Who is your slave in these dalliances who earns such merit and speaks so sweetly?

Life has been enhanced for those of us who have seen this beauty of yours which, with the exception of the ocean, cannot be found even in the world of heaven.

I think that, like a lotus whose nectar has been drunk by 5.70
bees on a bright day, you with your wealth of sweet fragrance are not unknown to a man.

As you have evidently stolen the glory of Shri, I think that Shri falsely fancies herself to be Shri and Vishnu in vain considers himself to be possessed of Shri.

n' ôdakaṇṭhiṣyat' âtyartham, tvām aikṣiṣyata cet Smaraḥ,
khelāyann aniśaṃ n' âpi sajūḥ|kṛtya Ratiṃ vaset.

valgūyantīṃ vilokya tvāṃ strī na mantūyat' îha kā?
kāntiṃ n' âbhimanāyeta ko vā sthāṇu|samo 'pi te?

duḥkhāyate janaḥ sarvaḥ sa ev' âikaḥ sukhāyate
yasy' ôtsukāyamānā tvaṃ na pratīpāyase 'ntike.

5.75 kaḥ paṇḍitāyamānas tvām ādāy' āmiṣa|saṃnibhām*
trasyan vairāyamāṇebhyaḥ śūnyam anvavasad vanam?»

ojāyamānā tasy' ârghyaṃ praṇīya Janak'|ātmajā
uvāca daśa|mūrdhānaṃ s'|ādarā gadgadaṃ vacaḥ.

«mahā|kulīna Aikṣvāke vaṃśe Dāśarathir mama
pituḥ priyaṃ|karo bhartā kṣemaṃ|kāras tapasvinām,

nihantā vaira|kārāṇāṃ satāṃ bahu|karaḥ sadā,
pāraśvadhika|Rāmasya śakter anta|karo raṇe.

adhvareṣv iṣṭināṃ pātā, pūrtī karmasu sarvadā
pitur niyogād rājatvaṃ hitvā yo 'bhyāgamad vanam.

5.80 patatri|kroṣṭu|juṣṭāni rakṣāṃsi bhaya|de vane
yasya bāṇa|nikṛttāni śreṇī|bhūtāni śerate.

dīvyamānaṃ śitān bāṇān, asyamānaṃ mahā|gadāḥ,
nighnānaṃ śātravān Rāmaṃ kathaṃ tvaṃ n' âvagacchasi?

If the god of love had seen you he would not have longed excessively for Rati and he would not have made her his companion and remained dallying with her day and night.

Seeing you so exultant what woman would not be jealous? Or what man even if he were like a post would not desire your beauty?

All men suffer but he alone is happy for whom you long and to whom you are not hostile when he is by.

What wise man has received you as his gift and, fearing his 5.75
rivals, has come to dwell in this empty forest?"

With all her strength, the daughter of Jánaka offered him the water due to a guest and respectfully spoke stuttering words to the ten-headed Rávana.

"The noble-born son of Dasha·ratha of the line of Ikshváku is my husband, the delight of my father and giver of safety to the ascetics,

The killer of his enemies and ever the benefactor for good people, he ended the power of the axe-wielding Párashu·rama in battle.

He protects the sacrificers during the *soma* rites and he always gives nourishment at rituals. He renounced his kingship at the command of his father and came to the forest.

In this fearsome forest demons who were cut down by his 5.80
arrows lie in heaps as leftovers for birds and jackals.

How do you not know of Rama who casts sharp arrows, hurls huge clubs and slays his enemies?

bhrātari nyasya yāto māṃ mṛgāvin mṛgayām asau,
eṣituṃ preṣito yāto mayā tasy' ânu|jo vanam.»

ath' āyasyan, kaṣāy'|âkṣaḥ, syanna|sveda|kaṇ'|ôlbaṇaḥ
saṃdarśit'|ântar|ākūtas, tām avādīd Daśānanaḥ:

«kṛte kāniṣṭhineyasya jyaiṣṭhineyaṃ vivāsitam
ko nagna|muṣita|prakhyaṃ bahu manyeta Rāghavam?

5.85 rākṣasān baṭu|yajñeṣu piṇḍī|śūrān nirastavān
yady asau kūpa|māṇḍūki! tav' âitāvati kaḥ smayaḥ?

mat|parākrama|saṃkṣipta|rājya|bhoga|paricchadaḥ
yuktaṃ mam' âiva kiṃ vaktuṃ daridrāti yathā Hariḥ?

nir|Laṅko vimadaḥ svāmī dhanānāṃ hṛta|Puṣpakaḥ
adhyāste 'ntar|giraṃ yasmāt, kas tan n' âvaiti kāraṇam?

bhinna|nauka iva, dhyāyan
 matto bibhyad Yamaḥ svayam
kṛṣṇimānaṃ dadhānena
 mukhen' āste nirudyatiḥ.

samudr'|ôpatyakā haimī parvat'|âdhityakā purī
ratna|pārāyaṇaṃ nāmnā Laṅk" êti mama Maithili.

5.90 āvāse sikta|saṃmṛṣṭe gandhais tvaṃ lipta|vāsitā
ārpit'|ôru|sugandhi|srak tasyāṃ vasa mayā saha.

saṃgaccha pauṃsni, straiṇaṃ māṃ
 yuvānaṃ, taruṇī śubhe.
Rāghavaḥ proṣya|pāpīyān:
 jahīhi tam a|kiṃ|canam.

That hunter left me with his brother and went hunting. His sibling has now gone to the forest, sent by me to find him."

Then, striving to control himself, with his eyes red, with a film of beads of sweat trickling down revealing his hidden intentions, the ten-faced Rávana said to her:

"Who would reckon much of Rama as the son of the elder wife exiled in favor of the son of the younger, like someone robbed and left naked?

O you frog-in-a-well! What pride can you take in this mat- 5.85
ter if he has merely cast out cake-hero* demons at the priestlings' sacrifices?

Is it proper that I myself should speak about how Indra became destitute when his kingdom and chattels were removed through my prowess?

Who does not know the reason why Kubéra the lord of wealth lost Lanka, lost his pride, had his chariot Púshpaka taken away and went to live on Mount Kailása?

As if shipwrecked, Yama himself brooding on me and fearing me sits with darkened visage, unable to act.

O Maithilí, my golden city is up on a mountain by the ocean, a study in gems, Lanka by name.

Live with me! There in my sprinkled and scoured house you 5.90
will be smeared and anointed with fragrances and you will wear a broad and perfumed garland.

O you who are worthy of a man, come to me who am fit for a woman and youthful, you tender beauty. Rama is an exiled sinner; leave him, he counts for nothing.

aśnīta|pibatīyantī, prasitā smara|karmaṇi,
vaśe|kṛtya Daśagrīvaṃ, modasva vara|mandire.

mā sma bhūr grāhiṇī bhīru, gantum utsāhinī bhava,
udbhāsinī ca bhūtvā me vakṣaḥ|saṃmārdinī bhava.»

tāṃ prātikūlikīṃ matvā jihīrṣur, bhīma|vigrahaḥ
bāh'|ûpapīḍam āśliṣya jagāhe dyāṃ niśā|caraḥ.

5.95 trasyantīṃ tāṃ samādāya yāto rātriṃ|car'|ālayam.
tūṣṇīṃ|bhūya bhayād āsāṃ cakrire mṛga|pakṣiṇaḥ.

uccai rārasyamānāṃ* tāṃ kṛpaṇāṃ Rāma|Lakṣmaṇau
Jaṭāyuḥ* prāpa pakṣ'|îndraḥ paruṣaṃ Rāvaṇaṃ vadan.

«dviṣan vane|car'|âgryāṇāṃ tvam ādāya|caro vane,
agre|saro jaghanyānāṃ: mā bhūḥ pūrva|saro mama.**

yaśas|kara|samācāraṃ
  khyātaṃ bhūvi dayā|karam,
pitur vākya|karaṃ Rāmaṃ,
  dhik tvāṃ dunvantam a|trapam.*

aham anta|karo nūnaṃ dhvāntasy' êva divā|karaḥ
tava rākṣasa, Rāmasya neyaḥ karma|kar'|ôpamaḥ!»*

5.100 satām aruṣ|karaṃ pakṣī vaira|kāraṃ nar'|âśinam
hantuṃ kalaha|kāro 'sau śabda|kāraḥ papāta kham.*

Giving orders for food and drink, devoted to acts of love, making me, the ten-headed Rávana your servant, revel in my excellent palace.

Do not be reluctant, O timid one, get ready to go, and when you are radiant, press yourself to my chest."

Thinking that she was opposing him and wishing to take her, the nightstalker of terrible form embracing her in a crushing grip shot into the sky.

He abducted the terrified girl and went to the demons' 5.95
abode. The birds and animals became silent and fell still from fear.

Finding the poor girl crying loudly and continually for Rama and Lákshmana, Jatáyu, the lord of the birds, spoke harshly to Rávana:

"O enemy of the best of the forest dwellers, you have snatched and run in the forest. You are the foremost of the worst; you will not go past me.

Rama's conduct makes him famous; he is known in the world as compassionate and obedient to his father's bidding. A curse on you for being shameless and distressing him.

As the sun destroys the night, so will I like a servant subject to Rama surely kill you, you demon!

The pugnacious bird flew into the air with a cry to kill the 5.100
wounder of the good, the enemy, the eater of men.

dhunvan sarva|pathīnaṃ khe vitānaṃ pakṣayor asau,
māṃsa|śoṇita|saṃdarśaṃ, tuṇḍa|ghātam, ayudhyata.

na bibhāya, na jihrāya, na caklāma, na vivyathe,
āghnāno vidhyamāno vā raṇān nivavṛte na ca.

piśāca|mukha|dhaureyaṃ sa|cchatra|kavacaṃ ratham
yudhi kad|rathavad bhīmaṃ babhañja dhvaja|śālinam.

saṃtrāsayāṃ cakār' ârim, surān piprāya paśyataḥ,
sa tyājayāṃ cakār' ârim Sītāṃ viṃśati|bāhunā.**

5.105 a|Sīto Rāvaṇaḥ kāsāṃ
cakre, śastrair nirākulaḥ,
bhūyas taṃ bebhidāṃ cakre
nakha|tuṇḍ'|āyudhaḥ khagaḥ.*

hantuṃ krodha|vaśād īhāṃ cakrāte tau parasparam,
na vā palāyāṃ cakre vir, dayāṃ cakre na rākṣasaḥ.*

upāsāṃ cakrire draṣṭuṃ deva|gandharva|kinnarāḥ
chalena pakṣau lolūyāṃ cakre Kravyāt patatriṇaḥ.

praluṭhitam avanau vilokya kṛttaṃ
Daśavadanaḥ kha|car'|ôttamaṃ prahṛṣyan
ratha|varam adhiruhya bhīma|dhuryaṃ,
sva|puram agāt parigṛhya Rāma|kāntām.

He fought flapping the all-encompassing extent of his wings in the sky, striking continually with his beak and exposing his flesh and blood.

He was not afraid or timid, he did not weary nor did he waver. As he struck and tore he did not hold back from the fight.

In the battle he broke up the terrible flag-furnished car with its demon-faced horses and its fine canopy and armor as if it were an old jalopy.

He terrified his foe and delighted the onlooking gods. With his twenty arms he made his enemy let go Sita.

Without Sita, Rávana reviled him, unfazed by his 5.105
weapons. The bird again tore at him with weapons of claw and beak.

Driven by anger each tried to kill the other; the bird could not protect himself, the demon showed no mercy.

The gods, *gandhárvas* and *kínnaras* were nearby to watch as Rávana tried to hack off the bird's wings by trickery.

When he saw the best of birds cut up rolling about on the ground, ten-faced Rávana laughed as he mounted that supreme chariot with its terrible steeds and, taking Rama's wife, he went to his own city.

CANTO 6

THE ALLIANCE WITH THE MONKEYS

6.1 OṢĀṂ CAKĀRA kām'|âgnir Daśavaktram ahar|niśam:
vidāṃ cakāra Vaidehīṃ Rāmād anya|nirutsukām.**

prajāgarāṃ cakār' ârer īhāsv aniśam ādarāt,
prabibhayāṃ cakār' âsau Kākutsthād abhiśaṅkitaḥ.*

na jihrayāṃ cakār' âtha Sītām abhyarthya tarjitaḥ,
n' âpy ūrjāṃ bibharām āsa Vaidehyāṃ prasito bhṛśam.*

vidāṃ kurvantu Rāmasya vṛttam ity avadat svakān,
rakṣāṃsi rakṣituṃ Sītām āśiṣac ca prayatnavān.*

6.5 Rāmo 'pi hata|Mārīco, nivartsyan khara|nādinaḥ
kroṣṭūn samaśṛṇot krūrān rasato 'śubha|śaṃsinaḥ.

āśaṅkamāno Vaidehīṃ khāditāṃ nihatāṃ mṛtām,
sa Śatrughnasya s'|ôdaryaṃ dūrād āyāntam aikṣata.

Sītāṃ Saumitriṇā tyaktāṃ
sadhrīcīṃ trasnum ekikāṃ
vijñāy', âmaṃsta Kākutsthaḥ:
«kṣaye kṣemaṃ su|durlabham.»

so 'pṛcchal Lakṣmaṇaṃ Sītāṃ yācamānaḥ śivaṃ surān.
Rāmaṃ yathā|sthitaṃ sarvaṃ bhrātā brūte sma vihvalaḥ.*

saṃdṛśya śaraṇaṃ śūnyaṃ, bhikṣamāṇo vanaṃ priyām
prāṇān duhann iv' ātmānaṃ, śokaṃ cittam avārudhat.

6.10 «gatā syād avacinvānā kusumāny āśrama|drumān,
ā yatra tāpasān dharmaṃ Sutīkṣṇaḥ śāsti, tatra sā.

THE FIRE OF passion burned ten-faced Rávana day and night; he knew that Sita desired none but Rama. 6.1

He watched with attention ever alert to the affairs of his enemy: he was worried and he feared Rama.

He had no shame entreating Sita and being rejected. Nevertheless, because he was so devoted to Sita he did not use force.

He told his henchmen that they should find out what Rama was up to. He took care to order the demons to guard Sita.

Even though Rama had killed Marícha, as he returned he 6.5
heard the terrible ass-like calls of the jackals sounding promise of evil.

Fearing that Sita had been eaten or assaulted or slain, he saw Shatrúghna's brother Lákshmana coming from afar.

When he realized that Lákshmana had left his timid companion alone, Rama thought: "Safety is all but impossible even at home."

Begging the gods for favor he asked Lákshmana about Sita. His perturbed brother told Rama everything just as it had happened.

Seeing their hut empty and begging the forest for his beloved as if milking himself of his own life, he contained his sorrow within his heart.

"Whilst collecting flowers from the ashram trees, she may 6.10
have gone to where Sutíkshna now teaches the law to the ascetics.

āḥ, kaṣṭaṃ, bata! hī|citraṃ, hūṃ. mātar! daivatāni dhik!
hā pitaḥ! kv' âsi he subhru?» bahv evaṃ vilalāpa saḥ.

«ih' āsiṣṭh' âśayiṣṭ' êha sā, sa|khelam ito 'gamat,»
aglāsīt saṃsmarann itthaṃ Maithilyā Bharat'|âgra|jaḥ.

«idaṃ naktaṃtanaṃ dāma pauṣpam etad divātanam.
śuc" êv' ôdbadhya śākhāyāṃ praglāyati tayā vinā.

aikṣiṣmahi muhuḥ suptāṃ yāṃ mṛt'|āśaṅkayā vayam,
a|kāle dur|maram aho, yaj jīvāmas tayā vinā.

6.15 a|kṣemaḥ parihāso 'yaṃ, parīkṣāṃ mā kṛthā mama
matto m" ântardhithāḥ Sīte: mā raṃsthā jīvitena naḥ.

ahaṃ nyavadhiṣaṃ bhīmaṃ rākṣasaṃ krūra|vikramam.
mā ghukṣaḥ patyur ātmānaṃ. mā na ślikṣaḥ priyaṃ priye!**

mā sma drākṣīr mṛṣā doṣaṃ. bhaktaṃ mā m" âticikliśaḥ.
śailaṃ nyaśiśriyad vāmā nadīṃ nu pratyadudruvat.*

ai vācaṃ dehi! dhairyaṃ nas tava hetor asusruvat.
tvaṃ no matim iv' âghāsīr naṣṭā. prāṇān iv' âdadhaḥ.*

rudato 'śiśvayac cakṣur āsyaṃ hetos tav' âśvayīt,
mriye 'haṃ māṃ nirāsthaś cen. mā na vocaś cikīrṣitam.*

Oh woe alas! How horribly strange! O mother! Oh fie upon you gods! O father! Where are you with your beautiful brows?" Thus did he make many lamentations.

"Here she sat and here she lay, from here she gently went." Remembering Sita thus Bharata's elder brother languished.

"This is her night-time garland and this her garland of daytime flowers. It has hung itself on a branch as if from grief and withers away without her.

We often looked upon her as she slept, fearing her to be dead. Oh what a hard untimely death it is which we have to live through without her.

This is an uncomfortable joke; do not test me. Do not hide 6.15
yourself from me Sita: do not play with my life.

I have killed a terrible demon of cruel prowess. Do not hide yourself from your husband. Do not not embrace your beloved my beloved!

Do not in vain point out my faults. Do not torment me so who am devoted to you. Perhaps the fair girl has taken herself to the mountain. Surely she has run towards the river.

Oh give us some word! Because of you our fortitude has drained away. Now you are gone, it is as if you have consumed my heart, as if you have caused my life breath to be sucked out.

As I weep my eyes have swollen up, my face too has swollen up because of you. I will die if you reject me. Please tell me what you are trying to do.

6.20 Lakṣmaṇ', ācakṣva yady ākhyat sā kiñ cit kopa|kāraṇam.
doṣe pratisamādhānam a|jñāte kriyatāṃ katham?

iha sā vyalipad gandhaiḥ,
  snānt" îh' âbhyaṣicaj jalaiḥ,
ih' âhaṃ draṣṭum āhvaṃ tāṃ»
  smarann evaṃ mumoha saḥ.*

tasy' âlipata śok'|âgniḥ svāntaṃ kāṣṭham iva jvalan,
alipt' êv' ânilaḥ śīto vane taṃ, na tv ajihladat.*

snān abhyaṣicat' âmbho 'sau rudan dayitayā vinā.
tath" âbhyaṣikta vārīṇi pitṛbhyaḥ śoka|mūrchitaḥ.

tath" ārto 'pi, kriyāṃ dharmyāṃ sa kāle n' âmucat kva cit,
mahatāṃ hi kriyā nityā chidre n' âiv' âvasīdati.

6.25 āhvāsta sa muhuḥ śūrān, muhur āhvata rākṣasān:
«eta Sītā|druhaḥ saṃkhye, pratyartayata Rāghavam.

sva|poṣam apuṣad yuṣmān yā pakṣi|mṛga|śāvakāḥ,
adyutac c' êndunā sārdhaṃ, tāṃ prabrūta, gatā yataḥ?»*

girim anvasṛpad Rāmo lipsur Janaka|saṃbhavām
tasminn āyodhanaṃ vṛttaṃ Lakṣmaṇāy' âśiṣan mahat.*

«Sītāṃ jighāṃsū Saumitre rākṣasāv āratāṃ dhruvam.
idaṃ śoṇitam abhyagraṃ saṃprahāre 'cyutat tayoḥ.*

O Lákshmana, tell me if she spoke of any cause for anger. 6.20
How can I make amends for an unknown wrong?

Here she anointed me with perfumes, here while bathing she splashed me with water, here I called her to see her." As he remembered these things he passed out.

The blazing fire of grief burned like kindling inside him, it was as if the cool breeze in the forest inflamed him rather than gladdened him.

Bathing, he sprinkled water while weeping, bereft of his wife. As he sprinkled water for his ancestors he remained stupefied with grief.

Even though so pained, he never abandoned his religious duty at its proper time, for the constant duty of great men does not lapse into neglect.

He repeatedly called upon the warriors, he repeatedly chal- 6.25
lenged the demons: "Come, you enemies of Sita, take on
Rama in battle.

O you young of the birds and animals, she who nourished you with her own food and who shone like the moon, tell me of her. Where has she gone?"

Rama went towards the mountain hoping to find Jánaka's daughter and told Lákshmana about the great fight that had happened there.

"O Lákshmana, two demons seeking to harm Sita certainly came here. This is their fresh blood shed in the conflict.

idaṃ kavacam acyotīt, s'|âśvo 'yaṃ cūrṇīto rathaḥ.
ehy amuṃ girim anveṣṭum avagāhāvahe drutam.

6.30 manyur manye mam' âstambhīd,
viṣādo 'stabhad udyatim,
ajārīd iva ca prajñā,
balaṃ śokāt tath" âjarat.*

gṛdhrasy' êh' âśvatāṃ pakṣau kṛttau, vīkṣasva Lakṣmaṇa,
jighatsor nūnam āpādi dhvaṃso 'yaṃ tāṃ niśā|carāt.»*

kruddho 'dīpi Raghu|vyāghro, rakta|netro 'jani kṣaṇāt,
abodhi duḥ|sthaṃ trailokyaṃ, dīptair āpūri bhānuvat.*

atāyy asy' ôttamaṃ sattvam, apyāyi kṛta|kṛtyavat:
upācāyiṣṭa sāmarthyaṃ tasya saṃrambhiṇo mahat.*

adoh' îva viṣādo 'sya, samaruddh' êva vikramaḥ,*
samabhāvi ca kopena, nyaśvasīc c' āyataṃ muhuḥ.*

6.35 ath' ālambya dhanū Rāmo jagarja gaja|vikramaḥ,
«ruṇadhmi savitur mārgaṃ, bhinadmi kula|parvatān.*

riṇacmi jala|dhes toyaṃ, vivinacmi divaḥ surān,
kṣuṇadmi sarpān pātāle, chinadmi kṣaṇadā|carān.

Yamaṃ yunajmi kālena samindhāno 'stra|kauśalam;
śuṣka|peṣaṃ pinaṣmy urvīm a|khindānaḥ sva|tejasā.

Here this armor fell, here is a pulverized chariot and horses. Come quickly, let us plunge into our search of the mountain.

I think that grief has stiffened me up, despair has blocked 6.30
up my energy. It's as if my intelligence has atrophied and likewise my strength has wasted with grief.

Look, Lákshmana, here is a pair of sawn-off vulture's wings spread out: surely he died because the nightstalker wished to eat her."

Angered, Raghu's tiger blazed. In an instant he became red-eyed, he understood the three worlds to be evil, he was filled with flame like the sun.

His true essence expanded, he swelled like one whose purpose has been achieved: wrathful, his great power was strengthened.

It was as of his despondency had been milked out, as if his course had checked itself. He was filled with anger, he sighed long and often.

Then, taking up his bow, with the strength of an elephant 6.35
Rama roared: "I will obstruct the course of the sun, I will smash the mountain ranges.

I will drain the waters of the ocean, I will deprive the gods of heaven, I will crush the serpents in hell, I will cut up the nightstalkers.

Rekindling my skill in arrows, I shall furnish Yama with death; untiring in my power, I shall crush the wide world into dry dust.

bhūtiṃ tṛṇadmi yakṣāṇāṃ, hinasm' Îndrasya vikramam,
bhanajmi sarva|maryādās, tanacmi vyoma vistṛtam.

na tṛṇehm' îti loko 'yaṃ māṃ vinte niṣ|parākramam,»
evaṃ vadan Dāśarathir apṛṇag dhanuṣā śaraṃ.

6.40 nyavartayat Sumitrā|bhūs taṃ cikīrṣuṃ jagat|kṣayam.
aikṣetām āśramād ārād giri|kalpaṃ patatriṇam.

taṃ Sītā|ghātinaṃ matvā hantuṃ Rāmo 'bhyadhāvata.
«mā vadhiṣṭhā Jaṭāyuṃ māṃ, Sītāṃ Rām' âham aikṣiṣi.»

upāsthit' âivam ukte taṃ sakhāyaṃ Rāghavaḥ pituḥ.
papraccha Jānakī|vārtāṃ saṃgrāmaṃ ca patatriṇam.

tato Rāvaṇam ākhyāya dviṣantaṃ patatāṃ varaḥ.
vraṇa|vedanayā glāyan mamāra giri|kandare.
tasy' âgny|ambu|kriyāṃ kṛtvā pratasthāte punar vanam.

sattvān ajasraṃ ghoreṇa bal'|âpakarṣam aśnatā
kṣudhyatā jagṛhāte tau rakṣasā dīrgha|bāhunā.

6.45 bhujau cakṛtatus tasya nistriṃśābhyāṃ Ragh'|ûttamau.
sa cchinna|bāhur apatad vihvalo hvalayan bhuvam.

I shall destroy the wealth of the *yakshas*, I shall kill off the prowess of Indra, I shall break all the boundaries, I shall contract the broad sky.

Thinking that I shall do no harm, the world considers me powerless," and as he said this the son of Dasha·ratha fixed an arrow to his bow.

Lákshmana the son of Sumítra stopped him as he sought to 6.40
destroy the world. Near the ashram they saw a mountain-like bird.

Thinking he was Sita's murderer, Rama rushed forward for the kill. "Do not kill me, I am Jatáyu. O Rama, I have seen Sita."

When he had said this Rama attended to him as a friend of his father. He asked the bird what had happened to Sita and about the battle.

Then the best of birds, once he had named the enemy Rávana, died in the mountain gorge, fainting from the pain of his wounds. When he had performed for him the rites with fire and water, Rama again set off into the forest.

They were seized by a fearsome ravenous long-armed demon who was always dragging creatures away by force and eating them.*

The two best of Raghu's line cut off his arms with their 6.45
swords. With his arms chopped off he fell flailing to the ground, making it shake.

praṣṭavyaṃ pṛcchatas tasya, kathanīyam avīvacat
ātmānaṃ, vana|vāsaṃ ca jeyaṃ c' ârim Raghūttamaḥ.**

«labhyā kathaṃ nu Vaidehī?
 śakyo draṣṭuṃ kathaṃ ripuḥ?
sahyaḥ kathaṃ viyogaś ca?
 gadyam etat tvayā mama.»*

«ahaṃ Rāma, śriyaḥ putro madya|pīta iva bhraman,
pāpa|caryo muneḥ śāpāj jāta» ity avadat sa tam.*

«prayātas tava yamyatvaṃ śastra|pūto bravīmi te.
Rāvaṇena hṛtā Sītā Laṅkāṃ nītā sur'|âriṇā.*

6.50 Ṛṣyamūke 'n|avadyo 'sti paṇya|bhrātṛ|vadhaḥ kapiḥ
Sugrīvo nāma, varyo 'sau bhavatā cāru|vikramaḥ.*

tena vahyena hant" âsi tvam aryaṃ puruṣ'|āśinām,
rākṣasaṃ krūra|karmāṇaṃ, Śakr'|ârim, dūra|vāsinam.*

āste smaran sa kāntāyā hṛtāyā Vālinā kapiḥ
vṛṣo yath" ôpasaryāyā goṣṭhe gor daṇḍa|tāḍitaḥ.

tena saṅgatam āryeṇa Rām' âjaryaṃ kuru drutam,
Laṅkāṃ prāpya tataḥ pāpaṃ Daśagrīvaṃ haniṣyasi.*

anṛt'|ôdyaṃ na tatr' âsti, satya|vadyaṃ bravīmy aham,
mitra|bhūyaṃ gatas tasya ripu|hatyāṃ kariṣyasi.*

As he asked about what he needed to know, Rama said what had to be told about himself, his residence in the forest and the enemy he had to conquer.

"How can I find Sita? How can my enemy be destroyed? How can I bear the separation? Tell me."

He said to him: "I, O Rama, am the son of Shri, wandering like a drunkard, born to do wrong because of the curse of a sage."

"I will tell you because I have come under your control and am purified by your weapons. Sita has been seized by Rávana, the enemy of the gods, and has been taken to Lanka.

On Rishya·muka mountain is an irreproachable monkey, 6.50
Sugríva by name, who seeks to procure the murder of his own brother. You should choose him as an ally of excellent valor.

With him as your attendant you will kill the master of the man-eaters, the demon whose deeds are cruel, the enemy of Indra, who dwells far away.

The monkey still remembers his wife stolen by his brother Valin, like a bull in a cowpen beaten away from his cow in season with a stick.

O Rama, quickly make an unbreakable alliance with this noble monkey. Then when you reach Lanka you will kill the evil ten-headed Rávana.

There is no dissembling in him, I tell you truly. When you have become friends with him you will kill your enemy.

6.55 ādṛtyas tena vṛtyena stutyo, juṣyeṇa saṃgataḥ,
ityaḥ śiṣyeṇa guruvad, gṛdhyam artham avāpsyasi.*

n' â|kheyaḥ sāgaro 'py anyas tasya sad|bhṛtya|śālinaḥ,
manyus tasya tvayā mārgyo, mṛjyaḥ śokaś ca tena te.»*

sa rājasūya|yāj" îva tejasā sūrya|sannibhaḥ
a|mṛṣ'|ôdyaṃ vadan rucyo jagāhe dyāṃ niśā|caraḥ.*

a|kṛṣṭa|pacyāḥ paśyantau tato Dāśarathī latāḥ
ratn'|ânna|pāna|kupyānām āṭatur naṣṭa|saṃsmṛtī.*

samuttarantāv a|vyathyau
  nadān Bhidy'|Ôddhya|sannibhān,
Sidhya|tārām iva khyātāṃ,
  śabarīm āpatur vane.*

6.60 vasānāṃ valkale śuddhe, vipūyaiḥ kṛta|mekhalām,
kṣāmām añjana|piṇḍ'|ābhāṃ, daṇḍinīm ajin'|āstarām.*

pragṛhya|padavat sādhvīṃ, spaṣṭa|rūpām, a|vikriyām,
a|gṛhyāṃ vīta|kāmatvād, deva|gṛhyām, a|ninditām.

dharma|kṛtya|ratāṃ nityam, a|kṛṣya|phala|bhojanām
dṛṣṭvā tām, amucad Rāmo yugy'|āyāta iva śramam.*

Honored and praised by that most cherished monkey, 6.55
united with him in whom one should rejoice, just like a teacher attended by his pupil, you will attain your longed-for goal.

It is not impossible to dig another ocean for someone well enough attended by servants. You will cleanse him of his anger and he will wipe away your grief."

Like one performing the coronation rite, similar to the sun in brilliance, that radiant demon who spoke the truth went to heaven.

Then the two sons of Dasha·ratha, seeing vines ripening uncultivated, wandered forgetting jewels, food, drink and metal ores.

Those imperturbable men crossed rivers resembling the Bhidya and the Uddhya and came across Shábari in the forest, famed like the constellation Sidhya.*

She was wearing two clean bark garments and a girdle made 6.60
of *munja* grass. She was lean, dark like a smudge of kohl, she bore a staff and she wore the skin of a blackbuck.

She was virtuous, of distinct form, unchangeable like a *pragríhya** word, independent because free from desire, acceptable to the gods, blameless.

When he saw her who always delighted in doing her religious duties and who ate only uncultivated fruits, Rama let go his weariness as if he had just arrived by chariot.

sa tām ūce 'tha «kaccit tvam amāvāsyā|samanvaye
pitṝṇāṃ kuruṣe kāryam a|pākyaiḥ svādubhiḥ phalaiḥ?*

avaśya|pāvyaṃ pavase kaccit tvaṃ deva|bhāgg haviḥ?
āsāvyam adhvare somaṃ dvijaiḥ kaccin namasyasi?*

6.65 ācāmyaṃ saṃdhyayoḥ kaccit samyak te na prahīyate?
kaccid agnim iv' ānāyyaṃ kāle saṃmanyase 'tithim?*

na praṇāyyo janaḥ kaccin nikāyyaṃ te 'dhitiṣṭhati
deva|kārya|vighātāya dharma|drohī mah"|ôdaye?*

kuṇḍa|pāyyavatāṃ kaccid agni|cityāvatāṃ tathā
kathābhī ramase nityam upacāyyavatāṃ śubhe?*

vardhate te tapo bhīru? vyajeṣṭhā vighna|nāyakān?
ajaiṣīḥ kāma|saṃmohau, saṃprāpthā vinayena vā?*

n' āyasyasi tapasyantī? gurūn samyag atūtuṣaḥ?
yamān n' ôdavijiṣṭhās tvaṃ? nijāya tapase 'tuṣaḥ?»

6.70 ath' ârghyaṃ madhu|park'|ādyam upanīy' ādarād asau
arcayitvā phalair arcyau, sarvatr' ākhyad an|āmayam.

«sakhyasya tava Sugrīvaḥ kārakaḥ kapi|nandanaḥ.
drutaṃ draṣṭ" âsi Maithilyāḥ,» s" âivam uktvā tiro 'bhavat.**

He then said to her: "At the time of the conjunction of the sun and moon do you perform the rite for the fathers with sweet fruits which need no cooking?

Do you purify the offering which is the gods' portion which certainly needs purifying? Do you bow down to the *soma* which must be pressed out by brahmins at the sacrifice?

Do you not neglect the sipping ceremony as is proper, 6.65
morning and evening? Do you honor a guest at the proper time as if he were the sacrificial fire?

Does no despicable person enter your dwelling for the purpose of obstructing the rites to the gods, harming righteousness, O glorious one?

O beautiful one, do you always delight in the tales of those who drink *soma* from the bowl, those who maintain the sacred fires and those who arrange the fires?

Does your austerity prosper, O modest lady? Have you overcome the foremost obstacles? Have you conquered desire and delusion and are you possessed of modesty?

Will you not tire in the performance of austerity? Have you properly satisfied your teachers? Do you shrink from death? Are you satisfied with your own asceticism?"

After respectfully presenting offerings of honey and milk 6.70
and honoring those two honorable men with fruits, she told them she was well in all respects.

"Sugríva, the delight of the monkeys will form an alliance with you. You will soon see Sita." Saying thus she vanished.

nandanāni mun'|îndrāṇāṃ ramaṇāni van'|âukasām
vanāni bhejatur vīrau tataḥ Pāmpāni Rāghavau.*

«bhṛṅg'|ālī|kokila|kruṅbhir vāśanaiḥ paśya Lakṣmaṇa,
rocanair bhūṣitāṃ, Pampām asmākaṃ hṛday'|āvidham.*

paribhāvīṇi tārāṇāṃ paśya manthīni cetasām
udbhāsīni jale|jāni, dunvanty a|dayitaṃ janam.

6.75 sarvatra dayit'|âdhīnaṃ su|vyaktaṃ rāmaṇīyakam,
yena jātaṃ priy'|âpāye kad|vadaṃ haṃsa|kokilam.

pakṣibhir vitṛdair yūnāṃ śākhibhiḥ kusum'|ôtkiraiḥ
a|jño yo, yasya vā n' âsti priyaḥ, praglo bhaven na saḥ.*

dhvanīnām uddhamair ebhir madhūnām uddhayair bhṛśam
ājighraiḥ puṣpa|gandhānāṃ patagair glapitā vayam.*

dhārayaiḥ kusum'|ōrmīṇāṃ pārayair bādhituṃ janān
śākhibhir hā hatā bhūyo hṛdayānām udejayaiḥ.*

dadair duḥkhasya mādṛgbhyo, dhāyair āmodam uttamam,
limpair iva tanor vātaiś cetayaḥ syāj jvalo na kaḥ?*

6.80 avaśyāya|kaṇ'|āsrāvāś cāru|muktā|phala|tviṣaḥ
kurvanti citta|saṃsrāvaṃ calat|parṇ'|âgra|saṃbhṛtāḥ.*

Then the heroes, descendants of Raghu, enjoyed the forests of lake Pampa which were delightful and pleasing to the best of the forest-dwelling sages.

"Lákshmana, look at the Pampa lake which pierces our heart, adorned with gladdening swarms of bees, koil birds and sandpipers all calling out.

Look at the bright lotuses which outshine the stars and disturb hearts, paining those without their lovers.

Everywhere happiness is obviously dependent on the 6.75
beloved, whence, in the absence of the lover the geese and koils come to be harsh sounding.

Only one who is insensate or who has no lover would not be wearied by the birds and the flower-scattering trees that wound the young.

We are so tortured by these bees which make humming noises, suck honey and smell the fragrance of the flowers.

Oh we have once again been struck by these trees which bear waves of flowers and are able to torment people, causing hearts to tremble.

What sentient being would not be inflamed by the breezes, bestowers of the finest perfume, anointers of the body, but givers of pain to such as me?

The streams of dewdrops shining like beautiful pearls as 6.80
they collect on the tips of trembling leaves make my heart melt.

avasāyo bhaviṣyāmi duḥkhasy' âsya kadā nv aham?
na jīvasy' âvahāro māṃ karoti sukhinaṃ Yamaḥ.*

dahye 'haṃ madhuno lehair dāvair ugrair yathā giriḥ.
nāyaḥ ko 'tra sa, yena syāṃ bat' âhaṃ vigata|jvaraḥ?*

samāviṣṭaṃ graheṇ' êva grāheṇ' êv' āttam arṇave
dṛṣṭvā gṛhān Smarasy' êva van'|ântān mama mānasam.*

vāt'|āhati|calac|chākhā nartakā iva śākhinaḥ.
duḥsahā hī parikṣiptāḥ kvaṇadbhir ali|gāthakaiḥ.»*

6.85 eka|hāyana|sāraṅga|gatī, Raghu|kul'|ôttamau,
lavakau śatru|śaktīnām Ṛṣyamūkam agacchatām.*

tau Vāli|praṇidhī matvā Sugrīvo 'cintayat kapiḥ:
«bandhunā vigṛhīto 'haṃ bhūyāsaṃ jīvakaḥ katham?»*

sa śatru|lāvau manvāno Rāghavau, Malayaṃ girim
jagāma sa|parīvāro vyoma|māyam iv' ôtthitam.**

śarma|daṃ Mārutiṃ dūtaṃ viṣama|sthaḥ kapi|dvipam
śok'|âpanudam a|vyagraṃ prāyuṅkta kapi|kuñjaraḥ.*

viśvāsa|prada|veṣo, 'sau pathi|prajñaḥ, samāhitaḥ,
citta|saṃkhyo jigīṣūṇām utpapāta nabhas|talam.*

When will I be rid of this grief? Yama, the taker of the soul, is not about to make me happy.

I am being burned by the honey-licking bees like a mountain by fierce fires. What means is there here by which I might be free of fever?

When I see the edges of the forest, like the dwellings of the love god, it is as if my heart is afflicted by a planet or as if eaten by a crocodile in the sea.

The trees are like dancers, their branches shaking as the breezes strike them. Oh they are unbearable, surrounded by bee singers humming."

The two best of Raghu's line, walking with the gait of young 6.85
deer and cutting down the forces of their enemies went on
to Mount Rishya·muka.

Assuming that they were spies for Valin, Sugríva the monkey thought: "I have been betrayed by my kinsman: how can I live any longer?"

Reckoning the two sons of Raghu to be destroyers of their enemies, he went with his retinue to Mount Málaya which rose up as if measuring the sky.

The foremost monkey in a state of despair employed as his envoy the joy-giving imperturbable Hánuman son of the wind, an elephant among monkeys, a dispeller of sorrow.

His attire inspired confidence, he knew the way, he was composed and he knew the hearts of those who sought victory. He flew up to the surface of the clouds.

6.90 surā|pair iva ghūrṇadbhiḥ śākhibhiḥ pavan'|āhataiḥ
Ṛṣyamūkam agād bhṛṅgaiḥ pragītaṃ Sāma|gair iva.*

taṃ mano|haram āgatya giriṃ varma|harau kapiḥ
vīrau sukh'|āharo 'vocad bhikṣur bhikṣ"|ârha|vigrahaḥ.*

«balināv amum adr'|îndraṃ yuvāṃ stambe|ramāv iva
ācakṣāthām ithaḥ kasmāc Chaṅkareṇ' âpi dur|gamam,*

vyāptaṃ guhā|śayaiḥ krūraiḥ kravy'|âdbhiḥ sa|niśā|caraiḥ,
tuṅga|śaila|taru|cchannaṃ mānuṣāṇām a|gocaram.*

sattvam|ejaya|siṃh'|āḍhyān stanaṃ|dhāya|sama|tviṣau
kathaṃ nāḍiṃ|dhamān mārgān āgatau viṣam'|ôpalān?**

6.95 uttīrṇau vā kathaṃ bhīmāḥ saritaḥ kūlam|udvahāḥ,
āsāditau kathaṃ brūtaṃ na gajaiḥ kūlam|udrujaiḥ.»*

Rāmo 'vocadd Hanūmantam «āvām abhraṃ|lihaṃ girim
aiva vidvan, pituḥ kāmāt pāntāv alpaṃ|pacān munīn.*

a|mitaṃ|pacam īśānaṃ sarva|bhogīṇam uttamam
āvayoḥ pitaraṃ viddhi khyātaṃ Daśarathaṃ bhuvi.*

chalena dayit" âraṇyād rakṣas" âruṃ|tudena naḥ
a|sūryaṃ|paśyayā mūrtyā hṛtā:* tāṃ mṛgayāvahe.»*

He went to Rishya·muka where the trees waved around like 6.90
drunkards as they were struck by the wind and the bees
droned as if chanting the Sama Veda.

The monkey came as a joy-bringing mendicant deserving alms to that delightful mountain and spoke to the armor-bearing heroes.

"You men mighty as elephants should declare why you have come together to this lord of mountains which is difficult for even Shiva to reach.

It is filled with cruel cave-dwelling carnivores and demons, covered in high cliffs and trees and inaccessible to men.

How did you two who glow as if newly born travel roughly paved roads which are filled with lions that terrify other creatures, making one's arteries pulse?

Explain how you crossed the terrible bank-breaking spates 6.95
and how you were not attacked by embankment-tearing
elephants."

Rama spoke to Hánuman: "O sage, we have come to this cloud-licking mountain at the behest of our father, to protect those sages who scarcely cook for themselves.

Know that our father who has sacrificial food prepared without limit is lordly, is generous to all, is the best, and is known to the world as Dasha·ratha.

By trickery a demon who wounds most painfully took my beloved from the forest; we are hunting for her whose body even the sun might not see."

pratyūce Mārutī Rāmam «asti Vāl" îti vānaraḥ
śamayed api saṃgrāme yo lalāṭaṃ|tapaṃ ravim.*

6.100 ugraṃ|paśyena Sugrīvas tena bhrātā nirākṛtaḥ.
tasya mitrīyato dūtaḥ saṃprāpto 'smi vaśaṃ|vadaḥ.*

priyaṃ|vado 'pi n' âiv' âhaṃ bruve mithyā paraṃ|tapa.
sakhyā tena Daśagrīvaṃ nihant" âsi dviṣaṃ|tapam.*

vācaṃ|yamo 'ham an|ṛte. satyam etad bravīmi te:
‹ehi, sarvaṃ|sahaṃ mitraṃ Sugrīvaṃ kuru vānaram.› »*

sarvaṃ|kaṣa|yaśaḥ|śākhaṃ Rāma|kalpa|taruṃ kapiḥ
ādāy', âbhraṃ|kaṣaṃ prāyān Malayaṃ phala|śālinam.*

meghaṃ|karam iv' āyāntam ṛtuṃ Rāmaṃ klam'|ânvitaḥ
dṛṣṭvā mene na Sugrīvo Vāli|bhānuṃ bhayaṃ|karam.*

6.105 up'|âgny akurutāṃ sakhyam anyo|'nyasya priyaṃ|karau.
kṣemaṃ|karāṇi kāryāṇi paryālocayatāṃ tataḥ.*

āśitaṃ|bhavam, utkruṣṭaṃ, valgitaṃ, śayitaṃ, sthitam,
bahv amanyata Kākutsthaḥ kapīnāṃ svecchayā kṛtam.*

tato Baliṃdama|prakhyaṃ kapir viśvaṃ|bhar'|âdhipam*
Sugrīvaḥ prābravīd Rāmaṃ Vālino yudhi vikramam.

Hánuman replied to Rama: "The monkey Valin could extinguish the head-burning sun in battle.

Ill-favored, he ousted his brother Sugríva. I, speaking under 6.100
his authority, am employed as an envoy to seek friendship with you.

Although I speak sweetly, I certainly do not speak falsely, O tormentor of your enemies. With this friend you will slay your ten-headed enemy.

I restrain myself from speaking untruth. I say this truly to you: 'Come, make the monkey Sugríva a friend who can endure anything.'"

The monkey brought the wish-granting tree that was Rama, the branches of whose fame touched all, and went to the cloud-scraping Mount Málaya so full of fruit.

Sugríva was filled with weariness, but seeing Rama coming like the approaching monsoon season he no longer thought of Valin as the fearsome sun.

That delightful pair made an alliance with each other over 6.105
the fire. They then considered what they could do to secure peace.

Rama much approved the spontaneous activity of the monkeys: eating to the full, calling, jumping about, sleeping and standing.

Then the monkey Sugríva spoke of Valin's prowess in battle to Rama, the lord of the earth who resembled Vishnu, the tamer of Bali.

«vasuṃ|dharāyāṃ kṛtsnāyāṃ n' âsti Vāli|samo balī.
hṛdayaṃ|gamam etat tvāṃ bravīmi, na parābhavam.*

dūra|gair anta|gair bāṇair bhavān atyanta|gaḥ śriyaḥ
api Saṃkrandanasya syāt kruddhaḥ, kim uta Vālinaḥ?*

6.110 vareṇa tu muner Vālī saṃjāto dasyu|ho raṇe.
a|vārya|prasaraḥ prātar|udyann iva tamo|'pahaḥ.*

atipriyatvān na hi me kātaraṃ pratipadyate
ceto Vāli|vadhaṃ Rāma, kleś'|âpaham upasthitam.*

śīrṣa|ghātinam āyātam arīṇāṃ tvāṃ vilokayan
patighnī|lakṣaṇ'|ôpetāṃ manye 'haṃ Vālinaḥ śriyam.**

śatru|ghnān yudhi hasti|ghno girīn kṣipyann a|kṛtrimān
śilpibhiḥ pāṇi|ghaiḥ kruddhas tvayā jayyo 'bhyupāyavān?*

āḍhyaṃ|karaṇa|vikrānto, Mahiṣasya sura|dviṣaḥ,
priyaṃ|karaṇam Indrasya, duṣ|karaṃ kṛtavān vadham.*

6.115 priyaṃ|bhāvukatāṃ yātas, taṃ kṣipan yojanaṃ mṛtam,
svarge priyaṃ|bhaviṣṇuś ca krtsnaṃ śakto 'py a|bādhayan.»*

jijñāsoḥ śaktim astrāṇāṃ Rāmo nyūna|dhiyaḥ kapeḥ
abhinat pratipatty|arthaṃ sapta vyoma|spṛśas tarūn.*

"In the entire world there is not one who is equal in strength to Valin. I tell you what is in my heart but I do not say it to disparage you.

With your far-going accurate arrows, in your anger you could put an end to the glory even of roaring Indra, so what of Valin?

By the boon of a sage, Valin has become a foe-slayer in bat- 6.110
tle. His irresistible power is like the dark-slaying sun that rises in the morning.

My mind now becomes hesitant, O Rama, because over-fond, and fails to believe that its dearest desire, the grief-dispelling slaughter of Valin, is at hand.

When I see you come as a beheader of your enemies I think that Valin's fortune bears the marks of a husband-killer.*

Can he, angry and well-prepared, killing elephants in battle and throwing actual enemy-killing mountains, be overcome by you with your skilled monkeys who strike with their hands?

He is bold in enriching himself, he has effected the very difficult slaughter of Máhisha, the enemy of the gods, that was so pleasing to Indra.

He became beloved when he threw that dead demon a mile 6.115
away, he became dear in heaven by not oppressing the world though able to do so."

In order to demonstrate the power of his weapons to that uncomprehending monkey who wished to understand, Rama split seven sky-touching trees.

tato Vāli|paśau vadhye Rāma|rtvig jita|sādhvasaḥ
abhyabhūn nilayaṃ bhrātuḥ Sugrīvo ninadan dadhṛk.*

guhāyā niragād Vālī siṃho mṛgam iva dyuvan,
bhrātaraṃ yuṅ bhiyaḥ saṃkhye ghoṣeṇ' āpūrayan diśaḥ.

vyāyacchamānayor mūḍho bhede sadṛśayos tayoḥ
bāṇam udyatam āyaṃsīd Ikṣvāku|kula|nandanaḥ.*

6.120 Ṛṣyamūkam agāt klāntaḥ
kapir mṛga|sadṛg drutam,
Kiṣkindh'|âdri|sad" âtyarthaṃ
niṣpiṣṭaḥ, koṣṇam ucchvasan.*

kṛtvā Vāli|druhaṃ Rāmo mālayā sa|viśeṣaṇam,
Aṅgada|svaṃ punar hantuṃ kapin" āhvāyayad raṇe.*

tayor vānara|senā|nyoḥ saṃprahāre tanu|cchidam
Vālino dūra|bhāg Rāmo bāṇaṃ prāṇ'|âdam atyajat.*

Vālinaṃ patitaṃ dṛṣṭvā vānarā ripu|ghātinam,
bāndhav'|ākrośino bhejur a|nāthāḥ kakubho daśa.*

«dhig Dāśarathim!» ity ūcur munayo vana|vartinaḥ.
upeyur madhu|pāyinyaḥ krośantyas taṃ kapi|striyaḥ.*

6.125 Rāmam uccair upālabdha śūra|mānī kapi|prabhuḥ,
vraṇa|vedanayā glāyan, sādhuṃ|manyam a|sādhuvat:*

Sugríva, with Rama as his sacrificial priest, overcame his qualms with regard to the killing of the sacrificial victim Valin. Yelling and resolute he approached his brother's lair.

Valin came out of his cave at his brother like a lion chasing a deer, causing terror in the battle and filling the quarters with his roars.

Rama, delight of the Ikshváku clan, stayed his upraised arrow, bewildered, as he tried to distinguish that similar pair as they fought.

The exhausted monkey quickly fled to Rishya·muka like a 6.120
deer, panting warmly, crushed completely by the resident of Kishkíndha mountain.

Marking out Valin's enemy Sugríva with a garland, Rama once again challenged Valin the father of Ángada to fight with the monkey in battle.

In the fight between the leaders of the two monkey armies Rama shot an arrow from afar which cut into Valin's body and consumed his life force.

When the monkeys saw that Valin, destroyer of his enemies, had fallen, leaderless they resorted to the ten directions, weeping for their kinsman.

"Fie upon Rama!" said the forest sages. The honey-drinking monkey wives came to him lamenting.

The monkey king, thinking himself a hero, swooning with 6.125
the pain of his wound, loudly reproached Rama as an evil person who thought himself good:

«mṛṣ" âsi tvaṃ havir|yājī Rāghava, cchadma|tāpasaḥ,
anya|vyāsakta|ghātitvād brahma|ghnāṃ pāpa|saṃmitaḥ.*

pāpa|kṛt su|kṛtāṃ madhye, rājñaḥ puṇya|kṛtaḥ sutaḥ,
mām a|pāpaṃ dur|ācāra, kiṃ nihaty' âbhidhāsyasi?*

agni|cit soma|sud rājā ratha|cakra|cid|ādiṣu
analeṣv iṣṭavān, kasmān na tvay" âpekṣitaḥ pitā?*

māṃsa|vikrayiṇaḥ karma vyādhasy' âpi vigarhitam
māṃ ghnatā bhavat" âkāri niḥśaṅkaṃ pāpa|dṛśvanā.*

6.130 buddhi|pūrvaṃ dhruvaṃ na tvā rāja|kṛtvā pitā khalam
saha|yudhvānam anyena yo 'hino mām an|āgasam.*

pañca pañca|nakhā bhakṣyā ye proktāḥ kṛta|jair dvijaiḥ:
Kauśalyā|ja, śaś'|ādīnāṃ teṣāṃ n' âiko 'py ahaṃ kapiḥ.*

kathaṃ duḥṣṭhuḥ svayaṃ dharme prajās tvaṃ pālayiṣyasi?
ātm'|ânujasya jihreṣi Saumitres tvaṃ kathaṃ na vā?

manye kiṃ|jam ahaṃ ghnantaṃ tvām a|kṣatriya|je raṇe
Lakṣmaṇ'|âdhija, dur|vṛtta, prayuktam anujena naḥ.»

"You offer oblations in vain, O Rama. Your austerity is false, your sin is comparable to that of a brahmin-killer because you killed someone engaged in combat with another.

You are a sinner in the midst of saints. You are the son of a virtuous king. What can you say, you malefactor, after slaying me innocent as I am?

Why do you not look to your father, a king who tended the fires and pressed *soma*, sacrificing in fires such as the "chariot-wheel" and others?

You are familiar with your own sin and by killing me you have without doubt done a deed that would be despicable even to a meat-selling hunter.

Your father certainly did not act with foresight when he 6.130
made a sinner like you the king, for you struck me down who am faultless while I fought with another.

There are five five-clawed animals declared by the brahmins of the golden age to be eatable. I am not one of those rabbits, I am a monkey, O son of Kaushalyá.

When you yourself are deficient in the practice of *dharma*, how can you protect your subjects? Are you not ashamed before your own younger brother Lákshmana?

O villainous brother of Lákshmana, I think you are of obscure parentage because you killed in a fight which did not originate among honorable warriors, put up to it by my younger brother."

pratyūce Vālinaṃ Rāmo: «n' â|kṛtaṃ kṛtavān aham
yajvabhiḥ sutvabhiḥ pūrvair jaradbhiś ca, kap'|īṣvara.

6.135 te hi jālair gale pāśais tiraścām upasedusām
ūṣuṣāṃ para|dāraiś ca sārdhaṃ nidhanam aiṣiṣuḥ.*

ahaṃ tu śuśruvān bhrātrā striyaṃ bhuktāṃ kanīyasā
upeyivān anūcānair ninditas tvaṃ latā|mṛga.»*

anvanaiṣīt tato Vālī trapāvān iva Rāghavam
nyakṣipac c' Âṅgadaṃ yatnāt Kākutsthe tanayaṃ priyaṃ.

mriyamāṇaḥ sa Sugrīvaṃ proce sad|bhāvam āgataḥ:
«saṃbhāviṣyāva ekasyām abhijānāsi mātari.

avasāva nag'|êndreṣu yat pāsyāvo madhūni ca,
abhijānīhi tat sarvaṃ, bandhūnāṃ samayo hy ayam.*

6.140 daivaṃ na vidadhe nūnaṃ yugapat sukham āvayoḥ,
śaśvad babhūva tad duḥ|sthaṃ yato na iti h' âkarot.»*

dadau sa dayitāṃ bhrātre mālāṃ c' âgryāṃ hiraṇmayīm,
rājyaṃ saṃdiśya bhogāṃś ca mamāra vraṇa|pīḍitaḥ.

tasya nirvartya kartavyaṃ Sugrīvo Rāghav'|ājñayā
Kiṣkindh'|âdri|guhāṃ gantuṃ manaḥ praṇidadhe drutam.

Rama replied to Valin: "I have done nothing that was not done before by the old *soma*-pressing sacrificers, O monkey-lord.

For they sought with nets and nooses for the destruction of 6.135
animals which tried to attack them and also of those who lived with others' wives.

But I have heard that you made advances towards a woman who had already been enjoyed by your younger brother and so you have been censured by the wise, you tree creature."

Then Valin as if ashamed conciliated Rama and carefully handed over his dear son Ángada to the descendant of Kakútstha.

As he was dying he repented and addressed Sugríva: "You remember that we were born of one mother.

We lived together in the mountains and we drank nectar together, remember all this for this is a time for family.

Fate certainly did not bestow happiness on us both in the 6.140
same degree. It was always ill disposed and so made us like this."

He gave his wife and the best of golden garlands to his brother. Assigning his kingdom and his worldly goods to him he died, overcome by his wound.

After he had performed the rites for him, Sugríva on Rama's order quickly set his mind on going to the cave on the Kishkíndha Mountain.

nāma|grāhaṃ kapibhir a|śanaiḥ
stūyamānaḥ samantād,
anvag|bhāvaṃ* Raghu|vṛṣabhayor
vānar'|êndro virājan,
abhyarṇe 'mbhaḥ|patana|samaye,
parṇalī|bhūta|sānuṃ,
Kiṣkindh'|âdriṃ nyaviśata, madhu|
kṣība|guñjad|dvirepham.

Sugríva the monkey-king being praised continually by the monkeys calling his name, glowing in the friendship of the two bulls of Raghu's line, and given that the time of the monsoon was approaching, resorted to Kishkíndha mountain whose slopes were covered in leaves, whose bees were humming drunk with nectar.

CANTO 7
THE SEARCH FOR SITA

7.1 Tataḥ kartā van'|ākampaṃ
vavau varṣā|prabhañjanaḥ,
nabhaḥ pūrayitāraś ca
samunnemuḥ payo|dharāḥ.**

tarpaṇaṃ prajaniṣṇūnāṃ śasyānām a|malaṃ payaḥ
rociṣṇavaḥ sa|visphūrjā mumucur bhinnavad ghanāḥ,*

nirākariṣṇavo bhānuṃ divaṃ vartiṣṇavo 'bhitaḥ,
alaṃ|kariṣṇavo bhāntas taḍitvantaś cariṣṇavaḥ.*

tān viloky' â|sahiṣṇuḥ san, vilalāp' ônmadiṣṇuvat,
vasan Mālyavati, glāsnū Rāmo jiṣṇur a|dhṛṣṇuvat.*

7.5 «bhramī kadamba|saṃbhinnaḥ pavanaḥ, śaminām api
klamitvaṃ kurute 'tyarthaṃ, megha|śīkara|śītalaḥ.*

saṃjvāriṇ" êva manasā dhvāntam āyāsinā mayā
drohi khadyota|saṃparki nayan'|âmoṣi duḥsaham.*

kurvanti parisāriṇyo vidyutaḥ paridevinam
abhyāghātibhir āmiśrāś cātakaiḥ parirāṭibhiḥ.*

saṃsargī paridāh' îva śīto 'py ābhāti śīkaraḥ,
soḍhum ākrīḍino 'śakyāḥ śikhinaḥ parivādinaḥ.*

etā daiv'|ânurodhinyo dveṣiṇya iva rāgiṇam
pīḍayanti janaṃ dhārāḥ patantyo 'n|apacāriṇam.**

7.10 kuryād yoginam apy eṣa sphūrjāvān parimohinam
tyāginaṃ sukha|duḥkhasya parikṣepy ambhasām ṛtuḥ.*

vikatthī yācate prattam a|viśrambhī muhur jalam
parjanyaṃ cātakaḥ pakṣī nikṛntann iva mānasam.*

THEN THE MONSOON winds blew making the forests 7.1
shake and water-laden clouds rose up filling the sky.

As if split, the crashing and flashing clouds released pure water to refresh the growing crops,

Keeping the sun at bay, rolling around the sky, wandering about and decorating it with flashing lighting.

Seeing them and being unable to bear it, crying like a madman, living on Mount Mályavat, weary Rama who always won seemed devoid of courage.

"Mingled with the scent of *kadámba* trees, the wander- 7.5
ing wind, cold with cloud-drizzle, exhausts even quiescent
men.

The torturing darkness filled with fireflies robs me of my sight; it is unbearable to me as I contend with my feverish mind.

As they call, the tormenting *chátaka* birds interweave the flashing lightning and it makes me weep.

The shining drizzle, though cold, seems to scald as it touches. The lekking peacocks are impossible to bear when they call out.

As they fall upon an unoffending man in love these downpours are in cahoots with fate and torment him like enemies.

When this season of thunder scatters its rain it would con- 7.10
found even a yogi who has transcended pleasure and pain.

As if cutting into my heart the vaunting and distrustful *chátaka* bird repeatedly begs the cloud for rain already given.

pralāpino bhaviṣyanti kadā nv ete 'palāṣiṇaḥ
pramāthino viyuktānāṃ hiṃsakāḥ pāpa|dardurāḥ.»*

nindako rajaniṃ|manyaṃ divasaṃ kleśako niśām
prāvṛṣy anaiṣīt Kākutsthaḥ kathaṃ cit paridevakaḥ.*

ath' ôpaśarade 'paśyat krauñcānāṃ ceṣṭanaiḥ kulaiḥ
utkaṇṭhā|vardhanaiḥ śubhraṃ ravaṇair ambaraṃ tatam.*

7.15 vilokya dyotanaṃ candraṃ Lakṣmaṇaṃ śocano 'vadat:
«paśya dandramaṇān haṃsān aravinda|samutsukān.

kapiś caṅkramaṇo 'dy' âpi n' âsau bhavati gardhanaḥ,
kurvanti kopanaṃ tārā maṇḍanā gaganasya mām.*

n' âvaity āpyāyitāraṃ kiṃ kamalāni raviṃ kapiḥ
dīpitāraṃ din'|ārambhe nirasta|dhvānta|saṃcayam?

atīte varṣuke kāle, pramattaḥ sthāyuko gṛhe
gāmuko dhruvam adhvānaṃ Sugrīvo Vālinā gatam.*

jalpākībhiḥ sah' āsīnaḥ strībhiḥ prajavinā tvayā
gatvā Lakṣmaṇa, vaktavyo jayinā niṣṭhuraṃ vacaḥ.*

7.20 śaile viśrayiṇaṃ kṣipram an|ādariṇam abhyamī
nyāyaṃ paribhavī brūhi pāpam a|vyathinaṃ kapim.*

spṛhayāluṃ kapiṃ strībhyo
  nidrālum a|dayāluvat
śraddhāluṃ bhrāmaraṃ dhāruṃ
  sadrum adrau vada drutam.»*

When will these wicked chattering frogs who torment and harm separated lovers be free from their urges?"

So Rama mourning and troubled somehow passed a night and a night-like day of the rainy season.

Then as fall began he saw the clear sky spread with moving flocks of curlews and their cries increased his longing.

When he saw the shining moon he said in sorrow to Lák- 7.15
shmana: "Do you see the migrating geese which long for
their lotuses?

That covetous monkey is still not yet on the move and the stars that decorate the sky are making me angry.

Does the monkey not understand that when the sun rises at daybreak, it dispels the mass of darkness and makes the lotuses open?

Now the monsoon has passed and Sugríva remains indifferent at home. He is certainly going the way Valin went.

O Lákshmana, while he sits with his prattling women you should go quickly as a conquistador and speak harshly to him.

Reproach him for being neglectful as he takes refuge on his 7.20
mountain, mock him and speak reason to that wicked and
indifferent monkey.

Hasten to speak pitilessly to that concupiscent monkey as he sits on his mountain and sleeps with his women and trustingly sips honey."

sṛmaro bhaṅgura|prajño, gṛhītvā bhāsuraṃ dhanuḥ,
viduro jitvaraḥ prāpa Lakṣmaṇo gatvarān kapīn.*

taṃ jāgarūkaḥ kāryeṣu dandaśūka|ripuṃ kapiḥ
a|kampraṃ Mārutir dīpraṃ namraḥ prāveśayad guhām.*

kamrābhir āvṛtaḥ strībhir, āśaṃsuḥ kṣemam ātmanaḥ,
icchuḥ prasādaṃ praṇayan Sugrīvaḥ prāvadan nṛpam:*

7.25 «ahaṃ svapnak prasādena tava vandārubhiḥ saha
a|bhīrur avasaṃ strībhir bhāsurābhir ih' eśvaraḥ.*

vidyun|nāśaṃ raver bhāsaṃ vibhrājaṃ śaśa|lāñchanam
Rāma|pratteṣu bhogeṣu n' âham ajñāsiṣaṃ rataḥ.

eṣa śoka|cchido vīrān prabho, samprati vānarān
dharā|śaila|samudrāṇām anta|gān prahiṇomy aham.»

Rāghavasya tataḥ kāryaṃ kārur vānara|puṅgavaḥ
sarva|vānara|senānām āśv āgamanam ādiśat.**

«vayam ady' âiva gacchāmo Rāmaṃ draṣṭuṃ tvar"|ânvitāḥ
kārakā mitra|kāryāṇi* Sītā|lābhāya,» so 'bravīt.*

7.30 tataḥ kapīnāṃ saṃghātā harṣād Rāghava|bhūtaye
pūrayantaḥ samājagmur bhaya|dāyā diśo daśa.*

Sugrīv'|ântikam āseduḥ «sādayiṣyāma ity arim!»
kariṣyanta iv' âkasmād bhuvanaṃ nir|Daśānanam.*

Swift Lákshmana who bore a shining bow, understanding such weakness, wise and victorious, came to the ever-moving monkeys.

The respectful monkey Hánuman, aware of his duties, led the steady and radiant enemy of the demons into his cave.

As he bowed down, Sugríva, surrounded by his loving wives and wishing for ease, sought his favor and spoke to the protector of men:

"By your favor I dwelt sleepily here with these adoring beau- 7.25
tiful women as their fearless lord.

I delighted in the enjoyments that Rama gave and I was unaware of the brightness of the sun that drove away the lightning or of the radiant moon.

O lord, I will now dispatch my grief-dispelling monkey heroes who will go to the ends of the mountains and the oceans of the earth."

Then the best of monkeys doing Rama's bidding quickly ordered the assembly of all the monkey armies.

"We are now going to see Rama with all speed as agents in our friend's task of finding Sita," he said.

Then, to ensure Rama's success, fear-inspiring hosts of mon- 7.30
keys joyfully assembled and filled the ten directions.

They met in the presence of Sugríva, and said, "We will kill the enemy thus!" as if about to rid the earth of Rávana in an instant.

«kart" âsmi kāryam āyātair ebhir» ity avagamya saḥ
Kākutstha|pādapa|cchāyāṃ sīta|sparśām upāgamat.*

kāryaṃ sāra|nibhaṃ dṛṣṭvā vānarāṇāṃ samāgamam
avain nāśaṃ Daśāsyasya nirvṛttam iva Rāghavaḥ.*

tataḥ kapi|samāhāram eka|niścāyam āgatam
upādhyāya iv' āyāmaṃ Sugrīvo 'dhyāpipad diśām.**

7.35 sa|jal'|âmbhoda|saṃrāvaṃ Hanumantaṃ, sah'|Âṅgadam
Jāmbava|Nīla|sahitaṃ cāru|sandrāvam abravīt:*

«yāta yūyaṃ Yama|śrāyaṃ diśaṃ nāyena dakṣiṇām
vikṣāvais toya|viśrāvaṃ tarjayanto mah"|ôdadheḥ.*

unnāyān adhigacchantaḥ pradrāvair vasudhā|bhṛtām,
van'|âbhilāvān kurvantaḥ svecchayā, cāru|vikramāḥ!*

sad" ôdgāra|sugandhīnāṃ phalānām alam āśitāḥ,
utkāreṣu ca dhānyānām an|abhīṣṭa|parigrahāḥ,*

saṃstāvam iva śṛṇvantaś chando|gānāṃ mah"|âdhvare
śiñjitaṃ madhu|lehānāṃ puṣpa|prastāra|śāyinām,*

7.40 ālocayanto vistāram ambhasāṃ dakṣiṇ'|ôdadheḥ,
svādayantaḥ phala|rasaṃ muṣṭi|saṃgrāha|pīḍitam,*

nyāyyaṃ yad yatra, tat kāryaṃ paryāyeṇ' â|virodhibhiḥ,
niś"|ôpaśāyaḥ kartavyaḥ phal'|ôccāyaś ca saṃhataiḥ.*

"I can do Rama's business with these assembled forces," he thought and came to the cool shade of the tree that was Rama.

When he saw the assembly of monkeys Rama understood that his task was sound and the death of Rávana was as good as done.

Then Sugríva like a teacher explained the vastness of the regions to the gathering of monkeys who had come together in one group.

He spoke to Hánuman of pleasing gait who roared like a 7.35
water-laden storm cloud and also to Ángada, Jámbava and
Nila:

"Go lawfully to the southern quarter, Yama's abode, and rival with your cries the roar of the waters of the great ocean.

Moving swiftly ascend the heights of the mountains, process and clear the forests at will, O you of beautiful prowess!

You are always well-enough sated with fragrant fruit and you do not wish to acquire harvests of grains

You hear the humming of the bees as they resort to the open flowers as if it were the chanting of the *chandóga* priests at the great sacrifice.

You see the extent of the waters of the southern ocean and 7.40
you taste the juice of fruit crushed in the clench of a fist.

You should do that which is proper in turn without arguing, you should sleep by turns at night and formed into groups you should gather fruits.

Sītā rakṣo|nikāyeṣu stoka|kāyaiś chalena ca
mṛgyā, śatru|nikāyānāṃ vyāvahāsīm an|āśritaiḥ.*

sāṃrāviṇaṃ na kartavyaṃ, yāvan n' āyāti darśanam,
saṃdṛṣṭāyāṃ tu Vaidehyāṃ nigrāho vo 'rthavān areḥ.*

pragrāhair iva pātrāṇām anveṣyā Maithilī kṛtaiḥ,
jñātavyā c' êṅgitair dharmyair dhyāyantī Rāghav'|āgamam.*

7.45 vedivat sa|parigrāhā yajñiyaiḥ saṃskṛtā dvijaiḥ,
dṛśyā māsatamād* ahnaḥ prāg a|nindita|veśa|bhṛt.*

nīvāra|phala|mūl'|āśān ṛṣīn apy atiśerate,
yasyā guṇā niruddrāvās, tāṃ drutaṃ yāta, paśyata.»*

ucchrāyavān ghan'|ārāvo vānaraṃ jalad'|âravam
dūr'|āplāvaṃ Hanūmantaṃ Rāmaḥ proce gaj'|āplavaḥ:*

«avagrāhe yathā vṛṣṭiṃ prārthayante kṛṣīvalāḥ,
prārthayadhvaṃ tathā Sītāṃ. yāta Sugrīva|śāsanam.*

vaṇik pragrāhavān yadvat kāle carati siddhaye,
deś'|âpekṣās tathā yūyaṃ yāt' āday' âṅgulīyakam.»*

7.50 abhijñānaṃ gṛhītvā te samutpetur nabhas|talam
vājinaḥ syandane bhānor vimukta|pragrahā iva.*

With your slight bodies and using guile you should search for Sita in the dwellings of the demons without resorting to mockery of the bodies of your foes.

So long as you have not had sight of her you should make no clamor together, but when you have seen Sita the defeat of the enemy should be your objective.

You should seek for Sita as if you were holding begging bowls. As she meditates upon the advent of Rama you will know her by her pious gestures.

Like the altar with its enclosing fence constructed by twice- 7.45
born brahmins, she will be seen wearing modest clothing before the last day of the month.

She surpasses even those sages that live on wild rice, fruits and roots. She has immovable virtues. Go quickly to her and see."

The noble cloud-voiced Rama who proceeded like an elephant spoke to the cloud-voiced far-leaping Hánuman:

"As plowmen long for rain in a drought, so should you yearn for Sita. Go at Sugríva's command.

As a merchant with his scales sets out at the proper time for success in business, so should you go and look in the various regions, taking this ring."

Taking the keepsake they flew together across the firma- 7.50
ment like the horses of the sun's chariot with the reins unloosed.

udak Śatavaliṃ koṭyā, Suṣeṇaṃ pakṣimāṃ tathā
diśaṃ prāsthāpayad rājā vānarāṇāṃ kṛta|tvaraḥ.

prācīṃ tāvadbhir a|vyagraḥ kapibhir Vinato yayau
a|pragrāhair iv' ādityo vājibhir dūra|pātibhiḥ.*

yayur Vindhyaṃ śaran|meghaiḥ
prāvāraiḥ pravarair iva
pracchannaṃ Māruti|prasthāḥ
Sītāṃ draṣṭuṃ plavaṅ|gamāḥ.*

paribhāvaṃ mṛg'|êndrāṇāṃ kurvanto naga|mūrdhasu
Vindhye tigm'|âṃśu|mārgasya ceruḥ paribhav'|ôpame.*

7.55 bhremuḥ śil"|ôccayāṃs tuṅgān, utterur a|tarān nadān,
āśaṃsavo lavaṃ śatroḥ Sītāyāś ca viniścayam.*

ādareṇa gamaṃ cakrur viṣamesv apy a|saṅghasāḥ
vyāpnuvanto diśo, 'nyādān kurvantaḥ sa|vyadhān harīn.*

saṃceruḥ sa|hasāḥ ke cid, a|svanāḥ ke cid āṭiṣuḥ,
saṃyāmavanto yativan nigadān apare 'mucan.*

atha klamād a|niḥkvāṇā narāḥ kṣīṇa|paṇā iva,
a|madāḥ sedur ekasmin nitambe nikhilā gireḥ.*

tataḥ sa|saṃmadās tatra niraikṣanta patatriṇaḥ
guhā|dvāreṇa niryātaḥ, samajena paśūn iva.*

7.60 vīnām upasaraṃ dṛṣṭvā, te 'nyony'|ôpahavā guhām
prāviśann āhava|prajñā āhāvam upalipsavaḥ.*

The king of the monkeys made haste and dispatched Shátavali to the north with a crore and also Sushéna to the west.

With as many monkeys, steady Vínata went east like the sun with his far-traveling horses unrestrained.

Other monkeys led by Hánuman went to the Vindhya range covered by fall clouds like fine cloaks to look for Sita.

In the Vindhya which seemed to be in contempt of the path of the sun they went, making mock of the lions on the mountain peaks.

They wandered over high mountains, they crossed unford- 7.55
able rivers, they wished for the reaping of the enemy and
the discovery of Sita.

They made careful going even over uneven ground, with no sustenance, filling the regions, making the stricken lions go without food.

Some went laughing together, some passed by without a sound, others in self-control uttered prayers in the manner of ascetics.

Then soundless from fatigue like destitute men, they all sat joyless on one flank of the mountain.

Then and there with joy they saw birds coming out through the entrance to a cave, like beasts in a herd.

As they watched the birds approach, the battle-wise mon- 7.60
keys called to each other as they entered the cave in search
of a pool.

kurvanto havam āptānāṃ, pipāsā|vadha|kāṅkṣiṇaḥ,
dvāraṃ tamo|ghana|prakhyaṃ guhāyāḥ prāviśan drutam.*

tasminn antarghaṇe 'paśyan praghāṇe saudha|sadmanaḥ,
lauh'|ôdghana|ghana|skandhā lalit'|âpaghanāṃ striyam.*

sā stamba|ghna|pada|nyāsān, vighan'|êndu|sama|dyutiḥ,
parigh'|ôru|bhujān, āha hasantī svāgataṃ kapīn.*

piprāy' âdri|guh'|ôpaghnān udghān saṃgha|samāgatān
phalair nānā|rasaiś citraiḥ svādu|śītaiś ca vāribhiḥ.*

7.65 nigh'|ânigha|taru|cchanne
tasmiṃs te labdhrimaiḥ phalaiḥ
tṛptās tāṃ bhrājathumatīṃ
papracchuḥ «kasya pūr iyam?*

«rakṣṇaṃ karoṣi kasmāt tvaṃ? yatnen' ākhyāyatāṃ śubhe,
svapne nidhivad ābhāti tava saṃdarśanaṃ hi naḥ.»*

tato jaladhi|gambhīrān vānarān pratyuvāca sā:
«iyaṃ dānava|rājasya pūḥ sṛṣṭir Viśvakarmaṇaḥ.*

nihataś ca sthitiṃ bhindan dānavo 'sau Bala|dviṣā.
duhitā Merusāvarṇer ahaṃ, nāmnā Svayaṃprabhā.*

jūtim icchatha cet tūrṇaṃ, kīrtiṃ vā pātum ātmanaḥ,
karomi vo bahir|yūtīn. pidhadhvaṃ pāṇibhir dṛśaḥ.»*

Calling to those who had reached it, seeking to kill their thirst, they quickly entered the door of the cave which seemed like a dense mass of darkness.

There at the entrance on the terrace of a stuccoed dwelling, the monkeys with shoulders solid like a carpenter's bench saw a woman of voluptuous figure.

She, shining like the cloudless moon, laughingly bade welcome to the monkeys who crushed the clumps of grass as they placed their feet and whose arms were thick like clubs.

With various fruits of diverse flavor and with sweet cool water she pleased those model monkeys who had come grouped together taking refuge in the mountain cave.

In that place obscured by trees of various sizes, sated with 7.65
the available fruits, they asked that brilliant lady, "Whose is this city?

How do you keep guard? Please tell us fully, O fair lady, for the sight of you seems to us like treasure in a dream."

Then she replied to the monkeys who were profound like the ocean: "This city is the creation of the demon king Vishva·karman.

And Indra the enemy of Bala killed this demon who broke the law. I am Meru·savárni's daughter Svayam·prabha by name.

If you wish for speedy progress or to increase your own glory, I will conduct you outside. Cover your eyes with your hands."

7.70 vrajyāvatī niruddh'|âkṣān vidy" êv' ânuṣṭhita|kriyān
niracikramad icchāto vānarāṃś caṅkramāvataḥ.

niṣkramya śikṣayā tasyās trapāvanto rasā|talāt
jñātvā māsam atikrāntaṃ vyathām avalalambire.*

cintāvantaḥ kathāṃ cakrur upadhā|bheda|bhīravaḥ:
«a|kṛtvā nṛ|pateḥ kāryaṃ, pūjāṃ lapsyāmahe katham?»

prāy'|ôpāsanayā śāntiṃ manvāno Vāli|saṃbhavaḥ,
yuktvā yogaṃ sthitaḥ śaile, vivṛṇvaṃś citta|vedanām.

praskandikām iva prāpto dhyātvā brūte sma Jāmbavān
«dhik śāla|bhañjikā|prakhyān viśayān kalpanā|rucīn.*

7.75 yāṃ kāriṃ rāja|putro 'yam anutiṣṭhati, tāṃ kriyām
aham apy anutiṣṭhāmi,» so 'py uktv" âivam upāviśat.*

uvāca Mārutir vṛddhe saṃnyāsiny atra vānarān:
«ahaṃ paryāya|saṃprāptāṃ kurve prāy'|ôpaveśikām.*

a|bhāve bhavatāṃ yo 'smin jīvet, tasy' âstv a|jīvaniḥ,»
ity uktvā sarva ev' āsthur baddhvā yog'|āsanāni te.*

«a|kleśyam asin" âgny|antaṃ
  Kabandha|vadham,» abhyadhuḥ,
«dhiṅ naḥ prapatanaṃ ghoraṃ
  kled'|ântatvam, a|nāthavat,»

As Vedic knowledge strives to ensure that those whose eyes 7.70
are obscured are successful in their undertakings, so that graceful woman ensured that those monkeys walking awkwardly left in accordance with their wish.

They emerged from the nether world by her instruction and they were ashamed to discover that a month had passed and fell into anguish.

Being worried and fearing failure in their trial they spoke together: "Without doing our duty to the king, how will we gain honor?"

Valin's son thought that there would be peace through practicing a fast unto death and sat on the mountain engaged in yoga, showing the pain in his heart.

As if he had had diarrhea Jámbavan said in contemplation: "Fie upon sensual enjoyments which, like the game *shala·bhánjika* have an imaginary splendor.

Whatever duty the prince should carry out, that also will I 7.75
carry out," when he had spoken thus he sat down.

When the old monkey had become a renunciant, Hánuman said to the other monkeys, "I will take my turn as it comes to fast until death.

When Your Honor no longer exists, may he who lives on have life no more." Saying thus and setting themselves in yogic postures they all sat down.

"Kabándha's death with a sword beside the fire was painless," they declared, "How terrible is this fall of ours ending in decay, like one without a master."

tato manda|gataḥ pakṣī teṣāṃ prāy'|ôpaveśanam
aśanīyam iv' āśaṃsur mahān āyād a|śobhanaḥ.*

7.80 deha|vraścana|tuṇḍ'|âgraṃ taṃ viloky' â|śubh'|ākaram
pāpa|gocaram ātmānam aśocan vānarā muhuḥ:*

«Jaṭāyuḥ puṇya|kṛt pakṣī Daṇḍak'|âraṇya|saṃcaraḥ
kṛtvā Rāghava|kāryaṃ yaḥ svar'|ārūḍho, 'gni|saṃskṛtaḥ.

narakasy' âvatāro 'yaṃ pratyakṣo 'smākam āgataḥ,
a|ceṣṭā yad ih' â|nyāyād anen' âtsyāmahe vayaṃ.*

hṛday'|ôdaṅka|saṃsthānaṃ,
  kṛtānt'|ānāya|sannibham,
śarīr'|ākhana|tuṇḍ'|âgraṃ,
  prāpy' âmuṃ śarma dur|labham.*

īṣad|āḍhyaṃkaro 'py eṣa na paratr' â|śubha|kriyaḥ,
asmān attum ito 'bhyeti pariglāno bubhukṣayā.»*

7.85 saṃprāpya vānarān pakṣī jagāda madhuraṃ vacaḥ:
«ke yūyaṃ dur|upasthāne manas" âpy adri|mūrdhani?*

ātmanaḥ paridevadhve, kurvanto Rāma|saṃkathām,
samān'|ôdaryam asmākaṃ Jaṭāyuṃ ca stuth' ādarāt.»

śaṅkā|dhavitra|vacanaṃ pratyūcur vānarāḥ khagam
«vayaṃ śatru|lavitr'|êṣor dūtā Rāmasya bhū|pateḥ.

ken' âpi dauṣkuleyena kulyāṃ māhākulīṃ priyām
hṛtāṃ māhākulīnasya tasya lipsāmahe vayam.

Then a great slow ugly bird came hoping for a meal as they fasted to death.

Seeing him as an abundance of evil, with the tip of his beak 7.80
ready to rip their flesh, the monkeys agonized still more that they had come within the scope of evil:

"The bird Jatáyu did good as he roamed round the Dándaka forest and having served Rama he ascended to heaven, cremated in the fire.

This is evidently an incarnation of hell which has come for us, for as we stay motionless he will eat us here for no reason.

Safety is impossible now he is here, he who resembles a heart extractor, who is like death's net, the tip of whose beak is a gouge for the body.

This evil-doer exhausted by hunger who is not going to do us the slightest good even in the hereafter, has come here to eat us."

When he reached the monkeys the bird spoke sweet words: 7.85
"Who are you here on the top of a mountain which is difficult even for the mind to reach?

You lament for yourselves, you speak of Rama, and you respectfully praise my co-uterine brother Jatáyu."

The monkeys replied to the bird whose voice blew away their fear, "We are messengers of King Rama whose arrows are scythes for the enemy.

We wish to find that noble well-born beloved of one of great family taken by one of vile tribe.

triṃśattamam ahar yātaṃ matvā pratyāgam'|âvadhim
a|kṛt'|ârthā viṣīdantaḥ para|lokam upāsmahe.

7.90 mriyāmahe, na gacchāmaḥ Kauśalyāyani*|vallabhām
upalambhyām a|paśyantaḥ kaumārīṃ, patatāṃ vara.»

jagāda vānarān pakṣī
  «n' âdhyagīḍhvaṃ dhruvaṃ smṛtim
yūyaṃ saṃkuṭituṃ yasmāt
  kāle 'sminn adhyavasyatha.*

n' âyam udvijituṃ kālaḥ svāmi|kāryād bhavādṛśām
hṛta|bhārye cyute rājyād Rāme paryutsuke bhṛśam.*

yatnaṃ prorṇavituṃ tūrṇaṃ diśaṃ kuruta dakṣiṇām.
prorṇuvitrīṃ divas tatra purīṃ drakṣyatha kāñcanīm,*

Laṅkāṃ nāmnā girer mūrdhni rākṣas'|êndreṇa pālitām
nirjitya Śakram ānītā dadṛśur yāṃ sura|striyaḥ.*

7.95 babhūva y" âdhi|śail'|êndraṃ mṛditv" êv' Êndra|gocaram
kuṣitvā jagatāṃ sāraṃ s" âikā śaṅke kṛtā bhuvi.*

a|mṛḍitvā Sahasrākṣaṃ, kliśitvā kauśalair nijaiḥ,
uditv" ‹âlaṃ!› ciraṃ yatnāt s" âikā Dhātrā vinirmitā.

muṣitvā Dhanadaṃ pāpo yāṃ gṛhītv" âvasad dviṣan,
tāṃ ruditv" êva Śakreṇa yāta Laṅkām upekṣitām.*

Considering that the thirtieth day, the limit for her return has passed, we wait, despairing, upon the next world, our object unaccomplished.

We will die, we will not go, as we have not seen the princess 7.90
most beloved of Rama, O best of birds."

The bird said to the monkeys, "You have certainly not studied the scriptures if you have resolved to die at this time.

This is not the time for such as you to shrink from service to your master while Rama whose wife has been taken and who has been deprived of his kingdom longs so ardently for them.

Quickly make an effort to cover the southern region and there you will see a golden city that fills the sky,

It is called Lanka, it is at the top of a mountain presided over by the chief of the demons. The women of the gods saw it when they were brought there after he conquered Indra.

Having surpassed the chief of mountains it came to resem- 7.95
ble Indra's domain and after the essence of the worlds had
been extracted it was, I think, created unique upon earth.

After displeasing Indra, after tormenting him with his own skills, after saying 'Enough!' the creator with prolonged effort fashioned this city, of which there is but one.

Go to Lanka which the evil enemy, robbing Kubéra the giver of wealth, took and dwelt in, and which Indra almost weeping ignored.

viditvā śaktim ātmīyāṃ, Rāvaṇaṃ vijighṛkṣavaḥ,
uktaṃ pipṛcchiṣūṇāṃ vo, mā sma bhūta suṣupsavaḥ.*

n' â|vividiṣum abhyeti sampad rurudiṣuṃ naram.
kiṃ mumuṣiṣuvad yāta dviṣo n' âpacikīrṣayā?*

7.100 bubhutsavo drutaṃ Sītāṃ
bhutsīdhvaṃ, prabravīmi vaḥ,
mā ca bhuddhvaṃ* mṛṣ"|ôktaṃ naḥ:
kṛṣīḍhvaṃ svāmine hitaṃ.*

samagadhvaṃ* puraḥ śatror, modayadhvaṃ Raghūttamam,
n' ôpāyadhvaṃ bhayaṃ, Sītāṃ n' ôpāyaṃsta Daśānanaḥ.»*

tataḥ prāsthiṣat' âdr'|îndraṃ Mahendraṃ vānarā drutam
sarve kilakilāyanto, dhairyaṃ c' ādhiṣat' âdhikam.*

nikuñje tasya vartitvā ramye prakṣveditāḥ param
maṇi|ratn'|âdhiśayitaṃ pratyudaikṣanta toya|dhim,*

a|marṣitam iva ghnantaṃ taṭ'|âdrīn salil'|ōrmibhiḥ,
Śriyā samagraṃ dyutitaṃ, maden' êva pralothitam,*

7.105 pūtaṃ śītair nabhasvadbhir, granthitv" êva sthitaṃ rucaḥ,
gumphitv" êva nirasyantaṃ taraṅgān sarvato muhuḥ,*

vañcitv" âpy ambaraṃ dūraṃ svasmiṃs tiṣṭhantam ātmani
tṛṣitv" êv' âniśaṃ svādu pibantaṃ saritāṃ payaḥ,*

Hence do I tell you who wish to enquire, who know your own power, who wish to fight Rávana. Do not try to sleep.

Success does not come to a man who doesn't wish to know but wishes to weep. Should you not go like a thief with a wish to harm your enemy?

In your quest to know quickly discover Sita. I tell you and 7.100
do not regard this as our lie: ensure your master's benefit.

I hope that you will unite before your enemy. You should make Rama delighted. Do not be afraid. May Rávana not have married Sita."

Then all the chattering monkeys quickly set out for Mahéndra, the chief of mountains, their fortitude further strengthened.

Then calling loudly as they abided in one of its delightful groves they watched the ocean, the repository of gems and jewels.

It struck the mountains of the shore with its waves as if angry, the whole lit up by Lakshmi, made to roll about as if by drink.

It was purified by cool winds, it stayed as if knotting light 7.105
together, it repeatedly threw its waves around as if it had strung them together.

It remained in its own form even though it reached far into the sky, it always drank the sweet waters of the rivers as if it were thirsty.

dyutitvā śaśinā naktam raśmibhiḥ parivardhitam,
Meror jetum iv' ābhogam uccair didyotiṣuṃ muhuḥ.*

vilokya salil'|ôccayān
adhi|samudram abhraṃ|lihān
bhraman|makara|bhīṣaṇaṃ
samadhigamya c' âdhaḥ payaḥ,
gam'|āgama|sahaṃ drutaṃ
kapi|vṛṣāḥ paripraiṣayan
gaj'|êndra|guru|vikramaṃ
taru|mṛg'|ôttamaṃ Mārutim.

It was swollen up by the moon at night and it shone with its rays, always seeking to shine higher as if to conquer the expanse of Mount Meru.

Seeing the masses of water scraping the sky above the ocean and understanding the water underneath to be fearful with wandering sharks, the chiefs of the monkeys dispatched the best of the tree creatures Hánuman, who was able to go and return and whose prowess was great like the lord of elephants.

CANTO 8

THE WRECKING OF THE GROVE

8.1 ĀGĀDHATA TATO vyoma Hanūmān uru|vigrahaḥ,
atyaśerata tad|vegaṃ na Suparṇ'|ârka|mārutāḥ.*

abhāyata yath" ârkeṇa su|prātena śaran|mukhe,
gamyamānaṃ na ten' āsīd a|gataṃ krāmatā puraḥ.*

viyati vyatyatanvātāṃ mūrtī hari|payonidhī,
vyatyaitāṃ c' ôttamaṃ mārgam ark'|Êndr'|êndu|niṣevitam.*

vyatijigye samudro 'pi na dhairyaṃ tasya gacchataḥ,
vyatyagacchan na ca gataṃ pracaṇḍo 'pi prabhañjanaḥ.

8.5 vyatighnantīṃ vyatighnan tāṃ
rākṣasīṃ pavan'|ātmajaḥ
jaghān' āviśya vadanaṃ
niryān bhittv" ôdaraṃ drutam.

anyonyaṃ sma vyatiyutaḥ śabdān śabdais tu bhīṣaṇān
udanvāṃś c' ânil'|ôddhūto mriyamāṇā ca rākṣasī.*

nyavikṣata mahā|grāha|saṃkulaṃ makar'|ālayam
s" âikā bahūnāṃ kurvāṇā nakrāṇāṃ sv|āśitaṃ|bhavam.*

kṛten' ôpakṛtaṃ vāyoḥ parikrīṇānam utthitam
pitrā saṃrakṣitaṃ Śakrāt sa Maināk'|âdrim aikṣata.*

khaṃ parājayamāno 'sāv unnatya pavan'|âtmajam
jagād' âdrir: «vijeṣīṣṭhā mayi viśramya vairiṇam.*

8.10 phalāny ādatsva citrāṇi, parikrīḍasva sānuṣu,
sādhv anukrīḍamānāni paśya vṛndāni pakṣiṇām.*

THEN HÁNUMAN OF broad frame took to the sky, not Gáruda nor the sun nor the wind exceeded his speed. 8.1

He shone like the early-morning sun at the beginning of fall, going forth he overtook it as it proceeded.

The monkey and the ocean vied with each other to stretch their bodies into the sky and they surpassed the high course followed by the sun, Indra and the moon.

Even the ocean did not outdo his unrelenting progress as he went, even the violent wind did not overtake him on his journey.

The son of the wind striking at the mouth of a demoness 8.5
who struck at him, entered her mouth and quickly leaving after splitting her belly, killed her.

The wind-churned ocean and the dying demoness mixed together noise with terrible noise.

She on her own satiating the many crocodiles, fell back into the lair of sharks teeming with great monsters.

He saw Mount Mainága which had been protected from Indra by his father rising up, by this action paying back the help rendered by the wind.

That mountain overwhelming the sky as it reared up said to Hánuman: "After resting on me may you overcome your enemy.

Eat the various fruits, play on the ridges, watch the flocks 8.10
of birds courting gracefully.

kṣaṇaṃ bhadr' âvatiṣṭhasva, tataḥ prasthāsyase punaḥ.
na tat saṃsthāsyate kāryaṃ dakṣeṇ' ôrī|kṛtaṃ tvayā?*

tvayi nas tiṣṭhate prītis, tubhyaṃ tiṣṭhāmahe vayam.
uttiṣṭhamānaṃ mitr'|ârthe kas tvāṃ na bahu manyate?*

ye sūryam upatiṣṭhante
mantraiḥ saṃdhyā|trayaṃ dvijāḥ,
rakṣobhis tāpitās, te 'pi
siddhiṃ dhyāyanti te 'dhunā.*

a|vyagram upatiṣṭhasva vīra, vāyor ahaṃ suhṛt,
ravir vitapate 'tyartham, āśvasya mayi gamyatām.*

8.15 tīvram uttapamāno 'yam a|śakyaḥ soḍhum ātapaḥ,
āghnāna iva saṃdīptair alātaiḥ sarvato muhuḥ.*

saṃśṛṇuṣva kape, matkaiḥ saṃgacchasva vanaiḥ śubhaiḥ,
samāranta mam' âbhīṣṭāḥ saṃkalpās tvayy upāgate.*

ke na saṃvidrate, vāyor Maināk'|âdrir yathā sakhā?
yatnād upāhvaye prītaḥ, saṃhvayasva vivakṣitam.»*

dyām iv' āhvayamānaṃ tam avocad bhū|dharaṃ kapiḥ
upakurvantam atyarthaṃ prakurvāṇo 'nujīvivat:*

«kula|bhāryāṃ prakurvāṇam ahaṃ draṣṭuṃ Daśānanam
yāmi tvarāvān śail'|êndra. mā kasya cid upaskṛthāḥ.

8.20 yo 'pacakre vanāt Sītām, adhicakre na yaṃ Hariḥ,
vikurvāṇaḥ svarān adya balaṃ tasya nihanmy aham.*

Stay a moment, friend, then you will go on again. Will not that task succeed which you have skillfully undertaken?

We remain affectionate towards you, we are ready for you. Who would not greatly esteem you as you strive in your friend's cause?

Those brahmins who worship the sun with mantras at the three junctures of the day, tormented by demons, also now hope for your success.

Stay here without disturbance, O hero, I am a friend of the wind. The sun burns too much, rest on me then go.

This heat impossible to be borne burns so fiercely, as if 8.15
launching repeated assaults with blazing coals on all sides.

Listen, monkey, mingle among my fair forests. When you arrived the good intentions which I wished for came to pass.

Who does not know how much of a friend of the wind the Mainága mountain is? Being pleased, I respectfully invite you to announce what you want to say."

Like the dedicated servant that he was, the monkey answered that extremely helpful mountain, which seemed to challenge the sky:

"I am hurrying on my journey, O chief of mountains, to see Rávana who is making advances to a virtuous wife. Do not prepare anything for me.

Making all manner of sounds I will now strike down the 8.20
power of him who took Sita from the forest and whom Indra did not overcome.

vikurve nagare tasya pāpasy' âdya Raghu|dviṣaḥ:
vineṣye vā priyān prāṇān udāneṣye 'tha vā yaśaḥ.*

vineṣye krodham atha vā kramamāṇo 'ri|saṃsadi,»
ity uktvā khe parākraṃsta tūrṇaṃ sūnur nabhasvataḥ.*

parīkṣitum upākraṃsta rākṣasī tasya vikramam
divam ākramamāṇ" êva ketu|tārā bhaya|pradā.*

jale vikramamāṇāyā Hanūmān śata|yojanam
āsyaṃ praviśya nirayād aṇū|bhūy' â|pracetitaḥ.*

8.25 draṣṭuṃ prakramamāṇo 'sau Sītām ambho|nidhes taṭam
upākraṃst' ākulaṃ ghoraiḥ kramamāṇair niśā|caraiḥ.*

ātmānam apajānānaḥ śaśa|mātro 'nayad dinam,
jñāsye rātrāv iti prājñaḥ pratyajñāsta kriyā|paṭuḥ.*

saṃjānānān pariharan Rāvaṇ'|ânucarān bahūn
Laṅkāṃ samāviśad rātrau vadamāno 'ri|durgamām.*

kaṃ cin n' ôpāvadiṣṭ' âsau, kena cid vyavadiṣṭa na,
śṛṇvan saṃpravadamānād Rāvaṇasya guṇān janāt.*

jalpit'|ôtkruṣṭa|saṃgīta|pranṛtta|smita|valgitaiḥ
ghoṣasy' ânvavadiṣṭ' êva Laṅkā Pūtakratoḥ puraḥ.*

8.30 aid vipravadamānais tāṃ saṃyuktāṃ Brahma|rākṣasaiḥ
tath" âvagiramāṇaiś ca piśācair māṃsa|śoṇitam.*

I will now take action in the city of that evil enemy of Rama: either I will expend my precious life breath or I will augment my fame.

Or else striving in the camp of the enemy I will spend my anger," speaking thus the son of the wind quickly went forth into the sky.

A demoness approached to observe his prowess, coming across the sky like a fearful comet.

Hánuman, making himself minute, entering her hundred-mile mouth as she made across the water, emerged undetected.

Striving to see Sita, he came to the shore of the ocean teem- 8.25
ing with terrible prowling demons.

Concealing himself he spent the day the size of a rabbit, being wise and cunning he realized he would find her at night.

Avoiding the many attendants of Rávana who were keeping watch, learning that it was difficult of access for enemies, he entered Lanka by night.

He spoke to no one and was challenged by no one, as he heard Rávana's qualities from the conversing people.

Like the city of the terrible Indra, Lanka resounded with talking, shouting, singing, dancing, laughing and jumping.

He went to that city filled with brahmin demons arguing 8.30
and also with *pishácha*s swallowing flesh and blood.

yathā|svaṃ saṃgirante sma goṣṭhīṣu svāmino guṇān
pāna|śauṇḍāḥ, pathaḥ kṣībā vṛndair udacaranta ca.*

yānaiḥ samacarant' ânye kuñjar'|âśva|rath'|ādibhiḥ,
saṃprāyacchanta bandībhir anye puṣpa|phalaṃ śubham.*

kopāt kāś cit priyaiḥ prattam upāyaṃsata n' āsavam;
prema jijñāsamānābhyas tābhyo 'śapsata kāminaḥ.*

prādidṛkṣata n' ô nṛtyaṃ, n' âśuśrūṣata gāyanān
Rāmaṃ susmūrṣamāṇo 'sau kapir viraha|duḥkhitam.*

8.35 anujijñāsat" êv' âtha Laṅkā|darṣanam, indunā
tamo|'paha|vimukt'|âṃśu pūrvasyāṃ diśy udaiyata.*

āśuśrūṣan sa Maithilyā vārtāṃ harmyeṣu rakṣasām
śīyamān'|ândha|kāreṣu samacārīd a|śaṅkitaḥ.*

śata|sāhasram ārakṣaṃ madhya|gaṃ rakṣasāṃ kapiḥ
dadarśa, yaṃ Kṛtānto 'pi mriyet' āsādya bhīṣaṇam.*

adhyāsisiṣamāṇe 'tha viyan|madhyaṃ niśā|kare
kāsāṃ cakre purī saughair atīv' ôdbhāsibhiḥ sitaiḥ*

induṃ caṣaka|saṃkrāntam upāyuṅkta yath" âmṛtam,
prayuñjānaḥ priyā vācaḥ samāj'|ânurato janaḥ.*

8.40 saṃkṣṇuvāna iv' ôtkaṇṭhām, upābhuṅkta surām alam,
jyotsnāyāṃ vigalan|mānas taruṇo rakṣasāṃ gaṇaḥ.*

In gatherings they were arrogating each to himself his master's virtues and intoxicated by liquor, the drunkards took to the streets in crowds.

Some went by means such as elephants, horses and chariots, others offered beautiful flowers and fruits to their slave girls.

Some women out of anger did not accept spirits offered by their beloveds; when they sought to know if their suitors loved them they swore they did.

Wishing only to remember Rama pained by his separation, the monkey did not wish to see dancing or to hear singing.

Then as if wishing to allow him a sight of Lanka, the moon 8.35
rose in the east releasing its dark-dispelling rays.

Wishing to hear news of Sita he went without fear into the mansions of the demons in the dwindling darkness.

At the center the monkey saw a fearsome guard of one hundred thousand demons, meeting which even Yama would be killed.

Then as the moon sought to rise up to the middle of the sky the city shone with its shining white stuccoed mansions.

The people speaking sweet words and delighting in company partook of the moon reflected in their cups as if it were the nectar of immortality.

A young group of demons, their self-respect slipping away 8.40
in the moonlight, drank wine to satiety as if sharpening their lust.

madhv apāyayata svacchaṃ s'|ôtpalaṃ, dayit"|ântike
ātmānaṃ surat'|ābhoga|viśrambh'|ôtpādanaṃ muhuḥ.*

abhīṣayanta ye Śakraṃ rākṣasā raṇa|paṇḍitāḥ,
a|vismāpayamānas tān kapir āṭīd gṛhād gṛham.*

Sītāṃ didṛkṣuḥ pracchannaḥ so 'gardhayata rākṣasān,
avañcayata māyāś ca sva|māyābhir nara|dviṣām,*

apalāpayamānasya śatrūṃs tasy' âbhavan matiḥ
«mithyā kārayate cārair ghoṣaṇāṃ rākṣas'|âdhipaḥ.»*

8.45 gūhamānaḥ sva|māhātmyam aṭitvā mantri|saṃsadaḥ
nṛbhyo 'pavadamānasya Rāvaṇasya gṛhaṃ yayau,*

diśo dyotayamānābhir divya|nārībhir ākulam,
śriyam āyacchamānābhir uttamābhir an|uttamām,*

nityam udyacchamānābhiḥ smara|saṃbhoga|karmasu,
jānānābhir alaṃ līlā|kilakiñcita|vibhramān,*

svaṃ karma kārayann āste niścinto yā Jhaṣadhvajaḥ
svārthaṃ kārayamāṇābhir yūno mada|vimohitān,

kāntiṃ svāṃ vahamānābhir, yajantībhiḥ sva|vigrahān,
netrair iva pibantībhiḥ paśyatāṃ citta|saṃhatīḥ.*

The sweet clear wine tinctured with lotuses, giving confidence for the enjoyment of sex, repeatedly ensured that it was drunk in the presence of the lover.

The monkey as he roamed from house to house managed not to surprise those demons expert at war who had terrified Indra.

Being concealed as he sought Sita he deceived the demons and he confounded the tricks of the enemies of men with his own tricks.

As he outwitted his enemies he thought, "The demon king is making a false proclamation through his agents."

Concealing his greatness, as he wandered through the cham- 8.45
bers of the ministers he entered the house of Rávana as he was disparaging men,

A house thronged with divine females lighting up the quarters, incomparable, possessing the highest beauty,

Always eager for acts of sensual pleasure, knowing well enough the motions of sex-play and seductive devices,

Who the carefree love god, whose symbol is a fish, keeps making do his own work and who make the youths befuddled by wine do their bidding,

Bearing their own light, offering their own bodies, drinking as it were with their eyes the multitude of hearts of those who gazed at them.

8.50 tā Hanūmān parākurvann agamat Puṣpakaṃ prati
vimānaṃ Mandarasy' âdrer anukurvad iva śriyam.*

tasmin Kailāsa|saṃkāśaṃ, śiraḥ|śṛṅgaṃ, bhuja|drumam,
abhikṣipantam aikṣiṣṭa Rāvaṇaṃ parvata|śriyam,*

pravahantaṃ sad" āmodaṃ, suptaṃ parijan"|ânvitam
Maghone parimṛṣyantam ārabhantaṃ paraṃ smare.*

vyaramat pradhanād yasmāt paritrastaḥ Sahasradṛk,
kṣaṇaṃ paryaramat tasya darśanān Mārut'|ātmajaḥ.*

upāraṃsīc ca saṃpaśyan vānaras taṃ cikīrṣitāt
ramyaṃ Merum iv' ādhūta|kānanaṃ śvasan'|ōrmibhiḥ*

8.55 dṛṣṭvā dayitayā sākaṃ rahī|bhūtaṃ Daśānanam,
«n' âtra Sīt"» êty upāraṃsta dur|manā vāyu|saṃbhavaḥ.*

tataḥ prākāram ārohat kṣapāṭān a|vibodhayan,
n' âyodhayat samartho 'pi, Sītā|darśana|lālasaḥ.*

adhyāsīd, «Rāghavasy' âhaṃ nāśayeyaṃ kathaṃ śucam?
Vaidehyā janayeyaṃ vā katham ānandam uttamam?

dṛṣṭvā Rāghava|kāntāṃ tāṃ drāvayiṣyāmi rākṣasān,
tasyā hi darśanāt pūrvaṃ, vikramaḥ kārya|nāśa|kṛt.»

cintayann ittham uttuṅgaiḥ prāvayantīṃ divaṃ vanaiḥ
aśoka|vanikām ārād apaśyat stabak'|ācitām.*

Disregarding them, Hánuman went towards the divine chariot Púshpaka which seemed to imitate the beauty of Mount Mándara. 8.50

In it he saw Rávana resembling Kailása, his heads like mountain peaks, his arms like tree trunks, excelling the luster of a mountain,

Always wearing scent, sleeping among his female retinue, angry at Indra, fixated fully on sex.

Hánuman delighted for a moment at the sight of him whom Indra for fear had ceased to fight.

And the monkey desisted from his intended course on seeing him shaking with the waves of his breath like the delightful Mount Meru with its forests waving in the gusts of wind.

Seeing that Rávana had retired with his lover, low in spirit 8.55
the son of the Wind paused thinking, "Sita is not here."

Then without waking the demons he mounted the ramparts, though capable he did not start a fight, desperate as he was to see Sita.

"How might I destroy Rama's grief ?" he wondered, "Or how could I produce the greatest happiness for Sita?

When I see Rama's wife then will I drive away the demons, for before seeing her my valor would overcome my duty."

Thinking thus he saw not far away an *ashóka* grove, a mass of blossom filling the sky with its high trees.

8.60 tāṃ prāviśat kapi|vyāghras, tarūn a|calayan, śanaiḥ,
a|trāsayan vana|śayān suptān śākhāsu pakṣiṇaḥ.*

avād vāyuḥ śanair yasyāṃ latāṃ nartayamānavat,
n' āyāsayanta saṃtrastā ṛtavo 'nyonya|saṃpadaḥ,*

jyotsn"|âmṛtaṃ śaśī yasyāṃ vāpīr vikasit'|ôtpalāḥ
apāyayata saṃpūrṇaḥ sadā Daśamukh'|ājñayā,*

prādamayanta puṣp'|êṣuṃ yasyāṃ, bandyaḥ samāhṛtāḥ,
parimohayamāṇābhī rākṣasībhiḥ samāvṛtāḥ,*

yasyāṃ vāsayate Sītāṃ kevalaṃ sma ripuḥ smarāt
na tv arocayat' ātmānaṃ caturo vṛddhimān api.*

8.65 mandāyamāna|gamano haritāyat|taruṃ kapiḥ
drumaiḥ śakaśakāyadbhir māruten' āṭa sarvataḥ.*

asyandann indu|maṇayo, vyarucan kumud'|ākarāḥ,
aloṭhiṣata vātena prakīrṇāḥ stabak'|ôccayāḥ.*

Sīt"|ântike vivṛtsantaṃ vartsyat|siddhiṃ plavaṅ|gamam
patatriṇaḥ śubhā mandram ānuvānās tv ajihladan.*

vartiṣyamāṇam ātmānaṃ Sītā patyur iv' ântike
udapaśyat tadā tathyair nimittair iṣṭa|darśanaiḥ.*

«niravartsyan na ced vārtā Sītāyā, vitath" âiva naḥ
akalpsyad udyatiḥ sarvā,» Hanūmān ity acintayat.*

That tiger of a monkey entered it quietly, not shaking the trees, or frightening the woodland birds asleep in the branches. 8.60

The wind blew gently through it seeming to make its creepers dance, the seasons, afraid of him, did not disturb each others' glories,

In which the moon, always full at Rávana's command, made the ponds of blooming lotuses drink the nectar of the moonlight,

Where the female prisoners collected together, surrounded by demonesses enticing them, tamed the flower-arrowed God of Love,

Where the enemy in his infatuation merely lodged Sita but could not make himself pleasing to her, be he ever so clever and powerful.

Going slowly the monkey wandered around the greening 8.65
wood with its trees rustling in the wind.

Moonstones oozed, clumps of lotuses shone and the piles of blossom scattered by the wind fluttered about.

Auspicious birds making low calls gladdened the monkey who wished to be near Sita and whose success was imminent.

Then through true omens showing her her desired object, Sita foresaw herself as if in the presence of her husband.

"If there were not about to be news of Sita then all my effort would have been to no purpose," thought Hánuman.

8.70 vṛkṣād vṛkṣaṃ parikrāman Rāvaṇād bibhyatīṃ bhṛśam,
śatros trāṇam a|paśyantīm a|dṛśyo Janakātmajām,**

tāṃ parājayamānāṃ sa prīte rakṣyāṃ Daśānanāt,
antar|dadhānāṃ rakṣobhyo, malināṃ mlāna|mūrdhajām,
Rāmād adhīta|saṃdeśo vāyor jātaś, cyuta|smitām,
prabhavantīm iv' ādityād, apaśyat kapi|kuñjaraḥ.*

rocamānaḥ kudṛṣṭibhyo, rakṣobhyaḥ prattavān śriyam,
ślāghamānaḥ para|strībhyas, tatr' āgād rākṣas'|âdhipaḥ.*

aśapta nihnuvāno 'sau Sītāyai smara|mohitaḥ,
dhārayann iva c' âitasyai vasūni pratyapadyata.*

8.75 tasyai spṛhayamāṇo 'sau bahu priyam abhāṣata,
s'|ânunītiś ca Sītāyai n' âkrudhyan, n' âpy asūyata:*

«saṃkrudhyasi mṛṣā kiṃ tvaṃ didṛkṣuṃ māṃ mṛg'|êkṣaṇe?
īkṣitavyaṃ para|strībhyaḥ sva|dharmo rakṣasām ayam.*

śṛṇvadbhyaḥ pratiśṛṇvanti madhyamā bhīru, n' ôttamāḥ!
gṛṇadbhyo 'nugṛṇanty anye 'kṛt'|ârthā, n' âiva mad|vidhāḥ.*

iccha snehena dīvyantī viṣayān bhuvan'|ēśvaram,
saṃbhogāya parikrītaḥ kart" âsmi tava n' â|priyam.*

Going round unseen from tree to tree towards Sita, who 8.70
was so terrified of Rávana she could not see what protection
she had from her enemy,

That elephant of a monkey born of the wind who received his orders from Rama saw her in need of protection from Rávana, rejecting his affection, hiding herself from the demons, dirty and with unkempt hair, bereft of a smile but as if issued from the sun.

There came the king of the demons, delighting those with evil eyes, giving glory to the demons, flattering the wives of others.

Deluded by love, dissembling, he vowed to Sita, and as if in debt he gave her gifts.

Longing for her he spoke so sweetly and being conciliatory 8.75
he was not angry with Sita, he did not even find fault with
her:

"O doe-eyed lady, why are you needlessly angry with me as I seek to gaze at you? It is the nature of demons to look at the wives of others.

Mediocrities make promises to those who will listen to them, O timid one, but not the best! Others who have not achieved their aims encourage flatterers, not those like me.

As you play with sensual things, accept me, the lord of the earth, affectionately. I have been made a hireling for your enjoyment, not for your displeasure.

āssva sākaṃ mayā saudhe, m" âdhiṣṭhā nirjanaṃ vanam
m" âdhivātsīr bhuvaṃ, śayyām adhiśeṣva smar'|ôtsukā.*

8.80 abhinyavikṣathās tvaṃ me yath" âiv' âvyāhatā manaḥ,
tav' âpy adhyāvasantaṃ māṃ mā rautsīr hṛdayaṃ tathā.*

m' âvamaṃsthā namasyantam a|kārya|jñe jagat|patim,
saṃdṛṣṭe mayi Kākutstham a|dhanyaṃ kāmayeta kā?*

yaḥ payo dogdhi pāṣāṇaṃ, sa Rāmād bhūtim āpnuyāt;
Rāvaṇaṃ gamaya prītiṃ bodhayantaṃ hit'|âhitaṃ.*

prīto 'haṃ bhojayiṣyāmi bhavatīṃ bhuvana|trayam,
kiṃ vilāpayase 'tyarthaṃ? pārśve śāyaya Rāvaṇam.

ājñāṃ kāraya rakṣobhir, mā priyāṇy upahāraya.
kaḥ Śakreṇa kṛtaṃ n' êcched adhi|mūrdhānam añjalim?»

8.85 vacanaṃ rakṣasāṃ patyur anu kruddhā pati|priyā
pāp'|ânuvāsitaṃ Sītā Rāvaṇaṃ prābravīd vacaḥ:**

«na bhavān anu Rāmaṃ ced upa śūreṣu vā, tataḥ
apavāhya cchalād vīrau kim arthaṃ mām ih' āharaḥ?*

upa|śūraṃ na te vṛttaṃ kathaṃ rātriṃ|car'|âdhama,
yat saṃpraty apa lokebhyo Laṅkāyāṃ vasatir bhayāt?*

ā Rāma|darśanāt pāpa, vidyotasva striyaḥ prati,
sad|vṛttān anu dur|vṛttaḥ para|strīṃ jāta|manmathaḥ.*

Stay with me in the palace, do not go to the unpeopled forest, do not lie on the ground. Recline on my bed eager for love.

As you have entered my heart without obstruction, so also do not obstruct me as I enter your heart. 8.80

O you ignorant of your duty, do not despise the lord of the world as he bows down to you. When I am in sight what woman would desire the wretched Rama?

He who can milk a stone can get glory from Rama; bring your affection to Rávana who enlightens as to good and ill.

As your lover I will enable you to enjoy the three worlds. Why lament so much? Let Rávana lie at your side.

Let your command be done by the demons, let me bring you your desired things. What man would not desire Indra himself to join his hands upon his head to him?"

Sita, devoted to her husband and angry at the demon king's 8.85
words, addressed a speech to Rávana who abided in sin:

"If you are not inferior to Rama or if you are superior to the warriors, then for what purpose did you bring me here after luring away the two heroes by guile?

How is your conduct not inferior to that of the heroes, O worst of the demons, when out of fear your dwelling is now in Lanka away from people?

Until you see Rama, O evil one, you may dazzle women, behaving badly towards the good and lusting after the wives of others.

abhi dyotiṣyate Rāmo bhavantam a|cirād iha,
udgūrṇa|bāṇaḥ saṃgrāme, yo Nārāyaṇataḥ prati.*

8.90 kuto 'dhiyāsyasi krūra, nihatas tena patribhiḥ?
na s'|ûktaṃ bhavat" âty|ugram ati Rāmaṃ mad'|ôddhata.*

pariśeṣaṃ na nām' âpi sthāpayiṣyati te vibhuḥ.
api Sthāṇuṃ jayed Rāmo, bhavato grahaṇaṃ kiyat?*

api stūhy api sedh' âsmāṃs tathyam uktaṃ nar'|âśana!
api siñceḥ kṛśānau tvaṃ darpaṃ, mayy api yo 'bhikaḥ.

adhi Rāme parākrāntam adhikartā sa te kṣayam,»
ity uktvā Maithilī tūṣṇīm āsāṃ cakre Daśānanam.

tataḥ khaḍgaṃ samudyamya Rāvaṇaḥ krūra|vigrahaḥ
Vaidehīm antarā kruddhaḥ kṣaṇam ūce viniśvasan:**

8.95 «cireṇ' ânuguṇaṃ proktā pratipatti|parāṅmukhī
na māse pratipatt" āse māṃ cen, mart" âsi Maithili.»*

prāyuṅkta rākṣasīr bhīmā mandirāya prativrajan
«bhayāni datta Sītāyai sarvā yūyaṃ kṛte mama.»*

gate tasmin samājagmur bhayāya prati Maithilīm
rākṣasyo, Rāvaṇa|prītyai krūraṃ c' ōcur alaṃ muhuḥ:*

«Rāvaṇāya namas|kuryāḥ, syāt Sīte, svasti te dhruvam,
anyathā prātar āśāya kuryāma tvām alaṃ vayam.»*

Soon Rama who is a proxy for Naráyana will outshine you here with his arrow upraised in battle.

Where will you go, O cruel one, struck by his arrows? What 8.90
you said about Rama when you were so fiercely puffed up with pride was not well spoken.

The lord will ensure that even your name does not endure. If Rama can conquer even Shiva, how easily could he take out you?

Praise me or blame me, O man-eater, my words are truly spoken! You may spill your pride in the fire which you tend as lust for me.

Valor inheres in Rama; he will be your destruction," speaking thus to Rávana, Sita sat down quietly.

Then angry Rávana of vicious form, raising his sword between himself and Sita, hissing for a moment said:

"Though addressed respectfully at length, you are still disin- 8.95
clined to acquiesce. If you do not accept me within a month you will die, O Sita."

Returning to his palace he exhorted the fierce demonesses: "All of you should serve me by giving Sita the horrors."

When he had gone the demonesses went together to Sita to frighten her and they repeatedly spoke cruelly enough to delight Rávana.

"You should obey Rávana, it would be to your eternal benefit, O Sita, otherwise we may prepare you as a satisfying breakfast."

tṛṇāya matvā tāḥ sarvā vadantīs Trijaṭ" âvadat:
«ātmānaṃ hata durvṛttāḥ, sva|māṃsaiḥ kurut' âśanam.*

8.100 adya Sītā mayā dṛṣṭā sūryaṃ candramasā saha
svapne spṛśantī madhyena tanuḥ* śyāmā su|locanā.»*

tās tayā tarjitāḥ sarvā, mukhair bhīmā yath"|āgatam
yayuḥ suṣupsavas talpaṃ bhīmair vacana|karmabhiḥ.*

gatāsu tāsu Maithilyā saṃjānāno 'nil'|ātmajaḥ
āyātena Daśāsyasya saṃsthito 'ntar|hitaś ciram,*

ṛṇād baddha iv', ônmukto viyogena Kratudviṣaḥ
hetor bodhasya Maithilyāḥ prāstāvīd Rāma|saṃkathām.*

taṃ dṛṣṭv" âcintayat Sītā «hetoḥ kasy' âiṣa Rāvaṇaḥ
avaruhya taror ārād aiti vānara|vigrahaḥ?*

8.105 pūrvasmād anyavad bhāti bhāvād Dāśarathiṃ stuvan,
ṛte krauryāt samāyāto māṃ viśvāsayituṃ nu kim?*

itaro Rāvaṇād eṣa Rāghav'|ânucaro yadi,
sa|phalāni nimittāni prāk prabhātāt tato mama.*

uttarāhi vasan Rāmaḥ samudrād rakṣasāṃ puram
avail lavaṇa|toyasya sthitāṃ dakṣiṇataḥ katham?

Thinking of them all as so much grass, Tríjata addressed those who spoke: "Kill yourselves, you evil beings, make a meal of your own flesh.

Today in a dream I saw the fair-eyed Sita, slender of waist 8.100
and youthful, touching the sun and moon."

All of them reviled by her, terrible in their faces and their terrible words and deeds, went as they had come to bed seeking sleep.

When they had gone Hánuman, who had recognized Sita and for a long time had remained hidden on account of the arrival of Rávana,

As if bound by a debt, was released by the absence of Rávana, hostile to sacrifice. In order to inform Sita he began to tell her of Rama.

Seeing him Sita thought, "Why is Rávana coming down from a nearby tree and approaching in the form of a monkey?

Surely he appears like someone other than he was before, 8.105
praising Rama with affection, approaching without cruelty, trying to reassure me.

If this is a follower of Rama's, rather than Rávana's, then the omens which appeared to me before dawn are bearing fruit.

How does Rama dwelling far to the north of the ocean know of the city of the demons situated in the south of the salt sea?

Daṇḍakān dakṣiṇen' âhaṃ sarito 'drīn vanāni ca
atikramy' âmbu|dhiṃ c' âiva puṃsām agamam āhṛtā.*

pṛthaṅ nabhasvataś caṇḍād Vainateyena vā vinā,
gantum utsahate n' êha kaś cit kim uta vānaraḥ?»*

8.110 iti cintāvatīṃ kṛcchrāt samāsādya kapi|dvipaḥ
muktāṃ stokena rakṣobhiḥ proce «'haṃ Rāma|kiṅkaraḥ.*

viprakṛṣṭaṃ Mahendrasya, na dūraṃ Vindhya|parvatāt
n' ân|abhyāśe samudrasya tava Mālyavati priyaḥ.*

a|saṃprāpte Daśagrīve praviṣṭo 'ham idaṃ vanam
tasmin pratigate draṣṭuṃ tvām upākraṃsy a|cetitaḥ.*

tasmin vadati ruṣṭo 'pi, n' âkārṣaṃ devi vikramam,
a|vināśāya kāryasya vicinvānaḥ par'|âparam.*

vānareṣu kapiḥ svāmī nareṣv adhipateḥ sakhā
jāto Rāmasya Sugrīvas, tato dūto 'ham āgataḥ.*

8.115 īśvarasya niśāṭānāṃ vilokya nikhilāṃ purīm
kuśalo 'nveṣaṇasy' âham āyukto dūta|karmaṇi,*

darśanīyatamāḥ paśyan strīṣu divyāsv api striyaḥ
prāpto vyālatamān vyasyan bhujaṅgebhyo 'pi rākṣasān.*

I have been taken to the south of the Dándaka forests after crossing rivers, mountains and forests and even the ocean to a place inaccessible to men.

Apart from the fierce wind or except for Gáruda, no one can come here, so how did a monkey?"

When that elephant of a monkey had with difficulty found 8.110
that unhappy lady, only just left by the demons, he said to her, "I am Rama's aide.

Your beloved is on Mount Mályavat far from Mount Mahéndra, not far from the Vindhya Range and near to the ocean.

I entered this grove when Rávana had not yet come and when he had gone I came unnoticed to see you.

Although furious with him as he talked, I performed no heroics, O queen, considering the immediate and the long-term consequences in order not to imperil my task.

The lord of monkeys, the ape Sugríva, has become a friend of Rama the lord of men, therefore I have come as his messenger.

Being skilled at careful investigation I was employed in the 8.115
function of an emissary and, after seeing the entire city of the lord of the demons,

I arrived having seen women more beautiful even than the women of heaven and having come through demons more vicious than even snakes.

bhavatyām utsuko Rāmaḥ prasitaḥ saṃgamena te.
Maghāsu kṛta|nirvāpaḥ pitṛbhyo māṃ vyasarjayat.*

ayaṃ Maithily abhijñānaṃ Kākutsthasy' âṅgulīyakaḥ
bhavatyāḥ smarat" âtyartham arpitaḥ s'|ādaraṃ mama.*

Rāmasya dayamāno 'sāv adhyeti tava Lakṣmaṇaḥ.
upāskṛṣātāṃ rāj'|êndrāv āgamasy' êha, mā trasīḥ.*

8.120 Rāvaṇasy' êha rokṣyanti kapayo bhīma|vikramāḥ.
dhṛtyā nāthasva Vaidehi, manyor ujjāsay' ātmanaḥ.*

rākṣasānāṃ mayi gate Rāmaḥ praṇihaniṣyati
prāṇānām apaṇiṣṭ' âyaṃ Rāvaṇas tvām ih' ānayan.*

adevīd bandhu|bhogānāṃ, prādevīd ātma|saṃpadam,
śata|kṛtvas tav' âikasyāḥ smaraty ahno Raghūttamaḥ.*

tav' ôpaśāyikā yāvad rākṣasyaś cetayanti na,
pratisaṃdiśyatāṃ tāvad bhartuḥ Śārṅgasya Maithili.»*

puraḥ praveśam āścaryaṃ buddhvā śākhā|mṛgeṇa, sā
cūḍā|māṇim abhijñānaṃ dadau Rāmasya saṃmatam.*

8.125 Rāmasya śayitaṃ bhuktaṃ jalpitaṃ hasitaṃ sthitam
prakrāntaṃ ca muhuḥ pṛṣṭvā Hanūmantaṃ vyasarjayat.*

asau dadhad abhijñānaṃ cikīrṣuḥ karma dāruṇam
gāmuko 'py antikaṃ bhartur manas" âcintayat kṣaṇam.*

«kṛtvā karma yath"|ādiṣṭaṃ pūrva|kāry'|âvirodhi yaḥ
karoty abhyadhikaṃ kṛtyaṃ, tam āhur dūtam uttamam.

Rama longs for you and is eager to be united with you. After making offerings to his ancestors under the constellation Magha, he dispatched me.

This ring, O Sita, is Rama's keepsake ring carefully entrusted to me by him in his acute remembrance of you.

Lákshmana who feels for Rama is thinking of you. The two kings have made preparations for coming here, do not fear.

The monkeys of terrible prowess will crush Rávana here. 8.120
Wish for fortitude, O Sita, defeat your own grief.

When I have gone Rama will destroy the demons. By bringing you here Rávana was bargaining with his own life.

He has staked the prosperity of his kinsmen, he has gambled with his own success. One hundred times a day Rama remembers you alone.

While the demonesses taking turns to sleep are not minding you, send a message to the lord of the Shárnga bow, O Sita."

Amazed that a monkey had entered the city, she gave him her crest jewel, a token most esteemed by Rama.

After asking repeatedly about Rama's sleeping, eating, recit- 8.125
ing, laughing, staying and moving, she sent Hánuman off.

Securing the token, keen to do his difficult task, although eager to go to the presence of his master, he pondered a moment in his mind.

"One who when he has done his job as directed then performs a more excellent action not opposed to the previous duty they call the best envoy.

Vaidehīṃ dṛṣṭavān karma kṛtv" ânyair api duṣkaram
yaśo yāsyāmy upādātā vārtām ākhyāyakaḥ prabhoḥ.*

rākṣas'|êndrasya saṃrakṣyaṃ mayā lavyam idaṃ vanam,»
iti saṃcintya, sadṛśaṃ Nandanasy' âbhanak kapiḥ.*

8.130 «Rāghavābhyāṃ śivaṃ, dūtas tayor aham» iti bruvan
«hito bhanajmi Rāmasya, kaḥ kiṃ brūte 'tra rākṣasaḥ?»

vilulita|puṣpa|reṇu|kapiśaṃ,
praśānta|kalikā|palāśa|kusumaṃ,
kusuma|nipāta|citra*|vasudhaṃ,
sa|śabda|nipatad|drum'|ôtka|śakunam,
śakuna|nināda|nādita*|kakub,
vilola|vipalāyamāna|hariṇaṃ,
hariṇa|vilocan'|âdhivasatiṃ
babhañja pavan'|ātmajo ripu|vanam.

I have seen Sita and after doing an action difficult for others to do, I will go gaining fame and tell the news to my master.

I should cut down this grove protected by the demon king," so thinking, the monkey destroyed the grove which resembled Nándana.*

Saying, "A blessing to the two Raghavas, I am their envoy, I 8.130
will break it up as a service to Rama. What can any demon
say about this?"

The son of the wind destroyed the enemy's forest where the doe-eyed Sita dwelt, which was dusty with the pollen of shaken flowers, where the *palása* blossom was blown from its bud, where the ground was mottled with fallen flowers, where the birds missed their noisily falling trees, where the quarters resounded with the calls of birds, the deer fleeing in agitation.

CANTO 9
THE CAPTURE OF HÁNUMAN

9.1 DRU|BHAṄGA|dhvani|saṃvignāḥ,
kuvat|pakṣi|kul'|ākulāḥ,
akārṣuḥ kṣaṇadā|caryo
Rāvaṇasya nivedanam:

«yad atāpsīc chanair bhānur, yatr' âvāsīn mitaṃ marut,
yad āpyānaṃ him'|ôsreṇa bhanakty upavanaṃ kapiḥ.»

tato 'śīti sahasrāṇi kiṅkarāṇāṃ samādiśat
Indrajit|sūr vināśāya Māruteḥ krodha|mūrcchitaḥ.

śakty|ṛṣṭi|parigha|prāsa|gadā|mudgara|pāṇayaḥ,
vyaśnuvānā diśaḥ prāpur vanaṃ dṛṣṭi|viṣ'|ôpamāḥ.

9.5 dadhvāna meghavad bhīmam ādāya parighaṃ kapiḥ
nedur dīpt'|āyudhās te 'pi taḍitvanta iv' âmbudāḥ.

kapin" âmbhodhi|dhīreṇa samagaṃsata rākṣasāḥ
varṣās' ûddhata|toy'|āughāḥ samudreṇ' êva sindhavaḥ.

lāṅgūlam uddhataṃ dhunvann, udvahan parighaṃ gurum,
tasthau toraṇam āruhya pūrvaṃ na prajahāra saḥ.

akṣāriṣuḥ śar'|âmbhāṃsi tasmin rakṣaḥ|payodharāḥ,
na c' âhvālīn, na c' âvrājīt trāsaṃ kapi|mahīdharaḥ.**

avādīt «tiṣṭhat'!» êty uccaiḥ, prādevīt parighaṃ kapiḥ
tathā, yathā raṇe prāṇān bahūnām agrahīd dviṣām.*

9.10 vraṇair avamiṣū raktaṃ, dehaiḥ praurṇāviṣur bhuvam,
diśaḥ praurṇāviṣuś c' ânye yātudhānā bhavad|bhiyaḥ.*

Terrified by the sound of breaking trees, confused by the flocks of birds screeching, the nocturnal demonesses made an appeal to Rávana: 9.1

"A monkey is destroying the grove which the sun gently warmed, where a mild breeze blew, and which is fostered by the moon."

Then the father of Índrajit, maddened with rage, ordered his eighty thousand minions to kill Hánuman.

Spears, swords, bludgeons, javelins, clubs and mallets in hand, the snake-like demons that filled the horizons reached the wood.

Taking up a terrible club, the monkey thundered like a 9.5
cloud. With their weapons flashing they also roared, rumbling like storm clouds.

Like rivers with their currents swollen in the rains meeting the ocean, the demons met with the monkey who was as steady as the ocean.

Waving his upraised tail, wielding a heavy club, he mounted the archway and stood but he did not strike first.

The cloud of demons poured a rain of arrows onto him but the mountain of a monkey did not tremble or become frightened.

The monkey cried loudly, "Stay!" and as he wielded his club he took many enemies' lives in the fight.

They spewed blood from their wounds, they cloaked the 9.10
earth with their bodies, and other fiends being terrified filled the horizons as they fled.

arāsiṣuś cyut'|ôtsāhā bhinna|dehāḥ priy'|âsavaḥ
kaper atrāsiṣur nādān mṛgāḥ siṃha|dhvaner iva.*

māyānām īśvarās te 'pi śastra|hastā rathaiḥ kapim
pratyāvavṛtire hantuṃ, hantavyā Māruteḥ punaḥ.**

tāṃś cetavyān kṣitau śritvā vānaras toraṇaṃ yutān
jaghān' ādhūya parighaṃ vijighṛkṣūn samāgatān.*

saṃjughukṣava āyūṃṣi, tataḥ pratirurūṣavaḥ,
Rāvaṇ'|ântikam ājagmur hata|śeṣā niśā|carāḥ.*

9.15 «ekena bahavaḥ śūrāḥ s'|āviṣkārāḥ pramattavat
vaimukhyaṃ cakṛm'» êty uccair ūcur Daśamukh'|ântike.*

māṃs'|ôpabhoga|saṃśūnān, udvignāṃs tān avetya, saḥ
udvṛtta|nayano minnān* mantriṇaḥ svān vyasarjayat.*

prameditāḥ sa|putrās te su|svāntā bāḍha|vikramāḥ
a|mliṣṭa|nādā niraguḥ, phāṇṭa|citr'|âstra|pāṇayaḥ.*

tān dṛṣṭv" âtidṛḍhān dhṛṣṭān prāptān parivṛḍh'|ājñayā
kaṣṭaṃ vinardataḥ krūrān śastra|ghuṣṭa|karān kapiḥ
a|vyarṇo giri|kūṭ'|ābhān abhyarṇān ārdidad drutam
vṛtta|śastrān mah"|ârambhān a|dāntāṃs tridaśair api.*

They cried out, fond of life but bereft of strength, and with their bodies broken they feared the roars of the monkey as deer fear the sound of the lion.

These masters of illusion too were going to be killed by Hánuman, they who, sword in hand, turned their chariots to kill the monkey.

Resorting to the archway, the monkey wielded his club and killed those groups that came together to kill him but which were soon to be piled upon the earth.

Then wishing to save their lives, wishing to speak, those demons, the remnant from the slain, came to Rávana.

They shouted in the presence of Rávana, "We many proud 9.15
heroes were made to turn tail like drunkards by one
monkey."

Understanding that they were terrified, he with his eyes bulging out sent his own fat ministers swollen with meat eating.

Fattened, accompanied by their sons, glad-hearted, of great courage, with clear-sounding cries they went off, brightly-colored weapons in hand.

The competent monkey quickly slew them as they came, seeing them so strong and bold, coming on the order of their chief and roaring horribly, cruel, their hands clattering with weapons, resembling mountain peaks, skilled in arms, of great undertakings, not subdued even by the thirty gods.

9.20 damit'|âriḥ, praśānt'|âujā, nād'|āpūrita|diṅ|mukhaḥ,
jaghāna ruṣito ruṣṭāṃs tvaritas tūrṇam āgatān.*

teṣāṃ nihanyamānānāṃ saṃghuṣṭaiḥ karṇa|bhedibhiḥ,
abhūd abhyamita|trāsam āsvānt'|âśeṣa|dig jagat.*

bhaya|saṃhṛṣṭa|romāṇas tatas te 'pacita|dviṣaḥ,
kṣaṇena kṣīṇa|vikrāntāḥ kapin' ânesata kṣayam.*

hatvā rakṣāṃsi lavitum akramīn Mārutiḥ punaḥ
aśoka|vanikām eva nigṛhīt'|âri|śāsanaḥ.**

āvarītum iv' ākāśaṃ varituṃ* vīn iv' ôtthitam
vanaṃ prabhañjana|suto n' âdayiṣṭa vināśayan.

9.25 variṣīṣṭa śivaṃ kṣipyan Maithilyāḥ kalpa|śākhinaḥ,
prāvāriṣur iva kṣoṇīṃ kṣiptā vṛkṣāḥ samantataḥ.*

saṃvuvūrṣuḥ svam ākūtam ājñāṃ vivariṣur drutam
avariṣṭ' Âkṣam a|kṣamyaṃ* kapiṃ hantuṃ Daśānanaḥ.**

ūce «saṃvariṣīṣṭhās tvaṃ gaccha śatroḥ parākramam,
dhvṛṣīṣṭhā yudhi māyābhiḥ, svaritā śatru|sammukham.*

drutaṃ saṃsvariṣīṣṭhās tvaṃ nirbhayaḥ pradhan'|ôttame.»
sa māyānām agāt sotā kaper vidhavituṃ dyutim.*

Taming his enemy, quelling their might, filling the mouths of the quarters with his roars, in anger he soon smote them as they came at speed enraged. 9.20

With all its directions resounding with the ear splitting cries of those demons being slain, the world became sick with fear.

Then in a moment the monkey destroyed those enemies of the honored sages, their hair on end with fear, their strength destroyed.

When he had killed the demons Hánuman again proceeded to cut down the ashoka grove, indifferent to the imperative of his enemy.

The son of the wind showed no mercy as he destroyed the grove which rose up as if to cover the sky and to enclose the birds.

He wished that the wish-granting trees would bless Sita as he threw them about. It was as if the cast-down trees cloaked the surrounding earth. 9.25

Because he wished to conceal his agitation and to show his authority, Rávana quickly ordered his irresistible son Aksha to kill the unpardonable monkey.

He said, "Go and obstruct the power of the enemy, deceive with your tricks in battle, roar in the face of the foe.

Attack at once without fear in the greatest of battles." So that begetter of miracles went to extinguish the monkey's brilliance.

vigāḍh" âraṃ vanasy' âsau śatrūṇāṃ gāhitā kapiḥ
Akṣaṃ radhitum ārebhe raddhā Laṅkā|nivāsinām.*

9.30 niṣkoṣitavyān niṣkoṣṭuṃ prāṇān Daśamukh'|ātmajāt
ādāya parighaṃ tasthau vanān niṣkuṣita|drumaḥ.*

eṣṭāram eṣitā saṃkhye soḍhāraṃ sahitā bhṛśam
reṣṭāraṃ reṣituṃ vyāsyad roṣṭ" Âkṣaḥ śastra|saṃhatīḥ.*

śastrair didevisuṃ saṃkhye dudyūṣuḥ parighaṃ kapiḥ
ardidhiṣur yaśaḥ kīrtim īrtsuṃ vṛkṣair atāḍayat.*

bhūyas taṃ dhipsum āhūya rāja|putraṃ didambhiṣuḥ
ahaṃs tataḥ sa mūrchāvān saṃśiśrīṣur abhūd dhvajam.*

āśvasy' Âkṣaḥ kṣaṇāl lokān bibhrakṣur iva tejasā
ruṣā bibhrajjiṣu|prakhyaṃ kapiṃ bāṇair avākirat.*

9.35 saṃyuyūṣuṃ diśo bāṇair Akṣaṃ yiyaviṣur drumaiḥ,
kapir māyām iv' âkārṣīd darśayan vikramaṃ raṇe.*

vānaraṃ prorṇunaviṣuḥ śastrair Akṣo vididyute,
taṃ prorṇunūṣur upalaiḥ sa|vṛkṣair ābabhau kapiḥ.*

Then that monkey, wrecker of the grove, destroyer of his enemies, tormentor of the denizens of Lanka, started to torment Aksha.

He who had torn up trees from the grove took up his club 9.30
and stood up to tear out the life breaths ready to be torn out from Rávana's son.

Aksha the striver in battle, greatly able to endure, a harmer, threw salvoes of weapons to harm Hánuman, also a striver, enduring and a harmer.

With trees the monkey who wished to win fame and to wield his club in battle struck Aksha who sought to wield his weapons and sought also to augment his fame.

As he wished to deceive that prince who himself wanted to deceive, he challenged him again and attacked, after which he sought refuge at his own standard.

Drawing breath as if seeking to scorch the worlds in an instant with his own brightness Aksha warded off the monkey with his arrows who appeared to seek to scorch the worlds with his rage.

Seeking to cover Aksha with trees as he sought to knit up 9.35
the quarters with his arrows, the monkey showing his valor in the battle seemed to cast a magical illusion.

Seeking to engulf the monkey with his weapons Aksha sparkled. The monkey wishing to enshroud him with rocks and trees shone out.

«svāṃ jijñāpayiṣū śaktiṃ? bubhūrṣū nu jaganti kim
śastrair?» ity akṛṣātāṃ tau paśyatāṃ buddhim āhave.*

māyābhiḥ su|ciraṃ kliṣṭvā rākṣaso '|kliśita|kriyam
saṃprāpya vānaraṃ bhūmau papāta parigh'|āhataḥ.*

pavito 'nuguṇair vātaiḥ śītaiḥ, pūtvā payo|nidhau,
babhañj' âdhyuṣitaṃ bhūyaḥ* kṣudhitvā patribhir vanam
9.40 uccair añcita|lāṅgūlaḥ śiro 'ñcitv" êva saṃvahan
dadhad vilubhitaṃ vātaiḥ keśaraṃ vahni|piṅgalam.*

jaritv" êva javen' ânye nipetus tasya śākhinaḥ,
vraścitvā vivaśān anyān balen' âpātayat tarūn.*

damitv" âpy ari|saṃghātān, a|śrāntvā kapi|keśarī
vanaṃ cacāra kartiṣyan nartsyann iva niraṅkuśaḥ.*

pāraṃ jigamiṣan so 'tha punar āvartsyatāṃ dviṣām
matta|dviradavad reme vane Laṅkā|nivāsinām.*

«yady akalpsyad abhiprāyo yoddhuṃ rakṣaḥ|pateḥ svayam,
tam apy akartsyam ady' âhaṃ» vadann ity acarat kapiḥ.*

9.45 «hate tasmin priyaṃ śrutvā kalptā prītiṃ parāṃ prabhuḥ,
toṣo 'dy' êva ca Sītāyāḥ paraś cetasi kalpsyati.»*

āhūya Rāvaṇo 'vocad ath' Êndrajitam antikāt:
«vane matta iva kruddho gajendraḥ pradhaneṣv aṭan,

"Are they trying to demonstrate their own power? Are they trying to fill the world with weapons?" as they fought they made the onlookers think thus.

After tormenting him with his tricks for a long time the demon reached the yet-unhindered monkey and fell to the ground struck by his club.

Freshened by the pleasant cool breezes, cleansed in the
ocean, with his tail curled high, holding his head turned up- 9.40
wards, bearing wind-blown hair reddish like fire, he again smashed up the forest that had been re-inhabited by the hungry birds.

Some trees fell quickly at his onslaught as if from old age. He cut down and felled other helpless trees by force.

Although he had tamed the hosts of his enemies, the lion of a monkey did not rest: as if about to dance he prepared to slash the forest and proceeded unrestrained.

Wishing to finish off his enemies as they were about to return he frolicked in the Lanka residents' grove like a musth elephant.

"If it were the intention of the demon chief himself to fight, then I would have to cut him down today," speaking thus the monkey continued:

"When the lord hears this pleasing news that he is slain, he 9.45
will be most delighted and Sita's heart will be full of joy."

Rávana summoned Índrajit to his presence and said: "As you wandered amid the fighting like an angry musth elephant in the forest

yayātha tvaṃ dviṣām antaṃ bhūyo yāt" âsi c' â|sakṛt:
śaśaktha jetuṃ tvaṃ devān, māyāḥ sasmartha saṃyati.*

tvaṃ sasarjitha śastrāṇi, dadraṣṭh' ârīṃś ca duḥ|sahān,
śastrair āditha śastrāṇi tvam eva mahatām api.*

sa tvaṃ haniṣyan dur|buddhiṃ kapiṃ, vraja mam' ājñayā:
mā n' âñjī rākṣasīr māyāḥ, prastāvīr mā na vikramam.*

9.50 mā na sāvīr mah"|âstrāṇi, mā na dhāvīr ariṃ raṇe,
vānaraṃ mā na saṃyaṃsīr, vraja tūrṇam a|śaṅkitaḥ.»*

anaṃsīc caraṇau tasya mandirād Indrajid vrajan,
avāpya c' āśiṣas tasmād āyāsīt prītim uttamām.*

gate tasminn upāraṃsīt saṃrambhād rakṣasāṃ patiḥ,
Indrajid|vikram'|âbhijño manvāno vānaraṃ jitam.

saṃsismayiṣamāṇo 'gān māyāṃ vyañjijiṣur dviṣaḥ
jagat pipaviṣur vāyuḥ kalp'|ânta iva durdharaḥ.*

lokān āśiśiṣos tulyaḥ Kṛtāntasya viparyaye
vane cikariṣor vṛkṣān balaṃ jigariṣuḥ kapeḥ.*

9.55 roditi sm' êva c' āyāti tasmin pakṣi|gaṇaḥ śucā
mukta|kaṇṭhaṃ hatān vṛkṣān bandhūn bandhor iv' āgame.*

You destroyed your enemies and you will do that many times again: you were able to conquer the gods, you remembered your tricks in battle.

You cast your missiles, you looked upon irresistible foes, you consumed even the weapons of the great with your weapons.

Go prepared to kill the imbecilic monkey, under my command. Do not fail to manifest your demonic tricks, do not fail to show your prowess.

Do not fail to fire your great weapons, do not fail to oppress 9.50
the enemy in battle, do not fail to capture the monkey. Go quickly and fearlessly."

Índrajit bowed to Rávana's feet and as he left the palace after receiving his blessings he was ecstatic with delight.

When he had gone, the lord of the demons, confident of Índrajit's power and considering the monkey as good as defeated, ceased to be agitated.

Índrajit left seeking to mock his enemies and to show them his magic power. He was irresistible like the wind about to purge the world at the end of the eon.

Like Yama about to eat the worlds at the dissolution, he sought to consume the monkey's strength as he was trying to cut down the trees in the grove.

And when he came the flocks of birds loosed their throats 9.55
and cried as if in sorrow for the fallen trees just as one weeps for fallen kinsmen on the arrival of a friend.

āśvasīd iva c', āyāti, tad vega|pavan'|āhatam,
vicitra|stabak'|ôdbhāsi, vanaṃ lulita|pallavam.

«na prāṇiṣi dur|ācāra, māyānām īśiṣe na ca
n' ēḍiṣe yadi Kākutsthaṃ» tam ūce vānaro vacaḥ.*

sa|sainyaś chādayan saṃkhye prāvartiṣṭa tam Indrajit
śaraiḥ kṣuraprair māyābhiḥ śataśaḥ sarvato muhuḥ.**

vānaraḥ kula|śail'|ābhaḥ prasahy' āyudha|śīkaram,
rakṣas|pāśān yaśas|kāmyaṃs tamas|kalpān adudruvat.*

9.60 dhanuṣ|pāśa|bhṛtaḥ saṃkhye jyotiṣ|kalp'|ôru|keśaraḥ
dudhāva nir|namas|kārān rākṣas'|êndra|puras|kṛtān.*

svāmino niṣkrayaṃ gantum āviṣ|kṛta|balaḥ kapiḥ
rarāja samare śatrūn ghnan, duṣkṛta|bahiṣ|kṛtaḥ.*

catuṣ|kāṣṭhaṃ kṣipan vṛkṣān tiras|kurvann arīn raṇe
tiras|kṛta|dig|ābhogo dadṛśe bahudhā bhraman.*

dviṣ|kurvatāṃ catuṣ|kurvann abhighātaṃ nagair dviṣām,
bahiṣ|kariṣyan saṃgrāmād ripūn, jvalana|piṅgalaḥ,*

jyotiṣ|kurvann iv' âiko 'sāv āṭīt saṃkhye parārdhyavat,
tam an|āyuṣ|karaṃ prāpa Śakra|śatrur dhanuṣ|karaḥ.*

As he came, the grove was struck by the wind of his impetus and seemed to revive, bright with its varied blossom, its buds aflutter.

The monkey said to him: "O evil-doer, you will breathe no more, you will not command your magic powers if you do not honor Rama."

Índrajit and his army continually advanced on him from all directions in the fight, enveloping him with sharp-edged arrows and magical devices by the hundred.

Wishing for fame, the monkey, resembling a mountain range, enduring a downpour of weapons, advanced upon those miserable dark-looking demons.

With his abundant hair like flames he shook up the fore- 9.60
most of the demon chiefs who bore bows and snares and refused obeisance.

The monkey, whose sins were purged, displaying his power to gain recompense for his master, shone in battle as he slew the enemy.

Throwing trees in the four directions, scorning the enemy in battle, obscuring the expanse of the horizons, he appeared manifold as he moved about.

Reddish like fire, making four strikes with his trees on his enemy as they made two, excising his foes from the fight,

He seemed to blaze as he roamed alone as if the most excellent in battle. The enemy of Indra, Índrajit, bow in hand found the death maker.

9.65 asyann aruṣ|karān bāṇān jyotiṣ|kara|sama|dyutiḥ,
yaśas|karo yaśas|kāmaṃ kapiṃ bāṇair atāḍayat.*

cakār' âdhas|padaṃ n' âsau caran viyati Mārutiḥ
marmā|vidbhis tamas|kāṇḍair vidhyamāno 'py an|ekadhā.*

Puruhūtadviṣo dhūrṣu yuktān yānasya vājinaḥ
āyūṃṣi tvakṣu nirbhidya Prābhañjanir amocayat.**

suṣupus te yadā bhūmau, Rāvaṇiḥ sārathiṃ tadā
āhartum anyān aśiṣat proṣita|trāsa|karkaśaḥ.**

pratuṣṭūṣuḥ punar yuddham āsiṣañjayiṣur bhayam,
ātasthau ratham ātmīyān utsisāhayiṣann iva.*

9.70 balāny abhiṣiṣikṣantaṃ tarubhiḥ kapi|vāridam
vijigīṣuḥ, punaś cakre vyūhaṃ dur|jayam Indrajit.*

abhiṣyantaḥ kapiṃ krodhād abhyaṣiñcann iv' ātmanaḥ
saṃprahāra|samudbhūtai raktaiḥ koṣṇair aruś|cyutaiḥ.

saṃgrāme tān adhiṣṭhāsyan niṣadya pura|toraṇam
a|viṣīdann avaṣṭabdhān vyaṣṭabhnān nara|viṣvaṇān.*

viṣahya rākṣasāḥ kruddhāḥ śastra|jālam avākiran
yan na vyaṣahat' Êndro 'pi; kapiḥ paryaṣahiṣṭa tat.*

viṣyandamāna|rudhiro rakta|visyanda|pāṭalān
viṣkantṝn parigheṇ' âhann a|viskantā kapir dviṣaḥ.*

Shining like the sun as he cast his wounding arrows, the 9.65
fame-causing Índrajit struck the fame-seeking monkey with
his arrows.

The son of the wind did not set his foot down as he went through the air though struck often by vitals-piercing dark-tipped arrows.

Hánuman pierced the hides of the horses yoked to the shafts of Índrajit's chariot and took their lives.

When his horses lay inert on the ground, Rávana's son fierce because free from fear ordered his driver to get others.

Then, to encourage the fighting again, making them cling to fear, he stood on his chariot as if to give his troops fortitude.

As he sought to defeat that rain cloud of a monkey who 9.70
was sprinkling his troops with trees, Índrajit again made an
indefatigable array of his forces.

As they destroyed themselves it was as if they sprinkled the monkey with warm blood spurting from their battle-engendered wounds.

Ready to overwhelm in battle the advancing man-eaters, he resorted to the arch of the city gate and waited undaunted.

The surviving angered demons sprayed down a multitude of weapons which even Indra had not overcome. That the monkey did withstand.

Streaming with blood the steadfast monkey struck with his club his swarming enemies who were already red with streams of blood.

9.75 Meghanādaḥ pariskandan pariṣkandantam āśv arim
abadhnād a|pariskandaṃ Brahma|pāśena visphuran.*

visphuladbhir gṛhīto 'sau niṣphulaḥ puruṣ'|âśanaiḥ
viṣkambhituṃ samartho 'pi n' âcalad Brahma|gauravāt.*

«kṛṣīḍhvaṃ bhartur ānandaṃ,
mā na proḍhvaṃ drutaṃ viyat
vānaraṃ netum» ity uccair
Indrajit prāvadat svakān.*

«gatam aṅguli|ṣaṅgaṃ tvāṃ bhīru|ṣṭhānād ih' āgatam
khādiṣyāma,» iti procur nayanto Mārutiṃ dviṣaḥ.*

«Agniṣṭom'|ādi|saṃstheṣu Jyotiṣṭom'|ādiṣu dvijān
yo 'rakṣīt, tasya dūto 'yaṃ mānuṣasy'» êti c' âvadan.*

9.80 «nāsāṃ mātṛ|ṣvaseyyāś* ca Rāvaṇasya lulāva yaḥ
mātuḥ svasuś ca tanayān Khar'|ādīn vijaghāna yaḥ,*

prāduḥ|ṣanti na saṃtrāsā yasya rakṣaḥ|samāgame,
tasya kṣatriya|duḥṣūter ayaṃ praṇidhir āgataḥ.*

dṛṣṭvā su|ṣuptaṃ rāj'|êndraṃ pāpo 'yaṃ viṣam'|âśayaḥ,
cāra|karmaṇi niṣṇātaḥ, praviṣṭaḥ pramadā|vanam.*

supratiṣṇāta|sūtrāṇāṃ Kapiṣṭhala|sama|tviṣām
sthitāṃ vṛtte dvijātīnāṃ rātrāv aikṣata Maithilīm,*

The thunderous active shining Índrajit quickly snared his moving enemy with his Brahma-noose, making him immobile. 9.75

Though able to escape, when bright Hánuman was seized by the thronging man-eaters he did not move out of respect for Brahma.

Índrajit loudly urged his troops: "Bring delight to your lord, do not fail to speed through the air to fetch the monkey."

The enemies brought Hánuman and said: "Now that you are in our hands and have come here from the land of the timid, we shall eat you."

And they said, "This is the envoy of the man who protected the twiceborn in rites such as the Jyoti·shtoma based on the Agni·shtoma,

And who cut off the nose of Rávana's maternal aunt's daugh- 9.80
ter and killed Khara and the other sons of his mother's sister,

Who came as a spy for that ill-begotten warrior who appears to have no fears in his battle with the demons.

When he saw the king fast asleep, this evil one of crooked disposition, expert in the art of the spy, entered the pleasure grove.

He saw Sita at night keeping to the practices of the twiceborn who are well learned in their texts and who have the same radiance as Kapi·shthala,*

sarva|nārī|guṇaiḥ prasṭhāṃ, viṣṭara|sthāṃ, gavi|ṣṭhirām,
śayānāṃ ku|ṣṭhale, tārāṃ divi|ṣṭhām iva nirmalām,*

9.85 su|ṣāmnīṃ, sarva|tejassu tanvīṃ jyotiṣṭamāṃ, śubhām,
niṣṭapantīm iv' ātmānaṃ jyotiḥsāt|kurvatīṃ vanam,*

madhusād|bhūta|kiñjalka|piñjara|bhramar'|ākulām
ullasat|kusumāṃ puṇyāṃ hema|ratna|latām iva,

vilocan'|âmbu muñcantīṃ kurvāṇāṃ pari|sesicām
hṛdayasy' êva śok'|âgni|saṃtaptasy' ôttama|vratām.*

dṛṣṭvā tām abhanag vṛkṣān dviṣo ghnan parisedhataḥ,
paritas tān vicikṣepa kruddhaḥ svayam iv' ânilaḥ.*

a|pratistabdha|vikrāntam a|nistabdho mah"|āhave,
visoḍhavantam astrāṇi vyatastambhad ghana|dhvaniḥ.»*

9.90 te vijñāy' âbhisoṣyantaṃ raktai rakṣāṃsi sa|vyathāḥ,
anyair apy āyataṃ nehur varatrā|śṛṅkhal'|ādibhiḥ.*

viṣasād' Êndrajid buddhvā bandhe bandh'|ântara|kriyām
divya|bandho viṣahate n' âparaṃ bandhanaṃ yataḥ.*

muṣṇantam iva tejāṃsi vistīrṇ'|ôraḥ|sthalaṃ puraḥ
upasedur Daśagrīvaṃ gṛhītvā rākṣasāḥ kapim.**

bahudhā bhinna|marmāṇo bhīmāḥ Kharaṇas'|ādayaḥ,
agre|vaṇaṃ vartamāne pratīcyāṃ candra|maṇḍale,
«nirvaṇaṃ kṛtam udyānam anen' āmra|vaṇ'|ādibhiḥ
devadāru|van'|āmiśrair» ity ūcur vānara|dviṣaḥ.*

Foremost of all women by her virtues, seated on a couch of leaves, firm in speech, sleeping on the bare ground, like a pure star in the heavens,

Singing sweetly, most light of all lights, slender, pale, light- 9.85
ing up the forest as if igniting her very self,

Like a holy vine of gold and gems with bright blossom thronged with bees golden from the honey filled stamens,

A woman of the highest vows, shedding tears as if making a libation over a heart burning on the fire of grief.

Seeing her he tore down the trees and, killing his surrounding foes, furious, he threw them round as if he were the wind itself.

Not checked in the great battle Índrajit of the storm cloud's roar stopped the unhindered warrior who withstood his weapons."

Fearfully thinking he was about to splash them with blood 9.90
they also bound him thoroughly with additional leather straps and chains.

Índrajit was vexed to see another bond on the binding as the divine bond would not tolerate another binding with it.

Bringing the monkey, the demons came before Rávana who seemed to steal the light with the broad expanse of his chest.

Just as the orb of the moon was setting beyond the grove in the west, the fearsome demons, the monkey's enemies, headed by Khara·nasa, with open wounds in many places said, "He has made the garden void of groves of trees such

9.95 upāsthiṣata saṃprītāḥ pūrv'|âhṇe roṣa|vāhanam
rākṣasāḥ kapim ādāya patiṃ rudhira|pāyiṇām.*

surā|pāṇa|parikṣībaṃ, ripu|darpa|har'|ôdayam,
para|strī|vāhinaṃ prāyuḥ s'|āviṣkāraṃ surā|piṇaḥ.*

saṃgharṣa|yogiṇaḥ pādau praṇemus tridaśa|dviṣaḥ,
prahiṇvanto Hanūmantaṃ pramīṇantaṃ dviṣan|matīḥ.*

«pravapāṇi śiro bhūmau vānarasya vana|cchidaḥ»
āmantrayata saṃkruddhaḥ samitiṃ rakṣasāṃ patiḥ.*

praṇyagādīt praṇighnantaṃ ghanaḥ praṇinadann iva
tataḥ praṇihitaḥ sv'|ârthe rākṣas'|êndraṃ Vibhīṣaṇaḥ:*

9.100 «praṇiśāmya, Daśagrīva, praṇiyātum alaṃ ruṣam,
praṇijānīhi: hanyante dūtā, doṣe na saty api.»*

prāṇayantam ariṃ proce rākṣas'|êndro Vibhīṣaṇam
«prāṇiṇiṣur na pāpo 'yaṃ, yo 'bhāṅkṣīt pramadā|vanam.*

prāghāniṣata rakṣāṃsi yen' āptāni vane mama,
na prahaṇmaḥ kathaṃ pāpaṃ vada pūrv'|âpakāriṇam?*

as mangos interspersed with stands of deodars."

As they brought the monkey, the delighted demons stood in the morning before the lord of the blood drinkers, a vector of rage. 9.95

The liquor-swilling fiends proudly approached Rávana the abductor of others' wives, who was intoxicated from drinking spirits, exalted by the removal of his enemies' pride.

Bringing Hánuman who frustrates his enemies' intentions, they bowed down emulously at the feet of the enemy of the thirty gods.

The enraged lord of the demons addressed the assembly: "I shall cast the head of this forest-scything monkey onto the ground."

Then Vibhíshana, having regard to his own purposes, roaring like a thundercloud, spoke to the murderous king of demons:*

"O Rávana, refrain, do not access your rage. Consider: ambassadors should not be killed, even when they are in the wrong." 9.100

The demon king spoke to Vibhíshana who was helping his enemy live: "This sinner who destroyed the courtesans' grove does not wish to live.

Tell me, how can we not kill this sinner who offended first, who killed the trusted demons in my grove?

veśm'|ântar|haṇanaṃ kopān mama śatroḥ kariṣyataḥ
mā kārṣīr antar|ayaṇaṃ. prayāṇ'|ârham avehy amum.*

prahīṇa|jīvitaṃ kuryur ye na śatrum upasthitam
nyāyyāyā api te lakṣmyāḥ kurvanty āśu prahāpaṇam.*

9.105 kaḥ kṛtvā Rāvaṇ'|āmarṣa|prakopaṇam avadya|dhīḥ
śakto jagati Śakro 'pi kartum āyuḥ|pragopaṇam?*

van'|ânta|preṅkhaṇaḥ pāpaḥ phalānāṃ pariṇiṃsakaḥ
praṇikṣiṣyati n' ô bhūyaḥ praṇindy' âsmān madhūny ayam.*

Hareḥ pragamanaṃ n' âsti, na prabhānaṃ hima|druhaḥ,
n' âti|pravepanaṃ vāyor, mayā gopāyite vane.*

duṣ|pānaḥ punar etena kapinā bhṛṅga|saṃbhṛtaḥ
pranaṣṭa|vinayen' âgryaḥ svāduḥ puṣp'|āsavo vane.»*

roṣa|bhīma|mukhen' âivaṃ kṣubhnat" ôkte, plavaṅgamaḥ
proce s'|ānunayaṃ vākyaṃ Rāvaṇaṃ sv'|ârtha|siddhaye:*

9.110 «dūtam ekaṃ kapiṃ baddham ānītaṃ veśma paśyataḥ,
loka|traya|pateḥ, krodhaḥ kathaṃ tṛṇa|laghus tava?*

agny|āhita|jana|prahve, vijigīṣā|parāṅmukhe,
kasmād vā nīti|niṣṇasya saṃrambhas tava tāpase?

Do not create an obstacle for me just as I am about to kill my enemy's spy in anger. Understand that he deserves to die.

Those who would not quickly deprive of life an enemy in their midst ensure the loss of even their rightful wealth.

What idiot is there in the world who, even were he Indra, 9.105
would be able to save his life if he had provoked Rávana's anger?

Now that the evil fruit eater who has reached the extremities of our grove has mocked us, he will never taste the sweet juices again.

While I protect the grove *the moon ⁝ Indra Vishnu (as Rama) ⁝ the monkey* will not come there, the sun will not shine and the wind will not gust.

Moreover this reprobate monkey will now find the choice sweet nectar of flowers collected by bees in the grove difficult to drink."

When he had said this the monkey, for the furtherance of his own purposes, made a courteous reply to Rávana who shook, his face terrible with anger:

"Surely this anger is as a straw to you, the lord of the three 9.110
worlds, as you see a solitary monkey envoy brought bound to your house?

Why are you who are so skilled in policy angry at an ascetic devoted to those who worship the fires, who has turned his face from the quest to conquer?

na sarva|rātra|kalyāṇyaḥ striyo vā ratna|bhūmayaḥ
yaṃ vinirjitya labhyante kaḥ kuryāt tena vigraham?

saṃgaccha Rāma|Sugrīvau bhuvanasya samṛddhaye,
ratna|pūrṇāv iv' âmbho|dhī Himavān pūrva|paścimau.

suhṛdau Rāma|Sugrīvau, kiṃkarāḥ kapi|yūtha|pāḥ,
para|dār'|ârpaṇen' âiva labhyante. muñca Maithilīm.

9.115 dharmaṃ pratyarpayan Sītām, arthaṃ Rāmeṇa mitratām,
kāmaṃ viśvāsa|vāsena Sītāṃ dattv": āpnuhi trayam.

Virādha|Tāḍakā|Vāli|Kabandha|Khara|Dūṣaṇaiḥ
na ca na jñāpito yādṛṅ Mārīcen' âpi te ripuḥ.

Khar'|ādi|nidhanaṃ c' âpi mā maṃsthā vaira|kāraṇam
ātmānaṃ rakṣituṃ yasmāt kṛtaṃ tan, na jigīṣayā.»

tataḥ krodh'|ânil'|āpāta|kampr'|āsy'|âmbhoja|saṃhatiḥ
mahā|hrada iva kṣubhyan kapim āha sma Rāvaṇaḥ.

«hata|rākṣasa|yodhasya virugṇ'|ôdyāna|śākhinaḥ
‹dūto 'sm'› îti bruvāṇasya kiṃ dūta|sadṛśaṃ tava?

9.120 paṅgu|bāla|striyo nighnan Kabandha|Khara|Tāḍakāḥ
tapasvī yadi Kākutsthaḥ, kīdṛk kathaya pātakī?

Who would make war with one from whom once conquered one would not gain women wanton all night, or gems, or lands?

Join Rama and Sugríva for the prosperity of the world, as the Himálaya joins the eastern and the western oceans full of jewels.

By giving back another's wife you will gain Rama and Sugríva and their attendants, the lords of the monkey hosts, as friends. Release Sita.

Returning Sita would be righteousness, friendship with 9.115
Rama would be gain, and giving up Sita would be pleasure
in that you would live without fear. Gain all three

The sort of enemy that he is cannot have been made known to you by Virádha, Tádaka, Valin, Kabándha, Khara, and Dúshana or even by Marícha.

And do not regard even the death of Khara and others as a cause of hostility since he did that to protect himself, not with a view to conquer."

Then rippling like a great pool of water, the masses of his lotus-like faces shaking as they were buffeted by the winds of his anger, Rávana spoke to the monkey:

"Are you fit to be an envoy, declaring yourself to be a messenger but killing warrior demons and ripping up the parkland trees?

If Rama who kills cripples, children and women such as 9.120
Kabándha, Khara and Tádaka is a saint, then say, what sort
of person is a sinner?

abhimāna|phalaṃ jānan mahattvaṃ, katham uktavān
ratn'|ādi|lābha|śūnyatvān niṣphalaṃ Rāma|vigraham?

para|strī|bhoga|haraṇaṃ dharma eva nar'|âśinām,
mukham ast' îty abhāṣiṣṭhāḥ: kā me s'|āśaṅkatā tvayi?

brūhi dūra|vibhinnānām ṛddhi|śīla|kriy"|ânvayaiḥ
Hanūman, kīdṛśaṃ sakhyaṃ nara|vānara|rakṣasām?

eko dvābhyāṃ Virādhas tu jitābhyām a|vivakṣitaḥ
hataś chalena mūḍho 'yaṃ, ten' âpi tava kaḥ smayaḥ?

9.125 man|niyogāc ca Mārīcaḥ palāyana|parāyaṇaḥ
yuyutsā|rahito, Rāmaṃ mamār' âpaharan vane.

nijaghān' ânya|saṃsaktaṃ satyaṃ Rāmo latā|mṛgam.
tvam eva brūhi saṃcintya, yuktaṃ tan mahatāṃ yadi?

puṃsā bhakṣyeṇa bandhūnām ātmānaṃ rakṣituṃ vadhaḥ
kṣamiṣyate Daśāsyena, kvaty" êyaṃ tava durmatiḥ?»

kapir jagāda «dūto 'ham upāyaṃ tava darśane
druma|rākṣasa|vidhvaṃsam akārṣaṃ buddhi|pūrvakam.

Knowing that greatness has as its reward honor, how can you say that my fight with Rama will be fruitless because there will be no gain of jewels or anything like that?

The righteousness of man-eaters consists in taking and enjoying the wives of others. It is mere mouth that you spoke: how can I have any fear of you?

Tell me, Hánuman, what sort of friendship can there be between men, monkeys and demons who are far distant from each other in accomplishment, character, behavior and race?

What pride can you take in the fact that the lonely Virádha, a fool not worth speaking for, was killed through guile by two who had already been defeated?

And it was at my injunction that Marícha, intent on flight 9.125
but suppressing his will to fight, was killed leading Rama away in the forest.

Rama killed the monkey Valin while he was engaged in battle with someone else. Consider carefully and tell me, is that fitting for the great?

Where do you get the stupid idea that Rávana in order to protect himself will forgive the killing of his relatives by a man himself fit to be eaten?"

The monkey said, "As an envoy I deliberately destroyed the trees and the demons as a means to get an audience with you.

ā|Trikūṭam akārṣur ye tvatkā nirjaṅgamaṃ jagat,
Daśagrīva, kathaṃ brūṣe tān a|vadhyān mahī|pateḥ?

9.130 abhimāna|phalaṃ proktaṃ yat tvayā Rāma|vigrahe
vineśus tena śataśaḥ kulāny asura|rakṣasām.

yat sva|dharmam a|dharmaṃ tvaṃ
  dur|balaṃ pratyapadyathāḥ
ripau Rāme ca niḥśaṅko
  n' âitat kṣemaṃ|karaṃ ciram.

anvay'|ādi|vibhinnānāṃ yathā sakhyam an|īpsitam,
n' āiṣīr virodham apy evaṃ sārdhaṃ puruṣa|vānaraiḥ.

Virādhaṃ tapasāṃ vighnaṃ jaghāna vijito yadi
varo dhanur|bhṛtāṃ Rāmaḥ, sa kathaṃ na vivakṣitaḥ?

praṇaśyann api n' âśaknod atyetuṃ bāṇa|gocaram
tvay" âiv' ôktaṃ, mahā|māyo Mārīco Rāma|hastinaḥ.

9.135 any'|āsaktasya yad vīryaṃ na tvaṃ smarasi Vālinaḥ,
mūrchāvān namataḥ saṃdhyāṃ dhruvaṃ tad|bāhu|pīḍitaḥ.

a|sad|bandhu|vadh'|ôpajñaṃ vimuñca bali|vigraham,
Sītām arpaya nantavye kośa|daṇḍ'|ātma|bhūmibhiḥ.»

O Rávana, how can you say that the lord of the earth should not kill those minions of yours who voided the world of living beings as far as Trikúta?

That which you said had honor as its reward in the war with 9.130
Rama has caused clans of demons and fiends to perish in their hundreds.

The fact that you own to an indefensible immorality as your moral right and the fact that you have no fears of your enemy Rama will not keep you safe for long.

Just as the friendship of those who are different in race and suchlike is undesirable, so also you should not seek conflict with these men and monkeys.

Although he had already lost, if Rama the best of archers slew Virádha who was an obstacle to his austerities, then how could he be someone not worth speaking of?

As you said, even while escaping Marícha the great illusionist was not able to get beyond arrow range of the elephant that is Rama.

You do not remember the courage of Valin when he was 9.135
engaged in combat with another, because you were certainly unconscious, squeezed in his arms as he bowed to the twilight.*

Give up your contest with the mighty enemy who is known for what he is by the killing of your evil relatives. Return Sita to the revered Rama along with your treasure, your scepter, yourself and your lands."

sphuṭa|paruṣam a|sahyam ittham uccaiḥ
sadasi marut|tanayena bhāṣyamāṇaḥ,
parijanam abhito vilokya dāhaṃ
Daśavadanaḥ pradideśa vānarasya.

Thus loudly addressed in public with insupportable words both clear and harsh by the son of the wind, Rávana looking around at his people, ordered the monkey to be burned.

CANTO 10
HÁNUMAN BURNS LANKA

10.1 ATHA SA VALKA|dukūla|kuth'|ādibhiḥ
parigato, jvalad|uddhata|vāladhiḥ,
udapatad divam ākula|locanair
nṛ|ripubhiḥ sa|bhayair abhivīkṣitaḥ.*

raṇa|paṇḍito 'grya|vibudh'|âri|pure
kalahaṃ sa Rāma|mahitaḥ kṛtavān,
jvalad|agni Rāvaṇa|gṛhaṃ ca balāt,
kala|haṃsa|rāmam, a|hitaḥ kṛtavān.**

nikhil" âbhavan na sa|hasā sahasā
jvalanena pūḥ prabhavatā bhavatā
vanitā|janena viyatā viyatā
Tripur'|āpadaṃ nagam itā gamitā.*

sarasāṃ sa|rasāṃ parimucya tanuṃ
patatāṃ patatāṃ kakubho bahuśaḥ
sa|kalaiḥ sakalaiḥ* paritaḥ karuṇair
uditai ruditair iva khaṃ nicitam.*

10.5 na ca kāṃ cana kāñcana|sadma|citiṃ
na kapiḥ śikhinā śikhinā samayaut,
na ca na dravatā dravatā parito
hima|hāna|kṛtā na kṛtā kva ca na.*

avasitaṃ hasitaṃ prasitaṃ, mudā
vilasitaṃ hrasitaṃ smara|bhāsitam,
na sa|madāḥ pramadā hata|saṃmadāḥ,
pura|hitaṃ vihitaṃ na samīhitam.*

samiddha|śaraṇā dīptā dehe Laṅkā mat'|ēśvarā
samid|dha|śaraṇ'|ādīptā dehe 'laṃ|kāmat"|ēśvarā.*

THEN CLOTHED IN bark, fine fabric and *kusha* grass, 10.1
with his upraised tail flaming, he flew up into the firmament watched by fearful fiends with rolling eyes.

That hostile expert in battle, honored by Rama, caused chaos in the city of the enemy of the foremost god and forcefully made Rávana's palace, already beautified by flamingoes, blaze with fire.

Suddenly with the splendid blaze, the whole city was bereft of laughter and being on a mountain it suffered the same misfortune as the Triple City* with the women scattering through the air.

It was as if the sky were completely filled with all the pitiful screams mixed with the sweet sounds of the birds flying in all directions as they left the watery body of the lakes.

There was no golden heap of buildings that the monkey 10.5
did not envelop with his flaming flame and nowhere anywhere was there not a rush of flow caused by the causer of snowmelt as he rushed.

The unceasing laughter ceased, the sport joyfully lit up by love ended, the forward women whose joy had been destroyed were not joyous, the weal of the city so desired was not bestowed.

Lanka, whose lord was honored, burned glowing with its burning houses. Able to give all pleasures to the body it was lit up by the protector of the kindling gatherers.

piśit'|âśinām anu|diśaṃ sphuṭatāṃ
sphuṭatāṃ jagāma parivihvalatā,
hvalatā janena* bahudhā caritaṃ
caritaṃ mahattva|rahitaṃ mahatā.*

na gajā naga|jā dayitā dayitā,
vi|gataṃ vigataṃ, lalitaṃ lalitam,
pramad" ā|pramad" āma|hatā, mahatām
a|raṇaṃ maraṇaṃ samayāt samayāt.**

10.10 na vānaraiḥ parākrāntāṃ mahadbhir bhīma|vikramaiḥ
na vā naraiḥ parākrāntāṃ dadāha nagarīṃ kapiḥ.*

drutaṃ drutaṃ vahni|samāgataṃ gataṃ,
mahīm ahīna|dyuti|rocitaṃ citam,
samaṃ samantād, apa|gopuraṃ puraṃ
paraiḥ parair apy a|nirākṛtaṃ kṛtam.*

naśyanti dadarśa vṛndāni kap'|îndraḥ
hārīṇy a|balānāṃ hārīṇy a|balānām.*

nārīṇām apanunudur na deha|khedān
ārīṇ'|âmala|salilā hiraṇya|vāpyaḥ,
n' ârīṇām anala|parīta|patra|puṣpān
nārīṇām abhavad upetya śarma vṛkṣān.*

atha lulita|patatri|mālaṃ,
rugṇ'|âsana|bāṇa|keśara|tamālam,
sa vanaṃ vivikta|mālaṃ,*
Sītāṃ draṣṭuṃ jagām' âlam.*

The bewilderment of the flesh eaters bursting forth in all directions burst forth and the great flailing crowd behaved variously with behavior bereft of nobility.

The treasured mountain-bred elephants were not tended, the birds stopped flying, dalliance was shaken, a wanton as if struck with fever lost her delight, death came timely to the warriors without a fight.

The monkey burned the city which had neither been at- 10.10
tacked by great monkeys of terrible prowess nor attacked by men.

Quickly the city in contact with fire melted, a mass shining with no small splendor on the ground, made level on all sides, bereft of its gate towers, never before destroyed even by mighty foes.

The lord of monkeys saw the captivating pearl-necklaced throngs of powerless women being destroyed.

The golden tanks with their pure spring water could not remove the bodily agonies of the women and there was no shelter for the wives of the enemy who had resorted to the trees rendered bereft of leaves and flowers by the fire.

To see Sita he went to the grove, its skeins of birds dispersed, its *ásana*, *bana*, *késara* and *tamála* trees broken, its clear lines disordered.

10.15 ghana|gir'|îndra|vilaṅghana|śālinā
vana|gatā vana|ja|dyuti|locanā*
jana|matā dadṛśe Janakātmajā
taru|mṛgeṇa taru|sthala|śāyinī.*

kāntā sahamānā* duḥkhaṃ, cyuta|bhūṣā,
Rāmasya viyuktā, kāntā saha|mānā.*

mitam avadad udāraṃ tāṃ Hanūmān mud" âraṃ:
«Raghu|vṛṣabha|sakāśaṃ yāmi devi, prakāśam,
tava vidita|viṣādo, dṛṣṭa|kṛtsn'|āmiṣ'|âdaḥ,
śriyam aniśam avantaṃ parvataṃ Mālyavantam.»*

udapatad viyad a|pragamaḥ parai
rucitam unnatimat pṛthu|sattvavat,
rucita|mun natimat* pṛthu|sattvavat
pratividhāya vapur bhaya|daṃ dviṣām.*

babhau Marutvān vi|kṛtaḥ sa|mudro;
babhau Marutvān vikṛtaḥ sa|mud|raḥ;
babhau Marutvān vikṛtaḥ samudro;
babhau Marutvān vikṛtaḥ samudraḥ.**

10.20 abhiyātā varaṃ tuṅgaṃ bhū|bhṛtaṃ ruciraṃ puraḥ
karkaśaṃ prathitaṃ dhāma sa|sattvaṃ puṣkar'|ēkṣaṇam,*
abhiy" *ât'|āvaraṃ* tuṅgaṃ bhū|bhṛtaṃ ruciraṃ puraḥ
karkaśaṃ prathitaṃ dhāma sa|sattvaṃ puṣkare kṣaṇam.*

citraṃ citram iv' āyāto vicitraṃ tasya bhū|bhṛtam,
harayo vegam āsādya saṃtrastā mumuhur muhuḥ.**

The monkey able to leap over great mountains of cloud 10.15
saw Jánaka's daughter in the wood, her eyes bright lotuses, beloved of the people, lying in a stand of trees.

The lovely lady, enduring pain, bereft of her ornaments, the lost beloved of Rama, kept her dignity.

In joy Hánuman quickly spoke measured and lofty words to her: "O Queen, I know your misery and now I have seen all these flesh eaters I shall go at once openly to Rama's presence, to Mount Mályavat which always nurtures glory.

Not to be overtaken by his enemies he leaped into the shining lofty sky full of huge beings, making his body delightful, reverent, of vast benignity and terrifying to his enemies.

Hánuman, of diverse deeds and possessed of the crest jewel, shone; Indra lord of the *Marut*s once undone now was glad in the company of the *ápsaras*es; the ocean with its accompanying winds seemed agitated; the cloud, companion of the wind, was spread out appearing as an ocean.

About to approach Rama—that excellent lofty king, beau- 10.20
tiful, of hairy chest, famed, a refuge, energetic and lotus-eyed—Hánuman, as he came from the city to the beautiful, high, solid, *sun-obscuring : wind-obstructing* mountain filled with creatures, spread his radiance in a moment through the sky.

The terrified monkeys feeling the surprising force of his arrival at the mountain, brightly colored like a picture, were momentarily bewildered.

gacchan sa vārīṇy akirat payodheḥ;
kūla|sthitāṃs tāni tarūn adhunvan;
puṣp'|āstarāṃs te 'ṅga|sukhān atanvan;
tān kinnarā manmathino 'dhyatiṣṭhan.**

sa giriṃ taru|khaṇḍa|maṇḍitaṃ
samavāpya tvarayā latā|mṛgaḥ
smita|darśita|kārya|niścayaḥ
kapi|sainyair muditair amaṇḍayat.*

10.25 Garuḍ'|ânila|tigma|raśmayaḥ
patatāṃ yady api saṃmatā jave,
a|cireṇa kṛt'|ârtham āgataṃ
tam amanyanta tath" âpy atīva te.*

vraṇa|kandara|līna|śastra|sarpaḥ,
pṛthu|vakṣaḥ|sthala|karkaś'|ôru|bhittiḥ,
cyuta|śoṇita|baddha|dhātu|rāgaḥ,
śuśubhe vānara|bhū|dharas tad" âsau.*

cala|piṅga|keśara|hiraṇya|latāḥ,
sphuṭa|netra|paṅkti|maṇi|saṃhatayaḥ,
kaladhauta|sānava iv' âtha gireḥ,
kapayo babhuḥ Pavanaj'|āgamane.

kapi|toya|nidhīn plavaṅgam'|êndur
madayitvā madhureṇa darśanena,
vacan'|âmṛta|dīdhitīr vitanvann,
akṛt' ānanda|parīta|netra|vārīn.

As he went he threw up the waters of the ocean; as they went they shook the trees standing on the shore; they then spread carpets of flowers pleasing to limb; and those the amorous *kínnaras* settled upon.

The monkey quickly reached the mountain adorned with groves of trees, showing with his smile his certainty of success, he adorned it with his happy soldiers.

Although Gáruda, the wind and the sun are esteemed among 10.25
fliers in point of speed, nevertheless they thought even more of Hánuman coming back so quickly with his object achieved.

Then that mountain of a monkey was adorned with snakes which were the weapons hiding in the gorges of his wounds, with a rough broad cliff that was his broad chest, and with the redness of ores which was produced by his shed blood.

Then, upon Hánuman's arrival, the monkeys with the golden vines which were their swaying yellow manes and with the seams of jewels which were their rows of open eyes, shone like the gold and silver ridges of the mountain.

The moon of a monkey Hánuman, bringing joy to the oceans of monkeys through his sweet aspect, spreading adoration through the nectar of his words, brought tears to eyes filled with bliss.

parikhedita|Vindhya|vīrudhaḥ
paripīt'|âmala|nirjhar'|âmbhasaḥ,
dudhuvur madhu|kānanaṃ tataḥ
kapi|nāgā mudit'|Âṅgad'|ājñayā.

10.30 viṭapi|mṛga|viṣāda|dhvānta|nud, vānar'|ârkaḥ,
priya|vacana|mayūkhair bodhit'|ârth'|âravindaḥ,
udaya|girim iv' âdriṃ sampramucy' âbhyagāt khaṃ
nṛpa|hṛdaya|guhā|khaṃ ghnan pramoh'|ândhakāram.*

Raghu|tanayam agāt tapo|vana|sthaṃ,
vidhṛta|jaṭ"|âjina|valkalaṃ, Hanūmān
param iva puruṣaṃ Nareṇa yuktaṃ,
sama|śama|veśa|samādhin" ânujena.

kara|puṭa|nihitaṃ dadhat sa ratnaṃ
pari|viral'|âṅguli|nirgat'|âlpa|dīpti,*
tanu|kapila|ghana|sthitaṃ yath" ênduṃ,
nṛpam anamat, paribhugna|jānu|mūrdhā.

*rucir'/ônnata/ratna/gauravaḥ**
paripūrṇ'/âmṛta/raśmi/maṇḍalaḥ
samadṛśyata jīvit'|āśayā
saha Rāmeṇa vadhū|śiro|maṇiḥ.*

avasanna/ruciṃ van'/āgataṃ
tam an|āmṛṣṭa|rajo|vidhūsaram
samapaśyad *apeta/Maithiliṃ*
dadhataṃ *gaurava/mātram* ātmavat.

The elephants of monkeys who had laid waste the shrubs of the Vindhya and drunk the pure waters of its torrents, then ravaged the nectar grove at the command of their beloved Ángada.*

Hánuman the monkey sun, leaving the mountain as if it 10.30
were the eastern range, driving out the darkness that was the monkeys' despair with the rays of his sweet speech and rousing the day lotuses of understanding, ascended the sky, slaying the darkness of delusion that was the space in the caverns of the king's heart.

Hánuman went to Rama residing in the holy grove, bearing matted locks, a buckskin and bark clothing, with his younger brother alike in tranquility, dress and spiritual absorption, like the supreme person Naráyana accompanied by Nara.

Holding the jewel placed in his enfolding hands, its faint light escaping through the gaps in his fingers, like the moon in a wispy ochre cloud, he bowed to the king, bending knee and head.

Rama saw hope in life as soon as he saw his wife's crest jewel *with a full circle of rays of immortality ⁝ like the orb of the full moon, heavy with jutting bright gems ⁝ rising bright, respectable as a gemstone.*

Holding it he gazed at it as if it where his very self, *its brightness dimmed ⁝ of diminished splendor, fresh from the forest ⁝ departed to the forest*, grimy with dust not yet wiped off, *come from Sita ⁝ bereft of Sita*, having *only its carat value ⁝ only dignity.*

10.35 «sāmarthya|saṃpādita|vāñchit'|ârthaś
cintā|maṇiḥ syān na kathaṃ Hanūmān?»
sa|Lakṣmaṇo bhūmi|patis tadānīṃ
śākhā|mṛg'|ânīka|patiś ca mene.

«yuśmān a|cetan kṣaya|vāyu|kalpān
Sītā|sphuliṅgaṃ parigṛhya jālmaḥ
Laṅkā|vanaṃ siṃha|samo 'dhiśete
martuṃ dviṣann» ity avadadd Hanūmān.

«ahṛta Dhaneśvarasya yudhi yaḥ
sameta|māyo dhanaṃ,
tam aham ito vilokya vibudhaiḥ
kṛt'|ôttam'|āyodhanam,
vibhava|madena nihnuta|hriy" â-
timātra|saṃpannakaṃ:
vyathayati sat|pathād adhigat" â-
tha v" êha saṃpan na kam.*

ṛddhimān rākṣaso mūḍhaś. citraṃ n' âsau yad uddhataḥ:
ko vā hetur an|āryāṇāṃ dharmye vartmani vartitum?*

tasy' âdhivāse tanur utsuk" âsau
dṛṣṭā mayā Rāma|patiḥ pramanyuḥ:
kāryasya sāro 'yam udīrito vaḥ,
proktena śeṣeṇa kim uddhatena?

10.40 samatāṃ śaśi|lekhay" ôpayāyād
avadātā pratanuḥ kṣayeṇa Sītā,
yadi nāma kalaṅka indu|lekhām
ativṛtto laghayen na c' âpi bhāvī.*

"How could Hánuman not appear to be my wish-granting 10.35
jewel, with his longed-for purpose achieved by his own power?" So thought at the time the king together with Lákshmana and the lord of the monkey forces.

"Not knowing that you are all like the wind of destruction, the reprobate who snatched the spark of fire Sita,* hostile, lies down like a lion to die in the grove at Lanka," said Hánuman.

"I have come here after seeing him who possessed of magic took in battle the wealth of Kubéra the lord of wealth, who made ultimate war with the gods, who is so very full of the madness of power that disowns shame. But after all, whom in this world does the arrival of wealth not cause to swerve from the right path?

A wealthy demon is a fool. It is no wonder that he is arrogant: what reason could there be for the ignoble to behave in a righteous manner?

I saw Rama's thin and anxious wife very sad in Rávana's dwelling. The essence of my actions has been related to you, what need is there to mention the rest of my roistering?

Immaculate Sita, so thin through waning, might become 10.40
like the digit moon if only no blemish—past or even future—did not already diminish the crescent moon.

a|parīkṣita|kāriṇā gṛhītāṃ
tvam, an|āsevita|vṛddha|paṇḍitena
a|virodhita|niṣṭhureṇa, sādhvīṃ
dayitāṃ trātum alaṃ ghaṭasva rājan.»*

sa ca *vihvala/sattva/saṃkulaḥ*
pariśuṣyann abhavan mahā|hradaḥ
paritaḥ *paritāpa/mūrchitaḥ*,
patitaṃ c' *âmbu* nirabhram īpsitam.*

atha Lakṣmaṇa|tulya|rūpa|veśaṃ,
gaman'|ādeśa|vinirgat'|âgra|hastam,
kapayo 'nuyayuḥ sametya Rāmaṃ,
nata|Sugrīva|gṛhīta|sādar'|ājñam.*

kapi|pṛṣṭha|gatau tato nar'|êndrau.
kapayaś ca jvalit'|âgni|piṅgal'|âkṣāḥ
mumucuḥ, prayayur, drutaṃ samīyur,
vasudhāṃ, vyoma, mahī|dharaṃ Mahendram,*

10.45 sthitam iva parirakṣituṃ samantād
udadhi|jal'|âugha|pariplavād dharitrīm,
gagana|tala|vasundhar"|ântarāle
jala|nidhi|vega|sahaṃ prasārya deham,*

viṣa|dhara|nilaye niviṣṭa|mūlaṃ,
śikhara|śataiḥ parimṛṣṭa|deva|lokam,
ghana|vipula|nitamba|pūrit'|āśaṃ
phala|kusum'|ācita|vṛkṣa|ramya|kuñjam,*

O king, you should exert yourself fully to protect your virtuous wife who has been snatched by one who does not consider his actions, who though he is learned has not served his elders and who is cruel though he has not been offended."

The great lake which was Rama *thronged with agitated creatures* ⁝ *was disturbed with his agitated spirits*, became *dried up* ⁝ *emaciated, thoroughly viscous with the intense heat* ⁝ *completely stupefied with intense suffering*, and then without clouds the longed-for *water* ⁝ *tears* fell.

The monkeys gathering round Rama followed him, in form and dress similar to Lákshmana, his forefinger held out in the command to go and whose respectful command was accepted with a bow by Sugríva.

Then the two lords of men set off on the monkey's back and the monkeys with their eyes red like blazing fires respectively left, traversed, and quickly came to the earth, the sky and Mount Mahéndra,

The mountain standing as if to protect the supporting earth 10.45
on all sides from the assault of the sea's waves, pushing up its body capable of withstanding the force of the ocean into the space between the vault of the sky and the earth,

With its roots entering the lair of the venom-bearing serpents, touching heaven with its hundreds of peaks, filling space with its solid broad flanks, its lovely bowers of trees filled with fruits and flowers,

madhu|kara|virutaiḥ priyā|dhvanīnāṃ
sarasi|ruhair dayit"|āsya|hāsya|lakṣmyāḥ
sphuṭam anuharamāṇam, ādadhānaṃ
puruṣa|pateḥ sahasā paraṃ|pramodam,*

graha|maṇi|rasanaṃ divo nitambaṃ
vipulam an|uttama|labdha|kānti|yogam
cyuta|ghana|vasanaṃ mano|'bhirāmaṃ
śikhara|karair madanād iva spṛśantam,*

pracapalam a|guruṃ bhar'|â|sahiṣṇuṃ
janam a|samānam an|ūrjitaṃ vivarjya,
kṛta|vasatim iv' ârṇav'|ôpakaṇṭhe
sthiram a|tul'|ônnatim ūḍha|tuṅga|megham,*

10.50 sphaṭhika|maṇi|gṛhaiḥ sa|ratna|dīpaiḥ
prataruṇa|kinnara|gīta|nisvanaiś ca,
amara|pura|matiṃ sur'|âṅganānāṃ
dadhatam a|duḥkham an|alpa|kalpa|vṛkṣam.*

atha dadṛśur udīrṇa|dhūma|dhūmrāṃ
diśam udadhi|vyavadhiṃ sameta|Sītām,
saha|Raghu|tanayāḥ plavaṅga|senāḥ
Pavanasut'|âṅguli|darśitām udakṣāḥ.*

jala|nidhim agaman Mahendra|kuñjāt
pracaya|tirohita|tigma|raśmi|bhāsaḥ,
salila|samudayair mahā|taraṅgair
bhuvana|bhara|kṣamam apy, a|bhinna|velam,

Clearly imitating the voice of his loved one with the humming of its bees, and the brilliance of the smile on her beloved face with its lotuses, suddenly imparting to the king the greatest joy,

As if in passion touching with the hands of its peaks the broad buttocks of the sky, with its jewel-girdle of planets, its union with beauty unsurpassed, its clothing of clouds slipped off, delighting the heart,

Shunning the lightweight unsteady people of the world who were unable to bear burdens, unequal and without strength, firm, seeming to make its residence beside the ocean, of unmatched height and bearing high clouds,

Making the *ápsaras*es think that it was the city of the im- 10.50
mortals with its crystal halls lit with jewels and its sounds of young *kínnara*s singing, free from sorrow and with many wish-granting trees.

Then the monkey army and the sons of Raghu with upraised eyes looked in the direction indicated by Hánuman's finger, cloudy with billowing smoke, separated by the ocean, where Sita had gone.

From the forests of Mahéndra, obscuring the light of the sun in their mass, they went to the ocean which though able to bear away the earth with its great floods of surging water, did not break its bounds,

pṛthu|guru|maṇi|śukti|garbha|bhāsā
glapita|rasātala|saṃbhṛt'|ândhakāram,
upahata|ravi|raśmi|vṛttim uccaiḥ
pralaghu|pariplavamāna|vajra|jālaiḥ,*

samupacita|jalaṃ vivardhamānair
a|mala|sarit|salilair vibhāvarīṣu,
sphuṭam avagamayantam ūḍha|vārīn
śaśadhara|ratna|mayān Mahendra|sānūn,*

10.55 bhuvana|bhara|sahān a|laṅghya|dhāmnaḥ
puru|ruci|ratna|bhṛto gur'|ûru|dehān
śrama|vidhura|vilīna|kūrma|nakrān
dadhatam udūḍha|bhuvo girīn ahīṃś ca.*

pradadṛśur uru|mukta|śīkar'|âughān
vimala|maṇi|dyuti|saṃbhṛt'|êndra|cāpān
jala|muca iva dhīra|mandra|ghoṣān
kṣiti|paritāpa|hṛto mahā|taraṅgān,*

vidruma|maṇi|kṛta|bhūṣā
muktā|phala|nikara|rañjit'|ātmānaḥ
babhur udaka|nāga|bhagnā
velā|taṭa|śikhariṇo yatra.*

«bhṛta|nikhila|rasā|talaḥ sa|ratnaḥ
śikhari|sam'|ōrmi|tirohit'|ântarīkṣaḥ
kuta iha param'|ârthato jal'|âugho?»
jala|nidhim īyur ataḥ sametya māyām.*

Which with the light of large heavy pearls from within oyster shells diminished the darkness concentrated in the underworld, and, high up, diffused the actions of the sun's rays with lattices of tiny floating diamonds,

With waters amassed from the pure waters of streams swelling up on the bright nights of the full moon, clearly showing that the ridges of Mount Mahéndra bear water and consist of moonstones,

Containing the earth-bearing mountains and serpents quite 10.55
up to the burden of the world, they of unsurpassable power, who, bearing abundant brilliant gems, their bodies broad and weighty, concealed tortoises and crocodiles helpless with exhaustion.

They beheld the huge waves like water-loosing clouds, releasing great fountains of spray, with rainbows produced by the light of faultless gems, with deep pleasant roars, relieving the earth of its great heat,

Where the shore and the mountains respectively appeared to have been lit up with coral and with gems, their bodies tinted with pearls and with fruits, and broken up by water and by elephants.

Then reaching the ocean they thought it an illusion: "Could this mass of water here really exist, pervading the entire underworld, filled with jewels and occluding the sky with its mountainous waves?

śaśi|rahitam api prabhūta|kāntiṃ,
vibudha|hṛta|śriyam apy a|naṣṭa|śobham,
mathitam api surair divaṃ jal'|âughaiḥ
samabhibhavantam, a|vikṣata|prabhāvam,*

10.60 kṣiti|kula|giri|śeṣa|dig|gajendrān
salila|gatām iva nāvam udvahantam,
dhṛta|vidhura|dharaṃ mahā|varāhaṃ
giri|guru|potram ap' īhitair jayantam,*

giri|parigata|cañcal'|âpag'|ântaṃ,
jala|nivahaṃ dadhataṃ mano|'bhirāmam,
galitam iva bhuvo vilokya Rāmaṃ
dharaṇi|dhara|stana|śukla|cīna|paṭṭam.*

a|parimita|mah"|âdbhutair vicitraś
cyuta|malinaḥ śucibhir mahān a|laṅghyaiḥ
taru|mṛga|pati|Lakṣmaṇa|kṣitīndraiḥ
samadhigato jala|dhiḥ paraṃ babhāse.*

na bhavati mahimā vinā vipatter
avagamayann iva paśyataḥ, payo|dhiḥ
a|viratam abhavat kṣaṇe kṣaṇe 'sau
śikhari|pṛthu|prathita|praśānta|vīciḥ.*

mṛdubhir api bibheda puṣpa|bāṇaiś,
cala|śiśirair api mārutair dadāha,
Raghu|tanayam an|artha|paṇḍito 'sau,
na ca Madanaḥ kṣatam ātatāna, n' ârciḥ.*

Although it is without the moon it abounds in luster, although Lakshmi has been snatched by the gods its beauty is undiminished, although churned by the demons it excels the sky with its masses of water. Its prowess is undiminished,

Bearing the earth, the mountain ranges, the primeval ser- 10.60
pent Shesha and the great elephants of the quarters like a ship at sea, outdoing with its motions the great boar who supported the troubled world despite having a snout heavy as a mountain,

Holding a delightful mass of water, the ends of which were the swirling rivers winding round the mountains, which on seeing Rama had seemed to slip down from the earth as a white silken garment from those breasts of the earth, the mountains.

When the lord of monkeys, Lákshmana and Rama, lord of the earth, incomparable great prodigies, pure and unsurpassable, came to the multi-colored, pure and great ocean, it shone supremely.

As if conveying to them as they watched that there is no greatness without downfall, the ocean continually had its broad, extended, mountainous waves calmed, moment by moment.

The love god, expert at mischief, pierced Rama with his flower arrows though they were soft, he burned him with his breezes though they were fickle and cool, and yet he made no wound nor used a flame.

10.65 atha mṛdu|malina|prabhau din'|ânte
jaladhi|samīpa|gatāv, atīta|lokau,
anukṛtim itar'|êtarasya mūrtyor
dina|kara|Rāghava|nandanāv akārṣṭām.*

apaharad iva sarvato vinodān,
dayita|gataṃ dadhad ekadhā samādhim,
ghana|ruci vavṛdhe tato 'ndhakāraṃ
saha Raghunandana|manmath'|ôdayena.*

adhi|jaladhi tamaḥ kṣipan himāṃśuḥ
paridadṛśe 'tha, dṛśāṃ kṛt'|âvakāśaḥ,
vidadhad iva jagat punaḥ pralīnam:
bhavati mahān hi par'|ârtha eva sarvaḥ.*

«aśanir ayam asau, kuto nirabhre?
śita|śara|varṣam a|sat tad apy a|śārṅgam,»
iti madana|vaśo muhuḥ śaś'|âṅke
Raghu|tanayo, na ca niścikāya candram.*

kumuda|vana|cayeṣu kīrṇa|raśmiḥ,
kṣata|timireśu ca dig|vadhū|mukheṣu,
viyati ca vilalāsa tadvad indur,
vilasati candramaso na yadvad anyaḥ.*

10.70 śaraṇam iva gataṃ tamo nikuñje
viṭapi|nirākṛta|candra|raśmy|arātau;
pṛthu|viṣama|śil"|ântarāla|saṃsthaṃ
sa|jala|ghana|dyuti bhītavat sasāda.*

The sun and Rama, their light soft and dim at dusk as they came to the ocean, their own realms abandoned, imitated of each others' forms. 10.65

Then as if completely removing distractions, allowing him to concentrate wholly on his dear-departed, the cloudy darkness waxed along with Rama's longing.

Then the moon appeared over the clouds dispelling darkness, creating a chance to see, seeming to make anew the occluded world: for all great ones exist for the benefit of others.

"This surely is lightning, but whence in a cloudless sky? There cannot be a shower of sharp arrows in the absence of a bow." So thought Rama momentarily overwhelmed by passion in the presence of the moon and he yet could not conclude that it was the moon.

Strewing its rays on the lotus clusters, and on the faces of those damsels the quarters whose darkness was driven away, and through the sky, the moon shone as none other than the moon can shine.

The darkness with its rain-cloud hue went as if for shelter into a grove where the trees kept its enemies the moonbeams at bay; it settled as if fearful into the fissures on the great rough rocks. 10.70

atha nayana|mano|haro 'bhirāmaḥ
Smara iva, citta|bhavo 'py a|vāma|śīlaḥ,
Raghu|sutam anujo jagāda vācaṃ
sa|jala|ghana|stanayitnu|tulya|ghoṣaḥ:*

«pati|vadha|parilupta|lola|keśīr,
nayana|jal'|âpahṛt'|âñjan'|âuṣṭha|rāgāḥ,
kuru ripu|vanitā, jahīhi śokaṃ:
kva ca śaraṇaṃ jagatāṃ bhavān, kva mohaḥ?*

adhigata|mahimā manuṣya|loke
vata sutarām avasīdati pramādī:
gaja|patir, uru|śaila|śṛṅga|varṣmā,
gurur, avamajjati paṅka|bhāṅ, na dāru.*

boddhavyaṃ kim iva hi, yat tvayā na buddhaṃ?
kiṃ vā te nimiṣitam apy a|buddhi|pūrvam?
labdh'|ātmā tava su|kṛtair an|iṣṭa|śaṅkī
sneh'|âugho ghaṭayati māṃ tath" âpi vaktum.»

10.75 Saumitrer iti vacanaṃ niśamya Rāmo
jṛmbhāvān bhuja|yugalaṃ vibhajya nidrān
adhyaṣṭhāc chiśayiṣayā pravāla|talpaṃ
rakṣāyai prati|diśam ādiśan plavaṅgān.

Then his younger brother, delightful to the eye and lovely like the love god, though in his heart not so perverse, spoke words to Rama with a sound like the thunder of a storm cloud:

"Make your enemy's wives cut off their flowing hair because of their husband's death, make them wash off their collyrium and lip gloss with their tears. Abandon grief. When you are the refuge of the people what place has bewilderment?

Alas one who has become great in the world of men falls hardest if he is careless: does not the lord of elephants unlike a tree, be his stature like a broad mountain peak, being heavy sink down when caught in the mud.

What is there to understand which you have not understood? Do you even blink without forethought? I am compelled to speak by the force of my love which has taken your soul to itself, through your good deeds, and which fears a dire outcome."

After hearing Lákshmana's words, Rama yawning sleepily 10.75
stretched out his arms and seeking repose got on his bed of fronds, and gave orders to the monkeys to protect every quarter.

CANTO 11
LANKA

11.1 ATH' ÂSTAM ĀSEDUṢI manda|kāntau
puṇya|kṣayeṇ' êva nidhau kalānām,
samālalambe ripu|mitra|kalpaiḥ
padmaiḥ prahāsaḥ kumudair viṣādaḥ.*

dūraṃ samāruhya divaḥ patantaṃ
bhṛgor iv'ênduṃ vihit'|ôpakāram,
baddh'|ânurāgo 'nupapāta tūrṇaṃ
tārā|gaṇaḥ saṃbhṛta|śubhra|kīrtiḥ.

«kva te kaṭ'|âkṣāḥ, kva vilāsavanti
proktāni vā tāni mam'?» êti matvā
Laṅk'|âṅganānām avabodha|kāle
tulām an|āruhya gato 'stam induḥ.

mānena talpeṣv a|yathā|mukhīnā
mithyā|prasuptair gamita|tri|yāmāḥ
strībhir, niś"|âtikrama|vihvalābhir,
dṛṣṭe 'pi doṣe patayo 'nunītāḥ.

11.5 īrṣyā|virugṇāḥ sthira|baddha|mūlā,
nirasta|niḥśeṣa|śubha|pratānāḥ,
āpyāyitā netra|jala|prasekaiḥ
prema|drumāḥ saṃruruhuḥ priyāṇām.

tataḥ samāśaṅkita|viprayogaḥ
punar navībhūta|raso '|vitṛṣṇaḥ
smarasya santaṃ punar ukta|bhāvaṃ
n' āvartamānasya viveda lokaḥ.

THEN WHEN THE moon of gentle light was sinking to its setting as if its merits were exhausted, the day lotuses smiled open as its enemies and the night lotuses desponded as its friends. 11.1

With feelings of affection for the moon which had rendered them a service by ascending far into the sky and was now falling as if from a cliff, the host of stars bearing their bright glory plunged quickly after it.

Thinking, "Where are those sidelong glances and where my flirtatious banter?" the moon, failing to reach compare with the beauties of Lanka, set at the time of their awakening.

The husbands who had passed three watches of the night in feigned sleep with faces turned away in pique were conciliated by their wives, distressed at the passing of the night, even though their faults had been found out.

The trees of their love, torn apart by jealousy, their pleas- 11.5
ing shoots completely removed, but bound firmly by their roots, they regenerated, nourished by showers of tears from their women.

Then the people afraid of separation, their passion renewed again, their avidity remaining, did not notice the recurrence of the roaming love god.

vṛttau prakāśaṃ hṛdaye kṛtāyāṃ
  sukhena sarv'|êndriya|saṃbhavena,
saṃkocam ev' â|sahamānam asthād
  a|śaktavad vañcita|māni cakṣuḥ.

pīne bhaṭasy' ôrasi vīkṣya bhugnāṃs
  tanu|tvacaḥ pāṇi|ruhān su|madhyā,
icchā|vibhaṅg'|ākula|mānasatvād
  bhartre nakhebhyaś ca ciraṃ jujūre.

srast'|âṅga|ceṣṭo vinimīlit'|âkṣaḥ,
  sved'|âmbu|rom'|ôdgama|gamya|jīvaḥ,
a|śeṣa|naṣṭa|pratibhā|paṭutvo
  gāḍh'|ôpagūḍho dayitair jano 'bhūt.

11.10 tamaḥ prasuptaṃ maraṇaṃ
  sukhaṃ nu mūrcchā nu māyā nu mano|bhavasya,
kiṃ tat kathaṃ v" êty upalabdha|saṃjñā
  vikalpayanto 'pi na saṃpratīyuḥ.

vakṣaḥ stanābhyāṃ, sukham ānanena,
  gātrāṇi gātrair ghaṭayann a|mandam,
smar'|âturo n' âiva tutoṣa lokaḥ:
  paryāptatā premṇi kuto viruddhā?

srast'|âṅga|yaṣṭiḥ parirabhyamāṇā,
  saṃdṛśyamān" âpy upasaṃhṛt'|âkṣī,
an|ūḍhamānā śayane nav'|ōḍhā,
  par'|ôpakār'|âika|ras" âiva tasthau.

When the condition produced in the heart by the pleasure that arose from all the senses made itself known, the eye thinking itself cheated remained closed as if incapable, unable to bear it.

A slender-waisted girl seeing her delicate fingernails broken on the stout chest of her lover, her mind troubled by her thwarted desire, was angry for a long time at her lover and at her nails.

The women tightly embraced by their husbands lost movement in their limbs, their eyes closed, their life was inferable only from the appearance of sweat and upraised hairs, their sharpness of mind was completely lost.

Even though they wondered if and how it could have been 11.10
darkness or sleep or death or happiness or a swoon or some spell of the love god, when the men also regained consciousness they could not come to a conclusion.

Urgently clasping chest to breast, mouth to mouth, limb to limb, the lovesick world is never satisfied; why is fulfillment in love forbidden?

The new bride, her slender form relaxed as she is embraced, though when looked at her glance is withheld, bashful she stays on the bed, her one desire to please her other.

āliṅgitāyāḥ sahasā, trapāvāṃs
  trās'|âbhilāṣ'|ânugato rat'|ādau,
viśvāsitāyā ramaṇena vadhvā
  vimarda|ramyo madano babhūva.

sām'|ônmukhen' ācchuritā priyeṇa,
  datte 'tha kā cit pulakena bhede,
antaḥ|prakop'|âpagamād vilolā,
  vaśī|kṛtā kevala|vikrameṇa.

11.15 gurur dadhānā paruṣatvam anyā,
  kānt" âpi, kānt'|êndu|kar'|âbhimṛṣṭā,
prahlāditā candra|śil" êva tūrṇaṃ
  kṣobhāt sravat|sveda|jalā babhūva.

śaśāṅka|nāth'|âpagamena dhūmrāṃ
  mūrcchā|parītām iva nir|vivekām
tataḥ sakh" îva prathit'|ânurāgā
  prābodhayad dyāṃ madhur'|âruṇa|śrīḥ.

a|vīta|tṛṣṇo 'tha parasparena,
  kṣaṇād iv' āyāta|niś"|âvasānaḥ
duḥkhena lokaḥ paravān iv' āgāt
  samutsukaḥ svapna|niketanebhyaḥ.

ardh'|ôtthit'|āliṅgita|sannimagno,
  ruddhaḥ punar yān gamane 'n|abhīpsuḥ,
vyājena niryāya punar nivṛttas,
  tyakt'|ânya|kāryaḥ sthita eva kaś cit.

For a woman suddenly embraced, love is shy at the beginning of lovemaking, attended by both fear and desire, but as she gains confidence from her lover it becomes a delightful friction.

One woman, being nail-scratched by her lover eager for her compliance, giving quarter by the bristling of her hairs, uncertain at the departure of her inner resistance, was taken by force alone.

Another, heavy of limb, showing some reluctance, though 11.15
lovely, being caressed by the bright rays of the moon became thrilled, quickly becoming like a moonstone, sweat streaming from her as she came.

Then the sweet beauty of the dawn spreading its redness awoke the sky, dark at the departure of its lord the moon as if sunk in a stupor and indistinguishable, like a female friend showing affection and awakening one gloomy at the departure of her lord and the moon, fainting and unable to distinguish things.

Then some with their desire for one another undiminished, with the end of the night come as if in an instant, came reluctantly out of their sleeping quarters still full of longing as if under the sway of the other.

Half risen then embraced and sunk down again, obstructed again when going and not wishing to go, leaving and again coming back on a pretext, with his other business abandoned he stays.

tālena saṃpādita|sāmya|śobhaṃ,
  śubh'|âvadhānaṃ svara|baddha|rāgam,
padair gat'|ârthaṃ, nṛpa|mandireṣu
  prātar jagur maṅgalavat taruṇyaḥ.

11.20 dur|uttare paṅka iv' ândha|kāre
  magnaṃ jagat, santata|raśmi|rajjuḥ,
pranaṣṭa|mūrti|pravibhāgam, udyan
  pratyujjahār' êva tato vivasvān.

pīt'|âuṣṭha|rāgāṇi hṛt'|âñjanāni
  bhāsvanti lolair alakair mukhāni,
prātaḥ kṛt'|ârthāni yathā
  virejus tathā na pūrve|dyur alaṃ|kṛtāni.

prajāgar'|ātāmra|vilocan'|āntā,
  nirañjan'|âlaktaka|patra|lekhāḥ,
tulyā iv' āsan parikheda|tanvyo
  vāsa|cyutāḥ sevita|manmathābhiḥ.

ābaddha|netr'|âñjana|paṅka|leśas,
  tāmbūla|rāgaṃ bahulaṃ dadhānaḥ,
cakāra kānto 'py adharo 'ṅganānāṃ
  sah'|ôṣitānāṃ patibhir laghutvam.

cakṣūṃṣi kāntāny api s'|âñjanāni
  tāmbūla|raktaṃ ca sa|rāgam oṣṭham
kurvan sa|vāsaṃ ca sugandhi vaktraṃ
  cakre janaḥ kevala|pakṣa|pātam.

Early in the morn the young women sang an auspicious song in the royal chambers, the beauty of the harmony brought about by the beat, the melody kept by the notes with fine attention, the meaning conveyed by the words.

When the world with its shapes indistinguishable was sunk 11.20
in darkness like cloying mud, the sun rising up with its ropes of rays extended drew it up and out.

The women's faces with the red of their lips drunk by their lovers, their kohl gone, shone with their disheveled hair. As their desires had been satisfied that morning they glowed as they had not done the previous day in their make-up.

With the corners of their eyes red with wakefulness, without kohl or cochineal or beauty marks, slender with fatigue, those women betrayed by their partners resembled those who had served the god of love.

Those ladies who had lain with their husbands had lower lips which, though lovely, bore the abundant redness of betel and small smears of kohl from their lovers' eyes, and were diminished thereby

The women putting kohl on already lovely eyes, reddening their lips with betel, though red already, and adding perfume to already sweet-scented mouths merely revealed their inclination.

11.25 kṣatair a|saṃcetita|danta|labdhaiḥ
saṃbhoga|kāle 'vagataiḥ prabhāte
aśaṅkat' ânyonya|kṛtaṃ vyalīkaṃ,
viyoga|bāhyo 'pi jano 'tirāgāt.

netr'|êṣubhiḥ saṃyuta|pakṣma|patraiḥ
karṇ'|ânta|kṛṣṭair, uru|keśa|śūlāḥ,
stan'|ōru|cakrās, tata|karṇa|pāśāḥ,
strī|yoddha|mukhyā jayino viceruḥ.

payo|dharāṃś candana|paṅka|digdhān
vāsāṃsi c' â|mṛṣṭa|mṛjāni dṛṣṭvā
strīṇāṃ sa|patnyo jahṛṣuḥ prabhāte
mandāyamān'|ânuśayair manobhiḥ.

smar'|āture cetasi labdha|janmā
rarāja, lolo 'pi guṇ'|âpahāryaḥ,
kutūhalān netra|gav'|âkṣa|saṃsthaḥ
paśyann iv' ânyonya|mukhāni rāgaḥ.

gate 'tibhūmiṃ praṇaye prayuktān
a|buddhi|pūrvaṃ, parilupta|saṃjñaḥ
ātm'|ânubhūtān api n' ôpacārān
smar'|āturaḥ saṃsmarati sma lokaḥ.

11.30 vastrair an|atyulbaṇa|ramya|varṇair,
vilepanaiḥ saurabha|lakṣmaṇīyaiḥ,
āsyaiś ca lokaḥ paritoṣa|kāntair
asūcayal labdha|padaṃ rahasyam.

With bite marks got unnoticed at the time of love-making but discovered in the morning they suspected each other of cheating, though because of their excessive passion there could have been no question of separation. 11.25

The foremost warrior women with spears in the form of long hair, broad discuses of breasts and snares of stretched ears advanced victorious, their eye-arrows drawn back to the tips of their ears with eyelashes attached for flights.

In the morning the co-wives of some women seeing their breasts still smeared with sandal paste and their clothes fresh without stain rejoiced with hearts less emulous.

Though it was fickle because removable by some other quality, the passion that found birth in lovelorn hearts shone forth and from curiosity established itself in the windows of their eyes as if looking at each others' faces.

The lovelorn did not remember actions which they themselves, bereft of consciousness, had experienced as they engaged in them without forethought when passion was at its height.

With scanty and colorful clothing, with unguents noticeable by their fragrance and with faces glowing with satisfaction, people showed that that secret state had been reached. 11.30

prātastarāṃ candana|lipta|gātrāḥ,
  pracchādya hastair adharān vadantaḥ,
śāmyan|nimeṣāḥ, sutarāṃ yuvānaḥ
  prakāśayanti sma nigūhanīyam.

«sāmn" âiva loke vijite 'pi vāme,
  kim udyataṃ bhrū|dhanur a|prasahyam?
hantuṃ kṣamo vā vada locan'|êṣur
  digdho viṣeṇ' êva: kim añjanena?»

«danta|cchade prajvalit'|âgni|kalpe
  tāmbūla|rāgas tṛṇa|bhāra|tulyaḥ
nyastaḥ kim?» ity ūcur upeta|bhāvā
  goṣṭhīṣu nārīs taruṇīr yuvānaḥ.

sukh'|âvagāhāni yutāni lakṣmyā
  śucīni saṃtāpa|harāṇy urūṇi
prabuddha|nārī|mukha|paṅkajāni
  prātaḥ sarāṃs' îva gṛhāṇi rejuḥ.

11.35 saṃmṛṣṭa|sikt'|ârcita|cāru|puṣpair
  āmodavad|dravya|sugandha|bhāgaiḥ
lakṣmīr* vijigye bhavanaiḥ sa|bhṛṅgaiḥ
  sevyasya devair api nandanasya.

akṣṇoḥ patan nīla|saroja|lobhād
  bhṛṅgaḥ, kareṇ' âlpa|dhiyā nirastaḥ,
dadaṃśa tāmr'|âmbu|ruh'|âbhisandhis
  tṛṣṇ"|āturaḥ* pāṇi|tale 'pi dhṛṣṇuḥ.

Still earlier the youths with their limbs* smeared with sandal, hiding their lips with their hands as they spoke, restraining their blinking, showed more clearly that which ought to be hidden.

"When the world has been conquered merely by your serenity, my beauty, why has your unendurable brow-bow been raised? Surely your eye-arrow is as lethal as if smeared with poison, tell me, what need is there for kohl?"

In the meeting places the young men roused to passion asked the slender girls: "Why put on the worthless red of betel when the coverings of your teeth are already like a blazing fire?"

In the morning the houses whose lotuses were the mouths of women just woken, shone like lakes pleasant to plunge into, furnished with beauty, clean, cool and extensive.

The beauty of even Indra's garden attended by the gods 11.35
was outdone by the mansions, with their bees and beautiful flowers wiped and watered and honored, and with places scented with fragrant objects.

A bold bee flying to her eyes in its longing for a dark lotus, brushed off thoughtlessly with her hand, tormented by thirst, thinking it was a red lotus, stung her on the palm of her hand.

vilolatāṃ cakṣuṣi, hasta|vepathuṃ,
 bhruvor vibhaṅgaṃ, stana|yugma|valgitam,
vibhūṣaṇānāṃ kvaṇitaṃ ca ṣaṭ|pado
 gurur yathā nṛtya|vidhau samādadhe.

ath' ânukūlān kula|dharma|saṃpado
 vidhāya veśān su|divaḥ purī|janaḥ.
prabodha|kāle Śatamanyu|vidviṣaḥ
 pracakrame rāja|niketanaṃ prati.

śail'|êndra|śṛṅgebhya iva pravṛttā
 vegāj jal'|âughāḥ pura|mandirebhyaḥ
āpūrya rathyāḥ sarito jan'|âughā
 rāj'|âṅgan'|âmbhodhim apūrayanta.

11.40 prabodha|kālāt tridaś'|êndra|śatroḥ
 prāg ūrdhva|śoṣaṃ,* pariśuṣyamāṇāḥ,
hīnā mahāntaś ca samatvam īyur,
 dvās|sthair avajñā|puruṣ'|âkṣi|dṛṣṭāḥ.

gur'|ûru|cañcat|kara|karṇa|jihvair,
 avajñay" âgr'|âṅguli|saṃgṛhītaiḥ,
rakṣāṃsy an|āyāsa|hṛtair upāsthuḥ,
 kapola|līn'|âli|kulair gaj'|êndraiḥ.

nikṛtta|matta|dvipa|kumbha|māṃsaiḥ
 saṃpṛkta|muktair harayo 'gra|pādaiḥ
āninyire śreṇi|kṛtās tath" ânyaiḥ
 parasparaṃ vāladhi|sannibaddhāḥ.

The bee like a teacher in a dancing lesson made her eyes roll, her hand wave, her brows bend, her breasts heave and her ornaments jangle.

Then the people of Lanka for whom the day was auspicious put on attire in keeping with their family, their position and their wealth and made their way towards the palace at the time when the enemy of Indra was waking up.

As streams of water swiftly flowing from great mountain peaks fill the rivers, so the masses of people filling the streets from the houses of the town filled the ocean that was the king's courtyards.

Before the enemy of the lord of the thirty gods woke up, 11.40
both the high and the low becoming more and more thirsty, drying up completely, became one and the same, watched with the harsh eye of disapproval by the gatekeepers.

Demons honored him with great elephants whose huge broad trunks, ears and tongues waved to and fro, led disdainfully by the tip of a finger, driven without care, on whose cheeks clung swarms of bees.*

Others brought lions arranged in lines, bound one to another by their tails, with pearls stuck between their front toes which had torn the flesh from the temples of musth elephants.

upekṣitā deva|gaṇais trasadbhir
niśā|carair vīta|bhayair nikṛttāḥ,
tasminn adṛśyanta sura|drumāṇāṃ
sa|jāla|puṣpa|stabakāḥ prakīrṇāḥ.

nirākariṣṇur dvija|kuñjarāṇāṃ,
tṛṇīkṛt'|âśeṣa|guṇo 'timohāt,
pāp'|âśayān abhyuday'|ârtham ārcīt
prāg brahma|rakṣaḥ|pravarān Daśāsyaḥ.

11.45 māyāvibhis trāsa|karair janānām
āptair upādāna|parair upetaḥ,
satāṃ vighāt'|âika|rasair, avikṣat
sadaḥ parikṣobhita|bhūmi|bhāgam.

vidhṛta|niśita|śastrais tad yutaṃ yātu|dhānair,
uru|jaṭhara|mukhībhiḥ saṃkulaṃ rākṣasībhiḥ,
śva|gaṇi|śata|vikīrṇaṃ vāgurāvan mṛgībhir
vanam iva sa|bhayābhir deva|bandībhir āsīt.

jalada iva taḍitvān prājya|ratna|prabhābhiḥ,
prati|kakubham udasyan nisvanaṃ dhīra|mandram,
śikharam iva Sumeror āsanaṃ haimam uccair
vividha|maṇi|vicitraṃ pronnataṃ so 'dhyatiṣṭhat.

Cared for by fearful groups of gods but cut by fearless demons, flowers and buds in clusters from sacred trees were seen scattered there.

Rávana, rejecting the most eminent of the twiceborn, in his great delusion holding all their virtues as straw, for the sake of his own aggrandizement first honored the evil-hearted leaders of the brahmin demons.

Accompanied by attendants with magical powers, who were 11.45
terrifying to men, whose chief object was gain and whose one delight was harming the good, he suddenly entered, shaking that portion of the earth.

It was filled with demons wielding sharpened weapons, thronged with demonesses with huge bellies and mouths, and with fearful goddess prisoners, like a forest of does full of traps and strewn with hundreds of hunters.

Throwing out a steady low sound in all directions, like a thundering rain cloud with many jewel-like flashes, he ascended to a golden throne raised high, inlaid with manifold gems like the peak of Suméru.

CANTO 12
THE DEFECTION OF VIBHÍSHANA

12.1 TATO VI|NIDRAM kṛta|devat"|ârcaṃ,
drṣṭy" âiva citta|praśamaṃ kirantam,
āviṣkṛt'|âṅga|pratikarma|ramyaṃ,
Vibhīṣaṇaṃ vācam uvāca mātā:

«prabādhamānasya jaganti dhīmaṃs,
tvaṃ sodarasy' âtimad'|ôddhatasya
ānandano nāka|sadāṃ praśāntiṃ
tūrṇaṃ, viṣasy' âmṛtavat* kuruṣva.

kuryās tathā, yena jahāti Sītāṃ
viṣāda|nīhāra|parīta|mūrtim,
sthitāṃ kṣitau śānta|śikhā|pratānāṃ
tārām iva, trāsa|karīṃ janasya.

yāvan na saṃtrāsita|deva|saṃghaḥ
piṇḍo viṣasy' êva Hareṇa bhīṣmaḥ
saṃgrasyate 'sau puruṣ'|âdhipena,
drutaṃ kul'|ānanda, yatasva tāvat.

12.5 hatā Janasthāna|sado nikāyāḥ;
kṛtā jit'|ôtkhāta|bhaṭa|drumā pūḥ;
sadāṃsi dagdhāni: vidheyam asmin
yad bandhunā, tad ghaṭayasva tasmin.»

cikīrṣite pūrvataraṃ sa tasmin,
kṣemaṃ|kare 'rthe muhur īryamāṇaḥ
mātr" âtimātraṃ śubhay" âiva buddhyā,
ciraṃ su|dhīr abhyadhikaṃ samādhāt.

Now to Vibhíshana who had woken up and performed his worship of the deities, who with a mere glance displayed the calmness of his heart, and who was a delight in his display of bodily decoration, his mother spoke these words: 12.1

"O wise one, you are the delight of the gods. You must quickly neutralize your brother who oppresses the worlds and who is swollen up with pride, just as nectar neutralizes poison.

You should act in such a way that he lets go Sita whose being is enveloped in a fog of despair, who stands on the soil of the earth with the braids of her hair dulled like a star fallen to earth, the diffusion of its rays dimmed, frightening the people.

Rávana who frightens the host of gods has not yet been swallowed up by Rama the king of men, as the terrible mouthful of poison was by Shiva. Therefore you should act quickly, O joy of your family.

The host of demons that lived in the Jana·sthana forest has 12.5
been killed; in the city the mercenaries are defeated and the trees uprooted; the houses have been burned: you should do your kindred duty in this matter.

When his mother with incredibly sound sense urged him repeatedly and vehemently to this peace-making purpose which he had even before wished to achieve, the wise Vibhíshana considered it long and deep.

dauvārik'|âbhyāhata|Śakra|dūtaṃ,
s'|ôpāyan'|ôpasthita|loka|pālam,
s'|āśaṅka|bhīṣm'|āpta|viśan|niśāṭaṃ,
dvāraṃ yayau Rāvaṇa|mandirasya.

dūrāt pratīhāra|nataḥ sa vārtāṃ
pṛcchann an|āvedita|sampraviṣṭaḥ,
sa|gauravaṃ datta|patho niśāṭair,
aikṣiṣṭa śail'|âgram iv' Êndra|śatrum,

kṛśānu|varṣmaṇy, adhirūḍham uccaiḥ
siṃh'|āsane, saṃkṣaya|megha|bhīmam,
nisarga|tīkṣṇaṃ, nayana|sphuliṅgaṃ,
yug'|ânta|vahner iva dhūma|rāśim,

12.10 prīty" âpi datt'|ēkṣaṇa|sannipātaṃ
bhayaṃ bhujaṅg'|âdhipavad dadhānam;
tamaḥ|samūh'|ākṛtim apy a|śeṣān
ūrjā jayantaṃ prathita|prakāśān.

taṃ ratna|dāyaṃ jita|mṛtyu|lokā
rātriṃ|carāḥ kānti|bhṛto 'nvasarpan
pramukta|muktāphalam ambu|vāhaṃ
saṃjāta|tṛṣṇā iva deva|mukhyāḥ.

sa kiṅkaraiḥ kalpitam iṅgita|jñaiḥ
saṃbādhakaṃ pūrva|samāgatānām
siṃh'|āsan'|ôpāśrita|cāru|bāhur
adhyāsta pīṭhaṃ vihita|praṇāmaḥ.

He went to the door of Rávana's palace where Indra's messengers had been struck down by the doormen, where the world guardians approached with gifts and wherein entering even the demons felt fear and terror.

The guards bowed to him from afar and he entered unannounced asking for news, he was respectfully given way by the demons. He saw Indra's enemy like a mountain peak,

Mounted high on a lion's throne, its form like fire, terrible like a cloud at the uncreation, harsh of nature, his eyes of sparks, like a mass of smoke from the fire at the end of the eon,

Whose glance encountered, even when given with affec- 12.10
tion, caused fear as if he were the king of the snakes. Even though his form was a mass of darkness, with his power he outdid anyone else who showed any light.

The lustrous demons who had conquered the mortal world followed him as the jewel-giver, just as the foremost of the gods, their thirst provoked, followed the cloud whose fruit was showers of pearls.

Vibhíshana who had made his obeisance, sat with his beautiful arms resting on the throne, on a seat brought by servants who understood Rávana's gestures, causing those who had come before to press back.

tato Daśāsyaḥ kṣubhit'|âhi|kalpaṃ
dīpr'|âṅgulīy'|ôpalam ūḍha|ratnam,
aneka|cañcan|nakha|kānti|jihvaṃ
prasārya pāṇiṃ, samitiṃ babhāṣe:

«śaktaiḥ suhṛdbhiḥ paridṛṣṭa|kāryair,
āmnātibhir nītiṣu, buddhimadbhiḥ
yuṣmad|vidhaiḥ sārdham upāya|vidbhiḥ,
sidhyanti kāryāṇi su|mantritāni.

12.15 upekṣite Vāli|Khar'|ādi|nāśe,
dagdhe pure, 'kṣe nihate sa|bhṛtye,
sainye dviṣāṃ sāgaram uttitīrṣāv,
anantaraṃ brūta yad atra yuktam.»

bhuj'|âṃsa|vakṣaḥ|sthala|kārmuk'|âsīn
gadāś ca śūlāni ca, yātu|dhānāḥ
parāmṛśantaḥ prathit'|âbhimānāḥ
procuḥ Prahasta|pramukhā Daśāsyam:

«a|khaṇḍya|mānaṃ parikhaṇḍya Śakraṃ
tvaṃ paṇḍitaṃ|manyam, udīrṇa|daṇḍaḥ,
nar'|âbhiyogaṃ nṛ|bhujāṃ pradhāna,
mantr'|ônmukhaḥ kiṃ nayase gurutvam?

niryat|sphuliṅg'|ākula|dhūma|rāśiṃ
kiṃ brūhi bhūmau pinaṣāma bhānum?
ā danta|niṣpīḍita|pītam induṃ
ṣṭhīvāma śuṣk'|êkṣu|lat"|âsthi|kalpam?

Then Rávana stretched forth his hand with jewels flashing on its fingers, in form like an enraged cobra laden with gems with many bright tongues in the form of his nails, and spoke to the assembly:

"Actions succeed which are well-advised by able friends who have given careful consideration to duty, who are versed in statecraft, who are intelligent such as yourselves and also who have knowledge of the right means.

The deaths of Valin, Khara and others have been disre- 12.15
garded, the city has been burned, Aksha and his attendants have been killed and the army of the enemy is about to cross over the ocean. Tell me immediately what is meet here."

Touching their arms, chests, bows and swords and their clubs and spears, the demons headed by Prahásta showed their respect to Rávana and said:

"O foremost of the eaters of men, whose staff is respected, having crushed Indra whose pride is unbreakable and who reckons himself wise, why do you who incline to counsel attribute such importance to a conflict with a man?

Tell us, shall we crush the sun upon the earth so that it emits a mass of smoke shot through with sparks? When the moon has been sucked after being crushed by our teeth shall we spew it out like a husk of drained sugar cane?

sa|Rāghavaiḥ kiṃ bata vānarais tair
  yaiḥ prātar|āśo 'pi na kasya cin naḥ?
sa|Sthāṇu|Kailāsa|dhar' âbhidhatsva,
  kiṃ dyaur adho 'stu, kṣitir antarīkṣe?

12.20 cāpalya|yuktasya hareḥ kṛśānuḥ
  samedhito vāladhi|bhāk tvadīyaiḥ
śastreṇa vadhyasya galann adhākṣīd
  rājan, pramādena nijena Laṅkām.»

ath' âñcit'|ôraskam udīrṇa|dṛṣṭiḥ
  kṛtvā vivakṣā|pravaṇaṃ śarīram
vivṛtta|pāṇir vihit'|ôttar'|ârthaṃ
  Vibhīṣaṇo 'bhāṣata yātu|dhānān:

«yuddhāya rājñā su|bhṛtair bhavadbhiḥ
  saṃbhāvanāyāḥ sadṛśaṃ yad uktam:
tat prāṇa|paṇyair vacanīyam eva,
  prajñā tu mantre 'dhikṛtā, na śauryam.

yac c' âpi yatn'|ādṛta|mantra|vṛttir
  gurutvam āyāti nar'|âbhiyogaḥ
vaśī|kṛt'|Êndrasya, kṛt'|ôttaro 'smin
  vidhvaṃsit'|âśeṣa|puro Hanūmān.

agniḥ pramādena dadāha Laṅkāṃ
  vadhyasya dehe svayam edhitaś cet,
vimṛśya tad deva|dhiy", âbhidhatta
  Brahm'|âstra|bandho 'pi yadi pramādaḥ.

What is the use of those monkeys and the sons of Raghu who would not even make a morning meal for any one of us? O bearer of Kailása and Shiva also, tell us, should the sky be below us and the earth in the air?

O king, it was the fire kindled by your own men as it took 12.20
to the tail of that fickle monkey who deserved to be slain with a weapon that burned Lanka by our own carelessness as it fell."

Then Vibhíshana, puffing out his chest, raising his eyes, and inclining his body in readiness to speak, holding his hand spread open, spoke to the demons with a message intended to be of the greatest significance:

"What you, who are maintained by the king for the sake of war, have said is worthy of honor: that should only be said by those who are offering their lives, for wisdom is valued in advice, not courage.

And as for it being said that conflict with a man conducted carefully and zealously according to counsel becomes significant: Hánuman who has laid waste the entire city has made his response to Indra's subjugator in this matter.

If fire lit on his body as he was about to be killed burned Lanka by mistake, once you have considered this with your god-like intellect, say if snaring him with the Brahma-weapon was also a mistake.

12.25 jaganty a|mey'|âdbhuta|bhāva|bhāñji,
jit'|âbhimānāś ca janā vicitrāḥ
kārye tu yatnaṃ kuruta prakṛṣṭaṃ
mā nīti|garbhān su|dhiyo 'vamandhvam.

vṛddhi|kṣaya|sthāna|gatām ajasraṃ
vṛttiṃ jigīṣuḥ prasamīkṣamāṇaḥ
ghaṭeta sandhy|ādiṣu yo guṇeṣu,
lLakṣmīr na taṃ muñcati, cañcal" âpi.

upekṣaṇīy" âiva parasya vṛddhiḥ
pranaṣṭa|nīter, a|jit'|êndriyasya,
mad'|ādi|yuktasya virāga|hetuḥ
sa|mūla|ghātaṃ vinihanti y" ânte.

jan'|ânurāgeṇa yuto 'vasādaḥ
phal'|ânubandhaḥ su|dhiy" ātmano 'pi,
upekṣaṇīyo 'bhyupagamya saṃdhiṃ
kām'|ādi|ṣaḍ|varga|jit'|âdhipena.

yadā vigṛhṇan na ca saṃdadhāno
vṛddhiṃ kṣayaṃ c' ânuguṇaṃ prapaśyet,
āsīta, rāj" âvasara|pratīkṣas
tadā, prayāsaṃ vitathaṃ na kuryāt.

12.30 saṃdhau sthito vā janayet sva|vṛddhiṃ,
hanyāt paraṃ v" ôpaniṣat|prayogaiḥ,
āsrāvayed* asya janaṃ, parair vā
vigrāhya kuryād avahīna|saṃdhim.

The worlds contain immeasurable and wonderful natures 12.25
and there are all sorts of men who have conquered pride,
but you should make particular effort in your duty and you
should not despise the wise who have a depth of political
knowledge.

Though fickle, Lakshmi does not abandon one who when he seeks victory unceasingly examines the conduct which the enemy resorts to in times of growth, decay and stability and who strives for virtues such as peace.

The prosperity of an enemy who has lost his morals, whose senses are not conquered and who is full of pride and the like is the cause of disaffection which in the end destroys, killing root and all. This should be disregarded.

Even one's own decline, accompanied by the affection of the people and dependent upon the outcome, should be overlooked by a wise king, who, contracting a truce, has overcome the six obstacles such as desire.

When a king does not see concomitant gain and loss as he fights and makes peace, he should rest, and then, looking for an opportunity, should not exert himself in vain.

Remaining at peace he should create his own gain, or he 12.30
should destroy the enemy by secret means, or he should
suborn his people, or, making war with his enemies, he
should discard peace.

saṃdarśita|sneha|guṇaḥ sva|śatrūn
  vidveṣayan maṇḍalam asya bhindyāt:
ity evam ādi pravidhāya saṃdhir
  vṛddher vidheyo 'dhigam'|âbhyupāyaḥ.

matvā sahiṣṇūn a|par'|ôpajapyān
  svakān adhiṣṭhāya jal'|ânta|durgān,
drum'|âdri|durlaṅghya|jal'|âpradhṛṣyān,
  vardheta rājā ripu|vigraheṇa.

śaknoti yo na dviṣato nihantuṃ
  vihanyate n' âpy a|balair dviṣadbhiḥ
sa śvā|varāhaṃ kalahaṃ vidadhyād
  āsīta durg'|ādi vivardhayaṃś ca.

prayāṇa|mātreṇa pare prasādye,
  varteta yānena kṛt'|âbhirakṣaḥ;
a|śaknuvan kartum arer vighātaṃ
  sva|karma|rakṣāṃ ca paraṃ śrayeta.

12.35 ekena saṃdhiḥ, kalaho 'pareṇa
  kāryo 'bhito vā prasamīkṣya vṛddhim;
evaṃ prayuñjīta jigīṣur etā
  nītīr, vijānann ahit'|ātma|sāram.

tvayā tu loke janito virāgaḥ,
  prakopitaṃ maṇḍalam Indra|mukhyam,
Rāme tu rājan, viparītam etat paśyāmi,
  ten' âbhyadhikaṃ vipakṣam.

By showing the virtue of love to his enemies and dividing them, he should break their coalition: with this consideration and by other means, one should establish peace as the means for the gain of prosperity.

Esteeming his own people who are capable and not traducible by the enemy and establishing his strongholds near water, unassailable because of forests, mountains and uncrossable waters, the king should make himself prosper through the conflict of his enemies.

He who is not able to kill his enemies and yet is not destroyed by weak adversaries should instigate strife as between dogs and a boar and continue to strengthen his fortresses and other assets.

When the enemy can be pacified merely by advancing upon him, he should proceed by marching once he has ensured his own security; if he is not able to ensure his enemy's destruction and his own protection by his own actions he should seek protection with another king.

Recognizing prosperity in either case, peace should be made 12.35
with one and conflict with the other; knowing his enemy's and his own strength, a king desirous of victory should adopt these policies.

But you have caused disaffection in the world. The alliance fronted by Indra has been angered, but I see the opposite in Rama's case, O king, whereby he is a superior adversary.

ekena Vālī nihataḥ śareṇa
  suhṛttamas te, racitaś ca rājā
yad" âiva Sugrīva|kapiḥ, pareṇa
  tad" âiva kāryaṃ bhavato vinaṣṭam.

prākāra|mātr'|āvaraṇaḥ prabhāvaḥ
  Khar'|ādibhir yo nihatais tav' âbhūt,
Laṅkā|pradāh'|Âkṣa|vadha|dru|bhaṅgaiḥ
  klāmyaty asāv apy adhun" âtimātram.

ṣaḍ|varga|vaśyaḥ, parimūḍha|bandhur,
  ucchinna|mitro, viguṇair upetaḥ
mā pāda|yuddhaṃ dvi|radena kārṣīr:
  nama kṣit'|îndraṃ praṇat'|ôpabhogyam.

12.40 Rāmo 'pi dār'|āharaṇena tapto,
  vayaṃ hatair bandhubhir ātma|tulyaiḥ,
taptasya taptena yath" âyaso naḥ
  saṃdhiḥ pareṇ' âstu: vimuñca Sītām.

saṃdhukṣitaṃ maṇḍala|caṇḍa|vātair
  amarṣa|tīkṣṇaṃ kṣiti|pāla|tejaḥ,
sām'|âmbhasā śāntim upaitu rājan:
  prasīda, jīvāma sa|bandhu|bhṛtyāḥ.

a|pakva|kumbhāv iva bhaṅga|bhājau,
  rājann iyātāṃ maraṇaṃ samānau;
vīrye sthitaḥ kiṃ tu kṛt'|ânurāgo
  Rāmo bhavaṃś c' ôttama|bhūri|vairī.

Your best friend Valin was killed with one arrow, and it was at that very point, when the monkey Sugríva was chosen as king, that your cause was lost.

That power of yours which was once a shield for the full length of your ramparts is now utterly exhausted by the slaying of Khara and others, by the burning of Lanka, by the death of Aksha and by the destruction of the forest.

You who are subject to the six vices, whose family is delusional, whose friends are base and who are attended by wickedness should not make war on foot against an elephant: bow to that lord of the earth who aids his supplicants.

That very Rama is fired up by his wife's abduction and we by 12.40
the killing of our kinsmen equal to ourselves. Let us meld peaceably with our enemy as heated iron with heated iron: release Sita.

May the fire of the king inflamed by the winds of his allies' wrath, sharp with impatience, be calmed with the waters of equity, O king: be content, may we and our kinsmen and servants live on.

Like two unfired jars being broken, two equals would both die, O king; Rama has been steady in valor and has made himself beloved but you have great and abundant enemies.

daṇḍena kośena ca manyase cet
  prakṛṣṭam ātmānam ares tath" âpi,
riktasya pūrṇena vṛthā vināśaḥ
  pūrṇasya bhaṅge bahu hīyate tu.

kliṣṭ'|ātma|bhṛtyaḥ parimṛgya|sampan
  mānī yatet' âpi sa|saṃśaye 'rthe,
saṃdeham ārohati yaḥ kṛt'|ârtho
  nūnaṃ ratiṃ tasya karoti na śrīḥ.

12.45 śakyāny a|doṣāṇi mahā|phalāni
  samārabhet' ôpanayan samāptim
karmāṇi rājā vihit'|ânurāgo,
  viparyaye syād vitathaḥ prayāsaḥ.

jetuṃ na śakyo nṛ|patiḥ su|nītir:
  doṣaḥ kṣay'|ādiḥ kalahe dhruvaś ca,
phalaṃ na kiṃ cin na śubhā samāptiḥ.
  kṛt'|ânurāgaṃ bhuvi saṃtyaj' ârim.

tvan|mitra|nāśo nija|mitra|lābhaḥ
  sameta|sainyaḥ sa ca mitra|kṛcchre
bhogyo vaśaḥ; paśya, śareṇa śatroḥ
  prasādhito Vāli|vadhe na ko 'rthaḥ?

lobhād bhayād v" âbhigataḥ kap'|îndro
  na Rāghavaṃ, yena bhaved vibhedyaḥ,
sthitaḥ satāṃ vartmani, labdha|rājyaḥ
  prati|priyaṃ so 'bhyagamac cikīrṣuḥ.

If nevertheless you consider yourself superior to your enemy in arms or treasure, then for you, a rich man, to destroy a poor man would be pointless whereas much would be lost in your own destruction as a wealthy man.

A proud man who has driven himself and his dependants and whose wealth has had to be sought for may strive after an uncertain outcome but surely Lakshmi does not favor a successful man who undertakes a doubtful venture.

A king who is regarded with affection should undertake ac- 12.45
tions that are achievable, devoid of sin and of great result, as he pursues success, for in the reverse scenario his effort would be futile.

It is not possible to conquer a king who has good policies: in conflict with him ruin and other evils are certain, there will be no fruit and no auspicious outcome. Leave alone an enemy who has made himself beloved to the world.

The death of your friend and my own gain of a friend along with his army are useful and serviceable in my friend's distress; see, as in the case of Valin's murder, what object cannot be achieved with an enemy arrow?

The lord of monkeys did not come to Rama out of greed or fear, through which he might be corrupted, he remains on the path of the good. He has obtained his kingdom and he came seeking to return a favor.

phal'|âśino nirjhara|kuñja|bhājo
  divy'|âṅgan"|ânaṅga|ras'|ânabhijñāḥ,
nyag|jātayo, ratna|varair a|labhyā,
  mukhyāḥ kapīnām api n' ôpajapyāḥ.

12.50 kṛt'|âbhiṣeko yuva|rāja|rājye
  Sugrīva|rājena sut'|âviśeṣam
Tārā|vidheyena, kathaṃ vikāraṃ
  Tārā|suto yāsyati rākṣas'|ârtham?

paśyāmi Rāmād adhikaṃ samaṃ vā
  n' ânyaṃ, virodhe yam upāśrayema.
dattvā varaṃ s'|ânuśayaḥ Svayambhūr
  Indr'|ādayaḥ pūrvataraṃ viruddhāḥ.

durg'|āśritānāṃ bahun" âpi rājan,
  kālena pārṣṇi|grahaṇ'|ādi|hetuḥ
durg'|ôparodhaṃ na ca kurvato 'sti
  śatroś cireṇ' âpi Daśāsya, hāniḥ.

śastraṃ tar'|ûrvīdharam, ambu pānaṃ,
  vṛttiḥ phalair, n' ô gaja|vāji|nāryaḥ,
rāṣṭraṃ na paścān, na jano 'bhirakṣyaḥ,
  kiṃ duḥ|stham, ācakṣva, bhavet pareṣām?

saṃdhānam ev' âstu pareṇa tasmān,
  n' ânyo 'bhyupāyo 'sti nirūpyamāṇaḥ;
nūnaṃ vi|saṃdhau tvayi sarvam etan
  neṣyanti nāśaṃ kapayo 'cireṇa.»

Eating only fruits, dwelling by streams and in groves, unacquainted with the joys of love with divine females, of a lower species, not to be bought with costly gems, the foremost of monkeys cannot be brought over.

Consecrated to the kingdom as crown prince no different 12.50
to his own son by king Sugríva who was influenced by Tara,
how will Tara's son adapt to change for the sake of the
demon?*

I do not see anyone better than or equal to Rama to whom we could surrender ourselves in dispute. The Self-created regrets having given you a boon and Indra and the others have been to you from the very first.

After a long time those who take refuge in a fortress are subject to death, occasioned by the seizure of the heel of the army and other such hazards, O king, but not the enemy who is long making the siege of the fortress, O Rávana.

For weapons they have trees and mountains, for drink they have water, they live off fruit, they have no elephants, horses or women, no kingdom to their rear, no people to protect. Say, what evil could befall the enemy?

There must therefore be only peace with the enemy, no other means can be considered; surely if you are bellicose the monkeys will soon bring everything to ruin."

12.55 Vibhīṣaṇ'|ôktaṃ bahu manyamānaḥ,
pronnamya dehaṃ pariṇāma|namram,
skhalad|valir, vārdhaka|kampra|mūrdhā,
mātā|maho Rāvaṇam ity uvāca:

«ekaḥ padātiḥ puruṣo dhanuṣmān
yo 'neka|māyāni viyad|gatāni
rakṣaḥ|sahasrāṇi caturdaś' ārdīt,
kā tatra vo mānuṣa|mātra|śaṅkā?

brahm'|arṣibhir nūnam ayaṃ sa|devaiḥ
saṃtāpitai rātri|cara|kṣayāya,
nar'|ākṛtir vānara|sainya|śālī,
jagaty a|jayyo, vihito 'bhyupāyaḥ.

vajr'|âbhighātair a|virugṇa|mūrteḥ
pheṇair jalānām asurasya mūrdhnaḥ
cakāra bhedaṃ mṛdubhir Mahendro
yathā, tath" âitat kim ap' îti bodhyam.

kva strī|viṣahyāḥ kara|jāḥ? kva vakṣo
daityasya śail'|êndra|śilā|viśālam?
saṃpaśyat' âitad dyu|sadāṃ su|nītaṃ:
bibheda tais tan nara|siṃha|mūrtiḥ.

12.60 pramādavāṃs, tvaṃ kṣata|dharma|vartmā,
gato munīnām api śatru|bhāvam,
kulasya śāntiṃ bahu manyase cet
kuruṣva rājendra, Vibhīṣaṇ'|ôktam.»

In consideration of Vibhíshana's lengthy speech, Rávana's 12.55
maternal grandfather, straightening his body bent with age, the folds of his skin tremulous, his head shaking in senescence, spoke thus to Rávana:

"Why do you believe that he is a mere man who alone and on foot killed, with his bow, fourteen thousand demons of infinite magic and airy flight?

Indefatigable in the world, with human form and possessed of an army of monkeys, he has been appointed by the tormented brahmin-sages and the gods as the means of eliminating the demons.

It should be understood as a wonder that with the soft foam of the waters the great lord broke off the head of a demon Námuchi whose body was invulnerable even to the blows of thunderbolts.*

Compare the strength of his nails which even a woman could endure with a demon's chest broad as a great mountain face. Behold this well executed act of the gods: in the form of the Man-lion he split it open with these very nails.*

You are deluded, you have strayed from the way of dharma, 12.60
you have even become an enemy of the sages. If you value the peace of your family highly then do as Vibhíshana has said, O best of kings."

ghoṣeṇa tena pratilabdha|saṃjño
nidr"|āvil'|âkṣaḥ śruta|kārya|sāraḥ
sphurad|ghanaḥ s'|âmbur iv' ântarīkṣe
vākyaṃ tato 'bhāṣata Kumbha|karṇaḥ:

«kriyā|samārambha|gato 'bhyupāyo,
nṛ|dravya|sampat, saha|deśa|kālā,
vipat|pratīkāra|yut", ârtha|siddhir
mantr'|âṅgam etāni vadanti pañca.

na niścit'|ârthaṃ samayaṃ ca deśaṃ
kriy'|âbhyupāy'|ādiṣu yo 'tiyāyāt
sa prāpnuyān mantra|phalaṃ, na mānī
kāle vipanne, kṣaṇadā|car'|êndra.

auṣṇyaṃ tyajen madhya|gato 'pi bhānuḥ;
śaityaṃ niśāyām atha vā him'|âṃśuḥ;
an|artha|mūlaṃ bhuvan'|âvamānī
manye na mānaṃ piśit'|âśi|nātha.

12.65 tath" âpi vaktuṃ prasabhaṃ yatante,
yan mad|vidhāḥ siddhim abhīpsavas, tvām
viloma|ceṣṭaṃ vihit'|âvahāsāḥ
parair hi tat snehamayais tamobhiḥ.

krūrāḥ kriyā grāmya|sukheṣu saṅgaḥ
puṇyasya yaḥ saṃkṣaya|hetur uktaḥ
niṣevito 'sau bhavat" âti|mātraṃ
phalaty a|valgu dhruvam eva rājan.

Then Kumbha·karna who had been brought back to consciousness through the noise, his eyes foggy with sleep, who had heard the essence of the matter, like a flashing storm cloud in the sky uttered a speech:

"They say that these five are the constituents of good advice: the means inherent in the undertaking of the action, the resources of men and equipment, the right place and time, possession of a contingency against disaster, and the success of the objective.

He who does not exceed his settled objective and the right time and place reaps the fruit of good counsel when the means of action and so forth are present. But not the arrogant man when the moment has passed, O lord of the demons, does not.

The sun even at the meridian may lose its heat; the cool-rayed moon may lose its chill at night; but I think that one who despises the world does not lose the pride which is the root-cause of his worthlessness, O Lord of the flesh-eaters.

That those such as I wishing for success, trying to speak 12.65
forcefully to you who are perverse in your actions, are made objects of derision by others is motivated by the darkness of attachment.

Cruel deeds and attachment to coarse pleasures which you have pursued to excess are said to cause total loss of merit and will certainly bring forth foul fruit, O king.

dattaṃ na kiṃ? ke viṣayā na bhuktāḥ?
sthito 'smi vā kaṃ paribhūya n' ôccaiḥ?
itthaṃ kṛt'|ârthasya mama dhruvaṃ syān
mṛtyus tvad|arthe yadi, kiṃ na labdham?

kiṃ dur|nayais tvayy uditair mṛṣ"|ârthair?
vīryeṇa vakt" âsmi raṇe samādhim.»
tasmin prasupte punar ittham uktvā,
Vibhīṣaṇo 'bhāṣata rākṣas'|êndram:

«nimitta|śūnyaiḥ sthagitā rajobhir
diśo, marudbhir vikṛtair vilolaiḥ
svabhāva|hīnair mṛga|pakṣi|ghoṣaiḥ
krandanti bhartāram iv' âbhipannam.

12.70 utpāta|jaṃ chidram asau vivasvān
vyādāya vaktr'|ākṛti, loka|bhīṣmam,
attuṃ janān, dhūsara|raśmi|rāśiḥ,
siṃho yathā kīrṇa|saṭo 'bhyudeti.

mārgaṃ gato gotra|gurur Bhṛgūṇām
Agastin" âdhyāsita|Vindhya|śṛṅgam.
saṃdṛśyate Śakra|purohito 'hni,
kṣmāṃ kampayantyo nipatanti c' ôlkāḥ.

māṃsaṃ hatānām iva rākṣasānām,
āśaṃsavaḥ krūra|giro ruvantaḥ
kravy'|āśino dīpta|kṛśānu|vaktrā,
bhrāmyanty a|bhītāḥ paritaḥ puraṃ naḥ.

What has not been given away? What things have not been enjoyed? Is there anyone I have not overcome to stand so tall? If death in your service were certain to be mine, when I have achieved such success, what would be lost?

What is the use of telling you bad policies with futile objectives? I shall with courage pronounce a solution in this conflict." After speaking thus he slept again, and Vibhíshana said to the lord of demons:

"It is as if the directions, obscured by swirling dust disturbed by the causeless winds, are bewailing their overpowered husband with the unnatural cries of animals and birds.

The sun with its mass of rays dimmed, opening wide the 12.70
mouth-shaped tear born of calamity, terrible to the world, rose up to eat men like a wild-maned lion.

Venus, teacher of the clan of the Bhrigus, has gone by way of the Vindhya peak occupied by Agástya. Jupiter, family priest to Indra, is seen during the day and meteors are falling causing the earth to shake.

Cruel voiced carnivores, their mouths lit up with fire, howling as if seeking the flesh of slain demons are wandering around our city unafraid.

payo ghaṭ'|ōdhnīr api gā duhanti
 mandaṃ vi|varṇaṃ vi|rasaṃ ca gopāḥ;
havyeṣu kīṭ'|ôpajanaḥ sa|keśo
 na dīpyate 'gniḥ, su|samindhano 'pi.

tasmāt kuru tvaṃ pratikāram asmin
 snehān mayā Rāvaṇa, bhāṣyamāṇaḥ,
vadanti duḥkhaṃ hy anujīvi|vṛtte
 sthitāḥ pada|sthaṃ pariṇāma|pathyam.

12.75 virugṇa|saṃkīrṇa|vipanna|bhinnaiḥ
 prakṣuṇṇa|saṃhrīṇa|śit'|âstra|vṛkṇaiḥ
yāvan nar'|āśair na ripuḥ śav'|āśān
 saṃtarpayaty ānama tāvad asmai.»

bhrū|bhaṅgam ādhāya, vihāya dhairyaṃ,
 Vibhīṣaṇaṃ bhīṣaṇa|rūkṣa|cakṣuḥ,
giraṃ jagād' ôgra|padām udagraḥ
 svaṃ sphāvayan* Śakra|ripuḥ prabhāvam:

«śilā tariṣyaty udake na parṇaṃ;
 dhvāntaṃ raveḥ syantsyati; vahnir indoḥ;
jetā paro 'haṃ yudhi jeṣyamāṇas:
 tulyāni manyasva Pulastya|naptaḥ.

a|nirvṛtaṃ bhūtiṣu, gūḍha|vairaṃ,
 satkāra|kāle 'pi kṛt'|âbhyasūyam,
vibhinna|karm'|āśaya|vāk, kule no
 mā jñāti|celaṃ, bhuvi kasya cid bhūt.

Though their udders are like jars, the cowherds barely milk the cows of their colorless, tasteless milk; though fed with the best fuel, the fire, a breeding place for insects and full of hair, does not blaze on the offerings.

Therefore, as I speak to you with love, O Rávana, you should make amends in this business, for those standing in a position of dependence speak to you in your office of an unhappy matter which will have consequences.

You should bow to the enemy while he has not yet sated 12.75
the corpse eaters with demons ripped up, minced, broken, split open, crushed, humiliated, and split with sharpened weapons."

Indra's haughty enemy, bending his brows, abandoning his forbearance, with his eyes fierce and harsh, inflating his own prowess, made a speech of cruel words to Vibhíshana:

"Understand that these things are equatable, O grandson of Pulástya: that a stone will float on water, not a leaf; that darkness will flow from the sun, fire from the moon; and that I, the supreme victor in war, am about to be defeated.

In this world may none in our family have a sham relative, discontented with his wealth, secretly hostile, indignant even at a time of hospitality, and whose actions, thoughts and words are inimical.

icchanty abhīkṣṇaṃ kṣayam ātmano 'pi
na jñātayas tulya|kulasya lakṣmīm,
namanti śatrūn na ca bandhu|vṛddhiṃ
saṃtapyamānair hṛdayaiḥ sahante.

12.80 tvay" âdya Laṅk"|âbhibhave 'tiharṣād
duṣṭo 'timātraṃ vivṛto 'ntarātmā.
dhik tvāṃ, mṛṣā te mayi dustha|buddhir»
vadann idaṃ tasya dadau sa pārṣṇim.

tataḥ sa kopaṃ kṣamayā nigṛhṇan,
dhairyeṇa manyuṃ, vinayena garvam,
mohaṃ dhiy" ôtsāha|vaśād a|śaktiṃ,
samaṃ caturbhiḥ sacivair udasthāt.

uvāca c' âinaṃ kṣaṇadā|car'|êndraṃ:
«sukhaṃ mahā|rāja, vinā may" āssva,
mūrkh'|āturaḥ pathya|kaṭūn an|aśnan
yat s'|āmayo 'sau, bhiṣajāṃ na doṣaḥ.

karoti vairaṃ sphuṭam ucyamānaḥ,
pratuṣyati śrotra|sukhair a|pathyaiḥ
viveka|śūnyaḥ prabhur ātma|mānī
mahān an|arthaḥ suhṛdāṃ bat' âyam.

krīḍan bhujaṅgena gṛh'|ânupātaṃ
kaś cid yathā jīvati saṃśaya|sthaḥ,
saṃsevamāno nṛ|patiṃ pramūḍhaṃ
tath" âiva yaj jīvati, so 'sya lābhaḥ.

Kinsmen always wish for the ruin of one of their own and not for wealth for one of the same family; they bow to enemies and they cannot bear the prosperity of their relatives in their tormented hearts.

Now when Lanka is being attacked you have revealed 12.80
through your high delight that your inner soul is excessively corrupted. A curse on you, your ignorant conception of me is false," saying this he gave him a kick.

Then containing his anger with patience, his grief with fortitude, his pride with modesty, his confusion with reason and his impotence through force of will, Vibhíshana stood up with his four ministers.

And he said to that lord of the nightstalkers: "Be happy without me, great king. It is not the fault of the doctors that a foolish patient who does not drink his bitter but wholesome draught remains sick.

When addressed plainly he shows his hostility; he is delighted with things pleasing to the ear but not to his benefit; the self-regarding king is devoid of reason and is certainly a great disaster to his friends.

As it remains in doubt how someone who goes from house to house performing with a snake continues to live, so also the fact that one who serves an insane king actually stays alive is his reward.

12.85 dattaḥ sva|doṣair bhavatā prahāraḥ
pādena dharmye pathi me sthitasya.
sa cintanīyaḥ saha mantri|mukhyaiḥ
kasy' āvayor lāghavam ādadhātu?»

iti vacanam asau rajani|cara|patiṃ
bahu|guṇam a|sakṛt prasabham abhidadhat,
niragamad a|bhayaḥ puruṣa|ripu|purān
nara|pati|caraṇau navitum ari|nutau.

atha tam upagataṃ vidita|sucaritaṃ
Pavanasuta|girā giri|guru|hṛdayaḥ
nṛ|patir amadayan mudita|parijanaṃ
sva|pura|pati|karaiḥ salila|samudayaiḥ.

Through your own evils you have dealt me a kick with your 12.85
foot because I abide on the righteous path. Together with your foremost counselors you should consider on which of us it confers insignificance?"

Forcefully delivering this speech replete with virtue more than once to the lord of the demons, fearless he left the city of the enemies of men to praise the feet of the lord of men which were praised even by his enemies.

Then the king, whose heart was great as a mountain, having heard of his good conduct from Hánuman, gladdened the approaching Vibhíshana by anointing him king of his own city to the delight of his retinue.

CANTO 13
THE INVASION OF LANKA

13.1 CĀRU|SAMĪRAṆA|ramaṇe
hariṇa|kalaṅka|kiraṇ'|āvalī|sa|vilāsā
ābaddha|Rāma|mohā
velā|mūle vibhāvarī parihīṇā.*

baddho vāsara|saṅge
bhīmo Rāmeṇa lavaṇa|salil'|āvāse
sahasā saṃrambha|raso
dūr'|ārūḍha|ravi|maṇḍala|samo lole.

gāḍha|guru|puṅkha|pīḍā|
sa|dhūma|salil'|âri|saṃbhava|mahā|bāṇe
ārūḍhā saṃdehaṃ
Rāme sa|mahī|dhārā mahī sa|phaṇi|sabhā.

ghora|jala|danti|saṃkulam
aṭṭa|mahā|paṅka|kāhala|jal'|āvāsam
ārīṇaṃ* lavaṇa|jalaṃ
samiddha|phala|bāṇa|viddha|ghora|phaṇi|varam.

13.5 sa|bhayaṃ pariharamāṇo
mah"|âhi|saṃcāra|bhāsuraṃ salila|gaṇam
ārūḍho lavaṇa|jalo
jala|tīraṃ hari|bal'|āgama|vilola|guham,

cañcala|taru|hariṇa|gaṇaṃ,
bahu|kusum'|ābandha|baddha|Rām'|āvāsam,
hari|pallava|taru|jālaṃ,
tuṅg'|ôru|samiddha|taru|vara|hima|cchāyam,

ON THE OCEAN shore pleasant with sweet breezes the 13.1
night faded as it sported rows of moonbeams and bewildered Rama.

Then suddenly at dawn as the orb of the sun was rising up far off, Rama conceived a terrible feeling of wrath at the fickle ocean.

When Rama gripped his great arrow such that it produced fire and smoke as he held it tight and close, the earth with its mountains and caves which were the assembly halls for cobras, was brought into jeopardy.

The ocean, crowded with fearsome water-elephants, with the fish flapping in the drained mudflats and the great snakes pierced by the flame-tipped arrow, flowed away.

The ocean fearfully abandoning the mass of water glistening 13.5
with the movements of great serpents took to the shore, the caves of which were fervid with the arrival of the monkey army,

Where gangs of monkeys roamed about, where Rama had a dwelling made from many woven flowers, where there were thickets of green-shooted trees, where the cool shade of the best high broad trees flared out,

vara|vāraṇaṃsalila|bhareṇa
  giri|mahī|maṇḍala|saṃvara|vāraṇam*
vasu|dhārayaṃtuṅga|taraṅga|
  saṅga|parihīṇa|lola|vasudhā|rayam.

praṇipatya tato vacanaṃ
  jagāda hitam āyatau patir vārīṇām
Gaṅg"|âvalambi|bāhū
  Rāmaṃ bahal'|ôru|hari|tamāla|cchāyam:

«tuṅgā giri|vara|dehā,
  a|gamamaṃ salilaṃ, samīraṇo rasa|hārī
a|himo ravi|kiraṇa|gaṇo
  māyā saṃsāra|kāraṇaṃ te paramā.

13.10 āyāsa|saṃbhav'|âruṇa,
  saṃhara saṃhāra|hima|hara|sama|cchāyam
bāṇaṃ, vāri|samūhaṃ
  saṃgaccha purāṇa|cāru|deh'|āvāsam.

a|sulabha|hari|saṃcāraṃ
  jala|mūlaṃ bahala|paṅka|ruddh'|āyāmam
bhaṇa kiṃ jala|parihīṇaṃ
  su|gamamaṃ timi|kambu|vāri|vāraṇa|bhīmam.

gantuṃ Laṅkā|tīraṃ
  baddha|mahā|salila|saṃcareṇa sa|helam
taru|hariṇā giri|jālaṃ
  vahantu giri|bhāra|saṃsahā guru|deham.

Where there were the best of elephants holding back the dam of mountains encircling the earth with its load of water containing treasure and where the motion of the shaking earth was obstructed by contact with the high waves.

Then, bowing down, the lord of the waters with his arms draped with the Ganges spoke words of future benefit to Rama whose shade was dense and broad like that of a green *tamála* tree:

"The great high bodies of the mountains, the uncrossable sea, the drying wind and the hot abundance of the sun's rays are your supreme magic, the cause of creation.

O you who are red with exertion, withdraw your arrow 13.10
whose luster is equal to the sun at the dissolution, be reconciled with the ocean, the ancient dwelling place of beautiful creatures.

Tell me, is the sea, usually difficult for monkeys to cross, easy to traverse when without its water, with its breadth obstructed by thick mud and fearsome with sea monsters, shellfish and sea elephants?

In order to go easily to the shore of Lanka by a causeway built over the sea, the monkeys who are able to bear mountains should bring a great mass of mountains.

Hara|hāsa|ruddha|vigamaṃ
  para|kaṇṭha|gaṇaṃ mah"|āhava|samārambhe,
chindantu Rāma|bāṇā
  gambhīre me jale mahā|giri|baddhe.

gacchantu cāru|hāsā
  vīra|ras'|ābandha|ruddha|bhaya|saṃbandham*
hantuṃ bahu|bāhu|balaṃ
  hari|kariṇo giri|var'|ôru|dehaṃ sahasā.»

13.15 jigamiṣayā saṃyuktā
  babhūva kapi|vāhinī mate Dāśaratheḥ,
buddha|jal'|ālaya|cittā
  giri|haraṇ'|ārambha|saṃbhava|samālolā.*

guru|giri|vara|haraṇa|sahaṃ,
  saṃhāra|him'|âri|piṅgalaṃ Rāma|balam
ārūḍhaṃ sahasā khaṃ
  Varuṇ'|ālaya|vimala|salila|gaṇa|gambhīram.

avagāḍhaṃ giri|jālaṃ
  tuṅga|mahā|bhitti|ruddha|sura|saṃcāram,
a|bhaya|hari|rāsa|bhīmaṃ,
  kari|parimala|cāru|bahala|kandara|salilam,

ali|gaṇa|vilola|kusumaṃ,
  sa|kamala|jala|matta|kurara|kāraṇḍava|gaṇam,
phaṇi|saṃkula|bhīma|guhaṃ,
  kari|danta|samūḍha|sa|rasa|vasudhā|khaṇḍam,

When my deep water has been blocked up by huge mountains at the start of the great battle, may Rama's arrows cut the crowd of the enemy's necks the removal of which was stopped by Shiva's laughter.*

May the sweetly laughing elephants of monkeys go quickly to slay the army of the many-armed Rávana, with its mass as broad as the best of mountains, its access to fear blocked by it being bound to heroism."

The monkey army in accordance with Rama's plan became 13.15
inflamed with the desire to go, knowing the mind of the ocean, and eager to begin moving the mountains.

Rama's army yellow like the fire of the dissolution, able to move the huge heavy mountains, suddenly mounted into the sky as high as the pure waters of the ocean are deep.

They plunged into the mass of the mountain which was an obstacle to the movements of the gods with its great high walls, fearsome with the roars of fearless lions, the waters of its abundant caves sweet with elephants' ichor,

Its flowers thronging with swarms of bees, with excited flocks of ospreys and *karándava* ducks at its lotus pools, its awesome caves seething with cobras, and heaped with moist earth dug up by elephants' tusks,

aravinda|reṇu|piñjara|
 sārasa|rava|hāri|vimala|bahu|cāru|jalam,
ravi|maṇi|saṃbhava|hima|hara|
 samāgam'|ābaddha|bahula|sura|taru|dhūpam,

13.20 hari|rava|vilola|vāraṇa|
 gambhīr'|ābaddha|sa|rasa|puru|saṃrāvam,
ghoṇā|saṃgama|paṅk'|ā-
 vila|subala|bhara|mah'|ôru|varāham.

uccakhnuḥ parirabdhān
 kapi|saṅghā bāhubhis tato bhūmi|bhṛtaḥ
niṣpiṣṭa|Śeṣa|mūrdhnaḥ
 śṛṅga|vikīrṇ'|ôṣṇa|raśmi|nakṣatra|gaṇān.*

tuṅga|mahā|giri|subharā
 bāhu|samāruddha|bhidura|ṭaṅkā bahudhā
lavaṇa|jala|bandha|kāmā
 ārūḍhā ambaraṃ mahā|pariṇāham,

bahu|dhavala|vāri|vāhaṃ
 vimal'|āyasa|mah"|âsi|deha|cchāyam,
baddha|vihaṅgama|mālaṃ
 hima|girim iva, matta|kurara|rava|saṃbaddham,

cāru|kalahaṃsa|saṃkula|
 sa|caṇḍa|saṃcāra|sāras'|ābaddha|ravam
sa|kusuma|kaṇa|gandha|vahaṃ
 samay'|āgama|vāri|saṅga|vimal'|āyāmam.

With its abundant sweet clear waters delightful with the cries of cranes yellowed with lotus pollen, with much smoke from the trees of the gods made by contact with the sun-stone-produced fire,

Where elephants alarmed by the roars of lions made many 13.20
deep trumpets full of emotion, where huge great boars, incredibly powerful bearers, were fouled by mud sticking to their snouts.

Then the hosts of monkeys, encircling them with their arms, dug up the mountains whose peaks were interspersed among the sun and starry constellations and which pressed down on the heads of Shesha the serpent lord.

As they repeatedly sought to span the sea, with the sharp peaks grasped in their arms they lifted the easy burden of the great high mountains up into the sky of vast dimensions,

Full of many white clouds, its luster embodied as a huge sword of pure steel, like the Himálaya with its garland made of birds, full of the sounds of excited ospreys,

Filled with the cries of gently moving cranes and thronged with lovely *kala·hansa* birds, its scent-bearing breezes full of flower pollen, its expanse pure by contact with the approaching monsoon.

13.25 sahasā te taru|hariṇā
giri|subharā lavaṇa|salila|bandh'|ārambhe
tīre girim ārūḍhā*
Rām'|āgama|ruddha|sa|bhaya|ripu|saṃcāram.

tataḥ praṇītāḥ kapi|yūtha|mukhyair
nyastāḥ kṛśānos tanayena samyak,
a|kampra|bradhn'|âgra|nitamba|bhāgā
mah"|ârṇavaṃ bhūmi|bhṛto 'vagāḍhāḥ.*

tene 'dri|bandhyo, vavṛdhe payo|dhis,
tutoṣa Rāmo, mumude kap'|îndraḥ,
tatrāsa śatrur, dadṛśe Suvelaḥ,
prāpe jal'|ânto, juhṛṣuḥ plavaṅgāḥ.

bhremur, vavalgur, nanṛtur,
jajakṣur, juguḥ, samutpupluvire, niṣeduḥ,
āsphoṭayāṃ cakrur, abhipraṇedū,
rejur, nanandur, viyayuḥ, samīyuḥ.

giri|paṅka|cāru|dehaṃ
kakkola|lavaṅga|badha|surabhi|parimalam
bahu|bahal'|ôru|taraṅgaṃ
parisaram ārūḍham uddharaṃ lavaṇa|jalam.

13.30 lolaṃ kūl'|âbhigame
khe tuṅg'|âmala|nibaddha|puru|pariṇāham
sura|Gaṅgā|bharaṇa|sahaṃ
giri|bandha|vareṇa lavaṇa|salilaṃ ruddham.

As they undertook to bridge the ocean, the monkeys with 13.25
their easy burden of mountains quickly reached the mountain on the shore where the activity of the terrified enemy was halted by Rama's arrival.

Then, brought by the foremost monkeys and placed properly by Nala the son of fire, the mountains, with their bases, peaks and flanks undisturbed, sank down into the ocean.

The mountain bridge was extended, the ocean swelled, Rama was pleased, the monkey lord rejoiced, the enemy was terrified, Mount Suvéla* was seen, the end of the water was reached and the monkeys exulted.

They spun round, leaped, danced, ate, sang, jumped up and sat down, clapped, roared out, shone, rejoiced, scattered and came together.

The salt water, its body beautiful with the mountain mud, with a lovely fragrance produced by *kakkóla* berries and cloves, with many broad high waves, rising up, mounted the surrounding shore.

Rolling, its abundant compass rising high and clear into 13.30
the sky right up to the shore, able to lift the burden of the divine Ganges, the salt water was blocked by that supreme mountain bridge.

ārūḍhaṃ ca Suvelaṃ
taru|māl"|ābandha|hāri|giri|vara|jālam,
Rāvaṇa|citta|bhayaṃ|karam
āpiṅgala|lola|kesaraṃ Rāma|balam.

Laṅk"|ālaya|tumul'|ārava|
subhara|gabhīr'|ôru|kuñja|kandara|vivaram,
vīṇā|rava|rasa|saṅgama|
sura|gaṇa|saṃkula|mahā|tamāla|cchāyam,

sa|rasa|bahu|pallav'|āvila|
kesara|hintāla|baddha|bahala|cchāyam,
Airāvaṇa|mada|parimala|
gandhavah'|ābaddha|danti|saṃrambha|rasam,

tuṅga|taru|cchāyā|ruha|
komala|hari|hāri|lola|pallava|jālam,
hariṇa|bhayaṃ|kara|sakusuma|
dāva|sama|cchavi|vilola|dāḍima|kuñjam,

13.35 kala|hari|kaṇṭha|virāvaṃ,
salila|mahā|bandha|saṃkula|mahā|sālam
cala|kisalaya|saṃbaddhaṃ
maṇi|jālaṃ salila|kaṇa|mayaṃ vivahantam,

tuṅga|maṇi|kiraṇa|jālaṃ,
giri|jala|saṃghaṭṭa|baddha|gambhīra|ravam,
cāru|guhā|vivara|sabhaṃ
sura|pura|samam amara|cāraṇa|susaṃrāvam,

Rama's army with its flowing tawny hair causing fear in the heart of Rávana, ascended Suvéla with its matrix of beautiful peaks bound by a girdle of trees,

The openings of its many deep wide caves and caverns were filled with the tumultuous howls of the denizens of Lanka, the shade of its great *tamála* trees was filled with hosts of deities come to savor the sound of lutes,

Where *késara* and *hintála* trees dark with their many moist fronds made abundant shade, where the wind fragranced with Airávana's ichor maddened the elephants,

With clusters of delicate green and lovely fluttering fronds growing in the shade of high trees, with flowering groves of pomegranate waving like a forest fire and scaring the deer,

With low roars from the throats of lions, with great sal trees 13.35
shaken in the great spanning of the sea and bearing networks of gems made of water droplets attached to their waving branches,

With high clusters of sparkles from jewels, with deep roars made by mountain cataracts, with halls formed from beautiful caves and chasms like those of a celestial city with the sweet harmonies of immortal musicians,

vimala|mahā|maṇi|ṭaṅkaṃ,
  sindūra|kalaṅka|piñjara|mahā|bhittim,
vīra|hari|danti|saṅgama|
  bhaya|ruddha|vibhāvarī|vihāra|samīham,

sa|mahā|phaṇi|bhīma|bilaṃ,
  bhūri|vihaṅgama|tumul'|ôru|ghora|virāvam,
vāraṇa|varāha|hari|vara|
  go|gaṇa|sāraṅga|saṃkula|mahā|sālam,

cala|kisalaya|sa|vilāsaṃ,
  cāru|mahī|kamala|reṇu|piñjara|vasudham,
sa|kusuma|kesara|bāṇaṃ,
  lavaṅga|taru|taruṇa|vallarī|vara|hāsam,

13.40 a|mala|maṇi|hema|ṭaṅkaṃ,
  tuṅga|mahā|bhitti|ruddha|ruru|paṅka|gamam,
amar'|ārūḍha|parisaraṃ
  Merum iv' āvila|sa|rasa|mandāra|tarum,

phala|bhara|manthara|taru|varam,
  a|vidūra|virūḍha|hāri|kusum'|āpīḍam,
hariṇa|kalaṅka|mahā|maṇi|
  saṃbhava|bahu|vāri|subhara|gambhīra|guham,*

jala|kāma|danti|saṃkula|
  sa|hema|rasa|cāru|dhavala|kandara|deham,
aṅkura|roha|sama|cchavi|
  ruru|gaṇa|saṃlīḍha|tarala|hari|maṇi|kiraṇam,

With its great pure cliffs of jewels, its great walls red with the stain of vermillion, with the longing for night-sport precluded by fear of meeting fierce lions and elephants,

With the fearsome holes of great serpents, with the tumultuous terrible great cries of many birds, with great sal forests filled with elephants, boar, the best of lions, cattle herds and deer,

Coquettish with waving sprays of flowers, where the earth was red with the pollen of lovely great land lotuses, with *késara* and *bana* trees full of flowers, laughing with splendid delicate shoots of *lavánga* trees,

With crags of flawless gems and gold, where the way through 13.40
the mud for the deer was blocked by great high cliffs, like Mount Meru with its thick charming coral trees, its slopes occupied by immortals,

With fine broad trees bearing fruit, where never far off lovely wreaths of flowers grew, where deep caves were filled with abundant water produced by huge moonstones,

Where the beautiful bodies of the caves were washed with gold, crowded with elephants in search of water, where the tremulous rays of emeralds appearing as fresh shoots were licked at by herds of deer,

gāḍha|samīraṇa|susahaṃ,
  bhīma|rav'|ôttuṅga|vāri|dhara|saṃghaṭṭam,
dhavala|jala|vāha|mālā|
  saṃbandh'|ābaddha|hima|dharā|dhara|līlam,

lavaṇa|jala|bandha|sa|rasaṃ,
  taru|phala|saṃpatti|ruddha|deh'|āyāsam,
Laṅkā|toraṇa|vāraṇam
  ārūḍhaṃ samara|lālasaṃ Rāma|balam.

13.45 guru|paṇava|veṇu|guñjā|
  bherī|pel'|ôru|jhallarī|bhīma|ravam,
ḍhakkā|ghaṇṭā|tumulaṃ,
  sannaddhaṃ para|balaṃ raṇ'|āyāsa|saham.

ārūḍha|bāṇa|ghoraṃ
  vimal'|āyasa|jāla|gūḍha|pīvara|deham,
cañcala|turaṅga|vāraṇa|
  saṃghaṭṭ'|ābaddha|cāru|pariṇāha|guṇam,

asi|tomara|kunta|mahā|
  paṭṭiśa|bhalla|vara|bāṇa|guru|puru|musalam,
vīra|ras'|âlaṅkāraṃ
  guru|saṃcāra|haya|danti|sa|mahī|kampam.

te Rāmeṇa sa|rabhasaṃ
  paritaralā hari|gaṇā raṇa|samārambhe
ruddhā Laṅkā|parisara|
  bhū|dhara|paribhaṅga|lālasā dhīra|ravam.

Well able to bear strong winds, where the clashes of high clouds thundered terribly, and whose resemblance to the Himálaya was occasioned by the garlands of white cloud.

Rama's army was delighted at the spanning of the ocean and, their bodily fatigue checked by the abundance of tree fruits, they mounted the outer gates of Lanka eager for battle.

The enemy force armed and ready to bear the trial of battle 13.45
was accompanied by the frightening sounds of large drums, flutes, kettle drums, gongs and cymbals large and small, as well as by the tumult of the great drums and bells.

The army was fearsome with mounted arrows, thick-set bodies hidden in spotless chain mail, the quality of its beautiful extent enhanced by the clash of thronging horses and elephants,

With swords, javelins, spears, massive axes, pikes, fine arrows and many heavy clubs, it was adorned with heroic emotion, and made the earth tremble with horses and elephants moving heavily.

Those monkeys so restless to start the battle, wanting to break down the trees surrounding Lanka, were forcibly restrained by Rama with his deep voice.

jala|tīra|tuṅga|taru|vara|
  kandara|giri|bhitti|kuñja|vivar'|āvāsam
bhīmaṃ taru|hariṇa|balaṃ
  susamiddha|himāri|kiraṇa|mālā|lolam,

13.50 Rāvaṇa|balam avagantuṃ
  jala|bhara|guru|salila|vāha|gaṇa|sama|cchāyam
aṭṭa|taru|mañca|mandira|
  toraṇa|mālā|sabhāsu samārūḍham.

The frightening force of monkeys occupying simultaneously the sea shore, tall trees, great caves, the mountain walls and thickets and hollows moved like a garland of light from a well fed fire,

Climbing into high trees, platforms, buildings, rows of 13.50
arches, and halls, to know Rávana's army that appeared like masses of heavy rain-bearing clouds.

CANTO 14

THE FIRST BATTLE

14.1 TATO DAŚĀSYAḤ smara|vihval'|ātmā,
cāra|prakāśī|kṛta|śatru|śaktiḥ,
vimohya māyāmaya|Rāma|mūrdhnā
Sītām anīkaṃ prajighāya* yoddhum.*

kambūn atha samādadhmuḥ, koṇair bheryo nijaghnire,*
veṇūn pupūrire, guñjā juguñjuḥ kara|ghaṭṭitāḥ,

vādayāṃ cakrire ḍhakkāḥ, paṇavā dadhvanur hatāḥ,
kāhalāḥ pūrayāṃ cakruḥ, pūrṇāḥ perāś ca sasvanuḥ,

mṛdaṅgā dhīram āsvenur, hataiḥ svene ca gomukhaiḥ
ghaṇṭāḥ śiśiñjire dīrghaṃ, jahrāde paṭahair bhṛśam.

14.5 hayā jiheṣire harṣād, gambhīraṃ jagajur gajāḥ,
saṃtrastāḥ karabhā reṭuś, cukuvuḥ patti|paṅktayaḥ.

turaṅgāḥ* pusphuṭur bhītāḥ, pusphurur vṛṣabhāḥ param,
nāryaś cukṣubhire mamlur mumuhuḥ śuśucuḥ patīn.

jagarjur, jahṛṣuḥ śūrā, rejus, tuṣṭuvire paraiḥ,
babandhur aṅguli|trāṇi, sannehuḥ, pariniryayuḥ.

dhanūṃṣy āropayāṃ cakrur, āruruhū rath'|ādiṣu,
asīn udvavṛhur dīptān, gurvīr ucckiṣipur gadāḥ.

śūlāni bhramayāṃ cakrur, bāṇān ādadire* śubhān,
bhremuś, cukurdire, resur vavalguś ca padātayaḥ.

THEN TEN-HEADED Rávana disturbed by desire, his enemy's power discovered by his spies, deceived Sita with an illusory head of Rama and sent out his army to fight. 14.1

Then they blew conches, drums were struck with sticks, they filled their pipes, kettle drums thrummed as they were struck by hand,

They made the great drums speak, their beaten cymbals sounded, they blew the *káhala*s, the air-filled *pera*s sang,

*Mridánga*s sounded deeply, beaten the *gómukha*s resounded, bells chimed long, tabors sounded fiercely.

Horses whinnied with excitement, elephants trumpeted 14.5
deeply, frightened camels grunted, the ranks of foot-soldiers roared.

The terrified steeds broke out, the bullocks were very restive, the women stumbled, wearied, swooned and bewailed their husbands.

Heroes shouted, exulted, were resplendent and were praised by their peers. They fastened their finger guards, armed themselves and marched about.

They took up their bows, ascended their chariots and other mounts, drew their bright swords and raised their heavy clubs.

The infantry waved their spears, took up their shining arrows, maneuvered, exulted, roared and pranced.

14.10 samutpetuḥ kaśā|ghātai, raśmy|ākarṣair mamaṅgire
aśvāḥ, pradudruvur mokṣe raktaṃ nijagaruḥ śrame.

gajānāṃ pradaduḥ śārīn, kambalān paritastaruḥ,
tenuḥ kakṣāṃ, dhvajāṃś c' âiva samucchiśriyur ucchikhān.

viśiśvāsayiṣāṃ cakrur ālilinguś ca yoṣitaḥ,
ājaghrur mūrdhni bālāṃś ca cucumbuś ca suta|priyāḥ.

gambhīra|vedinaḥ* saṃjñā gajā jagṛhur a|kṣatāḥ,
vavṛdhe śuśubhe c' âiṣāṃ mado, hṛṣṭaiś ca pupluve.

mṛgāḥ pradakṣiṇaṃ sasruḥ, śivāḥ samyag vavāśire,
a|vāmaiḥ pusphure dehaiḥ, prasede citta|vṛttibhiḥ.

14.15 prājyam āñjihiṣāṃ cakre* Prahasto Rāvaṇ'|ājñayā
dvāraṃ raraṅghatur yāmyaṃ Mahāpārśva|Mahodarau.

prayayāv Indrajit pratyag iyāya svayam uttaram,
samadhyāsisiṣāṃ cakre Virūpākṣaḥ pur'|ôdaram.

śuśrāva Rāmas tat sarvaṃ pratasthe ca sa|sainikaḥ,
visphārayāṃ cakār' âstraṃ babandh' âtha ca bāṇadhī.

īkṣāṃ cakre 'tha Saumitrim, anujajñe balāni ca,
namaś|cakāra devebhyaḥ parṇa|talpaṃ mumoca ca.

cakāsāṃ cakrur uttasthur, nedur, ānaśire* diśaḥ,
vānarā bhūdharān redhur,* babhañjuś ca tatas tarūn.

The horses leaped up at the whip strikes, they skittered to the reins' pull, ran forward on release and in their exertions swallowed down blood. 14.10

They put on the elephants' armor, they spread their saddle-cloths over them, they tightened their girths, and they raised their high crest banners.

They sought to give reassurance and embraced their women, they nuzzled their children on the head and kissed their sons affectionately.

Deep-thinking elephants took their signals without being goaded, their ichor increased and glistened and they surged forward in excitement.

Deer circled keeping them to the right, jackals howled auspiciously, the right sides of their bodies throbbed and their minds were well-disposed.

Prahásta at Rávana's command sought to go through the eastern gate, Maha·parshva and Mahódara hastened to the southern gate. 14.15

Índrajit proceeded to the west, Rávana himself to the north, Virupáksha sought to occupy the center of the city.

Rama heard all this and set out with his army. He strung his bow and bound on two quivers.

Then he looked at Lákshmana, commanded his forces, bowed to the gods and left his leaf couch.

Then the monkeys displaying themselves rose up, roared, filled the quarters, destroyed mountains and broke trees.

14.20 dadāla bhūr, nabho raktaṃ goṣpadapraṃ* vavarṣa ca,
mṛgāḥ prasasṛpur vāmaṃ, khagāś cukuvire '|śubham.

ulkā dadṛśire dīptā, ruruvuś c' â|śivaṃ śivāḥ,
cakṣmāye ca mahī: Rāmaḥ śaśaṅke c' â|śubh'|āgamam.

Rāvaṇaḥ śuśruvān* śatrūn rākṣasān abhyupeyuṣaḥ,
svayaṃ yuyutsayāṃ cakre, prākār'|âgre niṣedivān.*

nirāsū rākṣasā bāṇān, prajahuḥ śūla|paṭṭiśān,
asīṃś ca vāhayāṃ cakruḥ pāśaiś c' ācakṛṣus tataiḥ.

bhallaiś ca bibhidus tīkṣṇair vividhus* tomarais tathā,
gadābhiś cūrṇayāṃ cakruḥ,* śitaiś cakraiś ca cicchiduḥ.

14.25 vānarā muṣṭibhir jaghnur dadaṃśur daśanais tathā,
nirāsuś ca girīṃs tuṅgān, drumān vicakarus* tathā.

lāṅgūlair loṭhayāṃ cakrus, talair ninyuś ca saṃkṣayam,
nakhaiś cakṛtatuḥ kruddhāḥ pipiṣuś ca kṣitau balāt.

saṃbabhūvuḥ kabandhāni, prohuḥ śoṇita|toya|gāḥ,
terur* bhaṭ'|āsya|padmāni, dhvajaiḥ pheṇair iv' ābabhe,

rakta|paṅke gajāḥ sedur, na pracakramire rathāḥ,
nimamajjus turaṅgāś ca, gantuṃ n' ôtsehire bhaṭāḥ.

koṭyā koṭyā pura|dvāram ek'|âikaṃ rurudhe dviṣām,
ṣaṭ|triṃśadd hari|koṭyaś ca nivavrur vānar'|âdhipam.

14.30 tastanur, jahvalur, mamlur, jaglur, luluṭhire kṣatāḥ,
mumūrcchur, vavamū raktaṃ, tatṛṣuś c' ôbhaye bhaṭāḥ.

The earth split, the sky rained blood enough to fill the hoof print of a cow, deer passed by on the left, birds called inauspiciously. 14.20

Bright meteors were seen, jackals howled inauspiciously and the earth shook: Rama feared impending disaster.

Rávana hearing that the enemy were advancing on his demons, sitting on top of his ramparts, himself made them wish to fight.

The demons fired arrows, threw spears and javelins, wielded swords and drew in extended snares.

They split with sharp missiles and pierced with spears, they crushed with clubs and cut with sharp discuses.

The monkeys struck with their fists and bit with their teeth, 14.25
they hurled high mountains and scattered trees.

They beat them with their tails, destroyed them with their hands, ripped them with their nails and enraged they forcibly crushed them into the ground.

Headless trunks appeared, rivers of blood carried them, the lotus faces of soldiers passed by, banners shone like foam.

Elephants sank in the red mud, chariots could not move, horses went under and soldiers were unable to march.

Each one of the city gates was blockaded by a crore, thirty-six crore surrounded the monkey king.

On both sides the wounded soldiers groaned, staggered, 14.30
wearied, fainted, writhed, passed out, vomited blood and thirsted.

Sampātinā Prajaṅghas tu yuyudhe, 'sau drum'|āhataḥ
cakampe 'tīva cukrośa, jīva|nāśaṃ* nanāśa ca.

uccakhnāte* Nalen' ājau sphurat|Pratapan'|âkṣiṇī,
Jambumālī jahau prāṇān grāvṇā Mārutinā hataḥ.

Mitraghnasya pracukṣoda gaday" âṅgaṃ Vibhīṣaṇaḥ.
Sugrīvaḥ Praghasaṃ nebhe, bahūn Rāmas tatarda ca.

Vajramuṣṭer viśiśleṣa Mainden' âbhihataṃ śiraḥ,
Nīlaś cakarta cakreṇa Nikumbhasya śiraḥ sphurat.

14.35 Virūpākṣo jahe prāṇais tṛḍhaḥ Saumitri|patribhiḥ,
pramocayāṃ cakār' âsūn Dvividas tv Aśaniprabham.

gadā Śakrajitā jighye,* tāṃ pratīyeṣa Vāli|jaḥ,
rathaṃ mamantha sa|hayaṃ śākhin" âsya tato 'ṅgadaḥ.

tat karma Vāli|putrasya dṛṣṭvā viśvaṃ visiṣmiye,
saṃtresū rākṣasāḥ sarve bahu mene ca Rāghavaḥ.

Sugrīvo mumude, devāḥ «sādhv» ity ūcuḥ* sa|vismayāḥ,
Vibhīṣaṇo 'bhituṣṭāva* praśaśaṃsuḥ plavaṅgamāḥ.

«hī citraṃ» Lakṣmaṇen' ōde Rāvaṇiś ca tiro|dadhe,
vicakāra tato Rāmaḥ śarān, saṃtatrasur dviṣaḥ.

14.40 vibhinnā jughurur ghoraṃ, jakṣuḥ* kravy'|âśino hatān,
cuścyota vraṇināṃ raktaṃ, chinnāś celuḥ kṣaṇaṃ bhujāḥ.

kṛttair api dṛḍha|krodho vīra|vaktrair na tatyaje,
palāyāṃ cakrire* śeṣā, jihriyuḥ śūra|māninaḥ.

Prajángha fought with Sampáti, was struck by a tree and staggered roaring away to die his death.

In the battle Nala gouged out Prátapana's flashing eyes. Jambu·malin, struck by Hánuman with a rock, gave up his life.

Vibhíshana pulverized Mitrághna's body with a club, Sugríva tore open Prághasa and Rama eviscerated many.

Struck by Mainda, Vajra·mushti lost his head. Nila cut off the twitching head of Nikúmbha with a discus.

Virupáksha, minced by Lákshmana's arrows, was deprived 14.35
of life; Dvi·vida made Áshani·prabha give up the ghost.

Índrajit threw his club, Ángada the son of Valin took it, then he smashed his chariot and horses with a tree.

Seeing that deed of the son of Valin, everyone was amazed; all the demons trembled and Rama esteemed it highly.

Sugríva was delighted, the astonished gods pronounced it good, Vibhíshana praised it and the monkeys extolled it.

"How wonderful!" said Lákshmana and Índrajit hid himself. Then Rama deployed his arrows and the enemy were terrified.

Split open they howled horribly, scavengers ate the slain, 14.40
the blood of the wounded flowed, severed arms twitched sporadically.

Though cut off, the faces of the warriors did not loose their expressions of anger. The remainder fled, those who had boasted their valor were ashamed.

Rāghavo na dayāṃ cakre, dadhur dhairyaṃ na ke cana,
mamre pataṅgavad vīrair «hāh"» êti ca vicukruśe.

tiro|babhūve sūryeṇa, prāpe ca niśay" āspadam
jagrase kāla|rātr' îva vānarān rākṣasāṃś ca sā.

cukop' Êndrajid atyugraṃ sarp'|âstraṃ c' ājuhāva* saḥ,
ājuhuve* tiro|bhūtaḥ par'|ânīkaṃ jahāsa ca.

14.45 babādhe ca balaṃ kṛtsnaṃ nijagrāha ca sāyakaiḥ,
utsasarja śarāṃs, te 'sya sarpasāc ca prapedire.

ācicāya* sa taiḥ senām ācikāya ca Rāghavau
babhāṇa ca, «na me māyāṃ jigāy'* Êndro 'pi, kiṃ nṛbhiḥ.»

ācikyāte* ca bhūyo 'pi Rāghavau tena panna|gaiḥ;
tau mumuhatur udvignau vasudhāyāṃ ca petatuḥ.*

tato «Rām'» êti cakrandus, tresuḥ paridide vire,
niśaśvasuś ca senā|nyaḥ, procur «dhig» iti c' ātmanaḥ.

manyuṃ śekur na te roddhuṃ, n' âsraṃ saṃrurudhuḥ patat,
vividur n' Êndrajin|mārgaṃ, parīyuś ca plavaṅgamāḥ.

14.50 dadhāv' âdbhis tataś cakṣuḥ Sugrīvasya Vibhīṣaṇaḥ
vidāṃ cakāra* dhaut'|âkṣaḥ sa ripuṃ khe nanarda ca.

ujjugūre tataḥ śailaṃ hantum Indrajitaṃ kapiḥ
vihāya Rāvaṇis tasmād ānaṃhe* c' ântikaṃ pituḥ.

ācacakṣe ca vṛttāntaṃ prajaharṣa ca Rāvaṇaḥ,
gāḍhaṃ c' ôpajugūh'* âinaṃ śirasy upaśiśiṅgha ca.

Rama was not compassionate, no-one showed courage, heroes died like insects and cried out in pain.

The sun disappeared, and its place was taken by a night that swallowed up monkeys and demons like the night of death.

Índrajit became enraged and invoked the potent serpent missile, as he made himself invisible he challenged the enemy army and laughed.

He attacked the entire army and arrested it with missiles, 14.45
he fired arrows which, for that army, turned serpentine

He covered the army with them and he covered the two Rághava brothers and said, "Not even Indra could overcome my magic, let alone men!"

He covered the Rághava brothers once more with snakes, they were stupefied and overcome they fell to the earth.

Then the generals cried, "Rama," they trembled, wept and sighed and cursed themselves.

The monkeys were not able to stop their grief, they could not check their falling tears, they could not find Índrajit's trail and so they gathered together.

Then Vibhíshana washed Sugríva's eye with water and with 14.50
his doused eye he found his enemy in the sky and shouted.

Then the monkey raised up a mountain to kill Índrajit but Rávana's son escaped from him and went to his father.

He reported the news and Rávana rejoiced, embraced him tightly and kissed him on the head.

dhvajān uddudhuvus tuṅgān,
 māṃsaṃ cemur, jaguḥ, papuḥ,
kāmayāṃ cakrire kāntās,
 tatas tuṣṭā niśā|carāḥ.

darśayāṃ cakrire Rāmaṃ Sītāṃ rājñaś ca śāsanāt:
tasyā mimīlatur netre luluṭhe Puṣpak'|ôdare.

14.55 prāṇā dadhvaṃsire, gātraṃ tastambhe ca priye hate,
ucchaśvāsa cirād dīnā rurod' âsau rarāsa ca.

«lauha|bandhair babandhe nu vajreṇa kiṃ vinirmame
mano me na vinā Rāmād yat pusphoṭa sahasra|dhā?

utteritha samudraṃ tvaṃ mad|arthe 'rīn jihiṃsitha
mamartha c': âtighorāṃ māṃ dhig jīvita|laghū|kṛtām.

na jijīv' â|sukhī tātaḥ prāṇatā rahitas tvayā,
mṛte 'pi tvayi, jīvantyā kiṃ may" âṇaka|bhāryayā?»*

sā jugupsāṃ pracakre* 'sūn jagarhe lakṣaṇāni ca
deha|bhāñji tataḥ keśān luluñca luluṭhe muhuḥ.

14.60 jaglau, dadhyau, vitastāna, kṣaṇaṃ prāṇa* na, vivyathe,*
daivaṃ nininda, cakranda dehe c' âtīva manyunā.

āśvāsayāṃ cakār' âtha Trijaṭā tāṃ nināya ca.
tataḥ prajāgarāṃ cakrur* vānarāḥ sa|Vibhīṣaṇāḥ.

ciceta Rāmas tat kṛcchram oṣāṃ cakre* śuc" âtha saḥ,
manyuś c' âsya samāpipye* virurāva ca Lakṣmaṇam.

The nightstalkers raised up their high banners, they ate meat, sang, drank and made love to their beauties and then they were sated.

They showed Rama to Sita at their king's command: her eyes closed and she collapsed inside the Púshpaka chariot.

Her breath left her, her body stiffened at her slain beloved, 14.55
momentarily destroyed she recovered and wept and wailed.

"Is my heart bound with bonds of iron or is it made of diamond, my heart which without Rama does not shatter into one thousand pieces?

You have crossed the ocean for my sake and slain the enemy and now you have died: a curse on me for being so cruel and making light of life.

Bereft of you while you were alive, your father did not live. Now you are dead, why should I live on as a useless wife?"

She was disgusted with her own life and reproached her auspicious marks and then she tore her hair, repeatedly thrashing about.

She fainted, meditated, groaned, stopped breathing a while, 14.60
trembled, cursed her fate, yelled and was utterly burned up by grief.

Then Tríjata* comforted her and led her away. Then the monkeys and Vibhíshana roused themselves.

Rama realized what a terrible thing had happened, and burning with grief, his despair grew and he called to Lákshmana.

samīhe martum, ānarce* tena vāc" âkhilaṃ balam
āpapṛcche ca Sugrīvaṃ svaṃ deśaṃ visasarja ca.

ādideśa sa Kiṣkindhāṃ Rāghavau netum Aṅgadam
pratijajñe svayaṃ c' âiva Sugrīvo rakṣasāṃ vadham.

14.65 «nāg'|âstram idam etasya vipakṣas Tārkṣya|saṃsmṛtiḥ»
Vibhīṣaṇād iti śrutvā taṃ nidadhyau Raghūttamaḥ.

tato vijaghaṭe śailair, udvelaṃ pupluve 'mbu|dhiḥ,
vṛkṣebhyaś cucyute puṣpair, virejur* bhāsurā diśaḥ.

jagāhire 'mbu|dhiṃ nāgā, vavau vāyur mano|ramaḥ,
tejāṃsi śaṃśamāṃ cakruḥ,* śara|bandhā viśiśliṣuḥ.

bhrejire* '|kṣatavad yodhā,
  lebhe saṃjñāṃ ca Lakṣmaṇaḥ,
Vibhīṣaṇo 'pi babhrāje
  Garutmān prāpa c' ântikam.

saṃpaspars' âtha Kākutsthau jajñāte tau gata|vyathau,
tayor ātmānam ācakhyau,* yayau c' âtha yath"|āgatam.

14.70 svenus, titviṣur, udyemur uccakhnuḥ parvatāṃs tarūn,
vānarā dadramuś c' âtha saṃgrāmaṃ c' āśaśāsire.*

ḍuḍhaukire punar Laṅkāṃ bubudhe tān Daśānanaḥ
jīvataś ca vived' ârīn babhraṃśe 'sau dhṛtes tataḥ.

sasraṃse śara|bandhena divyen' êti bubunda saḥ
babhāj' âtha paraṃ moham ūhāṃ cakre jayaṃ na ca.

He sought to die, he praised his whole army with a speech and he took leave of Sugríva and sent him to his own country.

Sugríva ordered Ángada to take the Rághava brothers to Kishkíndha and he promised for himself the death of the demons.

Hearing from Vibhíshana that this was the serpent weapon 14.65
and its countermeasure was to recollect Gáruda, Rama concentrated on him.

The mountains broke up, the sea overflowed its banks, flowers fell from the trees and the bright horizons shone.

The snakes plunged into the ocean, a pleasant wind blew, the fires died down and the bonds of arrows were loosened.

The soldiers shone as if uninjured, Lákshmana regained consciousness, Vibhíshana too glowed and Gáruda approached.

Then he touched the two descendants of Kakútstha and they became free of pain, having announced himself to them he went as he had come.

The monkeys howled, shone, raised mountains and up- 14.70
rooted trees and then ran and sought battle.

They made for Lanka again and Rávana was awake to them and knew his enemy was alive and it was then that he lost his courage.

He understood that his divine arrow-bondage had failed and then suffered the greatest dejection and could no longer hope for victory.

Dhūmrākṣo 'tha pratiṣṭhāsāṃ cakre Rāvaṇa|saṃmataḥ.
siṃh'|āsyair yuyuje tasya vṛk'|āsyaiś ca rathaḥ khagaiḥ.

tvak|traiḥ saṃvivyayur* dehān, vāhanāny adhiśiśyire,*
ānarjur* nṛ|bhujo 'strāṇi vavañcuś c' āhava|kṣitim.

14.75 adhyuvāsa* rathaṃ, teye purāc, cukṣāva c' âśubham,
saṃśrāvayāṃ cakār' ākhyāṃ Dhūmrākṣas tatvare tathā.

nililye* mūrdhni gṛdhro 'sya, krūrā dhvāṅkṣā vavāśire,
śiśīke śoṇitaṃ vyoma, cacāla kṣmā|talaṃ tathā.

tataḥ prajaghaṭe yuddhaṃ śastrāṇy āsuḥ parasparam,
vavraścur ājughūrṇuś ca syemuś cukūrdire tathā.

rurujur, bhrejire, pheṇur bahudhā, hari|rākṣasāḥ,
vīrā na bibhayāṃ cakrur:* bhīṣayāṃ cakrire* parān.

raktaṃ pracuścutuḥ kṣaṇṇāḥ, śiśviyur* bāṇa|vikṣatāḥ,
asyatāṃ śuśuvur bāṇān bhujāḥ s'|âṅguṣṭha|muṣṭayaḥ.

14.80 raṇe cikrīḍa Dhūmrākṣas, taṃ tatarj' ânil'|ātmajaḥ:
ādade ca śilāṃ s'|âśvaṃ pipeṣ' âsya rathaṃ tayā.

papāta rākṣaso bhūmau rarāṭa ca bhayaṃ|karam
tutoda gadayā c' ârim taṃ dudhrāv' âdriṇā kapiḥ.

Then Dhumráksha got ready to set out with Rávana's approval. His chariot was yoked with wolf-faced and lion-faced birds.

The man-eaters covered their bodies in armor, settled on their mounts, got hold of their weapons and wended their way to the battle ground.

Dhumráksha mounted his chariot, passed out of the city 14.75
and sneezed inauspiciously; he spoke his own name and so hurried on.

A vulture settled on his head, cruel corvids croaked, the sky drizzled blood and the earth's surface shook.

When they set to battle they hurled weapons at each other, they slashed, they surged, they shrieked and exulted.

The monkeys and demons smashed each other, they shone and they sprang about diversely, the heroes were not frightened: they terrified their enemies.

The wounded shed blood, when pierced by arrows they became feverish and their arms, fists and thumbs swelled as they cast arrows.

Dhumráksha exulted in the battle but the son of the wind 14.80
challenged him: he took a rock and with it smashed his chariot and horses.

The demon fell to the ground and howled terrifyingly and struck at his enemy with his club but the monkey stilled him with a rock.

Akampanas tato yoddhuṃ cakame Rāvaṇ'|âjñayā:
sa rathen' âbhidudrāva jughure c' âtibhairavam.

paspande tasya vām'|âkṣi sasyamuś c' â|śivāḥ khagāḥ,
tān vavrāj' âvamaty' âsau babhāse ca raṇe śaraiḥ.

kham ūyur,* vasudhām ūvuḥ sāyakā rajjuvat tatāḥ.
tasmād balair apatrepe, puproth' âsmai na kaś cana.

14.85 sa bhasmasāc cakār'* ârīn, dudāva ca Kṛtāntavat.
cukrodha Mārutis, tālam uccakhne ca mahā|śikham.

Yamāy' Âkampanaṃ tena niruvāpa mahā|paśum.
babhrajja nihate tasmin śoko Rāvaṇam agnivat.

sa bibhreṣa, pracukṣoda, dantair oṣṭhaṃ cakhāda ca.
pragopāyāṃ cakār' āśu yatnena paritaḥ puram.

Prahastam arthayāṃ cakre yoddhum adbhuta|vikramam:
«kiṃ vicāreṇa, rāj'|êndra, yuddh'|ârthā vayam» ity asau
cakvāṇ' â|śaṅkito yoddhum utsehe ca mahā|rathaḥ:
niyemire* 'sya yoddhāraś cakḷpe c' âśva|kuñjaram.

14.90 yuyujuḥ syandanān aśvair, ījur devān purohitāḥ,
ānarcur brāhmaṇān samyag āśiṣaś c' āśaśaṃsire.

Then with Rávana's permission Akámpana sought to fight: he charged with his chariot and howled terribly.

His left eye twitched and birds of ill-omen screeched but dismissing them he advanced and his arrows shone in the battle.

Stretched out like threads his arrows made a warp of the sky and a weft of the earth. Armies shamefully turned from him, none withstood him.

He turned his enemies into ashes, like Yama he burned 14.85
them up. Hánuman became angry and uprooted a great-crowned *tala* palm.

With that palm he offered Akámpana as a great sacrificial victim to Yama. When he had been killed, grief roasted Rávana like fire.

He staggered and stomped and chewed off his lip with his teeth. He quickly made a careful defense of the city on all sides.

He exhorted Prahásta of astonishing valor to fight: "Why procrastinate, O great king? Our purpose is war," he cried and without qualm Prahásta of the great chariot prepared to fight: his warriors checked themselves and his horses and elephants were made ready.

They yoked horses to chariots, the priests worshipped the 14.90
gods, they honored the brahmins well and they prayed for intercessions.

ūhire mūrdhni siddh'|ârthā, gāvaś c' ālebhire bhaṭaiḥ,
pracukṣṇuvur mah"|âstrāṇi, jijñāsāṃ cakrire* hayān.

laluḥ khaḍgān mamārjuś* ca mamṛjuś ca paraśvadhān.
alaṃ|cakre, samālebhe, vavase, bubhuje, pape,
jahase ca kṣaṇaṃ yānair nirjagme yoddhṛbhis tataḥ.
viprān Prahasta ānarca juhāva ca Vibhāvasum.

saṃvargayāṃ cakār' āptān, candanena lilepa ca,
cacāma madhu mārdvīkam tvak|traṃ c' ācakace varam.

14.95 uṣṇīṣaṃ mumuce* cāru rathaṃ ca jujuṣe śubham,
ālalambe mah"|âstrāṇi gantuṃ pravavṛte tataḥ.

ājaghnus* tūrya|jātāni tuṣṭuvuś c' ânujīvinaḥ.
rajaḥ pravavṛdhe ghoraṃ ghoṣaś ca vyānaśe diśaḥ.

taṃ yāntaṃ dudruvur gṛdhrāḥ kravy'|âdaś ca siṣevire,
āvavur vāyavo ghorāḥ khād ulkāś ca pracakṣaruḥ.

sasyande śoṇitaṃ vyoma raṇ'|āṅgāni prajajvaluḥ,
rathāḥ pracaskhaluḥ s'|āśvā, na raraṃh' âśva|kuñjaram.

pratodā jagalur, vāmam ānañcur* yajñiyā mṛgāḥ,
dadāla bhūḥ pupūre dyauḥ kapīnām api niḥsvanaiḥ.

14.100 mimeha raktaṃ hasty|aśvaṃ rākṣasāś ca nitiṣṭhivuḥ.
tataḥ śuśubhatuḥ sene nirdayaṃ ca prajahratuḥ.

The soldiers bore white mustard on their heads and they took hold of cows, they whetted their great weapons and they tested their horses.

They took up their swords and polished them and polished their axes. The soldiers adorned, equipped and dressed themselves, ate and drank and laughed for a while and then came out with their mounts. Prahásta honored the brahmins and made offerings to Agni.

He gathered his comrades, smeared himself with sandal paste, sipped sweet wine and strapped on his fine armor.

He took off his beautiful turban and reveled in his fine char- 14.95
iot. He laid hold of his great weapons and started to go.

His followers beat anything that could be made an instrument and praised him. A terrible dust grew up and noise filled the horizons.

Vultures swooped at him as he went and scavengers attended him, fierce winds blew and meteors streamed down from the sky.

The sky dripped blood and the weapons of battle blazed, chariots and their horses crashed, horses and elephants did not sport.

Whips fell, sacrificial animals turned to the left, the earth split and the sky filled with the cries of monkeys.

Elephants and horses pissed blood and demons spat it out. 14.100
Then the two armies gleaming assailed each other without quarter.

didviśur, dudyuvuś, cacchuś, caklamuḥ, suṣupur, hatāḥ
cakhādire cakhāduś ca vilepuś ca raṇe bhaṭāḥ.

Prahastasya puro 'mātyān jihiṃsur dadhṛṣus tathā
vānarāḥ. karma senānī rakṣasāṃ cakṣame na tat.

ūrṇunāva sa śastr'|âughair vānarāṇām anīkinīm
śaśāsa ca bahūn yodhān jīvitena viveca ca.

āsasañja bhayaṃ teṣāṃ didyute ca yathā raviḥ,
n' āyayāsa, dviṣad|dehair jagāhe ca diśo daśa.

14.105 ke cit saṃcukuṭur bhītā, lejire 'nye par'|ājitāḥ,
saṃgrāmād babhraśuḥ ke cid yayācuś c' âpare '|bhayam.

evaṃ vijigye* tāṃ senāṃ Prahasto 'tidadarpa ca
śaśāma na ca saṃkruddho, nirjugopa niśā|carān.

cukrudhe tatra Nīlena taruś c' ôcciksipe mahān;
Prahasto 'bhihatas tena bāṇān visasṛje bahūn.

sehe kapī rath'|âśvāṃś ca ripos tatarha śākhinā.
dharitrīṃ musalī teye Prahastaś cikhide na ca.

saṃdudhukṣe tayoḥ kopaḥ, pasphāye śastra|lāghavam,
nunoda śākhinaṃ Nīla āvavre musalī tarum.

Soldiers in the battle fought, attacked, hacked and when wounded they fainted and became unconscious, they ate others and were themselves eaten and they screamed.

The monkeys struck Prahásta's ministers in front of him and so prevailed. The demons' general could not endure that act.

He covered the monkey army with a flood of arrows and he cut down many soldiers and separated them from life.

He struck fear into them and shone like the sun, he did not weary, he engulfed the ten directions with the bodies of his enemies.

Some turned away in fear, some beaten by the enemy were 14.105
ashamed, some fled from the battle and others begged shamelessly.

Thus Prahásta defeated that army and, exultant and full of anger, he did not calm down: he remained vigilant over the demons.

Then Nila became enraged and hurled a great tree; it struck Prahásta and he then fired many arrows.

The monkey survived and destroyed the enemy's chariot and horses with a tree. Prahásta alighted on the ground holding his club and he did not weary.

Anger ignited in them both, the speed of their weapons increased, Nila thrust at him with a tree but he with his club warded off the tree.

14.110 viyaty ānabhratur bhūmau maṇḍalāni viceratuḥ,
pradudruvatur anyonyaṃ vīrau śaśramatur na ca.

samīrayāṃ cakār' âtha rākṣasasya kapiḥ śilām
kṣatas tayā mamār' âsāv āśiśrāya ca bhū|talam.

tutuṣur vānarāḥ sarve, neśuś citrā niśā|carāḥ,
jerur āśā Daśāsyasya sainyaṃ Nīlaṃ nunāva ca.

yadā na pheluḥ kṣaṇadā|carāṇām
manorathā Rāma|bal'|âbhiyoge,
Laṅkāṃ tadā bhejur udīrṇa|dainyā
vyācakhyur uccaiś ca hataṃ Prahastam.

The two heroes dodged about in the air and circled each other on the ground, they assailed each other and they did not tire. 14.110

Then the monkey hurled a rock at the demon; struck by it he died and came to rest upon the ground.

All the monkeys rejoiced and the diverse demons vanished, Rávana's hopes faded and the army cheered Nila.

And when the dreams of the nightstalkers did not yield fruit in the encounter with Rama's army, increased in wretchedness they turned back to Lanka and loudly announced that Prahásta had been slain.

CANTO 15
KUMBHA·KARNA

15.1 RĀKṢAS'|ÊNDRAS TATO 'bhaiṣīd*
aikṣiṣṭa paritaḥ puram
prātiṣṭhipac* ca bodh'|ârthaṃ
Kumbhakarṇasya rākṣasān.*

te 'bhyagur* bhavanaṃ tasya suptaṃ c' âikṣiṣat' âtha tam,
vyāhārṣus tumulān śabdān daṇḍaiś c' âvadhiṣur drutam.

keśān aluñciṣus tasya, gajān gātreṣv acikraman,*
śītair abhyaṣicaṃs* toyair alātaiś c' âpy adambhiṣuḥ.

nakhair akartiṣus tīkṣṇair adāṅkṣur* daśanais tathā
śitair atautsuḥ śūlaiś ca bherīś c' âvīvadan śubhāḥ.

15.5 sa tān n' âjīgaṇat* sarvān icchay" âbuddha* ca svayam,
«abūbudhata kasmān mām?» aprākṣīc ca niśā|carān.

te 'bhāṣiṣata «rājā tvāṃ didṛkṣuḥ kṣaṇadā|cara.»
so 'snāsīd, vyalipan,* māṃsam apsāsīd, vāruṇīm apāt.*

nyavasiṣṭa tato draṣṭuṃ Rāvaṇaṃ prāvṛtad* gṛhāt;
rājā yāntaṃ tam adrākṣīd* udasthāc c' ēṣad āsanāt.

atuṣat pīṭham āsanne niradikṣac ca kāñcanam,
asmeṣṭa Kumbhakarṇo 'lpam upāvikṣad ath' ântike.

avādīn* «māṃ kim ity āhvo?»* rājñā ca pratyavādi* saḥ
«mā jñāsīs tvaṃ sukhī Rāmo yad akārṣīt sa rakṣasām.

15.10 udatārīd udanvantaṃ, puraṃ naḥ parito 'rudhat,
vyadyotiṣṭa raṇe śastrair anaiṣīd rākṣasān kṣayam.

THEN THE LORD of the demons was frightened and looked around the city and he dispatched his demons to awaken Kumbha·karna. 15.1

They went to his house and saw him sleeping there, they made cacophonic noises and beat him rapidly with sticks.

They pulled his hair and drove elephants over his limbs, they drenched him with cold water and then also wounded him with hot coals.

They cut him with their sharp nails and they bit him with their teeth and they struck him with sharpened spears and sounded clear drums.

He took no notice of any of this but woke of his own accord, 15.5
"Why did you try to wake me?" he asked the nightstalkers.

They said, "The king desires to see you, O nightstalker." He washed, anointed himself, and dined on meat and wine.

Then he dressed himself and set out from his house to see Rávana; the king saw him coming and rose slightly from his throne.

He was pleased and indicated a golden seat nearby, Kumbha·karna smiled a little and sat close by.

He said, "Why have you summoned me?" and the king replied to him, "Happy are you that you do not know what Rama has been doing to the demons.

He has crossed the ocean, he has blockaded our city, he has 15.10
shone in battle with his weapons and he has brought the demons to destruction.

na prāvocam ahaṃ kiṃ cit priyaṃ yāvad ajīviṣam,
bandhus tvam, arcitaḥ snehān, mā dviṣo na vadhīr* mama

vīryaṃ mā na dadarśas tvaṃ, mā na trāsthāḥ kṣatāṃ puram,
tav' âdrākṣma vayaṃ vīryaṃ, tvam ajaiṣīḥ purā surān.»

avocat Kumbhakarṇas taṃ «vayaṃ mantre 'bhyadhāma yat
na tvaṃ sarvaṃ tad aśrauṣīḥ, phalaṃ tasy' êdam āgamat.

prājña|vākyāny avāmaṃsthā mūrkha|vākyeṣv avāsthithāḥ.
adhyagīṣṭhāś ca śāstrāṇi pratyapatthā hitaṃ na ca.

15.15 mūrkhās tvām avavañcanta* ye vigraham acīkaran,
abhāṇīn Mālyavān yuktam akṣaṃsthās tvaṃ na tan madāt.

Rāghavasy' âmuṣaḥ kāntām āptair ukto na c' ārpipaḥ,*
mā n' ânubhūḥ svakān doṣān. mā muho, mā ruṣo 'dhunā.

tasy' âpy atyakramīt kālo yat tad" âham avādiṣam,
aghāniṣata rakṣāṃsi paraiḥ kośāṃs tvam avyayīḥ.*

sandhāna|kāraṇaṃ tejo nyag abhūt te 'kṛthās tathā,
yat tvaṃ vairāṇi, kośaṃ ca saha|daṇḍam ajiglapaḥ.»

akrudhac c' âbhyadhād vākyaṃ
  Kumbhakarṇaṃ Daśānanaḥ:
«kiṃ tvaṃ māṃ ajugupsiṣṭhā?*
  n' āididhaḥ* sva|parākramam?

I have not asked a favor as long as I have lived: you are a relative, honored out of affection, do not fail to kill my enemies.

You will not fail to show courage, you will not fail to protect the imperiled city: we have seen your courage, earlier you conquered the gods themselves."

Kumbha·karna said to him, "You did not listen to anything we said in council, this has come about as a result of that.

You have disregarded the words of the wise and you have resorted to the words of fools. You have studied the scriptures but you have not taken their counsel.

Fools who would have you make war have gulled you, 15.15
Mályavat spoke rightly but through pride you did not suffer that.

You have stolen Rama's wife and you have not returned her though told to by trusted friends; you will not fail to experience evils of your own making. Do not be stupid, do not rage now.

The time has passed for what I then advised, the enemy have killed the demons and you have lost your treasures.

You have acted so that your strength as the means to peace has diminished: you have exhausted your arguments, your treasury and your forces."

Rávana became angry and spoke to Kumbha·karna: "Why have you sought to offend me? Have you not enhanced your own prowess?

15.20 m" ôjjigrahaḥ su|nītāni, mā sma kraṃsthā na saṃyuge.
m" ôpālabdhāh kṛtair doṣair, mā na vākṣīr hitaṃ param.»

Kumbhakarṇas tato 'garjīd, bhaṭāṃś c' ânyān nyavīvṛtat,*
upāyaṃsta* mah"|âstrāṇi niragāc ca drutaṃ puraḥ.

mūrdhnā divam iv' âlekhīt khaṃ vyāpad vapuṣ" ôruṇā,
pādābhyāṃ kṣmām iv' âbhaitsīt, dṛṣṭy" âdhākṣīd iva dviśaḥ.

dagdha|śaila iv' âbhāsīt, prākraṃsta kṣaya|meghavat,
prācakampad udanvantaṃ rākṣasān apy atitrasat.

sa|pakṣo 'drir iv' âcālīn, nyaśvasīt kalpa|vāyuvat,
abhārṣīd dhvaninā lokān, abhrājiṣṭa kṣay'|âgnivat.

15.25 anaṃsīd* bhūr bhareṇ' âsya, raṃhasā śākhino 'luṭhan,*
siṃhāḥ prādudruvan* bhītāḥ, prākṣubhan kula|parvatāḥ.

utpātāḥ prāvṛtaṃs tasya, dyaur aśīkiṣṭa śoṇitam,
vāyavo 'vāsiṣur* bhīmāḥ krūrāś c' âkuṣata dvijāḥ.

aspandiṣṭ' âkṣi vāmaṃ ca, ghorāś c' ârāṭiṣuḥ śivāḥ,
nyapaptan* musale gṛdhrā, dīptay" âpāti c' ôlkayā.

āṃhiṣṭa tān a|saṃmānya darpāt sa pradhana|kṣitim
tato 'nardīd anandīc ca śatrūn āhvāsta* c' āhave.

prāśīn na c' âtṛpat krūraḥ, kṣuc c' âsy' âvṛdhad aśnataḥ,
adhād vasām adhāsīc* ca rudhiraṃ vana|vāsinām.

Do not extol good policy, you must not fail to exert yourself 15.20
in battle. Do not find fault with me, do not fail to carry out
the supreme purpose."

Kumbha·karna then roared and made the other soldiers turn, he took up his great weapons and quickly left the city.

As if scraping heaven with his head he filled space with his huge body; he seemed to shatter the earth with his feet, to burn the enemy with his glance.

He shone like a burning mountain, he advanced like a cloud of destruction, he made the ocean tremble and made even the demons quake.

He went like a winged mountain, he roared like the wind at the end of creation, he filled the worlds with his sound, he shone like the fire of destruction.

The earth buckled under his weight, trees shook with his 15.25
speed, lions roared in fear, mountain ranges shook.

Omens preceded him, the sky rained blood, terrible winds blew and cruel birds called.

His left eye twitched, vicious jackals howled, vultures landed on his club, a flaming meteor fell.

Arrogantly disregarding these portents he went on to the battle ground and roared and exulted and challenged his enemies in battle.

That cruel one ate and was never satisfied, and his hunger grew as he ate. He sucked out the fat and drank the blood of the monkeys.

15.30 māṃsen' âsy' âśvatāṃ* kukṣī, jaṭharaṃ c' âpy aśiśviyat,
bahūnām aglucat* prāṇān aglocīc ca raṇe yaśaḥ.

sāmarthyaṃ c' âpi so 'stambhīd,
  vikramaṃ c' âsya n' âstabhan,
śākhinaḥ ke cid adhyaṣṭhur,
  nyamāṅkṣur* apare 'mbu|dhau.

anye tv alaṅghiṣuḥ śailān, guhāsv anye nyaleṣata,
ke cid āsiṣata stabdhā, bhayāt ke cid aghūrṇiṣuḥ.

udatāriṣur ambho|dhiṃ vānarāḥ setun" âpare.
alajjiṣṭ' Âṅgadas tatra pratyavāsthita* c' ōrjitam.

sattvaṃ samadudhukṣac ca vānarāṇām ayuddha* ca,
tataḥ śailān udakṣaipsur udagūriṣata drumān.

15.35 anardiṣuḥ kapi|vyāghrāḥ samyak c' âyutsat'* āhave,
tān amardīd akhādīc ca nirāsthac* ca, tal'|āhatān.

prācucūrṇac ca pādābhyām abibhīṣata* ca drutam
atarhīc c' âiva śūlena Kumbhakarṇaḥ plavaṅgamān.

atautsīd gadayā gāḍham apiṣac c' ôpagūhanaiḥ,
jānubhyām adamīc c' ânyān hasta|vartam* avīvṛtat.

adāliṣuḥ śilā dehe, cūrṇy|abhūvan mahā|drumāḥ
kṣiptās tasya, na c' âcetīt tān asau, n' âpi c' âkṣubhat.

adrāṣṭāṃ taṃ Raghu|vyāghrau ākhyac c' âinaṃ Vibhīṣaṇaḥ,
«eṣa vyajeṣṭa Devendraṃ n' âśaṅkiṣṭa vivasvataḥ.

Both his flanks swelled with flesh, and his belly too swelled 15.30
up. He took the lives of many and he seized fame in battle.

They could not withstand his prowess in the manner that he withstood their force; some took to the trees, others plunged into the ocean.

Some leaped up cliffs, others hid in caves, some sat steady, others vacillated in fear.

Other monkeys crossed the ocean by the bridge. Among them Ángada was ashamed and recovered himself valiantly.

He ignited the monkeys' courage and fought; they then threw up mountains and pulled up trees.

Those tigers of monkeys roared and fought to the full in 15.35
the battle, but he crushed them and ate them and discarded them, swatted away with his hand.

Kumbha·karna crushed the monkeys with his feet and terrifying them immediately skewered them with his lance.

He struck them heavily with his club and crushed them with his embraces, others he mastered with his knees or rolled together in the movement of his hands.

Hurled rocks shattered against his body, great trees were crushed: he did not feel them and did not even twitch.

Those two tigers of Raghu saw him and Vibhíshana spoke of him: "He defeated Indra, the lord of the gods, and did not fear the sun.

15.40 yakṣ'|êndra|śaktim acchāsīn, n' âprothīd asya kaś cana,
Kumbhakarṇān na bhaiṣṭaṃ mā yuvām asmān nṛp'|ātmajau,

ghnantaṃ m" ôpekṣiṣāthāṃ ca, mā na kārṣṭam ih' ādaram.»
«amuṃ mā na vadhiṣṭ'»* êti Rāmo 'vādīt tataḥ kapīn.

te vyarāsiṣur* āhvanta* rākṣasaṃ c' âpy apiplavan,*
ababhāsan* svakāḥ śaktīr druma|śailaṃ vyakāriṣuḥ.

te taṃ vyāśiṣat' âkṣautsuḥ pādair dantais tath" âcchidan,
ārjijat Śarabho vṛkṣaṃ Nīlas tv ādita parvatam.

Ṛṣabho 'drīn udakṣaipsīt te tair arim atardiṣuḥ,
asphūrjīd giri|śṛṅgaṃ ca vyasrākṣīd Gandhamādanaḥ.

15.45 akūrdiṣṭa vyakārīc ca Gavākṣo bhū|dharān bahūn,
sa tān n' âjīgaṇad vīraḥ Kumbhakarṇo 'vyathiṣṭa na.

amanthīc ca par'|ânīkam aploṣṭa ca niraṅkuśaḥ
nihantuṃ c' âtvariṣṭ' ârīn ajakṣīc c' âṅkam āgatān.

vyakrukṣad vānar'|ânīkaṃ saṃpalāyiṣṭa c' āyati,
hastābhyāṃ naśyad akrākṣīd bhīme c' ôpādhit' ānane.

rakten' âciklidad bhūmiṃ sainyaiś c' âtastaradd* hataiḥ,
n' âtārpsīd bhakṣayan krūro n' âśramad ghnan plavaṅgamān.

The power of Kubéra the lord of the *yaksha*s could not 15.40
pierce him, no one could withstand him, you two princes
must be wary of this Kumbha·karna,

And do not ignore him as he kills, you must respect him now." Rama told the monkeys, "You must kill him."

They whooped and they baited the demon and made him jump, they displayed their own powers and hurled trees and rocks at him.

They reached him and pounded him with their feet and cut into him with their teeth, Shárabha got hold of a tree but Nila took up a mountain.

Ríshabha threw mountains and these harmed the enemy, Gandha·mádana roared and hurled a mountain peak.

Gaváksha played about and threw many mountains: the 15.45
hero Kumbha·karna did not reckon them and did not
budge.

And he churned up the enemy force and wanton he went about and he made haste to kill the enemy and he ate those that came within his sway.

As he came the monkey army screamed and fled, and as they disappeared he drew them up with his hands and placed them in his terrible mouth.

He drenched the ground with blood and strewed it with slain soldiers: the cruel Kumbha·karna was not sated as he ate and he did not weary in killing the monkeys.

na yoddhum aśakan ke cin, n' âḍhaukiṣata ke cana
prāṇaśan nāsikābhyāṃ ca vaktreṇa ca van'|âukasaḥ.

15.50 udare c' âjarann* anye tasya pātāla|sannibhe,
ākrandiṣuḥ sakhīn āhvan,* prapalāyiṣat' âsvidan.

raktam aścyotiṣuḥ kṣuṇṇāḥ kṣatāś ca kapayo 'tṛṣan,
upāsthāyi nṛpo bhagnair asau Sugrīvam aijihat.

yoddhuṃ so 'py aruṣac chatror airirac ca mahā|drumam,
taṃ prāptaṃ prāsahiṣṭ' âriḥ śaktiṃ c' ôgrām udagrahīt.

sa tām abibhramad bhīmāṃ, vānar'|êndrasya c' âmucat,
prāpaptan* Mārutis tatra tāṃ c' âlāsīd* viyad|gatām.

aśobhiṣṭ' âcakhaṇḍac ca śaktiṃ vīro na c' âyasat,
«lauha|bhāra|sahasreṇa nirmitā nirakāri me
15.55 śaktir,» ity akupad rakṣo, giriṃ c' ôdakhanīd gurum
vyasṛṣṭa taṃ kap'|îndrasya ten' âmūrcchīd asau kṣataḥ.

aloṭhiṣṭa* ca bhū|pṛṣṭhe, śoṇitaṃ c' âpy asusruvat,*
tam ādāy', âpalāyiṣṭa vyarociṣṭa ca rākṣasaḥ.

abhaiṣuḥ kapayo, 'nvārat* Kumbhakarṇaṃ Marut|sutaḥ,
śanair abodhi* Sugrīvaḥ so 'luñcīt karṇa|nāsikam
rākṣasasya na c' âtrāsīt pranaṣṭum ayatiṣṭa ca.
akrodhi Kumbhakarṇena peṣṭum ārambhi* ca kṣitau.

Some were unable to fight, some would not be drawn near and some monkeys fled through his nostrils and his mouth.

And others were digested in his hell-like belly, others cried 15.50
to their friends, fled and sweated.

The crushed monkeys oozed blood and the wounded suffered thirst, the king was surrounded by the broken and he urged on Sugríva.

He was also enraged at the enemy and to fight him threw a great tree, the foe was able to take it when it fell and took up a fearsome weapon.

He whirled that terrible weapon and loosed it at the monkey chief; Hánuman reached for it as it went through the air and caught it.

The hero shone and shattered the weapon with barely any 15.55
effort; the demon was enraged and said, "My weapon fashioned from one thousand weights of iron has been broken." He dug up a massive mountain and hurled it at the monkey lord who reeled when it struck him.

And he writhed on the ground and he also shed blood and, grabbing him, the demon went off exultant.

The monkeys were terrified, Hánuman followed Kumbha·karna, Sugríva awoke gradually and then lopped off the demon's ears and nose and he was not frightened and tried to disappear. Kumbha·karna became angry and began to pound the earth.

Sugrīvo 'sy' âbhraśadd hastāt samagāhiṣṭa c' âmbaram
tūrṇam anvasṛpad Rāmam ānanandac ca vānarān.

15.60 atatvarac* ca tān yoddhum aciceṣṭac* ca Rāghavau.
Kumbhakarṇo nyavartiṣṭa raṇe 'yutsanta vānarāḥ.

aviveṣṭan nṛp'|ādeśād ārukṣaṃś* c' āśu rākṣasam:
tān adhāvīt* samārūḍhāṃs te 'py asraṃsiṣat' ākulāḥ.

agrasiṣṭa, vyadhāviṣṭa samāślikṣac* ca nirdayam
te c' âpy aghoriṣur ghoraṃ raktaṃ c' âvamiṣur mukhaiḥ.

sa c' âpi rudhirair mattaḥ sveṣām apy adayiṣṭa na*
agrahīc* c' āyur anyeṣām aruddha ca parākramam.

saṃtrastānām apāhāri sattvaṃ ca vana|vāsinām.
acchedi Lakṣmaṇen' âsya kirīṭaṃ kavacaṃ tathā.

15.65 abhedi ca śarair dehaḥ prāśaṃsīt taṃ niśā|caraḥ
aspardhiṣṭa ca Rāmeṇa ten' âsy' âkṣipsat' êṣavaḥ.

yair aghāni Kharo, Vālī, Mārīco, Dūṣaṇas tathā,
avāmaṃsta sa tān darpāt prodayaṃsīc* ca mudgaram.

Vāyavy'|âstreṇa taṃ pāṇiṃ Rāmo 'cchaitsīt sah'|āyudham
ādīpi* taru|hasto 'sāv adhāvīc c' âri|saṃmukham.

sa|vṛkṣam acchidat tasya Śakr'|âstreṇa karaṃ nṛpaḥ,
jaṅghe c' âśīśatad* bāṇair aprāsīd iṣubhir mukham.

Sugríva slipped from his hand and plunged into the air and quickly pursued Rama and pleased the monkeys.

And he hastened them to fight and urged on the two Ragha- 15.60
vas. Kumbha·karna returned to the battle and the monkeys fought on.

At the king's command they surrounded the demon and quickly climbed up him. He shook off those that had ascended and they fell down in confusion.

He ate them, he assailed them and without pity he squeezed them and they screamed horribly and vomited blood from their mouths.

And, drunk with blood, he had no pity even for his own and took the lives of some and obstructed the prowess of others.

And the spirit of the terrified monkeys was taken from them. Lákshmana cut off his crown and his armor.

As arrows tore his body the demon lauded him and he 15.65
fought with Rama who was shooting arrows at him.

He arrogantly disdained those who had killed Khara, Valin, Marícha and Dúshana and raised his club.

With the arrow Vayu had given him, Rama severed that hand that bore the weapon and Kumbha·karna with tree in hand flared up and ran towards his enemy.

The king cut off the hand holding the tree with his Shakra weapon, shot arrows into his leg and stopped his mouth with shafts.

Aindreṇa hṛdaye 'vyātsīt so 'dhyavātsīc ca gāṃ hataḥ
apikṣātāṃ sahasre dve tad|dehena van'|âukasām.

15.70 astāviṣuḥ* surā Rāmaṃ, diśaḥ prāpan niśā|carāḥ,
bhūr akampiṣṭa s'|âdr'|îndrā, vyacālīd ambhasāṃ patiḥ.

hataṃ rakṣāṃsi rājānaṃ Kumbhakarṇam aśiśravan,
arodīd Rāvaṇo, 'śocīn mohaṃ c' âśiśriyat* param.

apaprathad* guṇān bhrātur acikīrttac* ca vikramam,
«kruddhena Kumbhakarṇena ye 'darśiṣata śatravaḥ
kathaṃ nv ajīviṣus te ca? sa c' âmṛta mahā|balaḥ?»
ayuyutsiṣat' āśvāsya kumārā Rāvaṇaṃ tataḥ.

Devāntako 'tikāyaś ca Triśirāḥ sa Narāntakaḥ
te c' āṃhiṣata saṃgrāmaṃ balino Rāvaṇ'|ātmajāḥ.

15.75 Yuddhonmattaṃ ca Mattaṃ ca rājā rakṣ"|ârtham āñjihat
sutānāṃ, niragātāṃ* tau rākṣasau raṇa|paṇḍitau.

tair ajeṣata sainyāni, dviṣo 'kāriṣat' ākulāḥ
parvatān iva te bhūmāv acaiṣur vānar'|ôttamān.

Aṅgadena samaṃ yoddhum aghaṭiṣṭa Narāntakaḥ,
praiṣiṣad rākṣasaḥ prāsaṃ, so 'sphoṭīd Aṅgad'|ôrasi.

aśvān Vāli|suto 'hiṃsīd atatāḍac ca muṣṭinā,
Rāvaṇiś c' â|vyatho yoddhum ārabdha ca mahīṃ gataḥ.

He pierced his heart with the Indra weapon. Slain, he sank to the ground and two thousand monkeys were crushed by his body.

The gods praised Rama, the nightstalkers took to the hori- 15.70
zons, the earth with its great mountains shook, the Ocean, Lord of the waters, churned.

The demons told their king about the slain Kumbha·karna: Rávana wept, grieved and went into deep torpor.

He extolled the virtues of his brother and praised his courage, "How can those enemies who the wrathful Kumbha·karna saw be alive? Has he of such great strength died?" Then the princes consoling Rávana readied themselves to fight.

Rávana's mighty sons, Devántaka, Atikáya, Tri·shiras and Narántaka himself, entered the battle.

The king sent for Yuddhonmátta and Matta to protect his 15.75
sons. Those two demons expert at battle went forth.

Rávana's sons bested the soldiers, they threw the enemy into disarray, they piled the best of the monkeys onto the earth like mountains.

Narántaka took on Ángada in battle: the demon threw a barbed missile and it shattered on Ángada's chest.

Valin's son Ángada struck his horses and crushed them with his fist: Rávana's son Narántaka, unmoved, got onto the ground and began to fight.

tasy' âhāriṣata prāṇā muṣṭinā Vāli|sūnunā.
prādudruvaṃs* tataḥ kruddhāḥ sarve Rāvaṇayo 'ṅgadam.

15.80 tato Nīla|Hanūmantau Rāvaṇīn avaveṣṭatām
akāriṣṭāṃ girīṃs tuṅgān arautsīt Triśirāḥ śaraiḥ.

parigheṇ' âvadhiṣṭ' âtha raṇe Devāntako balī
muṣṭin" âdadarat tasya mūrdhānaṃ Mārut'|ātmajaḥ.

adīdipat tato vīryaṃ Nīlaṃ c' âpīpiḍac charaiḥ
Yuddhonmattas tu Nīlena giriṇ" ānāyi saṃkṣayam.

ababhrājat tataḥ śaktiṃ Triśirāḥ pavan'|ātmaje
Hanūmatā kṣatās tasya raṇe 'mṛṣata vājinaḥ.

asrasac c' āhato mūrdhni, khaḍgaṃ c' âjīharad dviṣā
prāṇān aujjhīc ca, khaḍgena cchinnais ten' âiva mūrdhabhiḥ.

15.85 Matten' âmāri, saṃprāpya Śarabh'|âstāṃ mahā|gadām,
sahasra|hariṇ" âkrīḍīd Atikāyas tato raṇe.

rathen' âvivyathac c' ârīn vyacārīc ca niraṅkuśaḥ,
Vibhīṣaṇena so 'khyāyi Rāghavasya mahā|rathaḥ.

«atastambhad ayaṃ vajraṃ Svayaṃbhuvam atūtuṣat,
aśikṣiṣṭa mah"|âstrāṇi raṇe 'rakṣīc ca rākṣasān.

adhyagīṣṭ' ârtha|śāstrāṇi, Yamasy' âhnoṣṭa vikramam,
dev'|āhaveṣv adīpiṣṭa, n' âjaniṣṭ' âsya sādhvasam.

Valin's son took his life-breath with his fist, then all the enraged sons of Rávana attacked Ángada.

Then Nila and Hánuman encircled the sons of Rávana and 15.80
threw high mountains but Tri·shiras blocked them with his arrows.

Then in the battle the mighty Devántaka was struck by a club and Hánuman crushed his head with his fist.

Then Yuddhonmátta showed his courage and tormented Nila with his arrows but was wholly destroyed by Nila with a mountain.

Then Tri·shiras flashed his spear at the son of the wind but his horses, struck in the battle by Hánuman, died.

Being struck on the head he fell surrendering his sword to his enemy, and his foe took his life, severing his heads with that very sword.

Matta died, after getting a great club thrown by Shárabha, 15.85
then Atikáya jousted in the battle with a thousand-horse chariot.

And he oppressed his foes with the chariot and went about freely, Vibhíshana nominated the great chariot for Rama.

"He stopped a thunderbolt and delighted the Self-existent one, he studied great weapons and defended the demons in battle.

He studied the science of wealth, he warded off Yama's prowess, he shone in the wars of the gods, he is not known to fear.

eṣa Rāvaṇir āpādi vānarāṇāṃ bhayaṃ|karaḥ.»
āhvat' âtha sa Kākutsthaṃ dhanuś c' âpusphurad guru.

15.90 Saumitriḥ sarpavat siṃham ārdidat taṃ mah"|āhave,
tau prāvīvṛtatāṃ jetuṃ śara|jālāny an|ekaśaḥ.

acchaittāṃ ca mah"|ātmānau ciram aśramatāṃ na ca,
tathā tāv āsthatāṃ* bāṇān atāniṣṭāṃ tamo yathā.

saury'|āgneye vyakāriṣṭām astre rākṣasa|Lakṣmaṇau
te c' ôpāgamatāṃ nāśaṃ samāsādya parasparam.

abibhrajat tataḥ śastram Aiṣīkaṃ rākṣaso raṇe
tad apy adhvasad āsādya Māhendraṃ Lakṣmaṇ'|êritam.

tataḥ Saumitrir asmārṣīd adeviṣṭa ca durjayam
Brahm'|âstraṃ tena mūrdhānam adadhvaṃsan nara|dviṣaḥ.

15.95 tato 'krandīd Daśagrīvas tam āśiśvasad Indrajit
nirayāsīc ca saṃkruddhaḥ prārcicac ca Svayaṃbhuvam.

ahauṣīt Kṛṣṇavartmānaṃ samayaṣṭ' âstra|maṇḍalam,
so 'labdha Brahmaṇaḥ śastraṃ syandanaṃ ca jay'|āvaham.

tam adhyāsiṣṭa dīpr'|âgram amodiṣṭa ca Rāvaṇiḥ,
channa|rūpas tato 'kartīd dehān Rāvaṇa|vidviṣām.

This son of Rávana has become a cause of terror for the monkeys." Then he challenged Rama and made his heavy bow twang.

Lákshmana attacked him in the great battle as a snake does 15.90
a lion, many times those two sent forth skeins of arrows in order to win.

And those two great-souled ones cut at each other and for a long time did not rest, they fired so many arrows that they brought on darkness.

The demon fired the solar weapon and Lákshmana fired the fire weapon and when these met each other they were destroyed.

Then the demon made his Aishíka weapon flash in the fight and that also fell apart when it encountered the Mahéndra weapon fired by Lákshmana.

Then Lákshmana remembered and deployed the invincible Brahma-weapon with which he shattered the head of the demon.

Then Rávana wept and Índrajit gave succor and went out 15.95
enraged and propitiated the Self-existent one.

He sacrificed to Agni whose path is black and dedicated his range of weapons: he obtained Brahma's weapon and a victory-bringing chariot.

Rávana's son sat in it with its shining prow and gloated, then concealing his identity he cut the bodies of Rávana's foes.

sapta|ṣaṣṭiṃ plavaṅgānāṃ koṭīr bāṇair asūṣupat,
niś"|ânte Rāvaṇiḥ kruddho Rāghavau ca vyamūmuhat.

apisphavat* sva|sāmarthyam agūhīt sāyakair diśaḥ
aghorīc ca mahā|ghoraṃ gatvā praiṣīc ca Rāvaṇam.

15.100 Vibhīṣaṇas tato 'bodhi sa|sphurau Rāma|Lakṣmaṇau
apārīt sa gṛhīt'|ôlko hata|śeṣān plavaṅgamān.

«mā śociṣṭa, Raghu|vyāghrau n' âmṛṣātām» iti bruvan
avābuddha sa Nīl'|ādīn nihatān kapi|yūtha|pān.

tatr' ēṣaj Jāmbavān prāṇīd udamīlīc ca locane
Paulastyaṃ c' âgadīt «kaccid ajīvīn Mārut'|ātmajaḥ?

tasya kṣeme mahā|rāja, n' âmṛṣmahy* akhilā vayam,»
Paulastyo 'śiśravat taṃ ca jīvantaṃ Pavan'|ātmajam.

āyiṣṭa Mārutis tatra tau c' âpy ahṛṣatāṃ tataḥ,
prāhaiṣṭāṃ Himavat|pṛṣṭhe Sarvauṣadhi|giriṃ tataḥ
15.105 tau Hanūmantam ānetum oṣadhīṃ mṛta|jīvinīm,
sandhāna|karaṇīṃ c' ânyāṃ, vi|śalya|karaṇīṃ tathā.

prodapāti nabhas tena sa ca prāpi mahā|giriḥ
yasminn ajvaliṣū rātrau mah"|âuṣadhyaḥ sahasraśaḥ.

niracāyi yadā bhedo n' âuṣadhīnāṃ Hanūmatā,
sarva eva samāhāri tadā śailaḥ sah'|âuṣadhiḥ.

The son of Rávana put to sleep sixty-seven crore of monkeys with his arrows, enraged at the night's end he confronted the two Rághava brothers.

He augmented his own powers and obscured the horizons with his arrows and he roared a great roar and went and called upon Rávana.

Vibhíshana realized that Rama and Lákshmana were still 15.100
alive and taking a torch he protected the monkeys that re-
mained from the slaughter.

Saying, "Do not grieve! The two tigers of Raghu are not dead," he became aware that Nila and the other monkey chiefs had been slain.

And there Jámbavan revived a little and opened his eyes and he said to Vibhíshana, "Has Hánuman survived?

While he survives, O great king, we will not all die," and Vibhíshana told him that Hánuman was alive.

The son of the wind came there and then the two brothers
were delighted, and they sent Hánuman to the Mount of 15.105
All-herbs on a ridge of the Himálaya to bring the life-from-
death herb, that other, the healing herb and similarly the
healer-of-arrow-wounds herb.

He flew up into the sky and reached the great mountain on which at night the great herbs shone by the thousand.

As Hánuman could not discern the difference between the herbs, he took the entire mountain together with its herbs.

prāṇiṣur nihatāḥ ke cit, ke cit tu prodamīliṣuḥ,
tamo 'nye 'hāsiṣur yodhā vyajṛmbhiṣata c' âpare.

ajighrapaṃs tath" âiv' ânyān oṣadhīr ālipaṃs tathā,
evaṃ te' cetiṣuḥ sarve vīryaṃ c' âdhiṣat' âdhikam.

15.110 ajihladat sa Kākutsthau śeṣāṃś c' âjījivat kapīn
Hanūmān, atha te Laṅkām agnin" âdīdipan drutam.

samanātsīt* tataḥ sainyam amārjīd bhalla|tomaram
amārkṣīc* c' âsi|patr'|ādīn ababhāsat* paraśvadhān.

Kumbhakarṇa|sutau tatra samanāddhāṃ* mahā|balau
Nikumbhaś c' âiva Kumbhaś ca, prāpatāṃ tau plavaṅgamān.

agopiṣṭāṃ purīṃ Laṅkām agauptāṃ rakṣasāṃ balam,
atyāktām āyudh'|ânīkam anaiṣṭāṃ ca kṣayaṃ dviṣaḥ.

akokūyiṣṭa* tat sainyaṃ prapalāyiṣṭa c' ākulam
acyutac ca kṣataṃ raktaṃ, hataṃ c' âdhyaśayiṣṭa gām.

15.115 Aṅgaden' âhasātāṃ tau yudhy Akampana|Kampanau.
abhyārdīd Vālinaḥ putraṃ Prajaṅgho 'pi sa|matsaraḥ.

tasy' âpy abebhidiṣṭ'* âsau mūrdhānaṃ muṣṭin" Âṅgadaḥ
ahārṣīc ca śiraḥ kṣipraṃ Yūpākṣasya Nirākulaḥ.

śarīraṃ Lohitākṣasya
  nyabhāṅkṣīd Dvividas tadā,
kruddhaḥ Kumbhas tato 'bhaitsīn
  Maindaṃ sa|Dvividaṃ śaraiḥ.

Some that were slain revived, others opened their eyes, some soldiers emerged from the darkness and others yawned.

They made others smell the herbs and anointed them, thus they all became conscious and regained greater vigor.

Hánuman delighted Rama and Lákshmana and he revivi- 15.110
fied the rest of the monkeys, then they quickly set Lanka ablaze with fire.

Then the army prepared itself, polished its lances and javelins and wiped the blades of its swords and made its axes shine.

Kumbha·karna's sons of great strength, Nikúmbha and Kumbha, prepared themselves and approached the monkeys.

They guarded the city of Lanka and they protected the army of demons, they loosed an array of weapons and brought their enemy to ruin.

That army was made to cry aloud and to flee in confusion and wounded it shed blood and slain it lay prone on the ground.

Akámpana and Kámpana were killed in the fight by Án- 15.115
gada. Prajángha full of hostility wounded Valin's son Ángada.

Ángada in turn split his head with his fist and Nirákula quickly took Yupáksha's head.

Then Dvi·vida split open Lohitáksha's body and then Kumbha, enraged, wounded Mainda together with Dvi·vida using arrows.

āghūrṇiṣṭāṃ kṣatau kṣmāṃ ca tāv āśiśriyatām ubhau.
mātulau vihvalau dṛṣṭvā Kumbhaṃ Vāli|suto nagaiḥ
praurṇāvīc: chara|varṣeṇa tān aprauhīn niśā|caraḥ.
vānarān aijihad Rāmas tūrṇaṃ rakṣitum Aṅgadam.

15.120 drutam atrāsta Sugrīvo bhrātṛvyaṃ śatru|saṃkaṭāt
muṣṭinā Kaumbhakarṇiṃ ca kruddhaḥ prāṇair atityajat.

Nikumbho vānar'|êndrasya prāhaiṣīt parighaṃ tataḥ
Hanūmāṃś c' āpatantaṃ tam abhāṅkṣīd bhogi|bhīṣaṇam.

praurṇuvīt tejas" ârātim arāsīc ca bhayaṃ|karam,
grīvāṃ c' âsya tath" âkrākṣīd ajijīvad yathā na tam.

samagata kapi|sainyaṃ sammaden' âtimātraṃ,
viṭapa|hariṇa|nāthaḥ siddhim auhiṣṭa nityām:
nṛ|pati|matir araṃsta prāpta|kām" êva harṣāt,
rajani|cara|patīnāṃ santato 'tāyi śokaḥ.

Being struck they both spun round and fell to the ground. Ángada the son of Valin seeing his maternal uncles in distress covered Kumbha with trees; the demon brought them down with a rain of arrows. Rama quickly urged the monkeys to protect Ángada.

Sugríva swiftly protected his nephew Ángada from the peril 15.120
of the enemy and in anger took Kumbha's life with his fist.

Then Nikúmbha threw a club at the lord of monkeys and Hánuman broke that weapon as fearsome as a snake as it fell.

He overcame the enemy with his power and made a frightful noise, and he pulled his neck in such a way that he killed him.

The monkey army came together in excessive joy and the monkey lord believed success certain: it was as if the king's mind with its wishes fulfilled was ecstatic with joy and the continuous grief of the demon lords increased.

CANTO 16
RÁVANA'S LAMENT

16.1 Tataḥ prarudito rājā rakṣasāṃ hata|bāndhavaḥ,
«kiṃ kariṣyāmi* rājyena? Sītayā kiṃ kariṣyate?*

Atikāye hate vīre protsahiṣye na jīvitum.
hrepayiṣyati* kaḥ śatrūn? kena jāyiṣyate Yamaḥ?

Atikāyād vinā pāśaṃ ko vā chetsyati Vāruṇam?
Rāvaṇaṃ maṃsyate ko vā? Svayambhūḥ kasya tokṣyati?*

ślāghiṣye kena? ko bandhūn neṣyaty unnatim unnataḥ?
kaḥ preṣyati pitṝn kāle? kṛtvā katthiṣyate na kaḥ?

16.5 udyaṃsyati Harir vajraṃ, vicariṣyati nirbhayaḥ,
bhokṣyate* yajña|bhāgāṃś ca śūra|mānaṃ ca vakṣyati.*

ravis tapsyati niḥśaṅkaṃ, vāsyaty a|niyataṃ marut,
nirvartsyaty ṛtu|saṃghātaḥ, sv'|êcchay" êndur udeṣyati.

tīvraṃ syandiṣyate meghair, ugraṃ vartiṣyate* Yamaḥ,
Atikāyasya maraṇe, kiṃ kariṣyanti n' ânyathā?

unmīliṣyati cakṣur me vṛthā yad vinay'|āgatam
ājñā|lābh'|ônmukhaṃ namraṃ na drakṣyati Narāntakam.

dhiṅ māṃ Triśirasā n' âhaṃ saṃdarśiṣye 'dya yat punaḥ.
ghāniṣyante dviṣaḥ kena tasmin pañcatvam āgate?*

16.10 śatrubhir nihate Matte, drakṣye 'haṃ saṃyuge sukham.
Yuddhonmattād vinā śatrūn samāskantsyati ko raṇe?

THEN WITH HIS relatives slain, the king of the demons 16.1
lamented: "What shall I do with my kingdom? What
is to be done with Sita?

Now the brave Atikáya is slain I cannot bear to live. Who will humiliate the enemy? Who will conquer Yama?

Who will cut Váruna's noose except Atikáya? Who will esteem Rávana? Whom will the Self-existent favor?

By whom will I be eulogized? What noble person will lead my kinsmen to glory? Who will propitiate the ancestors at the right time? After action, who will not boast?

Indra will raise up his thunderbolt, he will go about without 16.5
fear, he will enjoy his portion of the sacrifice and he will
bear his pride as a hero.

Without doubt the sun will shine, the wind will always blow, the cycle of seasons will roll on, the moon will rise of its own will.

The clouds will rain heavily, Yama will proceed fiercely, now Atikáya is dead, what will they not do differently?

In vain will my eye open, for it will not see Narántaka coming obediently with face upraised to recieve my orders submissively.

A curse on me that I will never now again be seen by Tri·shiras. Who will kill my enemies now he is dead?

Now that Matta has been killed by the enemy, I shall be 16.10
easily visible in the fray. Who will attack the enemy in battle
without Yuddhonmátta?

āhvāsyate viśaṅko māṃ yotsyamānaḥ Śatakratuḥ,
prakalpsyati ca tasy' ârtho Nikumbhe durhaṇe hate.

kalpiṣyate* Hareḥ prītir Laṅkā c' ôpahaniṣyate.
Devāntaka tvayā tyakto, ripor yāsyāmi vaśyatām.

mariṣyāmi vijeṣye vā, hatāś cet tanayā mama,
haniṣyāmi ripūṃs tūrṇaṃ, na jīviṣyāmi duḥkhitaḥ.

smeṣyante munayo devāḥ kathayiṣyanti c' âniśam
Daśagrīvasya dur|nīter vinaṣṭaṃ rakṣasāṃ kulam.

16.15 kena saṃbhāvitaṃ tāta,* Kumbhakarṇasya Rāghavaḥ
raṇe kartsyati gātrāṇi marmāṇi ca vitartsyati?

patiṣyati kṣitau bhānuḥ, pṛthivī tolayiṣyate,
nabhasvān bhaṅkṣyate, vyoma muṣṭibhis tāḍayiṣyate,

indoḥ syandiṣyate vahniḥ, samucchokṣyati* sāgaraḥ,
jalaṃ dhakṣyati* tigm'|âṃśoḥ syantsyanti tamasāṃ cayāḥ.

Kumbhakarṇo raṇe puṃsā kruddhaḥ paribhaviṣyate
saṃbhāvitāni n' âitāni kadā cit kena cij jane.

Kumbhakarṇe hate, Laṅkām ārokṣyanti plavaṅgamāḥ,
daṅkṣyanti rākṣasān dṛptā, bhaṅkṣyanti ca mam' āśramān.

Indra of the hundred rites, ready to fight and fearless, will challenge me and he will achieve his purpose now that the invulnerable Nikúmbha has been killed.

Indra will get what he wants and Lanka will be destroyed. Abandoned by you, O Devántaka, I will come under the sway of the enemy.

I shall die or I shall conquer. If my sons have been killed, then I shall quickly kill my enemies, I shall not live in misery.

The sages will smile and the gods will always tell the story of how the tribe of demons was destroyed by ten-necked Rávana's ill-advised counsel.

Who could imagine, O father, that Rama would cut off 16.15
Kumbha·karna's limbs in battle and pierce his vital organs?

The sun might as well fall to earth, the earth be weighed, the wind be cut, the air be squeezed in fistfuls,

Fire might as well stream from the moon, the ocean be dried up, water burn or masses of darkness stream from the sun,

As that Kumbha·karna enraged in battle might be bested by a man. These things are unimaginable at any time, by anyone in the world.

Now Kumbha·karna has been killed, the monkeys will overrun Lanka, they will impudently bite my demons, they will destroy my refuges.

16.20 cartsyanti bāla|vṛddhāṃś ca nartsyanti ca mudā yutāḥ:
tena rākṣasa|mukhyena vinā, tān ko nirotsyati?

a|marṣo me paraḥ, Sītāṃ Rāghavaḥ kāmayiṣyate:
cyuta|rājyāt sukhaṃ tasmāt kiṃ kil' âsāv avāpsyati?*

mārayiṣyāmi Vaidehīṃ khādayiśyāmi rākṣasaiḥ
bhūmau vā nikhaniṣyāmi vidhvaṃsasy' âsya kāraṇam.

n' ânurotsye jagal|lakṣmīṃ ghaṭiṣye jīvituṃ na vā,
na raṃsye viṣayaiḥ śūnye bhavane bāndhavair aham.

modiṣye kasya saukhye 'haṃ? ko me modiṣyate sukhe?
ādeyāḥ kiṃ|kṛte bhogāḥ Kumbhakarṇa, tvayā vinā?

16.25 yāḥ suhṛtsu vipanneṣu mām upaiṣyanti saṃpadaḥ,
tāḥ kiṃ manyu|kṣat'|ābhogā na vipatsu vipattayaḥ?

‹vinaṅkṣyati* purī kṣipraṃ,* tūrṇam eṣyanti vānarāḥ
a|sandhitsos tav'› êty etad Vibhīṣaṇa|subhāṣitam.

‹arthena saṃbhṛtā rājñā na bhāṣiṣyāmahe vayam,
saṃyotsyāmaha,› ity etat Prahastena ca bhāṣitam.

mānuṣo nāma pat|kāṣī* rājānaṃ puruṣ'|âśinām
yodhayiṣyati saṃgrāme, divy'|âstra|ratha|durjayam.

saṃnatsyāmy* atha vā yoddhuṃ, na koṣye sattva|hīnavat,
adya tarpsyanti māṃs'|âdā, bhūḥ pāsyaty ari|śoṇitam.

And they will ravage both young and old and ecstatic they 16.20
will dance: without the foremost demon, who will restrain
them?

I absolutely cannot bear the fact that Rama will make love to Sita: what happiness can she get from him when he has lost his kingdom?

I will have the demons kill Sita and then eat her or I will bury her, the cause of this ruin, in the ground.

I shall not covet worldly wealth or even try to live, I shall not enjoy sensory pleasures in a palace without my kinsmen.

Whose happiness shall I delight in? Who will delight in my pleasure? How can pleasures be enjoyed without you, O Kumbha·karna?

Those successes that will come to me when my friends have 16.25
fallen, will they not be misfortunes piled on misfortunes,
their enjoyment destroyed by grief?

It was well said by Vibhíshana: 'Until and unless you seek peace the city will quickly be lost and the monkeys will soon come.'

And Prahásta said, 'We who the king maintains in prosperity will not talk, we will fight.'

A mere man on foot will fight in battle the king of the eaters of men, invincible by virtue of his divine weapons and chariot.

I will get ready to fight, I will not cry out like some lesser being. The carnivores will now be delighted, the earth will drink the blood of our enemies.

16.30 ākarkṣyāmi yaśaḥ, śatrūn apaneṣyāmi karmaṇā,
anubhāviṣyate śoko Maithily" âdya pati|kṣayāt.

mantūyiṣyati yakṣ'|êndro, valgūyiṣyati n' ô Yamaḥ
glāsyanty a|pati|putrāś ca vane vānara|yoṣitaḥ.

sukhaṃ svapsyanti rakṣāṃsi bhramiṣyanti ca nirbhayam,
na vikrokṣyanti rākṣasyo narāṃś c' âtsyanti harṣitāḥ.

prāṅ muhūrtāt prabhāte 'haṃ bhaviṣyāmi dhruvaṃ sukhī,
āgāmini tataḥ kāle yo dvitīyaḥ kṣaṇo 'paraḥ,
tatra jetuṃ gamiṣyāmi tridaś'|Êndraṃ sah'|âmaram,
tataḥ pareṇa bhūyo 'pi Laṅkām eṣyāmy a|matsaraḥ»

16.35 tam evaṃ|vādinaṃ mūḍham Indrajit samupāgataḥ
«yuyutsiṣye 'ham» ity evaṃ vadan, ripu|bhayaṃ|karaḥ.

«n' âbhijñā te mahārāja, jeṣyāvaḥ Śakra|pālitam
dṛpta|deva|gaṇ'|ākīrṇam āvāṃ saha sur'|ālayam?*

n' âbhijñā te sa|yakṣ'|êndraṃ bhaṅkṣyāvo yad Yamaṃ balāt,
ratnāni c' āhariṣyāvaḥ prāpsyāvaś ca purīm imām?

eṣa pekṣyāmy arīn bhūyo, na śociṣyasi Rāvaṇa,
jagad drakṣyasi nī|Rāmam avagāhiṣyase diśaḥ.

I shall obtain fame, I shall drive away my enemies by my deeds, Sita will now experience the grief of her husband's death. 16.30

The lord of the *yaksha*s will be angry; Yama will be displeased; and without their lords and their sons the monkey women will despair in the forest.

Demons will sleep happily and will wander without fear, the demonesses will not weep and they will delight to eat men.

In the morning before an hour is up I will certainly be happy, then in the ensuing time during the second hour, I shall go to conquer Indra lord of the thirty gods and the other gods and after that I will come once more to Lanka without rivals.

As he spoke thus in his delusion, Índrajit, the terror of his 16.35
enemies, approached saying, "I wish to fight.

Do you not recollect, O great king, that we conquered the abode of the gods guarded by Indra and full of hosts of proud deities?

Do you not remember that we crushed Yama by force and also Kubéra lord of the *yaksha*s and took their jewels and won this city.

I shall crush my enemies once more. Do not grieve, Rávana, you will see a world without Rama and you will occupy every region.

saha|bhṛtyaḥ sur'|āvāse bhayaṃ bhūyo vidhāsyasi,
praṇaṃsyaty adya Devendras tvāṃ, vakṣyati sa sannatim.

16.40 bheṣyate munibhis tvattas, tvam adhiṣṭhāsyasi dviṣaḥ,
jñāsye 'ham adya saṃgrāme samastaiḥ śūra|mānibhiḥ!

jñāyiṣyante mayā c' âdya vīraṃ|manyā dviṣad|gaṇāḥ,
gūhiṣyāmi kṣitiṃ kṛttair adya gātrair van'|âukasām.

ārokṣyāmi yugānta|vārida|ghaṭā|
    saṃghaṭṭa|dhīra|dhvanim
niryāsyan ratham ucchrita|dhvaja|dhanuḥ|
    khaḍga|prabhā|bhāsuram.
śroṣyasy adya vikīrṇa|vṛkṇa|vimukha|
    vyāpanna|śatrau raṇe
tṛptāṃś choṇita|śoṇa|bhīṣaṇa|mukhān
    kravy'|âśinaḥ krośataḥ.»

With your retinue you will once again bestow fear on heaven, the lord of the gods will bow down to you, he will utter homage to you.

The sages will fear you, you will overpower your enemies, I 16.40
will be known to all those who pride themselves on being heroes!

Today I will show up the hosts of the enemy who take pride in their courage, today I will conceal the earth with the severed limbs of monkeys.

Ready to go forth, I will mount my chariot whose deep sound is like the clashing of storm clouds at the world's end, shining with the light of upraised banners, bows and swords. Presently, you will hear the carrion eaters howling in delight with their terrible faces red with blood on the battlefield where the fallen enemy lie strewn, hacked up and headless."

CANTO 17

THE BATTLE FOR LANKA

17.1 ĀŚĀSATA TATAḤ śāntim,
asnur, agnīn ahāvayan,
viprān avācayan, yodhāḥ
prākurvan maṅgalāni ca.*

apūjayan kula|jyeṣṭhān, upāgūhanta bālakān,
strīḥ samāvardhayan s'|âsrāḥ kāryāṇi prādiśaṃs tathā.

ācchādayan vyalimpaṃś ca
prāśnann atha sur'|āmiṣam,
prāpiban madhu mādhvīkaṃ
bhakṣyāṃś c' ādan yath''|ēpsitān.

nyaśyan* śastrāṇy abhīṣṭāni samanahyaṃś ca varmabhiḥ,
adhyāsata su|yāgāni dviṣadbhyaś c' âśapaṃs tathā.

17.5 apūjayaṃś Caturvaktraṃ, viprān ārcaṃs tath'' âstuvan.
samālipata Śakr'|ârir yānaṃ c' âbhyalaṣad varam.

āmuñcad* varma ratn'|āḍhyam abadhnāt khaḍgam ujjvalam,
adhyāsta syandanaṃ ghoraṃ, prāvartata tataḥ puraḥ.

āghnan bherīr mahā|svānāḥ,
kambūṃś c' âpy adhaman śubhān,
atāḍayan mṛdaṅgāṃś ca,
perāś c' âpūrayan kalāḥ.

astuvan bandinaḥ śabdān anyonyaṃ c' ôdabhāvayan,
anadan siṃha|nādāṃś ca prādrekata haya|dvipam.

a|nimittāny ath' âpaśyann: asphuṭad ravi|maṇḍalam,
aukṣan śoṇitam ambhodā, vāyavo 'vān su|duḥsahāḥ.

Then the soldiers prayed for peace, bathed, had offerings made into the fires, had the priests recite and themselves performed auspicious rites. 17.1

They honored the eldest in their families, they hugged their children, consoled their tearful wives and directed them in their duties.

They clothed and anointed themselves and ate the flesh of the gods,* drank *madhvíka*-flower mead and ate such comestibles as they desired.

They whetted their chosen weapons and fastened on their armor, they settled in their fine chariots and cursed their enemies.

They worshipped four-faced Brahma and they honored and 17.5
praised the priests. The enemy of Indra anointed himself and sought his best chariot.

He put on his jewel-studded armor and bound on his shining sword, mounted his fearsome chariot and then set out in the van.

They struck deep-sounding drums, they blew pure pipes, they beat tabors and played melodious instruments.

The bards sang praises and called out to each other, they roared lions' roars and horses and elephants neighed and trumpeted.

They saw inauspicious omens: the orb of the sun split, the clouds rained blood, the winds blew with unbearable force.

17.10 ārcchan vāmaṃ mṛgāḥ kṛṣṇāḥ,
śastrāṇāṃ vyasmaran bhaṭāḥ,
raktaṃ nyaṣṭhīvad aklāmyad
akhidyad vāji|kuñjaram.

na tān agaṇayan sarvān āskandaṃś ca ripūn dviṣaḥ,
acchindann asibhis tīkṣṇair abhindaṃs tomarais tathā.

nyakṛntaṃś cakra|dhārābhir atudan śaktibhir dṛḍham,
bhallair avidhyann ugr'|âgrair atṛṃhaṃs tomarair alam.

āsyan plavaṅgamā vṛkṣān, adhunvan bhū|dharair bhṛśam,
ahiṃsan muṣṭibhiḥ krodhād adaśan daśanair api.

prādunvan jānubhis tūrṇam atudaṃs tala|kūrparaiḥ
prāhiṇvann ari|muktāni śastrāṇi vividhāni ca.

17.15 atṛṇeṭ* Śakrajic chatrūn abhrāmyac ca samantataḥ,
adhvanac ca mahā|ghoraṃ na ca kaṃ cana n' âdunot.

n' âjānan sandadhānaṃ taṃ, dhanur n' āikṣanta bibhratam,
n' êṣūn acetann asyantaṃ hatās ten' âvidur dviṣaḥ.*

aśṛṇvann anyataḥ śabdaṃ, prapalāyanta c' ânyataḥ,
ākrandam anyato 'kurvaṃs ten' âhanyanta c' ânyataḥ.

prāloṭhanta, vyabhidyanta, parito raktam asravan,
paryaśrāmyann atṛṣyaṃś ca kṣatās ten' âmriyanta ca.

Blackbuck came round to the left, soldiers were forgetful of 17.10
their weapons, horses and elephants spat blood and grew
weary and listless.

The enemy took no account of all these things and attacked their foes, cut them with sharp swords and skewered them with spears.

They hewed them down with discus knives, they stuck them firmly with javelins, they pierced them with sharp-tipped arrows and ran them through with lances.

The monkeys hurled trees, they struck them forcibly with mountains, killed them angrily with their fists and even bit them with their teeth.

They pummeled them rapidly with their legs and hit them with their elbows and hands and they threw back the multifarious weapons loosed by the enemy.

Índrajit crushed his enemies and he ranged all around, he 17.15
made a terrible noise and he spared no one.

The enemy did not realize he was setting his arrows, they did not see him raising his bow, they did not cognize him shooting arrows but they knew when they had been hit by him.

They heard the sound in one place, they fled to another, they cried out here and he slew them there.

They writhed, they were cleaved open, they spewed blood in all directions, they were exhausted and dehydrated and struck by him they died.

Saumitrir ākulas tasmin Brahm'|âstraṃ sarva|rakṣasām
nidhanāy' ājuhūṣat* taṃ vyaṣṭabhnād* Raghunandanaḥ.

17.20 tato māyāmayīṃ Sītāṃ ghnan khaḍgena viyad|gataḥ
adṛśyat' Êndrajid, vākyam avadat taṃ Marut|sutaḥ.

«m" âparādhnod* iyaṃ kiṃ cid, abhraśyat patyur antikāt,
Sītāṃ rākṣasa, mā sm' âināṃ nigṛhṇāḥ pāpa duḥkhitām.»

«pīḍā|karam a|mitrāṇāṃ kartavyam» iti Śakrajit
abravīt, khaḍga|kṛṣṭaś* ca tasyā mūrdhānam acchinat.

«yat|kṛte 'rīn vyagṛhṇīma samudram atarāma ca
sā hat"» êti vadan Rāmam upātiṣṭhan Marut|sutaḥ.

tataḥ prāmuhyatāṃ vīrau Rāghavāv arutāṃ tathā,
uṣṇaṃ ca prāṇatāṃ dīrgham uccair vyākrośatāṃ tathā.

17.25 tāv abhāṣata Paulastyo «mā sma praruditaṃ yuvām.
dhruvaṃ sa mohayitv" âsmān pāpo 'gacchan Nikumbhilām.

mā sma tiṣṭhata. tatra|stho vadhyo 'sāv a|hut'|ânalaḥ
astre Brahma|śirasy ugre syandane c' ân|upārjite.

Brahm" âdadhād vadhaṃ tasya tasmin karmaṇy a|saṃsthite»
prāyacchad ājñāṃ Saumitrer yūtha|pānāṃ ca Rāghavaḥ.

Distressed by this, Lákshmana sought to invoke the Brahma-weapon to kill all the demons and Rama encouraged him.

Then Índrajit was seen killing an illusory Sita with his sword 17.20
as he went through the air and Hánuman said to him:

"She has not done anything wrong, she was taken away from her husband, do not kill the unhappy Sita, O evil demon."

"Whatever can harm the enemy has to be done," said Índrajit and drawing his sword he cut off her head.

Hánuman approached Rama saying, "She for whose sake we fought the foe and crossed the ocean, she has been killed."

Then the two Rághava heroes became bewildered and so wept and sighed long and hot and howled loudly.

Then Vibhíshana spoke to them: "You should not weep 17.25
so. That evil one has certainly deluded us and gone to Nikúmbhila.

Do not stand here. While he stays there without having made his fire-offering and while he has not yet obtained the mighty Brahma-tipped weapon and his chariot he can be killed.

Brahma ordained his death to be at a time when that rite was still unaccomplished." Rama gave his order to Lákshmana and the generals.

tāṃ pratyaicchan su|saṃpritās tatas te sa|Vibhīṣaṇāḥ
Nikumbhilāṃ samabhyāyan nyarudhyanta ca rākṣasaiḥ
dik|pālaiḥ, kadanaṃ tatra sene prākurutāṃ mahat
aitāṃ rakṣāṃsi nirjitya drutaṃ Paulastya|Lakṣmaṇau.

17.30 tatr' Êndrajitam aikṣetāṃ kṛta|dhiṣṇyaṃ samāhitam,
so 'juhot kṛṣṇa|vartmānam āmanan mantram uttamam.

adhyāyac Chakrajid Brahma, samādher acalan na ca,
tam āhvayata Saumitrir agarjac ca bhayaṃ|karam.

akupyad Indrajit tatra pitṛvyaṃ c' âgadad vacaḥ
«tvam atr' âjāyathā deha ih' âpuṣyat sur'|āmiṣaiḥ,

ih' âjīva, ih' âiva tvaṃ
   krūram ārabhathāḥ katham?
n' âpaśyaḥ pāṇim ārdraṃ tvaṃ,
   bandhutvaṃ n' âpy apaikṣathāḥ.

a|dharmān n' âtrasaḥ pāpa? loka|vādān na c' âbibheḥ?
dharma|dūṣaṇa, nūnaṃ tvaṃ n' âjānā* n' âśṛṇor idam.

17.35 nirākṛtya yathā bandhūn laghutvaṃ yāty a|saṃśayam.»
pitṛvyeṇa tato vākyam abhyadhīyata Śakrajit:

«mithyā mā sma vyatikrāmo,
   mac|chīlaṃ mā na budhyathāḥ?
satyaṃ samabhavaṃ vaṃśe
   pāpānāṃ rakṣasām aham,

Then with great delight they and Vibhíshana accepted that order and went up to Nikúmbhila and were obstructed by the demon guards. There the two armies engaged in a great slaughter and Vibhíshana and Lákshmana having fast overcome the demons proceeded.

There they saw Índrajit in meditation, his altar prepared he 17.30
was offering into the fire and reciting his most important mantra.

Índrajit meditated on Brahman and did not budge from his concentration; Lákshmana challenged him and roared fearsomely.

Then Índrajit became angry and said to his uncle, "You were born here and here your body was nourished with meat intended for the gods.*

You have lived here, how can you have undertaken a cruel act here? You do not see that your hand is still wet,* you have no regard even for kinship.

Do you not tremble at unrighteousness, you evil one? Do you not fear the censure of the world? O bespoiler of merit, surely you cannot listen to this without recognizing it?

There is no doubt that in spurning one's kinsmen one gains 17.35
dishonor." Then his uncle had words with Índrajit:

"Do not go too far in your falsehood, do you not know my character? It is true that I was born in this line of evil demons,

na tv ajāyata me śīlaṃ tādṛg yādṛk pitus tava.
kṣay'|āvaheṣu doṣeṣu vāryamāṇo may" âramat
Daśagrīvo; 'ham etasmād atyajaṃ, na tu vidviṣan:
para|svāny ārjayan nārīr anyadīyāḥ parāmṛśat.

vyajighṛkṣat surān nityaṃ, prāmādyad guṇināṃ hite,
āśaṅkata suhṛd|bandhūn, a|vṛddhān bahv amanyata.

17.40 doṣair aramat' âibhis te pit" âtyajyata yair mayā.»
tato 'ruṣyad anardac ca dvi|viṃśatibhir eva ca
śarair atāḍayad bandhuṃ pañca|viṃśatibhir nṛpam
Rāvaṇis. tasya Saumitrir amathnāc caturo hayān.

sārathiṃ c' âlunād bāṇair abhanak syandanaṃ tathā,
Saumitrim akirad bāṇaiḥ parito Rāvaṇis tataḥ.

tāv asphāvayatāṃ* śaktīr, bāṇāṃś c' âkiratāṃ muhuḥ,
Vāruṇaṃ Lakṣmaṇo 'kṣipyad,* akṣipad Raudram Indrajit.

te parasparam āsādya śastre nāśam agacchatām,
Āsuraṃ rākṣasaḥ śastraṃ tato ghoraṃ vyasarjayat,

17.45 tasmān nirapatad bhūri śilā|śūl'|êṣṭi|mudgaram,
Māheśvareṇa Saumitrir astabhnāt tat su|durjayam.

tato Raudra|samāyuktaṃ Māhendraṃ Lakṣmaṇo 'smarat
ten' āgamyata ghoreṇa, śiraś c' âhriyata dviṣaḥ.

But my character was not made like that of your father. Even though I restrained him, Rávana enjoyed vices that brought him to ruin. But my character was not made like that of your father. Because of this I left but without malice. He appropriated his enemies' goods and violated the wives of others.

He always sought to attack the gods, he was dismissive of the counsel of the virtuous, he was mistrustful of his friends and relatives, he esteemed highly those who were immature.

Your father delighted in those very vices for which I aban- 17.40
doned him." Thus Índrajit was insulted and he roared and attacked his kinsman with two-score arrows and the prince with five-score. Lákshmana pulverized his four horses.

And he cut down his charioteer with arrows and broke his chariot. Índrajit then showered Lákshmana all over with arrows.

They both augmented their powers and repeatedly showered arrows; Lákshmana cast the Váruna weapon, Índrajit cast the Raudra weapon.

The two weapons falling on each other were destroyed, then the demon discharged his terrible Ásura weapon.

Rocks, spears, swords and clubs fell from it to the ground; 17.45
Lákshmana prevented that almost undefeatable weapon with his Mahéshvara weapon.

Then Lákshmana brought to mind the Mahéndra weapon in conjunction with the Raudra weapon and when that terrible instrument came his enemy's head was taken off.

atuṣyann amarāḥ sarve, prāhṛṣyan kapi|yūtha|pāḥ,
paryaṣvajata Saumitriṃ mūrdhny ajighrac ca Rāghavaḥ.

arodīd* rākṣas'|ânīkam, arodan nṛ|bhujāṃ patiḥ
Maithilyai c' âśapadd hantuṃ tāṃ prākramata c' āturaḥ.

«a|yuktam idam» ity anye tam āptāḥ pratyavārayan
nyarundhaṃś* c' âsya panthānaṃ bandhutā śucam āruṇat.

17.50 āsphāyat' âsya vīratvam amarṣaś c' âpy atāyata
Rāvaṇasya, tataḥ sainyaṃ samastam ayuyutsayat.

agnīn avarivasyaṃś ca te, 'namasyaṃś ca Śaṅkaram
dvijān aprīṇayan śāntyai yātu|dhānā bhavad|bhiyaḥ.

paritaḥ paryavād vāyur ājya|gandhir mano|ramaḥ,
aśrūyata sa|puṇy'|âhaḥ svasti|ghoṣaḥ samuccaran.

yoddhāro 'bibharuḥ śāntyai s'|âkṣataṃ vāri mūrdhabhiḥ
ratnāni c' âdadur gāś ca samavāñchann ath' āśiṣaḥ.

adihaṃś candanaiḥ śubhrair, vicitraṃ samavastrayan,
adhārayan srajaḥ kāntā varma c' ânye 'dadhur drutam.

17.55 samakṣṇuvata śastrāṇi, prāmṛjan khaḍga|saṃhatīḥ,
gaj'|ādīni samārohan, prātiṣṭhant' ātha sa|tvarāḥ

apūrayan nabhaḥ śabdo bala|saṃvarta|saṃbhavaḥ,
apūryanta ca dig|bhāgās tumulais tūrya|nisvanaiḥ.

All the immortals rejoiced, the monkey generals exulted and Rama embraced Lákshmana and kissed his head.

The demon army wept, the lord of the man-eaters wept and cursed Sita and in his agony prepared to kill her.

Some of his allies stopped him saying, "This is not right," obstructing his path, and his kinsmen assuaged his grief.

Rávana swelled in strength and his anger increased also and 17.50
then he exhorted his army to fight.

The demons tended the fires fearfully, paid homage to Shiva and gratified the twiceborn in order to propitiate them.

A delightful breeze scented by the oblations wafted around, the rising sounds "auspicious day" and "blessings" were heard.

For the sake of propitiation the soldiers bore unmilled grain mixed with water on their heads and gave jewels and kine and then wished for blessings.

They anointed themselves with white sandal paste, they dressed colorfully, some put on beautiful garlands and others quickly put on their armor.

They honed their weapons, they polished their collections 17.55
of swords, they mounted their elephants and other conveyances and then set out with haste.

The sound that rose as the army mustered together filled the air, the divisions of the quarters were filled with the tumultuous sounds of instruments.

āsīd dvāreṣu saṃghaṭṭo rath'|âśva|dvipa|rakṣasām
su|mahān, a|nimittaiś ca samabhūyata bhīṣaṇaiḥ.

kapayo 'bibhayus tasminn abhañjaṃś ca mahā|drumān,
prodakhāyan girīṃs tūrṇam agṛhṇaṃś ca mahā|śilāḥ.

tataḥ samabhavad yuddhaṃ, prāharan kapi|rākṣasāḥ,
anyonyen' âbhyabhūyanta, vimardam asahanta ca.

17.60 prāvardhata rajo bhaumaṃ, tad vyāśnuta diśo daśa
par'|ātmīya|vivekaṃ ca prāmuṣṇāt kapi|rakṣasām.

tato 'dviṣur* nirāloke svebhyo 'nyebhyaś ca rākṣasāḥ
adviṣan, vānarāś c' âiva vānarebhyo 'pi nirdayāḥ.

aghuraṃs te mahā|ghoram aścyotann atha śoṇitam
samapadyata raktena samantāt tena kardamaḥ.

gambhīrāḥ prāvahan nadyaḥ samajāyanta ca hradāḥ
vṛddhaṃ ca tad rajo 'śāmyat samavedyanta ca dviṣaḥ.

tato 'citrīyat' âstr'|âughair dhanuś c' âdhūnayan mahat
Rāmaḥ, samīhitaṃ tasya n' âcetan sve na c' âpare.

17.65 chinnān aikṣanta bhinnāṃś ca samantād Rāma|sāyakaiḥ
kruṣṭaṃ «hāh"» êti c' âśṛṇvan na ca Rāmaṃ nyarūpayan.

abhinac chatru|saṃghātān akṣuṇad vāji|kuñjaram,
apinaṭ ca rath'|ânīkaṃ, na c' âjñāyata saṃcaran.

At the gates there was an enormous clash of chariots, horses, elephants and demons, and terrifying ill-omens appeared.

When that happened the monkeys were frightened and broke great trees, they quickly dug up mountains and seized great rocks.

Then the fight started, the monkeys and the demons struck and overwhelmed each other and endured the chaos.

The dust from the earth grew, it filled the ten directions 17.60
and it removed the distinction between enemy and friend, between monkey and demon.

Then in the darkness the demons became hostile towards their own and towards others and the pitiless monkeys also attacked other monkeys.

They groaned huge groans and shed blood and everything mixed with that redness turned to mud.

The rivers flowed deep and pools formed and the blown up dust settled and they found the enemy.

Then Rama wondrous with his mass of weapons made his great bow resound: neither his own men nor the others understood what he strove for.

They saw others cut and split on all sides by Rama's arrows 17.65
and they heard cries of "Aargh!" but they could not make out Rama.

He split the multitudes of the enemy, he crushed horses and elephants, he smashed a battalion of chariots and as he moved he was unperceived.

daśa danti|sahasrāṇi rathināṃ ca mah"|ātmanām
caturdaśa sahasrāṇi, s'|ārohāṇāṃ ca vājinām
lakṣe ca dve padātīnāṃ Rāghaveṇa dhanur|bhṛtā
anīyant' âṣṭame bhāge divasasya parikṣayam.

Yama|lokam iv' âgrathnād, Rudr'|ākrīḍam iv' âkarot,
śailair iv' âcinod bhūmiṃ bṛhadbhī rākṣasair hataiḥ.

17.70 astuvan deva|gandharvā, vyasmayanta plavaṅgamāḥ,
kap'|îndre 'tanyata prītiḥ, Paulastyo 'manyat' âdbhutam.

rākṣasyaḥ prārudann uccaiḥ, prājugupsanta Rāvaṇam,
amuhyad bāla|vṛddhaṃ ca, samaraud* itaro janaḥ.

«sarvataś c' â|bhayaṃ prāpnon
n' āicchan nṛbhyas tu Rāvaṇaḥ:
phalaṃ tasy' êdam abhyāyād
dur|uktasy'» êti c' âbruvan.

tato 'dhāvan mahā|ghoraṃ ratham āsthāya Rāvaṇaḥ,
akṣmāyata mahī gṛdhrāḥ samārāryanta* bhīṣaṇāḥ.

meghāḥ sa|vidyuto 'varṣaṃś cela|knopaṃ* ca śoṇitam,
avān bhīmā nabhasvantaḥ, prāruvann a|śivāḥ śivāḥ

17.75 āṭāṭyat' âvamaty' âsau dur|nimittāni saṃyuge,
adhunod dhanur astr'|âughaiḥ praurṇonūyata vidviṣaḥ.

vyanāśayaṃs tataḥ śatrūn Sugrīv'|âstā mahī|bhṛtaḥ
tato vyarasad, aglāyad, adhyaśeta mahī|talam,
āścyotad rudhiraṃ, toyam alasac c' âtivihvalam,
aśīyata* nṛ|māṃs'|âdāṃ balaṃ Sugrīva|bādhitam.

In the eighth part of the day Rama bearing his bow destroyed ten thousand elephants, fourteen thousand noble charioteers and horses with their riders and twenty thousand foot soldiers.

It was as if he had fashioned a world of the dead with huge slain demons, as if he had created a playground for Rudra, as if he had heaped the earth with mountains.

The gods and *gandhárvas* praised him, the monkeys were 17.70
awestruck, the monkey lord's delight grew, Vibhíshana thought it marvelous.

The demonesses lamented loudly and reviled Rávana, the young and the elderly were bewildered and others sobbed.

They said, "Rávana had got immunity from fear from everything but he had not sought immunity from men: the fruit of that ill-articulated boon has now come."

Then Rávana mounting his roaring chariot charged, the earth was shaken and fierce raptors flocked together.

Lightning clouds rained blood enough to soak cloth, terrible winds blew, unholy jackals howled.

Disregarding these ill-omens he moved about continually 17.75
in the battle, made his bow vibrate and continually covered his enemies with masses of arrows.

Then the mountains thrown by Sugríva destroyed the enemy and thereafter the army of man-eating demons attacked by Sugríva screamed, fainted, fell to the ground, shed blood, craved water in great affliction and was cut down.

Virūpākṣas tato 'krīḍat saṃgrāme matta|hastinā,
muṣṭin" âdālayat tasya mūrdhānaṃ vānar'|âdhipaḥ
acūrṇayac ca Yūpākṣaṃ śilayā tad|anantaram.
saṃkruddho muṣṭin" âtubhnād Aṅgado 'laṃ Mahodaram.

17.80 tato 'kuṣṇād Daśagrīvaḥ kruddhaḥ prāṇān van'|âukasām
agopāyac ca rakṣāṃsi diśaś c' ârīn abhājayat.

ālokayat sa Kākutstham adhṛṣṇod, ghoram adhvanat,
dhanur abhramayad bhīmam abhīṣayata vidviṣaḥ.

āskandal Lakṣmaṇaṃ bāṇair atyakrāmac ca taṃ drutam,
Rāmam abhyadravaj jiṣṇur askunāc* c' êṣu|vṛṣṭibhiḥ.

apauhad bāṇa|varṣaṃ tad bhallai Rāmo nirākulaḥ,
pratyaskunod daṣa|grīvaṃ śarair āśī|viṣ'|ôpamaiḥ.

maṇḍalāny āṭatāṃ citram, acchittāṃ śastra|saṃhatīḥ,
jagad vismāpayetāṃ tau na ca vīrāv asīdatām.

17.85 vyoma prācinutāṃ bāṇaiḥ, kṣmām akṣmāpayatāṃ gataiḥ,
abhittāṃ tūrṇam anyonyaṃ śikṣāś c' âtanutāṃ muhuḥ.

samādhatt' Āsuraṃ śastraṃ rākṣasaḥ krūra|vikramaḥ
tad akṣaran mahā|sarpān vyāghra|siṃhāṃś ca bhīṣaṇān.

nyaṣedhat pāvak'|âstreṇa Rāmas tad, rākṣasas tataḥ
adīvyad Raudram aty|ugraṃ musal'|ādy agalat tataḥ.

Then Virupáksha sported in the battle with a musth elephant, the monkey king split his head with his fist then immediately crushed Yupáksha with a rock. Enraged Ángada felled Mahódara fully with his fist.

Then Rávana enraged tore out the lives of the monkeys 17.80
and guarded his demons and scattered his enemies to the horizons.

He saw Rama and attacked; he sounded a roar, wielded his fearful bow and terrified the enemy.

He attacked Lákshmana with arrows and quickly overpowered him, he charged triumphantly at Rama and enveloped him in showers of arrows.

Rama unfazed by missiles repelled that arrow shower: in response he covered Rávana with arrows like poisonous snakes.

The two warriors moved wondrously in circles, they cut off the volleys of weapons, they astonished the world and did not weary.

They filled the sky with arrows, they made the earth shake 17.85
with their movements, they rapidly cut each other and they continually extended their skills.

That demon of cruel prowess dispatched his Ásura weapon that streamed out great snakes and ferocious tigers and lions.

Rama warded it off with the fire weapon then the demon wielded his horribly cruel Raudra weapon and out of it fell clubs and suchlike.

Gāndharveṇa nyavidhyat tat kṣit'|îndro, 'tha nar'|âśanaḥ
sarva|marmasu Kākutstham aumbhat tīkṣṇaiḥ śilī|mukhaiḥ.

tatas Triśirasaṃ tasya prāvṛścal Lakṣmaṇo dhvajam,
amathnāt sārathiṃ c' āśu bhūribhiś c' âtudac charaiḥ.

17.90 aśvān Vibhīṣaṇo 'tubhnāt syandanaṃ c' âkṣiṇod drutam,
n' âkṣubhnād rākṣaso bhrātuḥ śaktiṃ c' ôdavṛhad gurum.

tām āpatantīṃ Saumitris tridh" âkṛntac chilī|mukhaiḥ,
aśabdāyanta paśyantas tataḥ kruddho niśā|caraḥ
Aṣṭaghaṇṭāṃ mahā|śaktim udayacchan mahattarām
Rāmānujaṃ tay" âvidhyat sa mahīṃ vyasur āśrayat.

Rāghavasy' âbhṛśāyanta sāyakās tair upadrutaḥ
tatas tūrṇaṃ Daśagrīvo raṇa|kṣmāṃ paryaśeṣayat.

sa|sphurasy' ôdakarṣac ca Saumitreḥ śaktim agra|jaḥ
asiñcad oṣadhīs tā yāḥ samānītā Hanūmatā.

17.95 udajīvat Sumitrā|bhūr bhrāt" āśliṣyat tam āyatam
samyaṅ mūrdhany upāśiṅghad apṛcchac ca nirāmayam.

tataḥ prodasahan sarve yoddhum abhyadravat parān
akṛcchrāyata ca prāpto rathen' ânyena Rāvaṇaḥ.

The lord of the earth struck it down with his Gandhárva weapon, then the man-eater filled Rama in all his vital organs with sharpened arrows.

Then Lákshmana tore to pieces his triple-headed banner, quickly crushed his charioteer and struck him with many arrows.

Vibhíshana killed his horses and quickly smashed his char- 17.90
iot; the demon was not shaken and drew out his heavy spear against his brother.

Lákshmana cut it in three with his arrows as it fell: those who were watching shouted and then the enraged night-stalker raised his even larger Eight-bell spear and struck Lákshmana, younger brother of Rama. Lifeless he fell to the ground.

Rama's arrows increased and when Rávana was struck by them he quickly left the battlefield.

Rama the firstborn pulled the spear out of Lákshmana as he writhed and he smeared on those herbs which Hánuman had brought.

Lákshmana born of Sumítra recovered and his brother long 17.95
embraced him and kissed him properly on the head and asked if he was well.

Then all boldly prepared to fight and Rávana equipped with another chariot attacked his enemies and tormented them.

«bhūmi|ṣṭhasy' â|samaṃ yuddhaṃ ratha|sthen',» êti Mātaliḥ
āharad ratham atyugraṃ sa|śastraṃ Maghav'|ājñayā.

so 'dhyaṣṭhīyata Rāmeṇa śastraṃ Pāśupataṃ tataḥ
nirāsyata Daśāsyas tac Chakr'|âstreṇ' âjayan nṛpaḥ.

tataḥ śata|sahasreṇa Rāmaḥ praurṇon niśā|caram
bāṇānām, akṣiṇod dhuryān* sārathiṃ c' âdunod drutam.

17.100 adṛśyant' â|nimittāni prāhvalat kṣiti|maṇḍalam,
Rāvaṇaḥ prāhiṇoc chūlaṃ śaktiṃ c' Āindrīṃ mahī|patiḥ.

tābhyām anyonyam āsādya samavāpyata saṃśamaḥ,
lakṣeṇa patriṇāṃ vakṣaḥ kruddho Rāmasya rākṣasaḥ
astṛṇād, adhikaṃ Rāmas tato 'devata sāyakaiḥ,
aklāmyad Rāvaṇas tasya sūto ratham anāśayat.

rākṣaso 'tarjayat sūtaṃ punaś c' âḍhaukayad ratham.
nirāsyetām ubhau bāṇān ubhau dhuryān avidhyatām.

ubhāv akṛntatāṃ ketūn, āvyathetām ubhau na tau,
adīpyetām ubhau dhṛṣṇū prāyuñjātāṃ ca naipuṇam.

17.105 ubhau māyāṃ vyatāyetāṃ, vīrau n' âśrāmyatām ubhau,
maṇḍalāni vicitrāṇi kṣipram ākrāmatām ubhau.

na c' ôbhāv apy alakṣyetāṃ, yantārāv āhatām ubhau,
syandanau samapṛcyetām ubhayor dīpta|vājinau.

At the command of Indra, who said, "A battle between one standing on the ground and one standing on a chariot is unequal," Mátali his charioteer brought a fearsome chariot furnished with weapons.

Rama mounted it and then Rávana cast the Pashu·pata weapon but the king overcame it with his Indra-weapon.

Then Rama enveloped the nightstalker in one hundred thousand arrows, killed his horses and quickly attacked his charioteer.

Ill omens were seen and the earth's orb shook, Rávana cast 17.100
a lance and the king his weapon given by Indra.

The two weapons stopped as they fell on each other; the demon in his rage strewed Rama's chest with a lakh of arrows and then Rama plied still more arrows; Rávana was exhausted as his driver drove away his chariot.

The demon rebuked his driver and once again made him bring back his chariot. Both fired arrows and both pierced each others' horses.

They both cut down each others' banners, neither yielded, they both displayed fortitude and they both used skill.

They both exhibited magical power, neither hero wearied, 17.105
both moved rapidly in wondrous arcs.

And neither could be distinguished, both struck each others' drivers, their two chariots with their shining horses crashed together.

tato māyāmayān mūrdhno rākṣaso 'prathayad raṇe,
Rāmeṇ' âika|śataṃ teṣāṃ prāvṛścyata śilī|mukhaiḥ.

samakṣubhnann udanvantaḥ, prākampanta mahī|bhṛtaḥ,
santrāsam abibhaḥ Śakraḥ praiṅkhac ca kṣubhitā kṣitiḥ.

tato Mātalinā śastram asmaryata mahī|pateḥ
vadhāya Rāvaṇasy' ôgraṃ Svayaṃbhūr yad akalpayat.

17.110 nabhasvān yasya vājeṣu, phale tigm'|âṃśu|pāvakau,
gurutvaṃ Meru|saṅkāśaṃ, dehaḥ sūkṣmo viyanmayaḥ,
rājitaṃ Gāruḍaiḥ pakṣair, viśveṣāṃ dhāma tejasām,
smṛtaṃ, tad Rāvaṇaṃ bhittvā su|ghoraṃ bhuvy aśāyayat.

ābadhnan kapi|vadanāni saṃprasādaṃ,
prāśaṃsat sura|samitir nṛpaṃ jit'|ârim.
anyeṣāṃ vigata|pariplavā dig|antāḥ.
Paulastyo 'juṣata śucaṃ vipanna|bandhuḥ.

Then the demon displayed his illusory heads in the battle, Rama cut off one hundred and one of them with his arrows.

The oceans shook violently, the mountains trembled, Indra shook in fear and the tremulous earth shook.

Then Mátali reminded the lord of the earth of the terrible weapon which the self-existent Brahma had fashioned for killing Rávana.

That terrible weapon at whose sides was the wind, in whose 17.110
issue was the sun and fire, which resembled Mount Meru in weight, whose body was subtly crafted of sky, which shone with wings like those of Gáruda, which was the seat of universal brilliance, cut, when remembered, the very terrible Rávana and felled him to the earth.

The faces of the monkeys showed serenity and the assembly of the gods was delighted that the king had defeated his enemy. To others the extremities of every direction became free from tyranny. Vibhíshana, his brother lost, suffered grief.

CANTO 18

VIBHÍSHANA'S LAMENT FOR RÁVANA

18.1 VYAŚNUTE SMA tataḥ śoko
nābhi|sambandha|sambhavaḥ
Vibhīṣaṇam asāv uccai
roditi sma Daśānanam.*

«bhūmau śete Daśagrīvo mah"|ârha|śayan'|ôcitaḥ,
n' ēkṣate vihvalaṃ māṃ ca na me vācaṃ prayacchati.

vipāko 'yaṃ Daśagrīva, saṃdṛṣṭo 'n|āgato mayā,
tvaṃ ten' âbhihitaḥ pathyaṃ. kiṃ kopaṃ na niyacchasi?

bhajanti vipadas tūrṇam, atikrāmanti sampadaḥ
tān, madān n' âvatiṣṭhante ye mate nyāya|vādinām.

18.5 a|pathyam āyatau lobhād āmananty anujīvinaḥ
priyaṃ, śṛṇoti yas tebhyas tam ṛcchanti na sampadaḥ.

prājñās tejasvinaḥ samyak paśyanti ca vadanti ca
te 'vajñātā mahārāja, klāmyanti viramanti ca.

leḍhi bheṣajavan nityaṃ yaḥ pathyāni kaṭūny api,
tad|arthaṃ sevate c' āptān, kadā cin na sa sīdati.

sarvasya jāyate mānaḥ sva|hitāc ca pramādyati
vṛddhau bhajati c' âpathyaṃ naro yena vinaśyati.

dveṣṭi prāyo guṇebhyo yan na ca snihyati kasya cit
vairāyate mahadbhiś ca śīyate vṛddhimān api.

THEN GRIEF growing from their co-uterine connection 18.1
filled Vibhíshana and he loudly wept for Rávana.

"Used to a very splendid bed, Rávana lies on the ground, he can neither see me in distress nor offer words to me.

O Rávana, I saw this fulfillment before it came: for that reason you were told the right path. Why did you not control your anger?

Those who misfortunes quickly break, who successes pass by, are those who out of pride do not give credence to the thoughts of their counselors.

Successes do not come to one who listens to that pleasing 18.5
but misleading course which courtiers greedily counsel for
the future.

When those wise luminaries who see and speak rightly are held in contempt, O great king, they become weary and they stop.

He who always tries the better course, though it be bitter as medicine, and for that purpose resorts to his true friends, never sinks down.

In prosperity all become proud and are heedless of their own welfare and indulge in that evil course by which a man is destroyed.

Even a prosperous man sinks if he generally despises the virtues and has no affection for anyone and contends with the great.

18.10 samāśvasimi ken' âhaṃ? kathaṃ prāṇimi dur|gataḥ
loka|traya|patir bhrātā yasya me svapiti kṣitau?

aho jāgarti kṛcchreṣu daivaṃ, yad Balabhij|jitaḥ,
luṭhyanti bhūmau klidyanti bāndhavā me svapanti ca.

śivāḥ kuṣṇanti māṃsāni, bhūmiḥ pibati śoṇitam,
Daśagrīva|sa|nābhīnāṃ samadanty āmiṣaṃ khagāḥ.

yena Pūtakrator mūrdhni sthīyate sma mah"|āhave,
tasy' âp' Îndrajito daivād dhvāṃkṣaiḥ śirasi līyate.

Svarbhānur bhāskaraṃ grastaṃ niṣṭhīvati, kṛt'|âhnikaḥ,
abhyupaiti punar bhūtiṃ Rāma|grasto na kaś cana.

18.15 tvam a|jānann idaṃ, rājann, īḍiṣe sma sva|vikramam,
dātuṃ n' êcchasi Sītāṃ sma, viṣayāṇāṃ ca n' ēśiṣe.

mantre jātu vadanty a|jñās tvaṃ tān apy anumanyase!
kathaṃ nāma bhavāṃs tatra n' âvaiti hitam ātmanaḥ?*

a|pṛṣṭo nu bravīti* tvāṃ mantre mātā|maho hitam,
‹na karom' îti Paulastya› tadā mohāt tvam uktavān?

tvaṃ sma vettha mahārāja, yat sm' āha na Vibhīṣaṇaḥ,
purā tyajasi* yat kruddho māṃ nirākṛtya saṃsadi.

With whom can I take courage? How can I live who am 18.10
ill-fated, whose brother the lord of the three worlds sleeps
on the ground?

Oh fate wakes up to miseries now my kinsmen, the conquerors of Indra slayer of Bala, writhe on the ground and rot and sleep.

Jackals gnaw at meat, the earth drinks blood, birds eat the flesh of Rávana's brothers.

Because of him crows settled on pure-intentioned Indra's head in the great battle: so fatefully do they alight on Índrajit's head now.

Rahu,* his day's work done, spits out the eclipsed sun, but none eclipsed by Rama gains glory again.

O king, in ignorance of this you praised your own prowess, 18.15
you did not wish to give Sita back and you had no sover-
eignty over the realms of the senses.

Even the ignorant speak in your council and you agree with them too! How can you possibly not appreciate your own best interests?

Your maternal grandfather unsolicited did indeed speak good advice to you in council. You then spoke in error, O Rávana, saying, "I will not do it."

O great king, you did not understand what I, Vibhíshana, said—that which in the past you rejected in anger after repudiating me in the assembly.

havir jakṣiti niḥśaṅko makheṣu Maghavān asau,
pravāti sv'|êcchayā vāyur udgacchati ca bhāskaraḥ.

18.20 dhanānām īśate yakṣā, Yamo dāmyati rākṣasān,
tanoti Varuṇaḥ pāśam indun" ôdīyate 'dhunā.

śāmyaty ṛtu|samāhāras, tapasyanti van'|âukasaḥ,
n' ô namasyanti te bandhūn varivasyanti n' âmarāḥ.

Śrīr niṣkuṣyati Laṅkāyāṃ, virajyanti samṛddhayaḥ,
na veda* tan na yasy' âsti mṛte tvayi viparyayaḥ.

śaktiṃ saṃsvajate Śakro, gopāyati Hariḥ Śriyam,
deva|vandyaḥ pramodante citrīyante ghan'|ôdayāḥ.

bibhraty astrāṇi s'|âmarṣā raṇa|kāmyanti c' âmarāḥ,
cakāsati ca māṃs'|âdāṃ tathā randhreṣu jāgrati.

18.25 cañcūryate* 'bhito Laṅkām asmāṃś c' âpy atiśerate,
bhūmayanti* sva|sāmarthyaṃ kīrtiṃ naḥ kanayanti* ca.

diśo vyaśnuvate dṛptās, tvat|kṛtāṃ jahati sthitim,
kṣodayanti ca naḥ kṣudrā hasanti tvāṃ vipad|gatam.

śamaṃ śamaṃ, nabhasvantaḥ punanti parito jagat.
ujjihīṣe,* mahā|rāja, tvaṃ praśānto na kiṃ punaḥ?

prorṇoti śokas cittaṃ me, sattvaṃ saṃśāmyat' îva me,
pramārṣṭi duḥkham ālokaṃ, muñcāmy ūrjaṃ tvayā vinā.

Fearless Indra eats the oblation at sacrifices, the wind blows of its own will and the sun rises.

The *yakshas* are lords of wealth, Yama controls the demons, 18.20
Váruna extends his noose and now the moon rises.

The mixing of the seasons ends, the forest dwellers practice penance, the immortals neither bow down to your kinsmen nor do they wait upon them.

Lakshmi does damage in Lanka, prosperity becomes indifferent, I do not know of anything for which the opposite is not true now you are dead.

Indra embraces his power, Vishnu protects Lakshmi, the captive goddesses rejoice and the cloud-tops dazzle.

Angered gods bear weapons and seek battle, bright they are awake to the weaknesses of the meat-eating demons.

They wander contemptuously around Lanka and surpass 18.25
us, they increase their own potency and diminish our fame.

Made proud, they occupy the quarters, they discard the status you determined for them, those lightweights diminish us and they mock you in your misfortune.

Ever calming, the winds purify the world all over. O great king, you have been tranquilized, why do you not again rise up?

Grief envelops my heart, it is as if my being ceases, grief wipes out my sight, without you I lose my strength.

ke na saṃvidrate* n' ânyas tvatto bāndhava|vatsalaḥ?
viraumi śūnye, prorṇaumi kathaṃ manyu|samudbhavam?

18.30 rodimy a|nātham ātmānaṃ, bandhunā rahitas tvayā,
pramāṇaṃ n' ôpakārāṇām avagacchāmi yasya te.

n' êdānīṃ Śakra|Yakṣendrau bibhīto, na daridritaḥ,
na garvaṃ jahito, dṛptau na kliśnīto Daśānana.

tvay" âpi nāma rahitāḥ kāryāṇi tanumo vayam
kurmaś ca jīvite buddhiṃ: dhik tṛṣṇāṃ kṛta|nāśinīm.

tṛṇehmi deham ātmīyaṃ tvaṃ vācaṃ na dadāsi cet,
drāghayanti hi me śokaṃ smaryamāṇā guṇās tava.

unmucya srajam ātmīyāṃ māṃ srajayati ko hasan?
nedayaty āsanaṃ ko me? ko hi me vadati priyam?

18.35 na gacchāmi purā Laṅkām āyur yāvad dadhāmy aham.
kadā bhavati me prītis tvāṃ paśyāmi na ced aham?

ūrdhvaṃ mriye muhūrtādd hi vihvalaḥ, kṣata|bāndhavaḥ.
mantre sma hitam ākhyāmi, na karomi tav' â|priyam.

antaḥ|purāṇi Paulastyaṃ paurāś ca bhṛśa|duḥkhitāḥ
saṃśrutya sm' âbhidhāvanti hataṃ Rāmeṇa saṃyuge.

Who does not know that no one else but you was so fond of his relatives? I call into the void, how can I smother my rising anguish?

Deprived of you, my kinsman, I weep for my lordless self, 18.30
I have no comprehension of the extent of the favors which you rendered.

Now Indra and Kubéra are not afraid, nor are they poor, nor do they dispose of their haughtiness, nor being proud do they have any anxiety, O Rávana.

Even though bereft of you we continue with our duties and we decide on life: a curse on the greed that wrecks obligation.

If you do not give me word I will crush my own body, for the recollection of your virtues is increasing my grief.

Who will laughingly take off his own garland and garland me? Who will bring me near to his seat? Who will speak sweetly to me?

I shall not go back to Lanka so long as I live. When will I 18.35
have delight if I never see you?

For within an hour I will die afflicted, my kinsmen slain. I gave good advice in council, I never did anything displeasing to you."

The women of the harem and the citizens in heavy sorrow heard that Rama had killed Rávana and rushed out upon the battlefield.

mūrdha|jān sma viluñcanti, krośanti sm' âtivihvalam,
adhīyanty upakārāṇāṃ muhur bhartuḥ pramanyu ca.

Rāvaṇasya namanti sma paurāḥ s'|âsrā rudanti ca.
bhāṣate sma tato Rāmo vacaḥ Paulastyam ākulam:

18.40 «dātuḥ sthātur dviṣāṃ mūrdhni, yaṣṭus, tarpayituḥ pitṝn,
yuddh'|âbhagn'|âvipannasya, kiṃ Daśāsyasya śocasi?

bobhavīti na sammoho vyasane sma bhavādṛśām,
kiṃ na paśyasi sarvo 'yaṃ janas tvām avalambate?

tvam arhasi bhrātur anantarāṇi
kartuṃ janasy' âsya ca śoka|bhaṅgam.
dhurye vipanne tvayi, rājya|bhāro
majjaty an|ūḍhaḥ, kṣaṇadā|car'|êndra.»

They ripped out their hair, they wailed in great affliction, they dwelt on the kindnesses of their lord in perpetual sorrow.

The citizens bowed down to Rávana and tearfully wept. Then Rama addressed words to the distressed Vibhíshana:

"Why do you mourn Rávana, the patron who stood on the 18.40
heads of his enemies, sacrificed, satisfied his ancestors and who was never beaten or troubled in battle?

Someone such as you should never be perplexed in calamity, do you not see that all these people depend on you?

You are worthy to perform the final rites for your brother and break the grief of these people. Capable as you are, if you are lost, then the burden of the kingdom unsupported will sink, O lord of the demons.

CANTO 19
THE CORONATION OF VIBHÍSHANA

19.1 Apa|manyus tato vākyaṃ
Paulastyo Rāmam uktavān
«a|śocyo 'pi vrajann astaṃ
sa|nābhir dunuyān na kim?*

taṃ no devā vidheyāsur yena, Rāvaṇavad, vayam
sapatnāṃś c' âdhijīyāsma saṃgrāme ca mṛṣīmahi.

kriyeraṃś ca Daśāsyena yath" ânyen' âpi naḥ kule
devadryañco* nar'|âhārā, nyañcaś ca dviṣatāṃ gaṇāḥ.

sa eva dhārayet prāṇān īdṛśe bandhu|viplave
bhaved āśvāsako yasya suhṛc chakto bhavādṛśaḥ.

19.5 mriyey' ôrdhvaṃ muhūrtādd hi, na syās tvaṃ yadi me gatiḥ,
āśaṃsā na hi naḥ, prete jīvema Daśamūrdhani.

prakuryāma* vayaṃ deśe garhyāṃ tatra kathaṃ ratim
yatra viṃśati|hastasya na s'|ôdaryasya sambhavaḥ?»

āmantrayeta* tān prahvān mantriṇo 'tha Vibhīṣaṇaḥ
«gaccheta tvaritaṃ Laṅkāṃ rāja|veśma viśeta ca.

ādadīdhvaṃ mah"|ârhāṇi, tatra, vāsāṃsi sa|tvarāḥ,
uddhunīyāta sat|ketūn nirharet' âgrya|candanam.

muñcet' ākāśa|dhūpāṃś ca, grathnīyāta srajaḥ śubhāḥ,
ānayet' âmitaṃ dāru, karpūr'|âguru|kuṅkumam.

19.10 uhyeran yajña|pātrāṇi, hriyeta ca vibhāvasuḥ,
bhriyeta c' ājyam ṛtvigbhiḥ, kalpyeta ca samit|kuśam.

snānīyaiḥ snāpayet' āśu, ramyair limpeta varṇakaiḥ,
alaṅ|kuryāta ratnaiś ca Rāvaṇ'|ârhair Daśānanam.

THEN FREE FROM cares, Vibhíshana spoke to Rama, 19.1
"Though he may not deserve to be lamented, will not
a co-uterine brother cause distress when he dies?

May the gods provide us with that by which we, like Rávana, may prevail over our enemies and die in battle.

May the demons be made to turn against the gods by someone else in our family just as they were by Rávana; may the hosts of the enemy be brought down.

He alone would be able to save lives in such a rout of his kinsmen who had a friend able to give comfort such as yourself.

For I might be dead within the hour if I could not come to 19.5
you, for we have no desire to live now that Rávana is dead.

How could we place such shameful affection on that place where our twenty-handed brother exists no more?"

Then Vibhíshana instructed those devoted ministers, "Go quickly to Lanka and enter the king's palace.

When there, quickly take clothes of great price, shake out the huge banners and bring the best sandalwood.

Waft incense, weave auspicious garlands, bring wood without limit, camphor, aloe and saffron.

The sacrificial vessels must be fetched, fire brought, ghee 19.10
carried by the priests, and kindling and *kusha* grass prepared.

Quickly have Rávana washed with cleansing ointments, smear him with pleasing unguents and adorn him with jewels worthy of him.

vāsayeta su|vāsobhyāṃ medhyābhyāṃ rākṣas'|âdhipam,
ṛtvik sragviṇam ādadhyāt, prāṅ|mūrdhānaṃ mṛg'|âjine.

yajña|pātrāṇi gātreṣu cinuyāc ca yathā|vidhi,
juhuyāc ca havir vahnau, gāyeyuḥ Sāma sāma|gāḥ.»

gatv" âtha te purīṃ Laṅkāṃ kṛtvā sarvaṃ yath"|ôditam,
samīpe 'nty'|āhuteḥ s'|âsrāḥ proktavanto Vibhīṣaṇam:

19.15 «kṛtaṃ sarvaṃ yath"|ôddiṣṭaṃ, kartuṃ vahni|jala|kriyām
prayatethā mahārāja, saha sarvaiḥ sva|bandhubhiḥ.

ajñavan n' ôtsahethās tvaṃ,* dheyā dhīratvam a|cyutam,
stheyāḥ kāryeṣu bandhūnāṃ, heyāḥ śok'|ôdbhavaṃ tamaḥ.

n' âvakalpyam idaṃ glāyed yat kṛcchreṣu bhavān api,
na pṛthag|janavaj jātu* pramuhyet paṇḍito janaḥ.

yacca* yatra bhavāṃs tiṣṭhet tatr' ânyo Rāvaṇasya na,
yacca yatra bhavān sīden mahadbhis tad vigarhitam.

āścaryaṃ yacca* yatra tvāṃ prabrūyāma vayaṃ hitam.
api sākṣāt praśiṣyās* tvaṃ kṛcchreṣv Indra|purohitam.

19.20 kāmo janasya «jahyās* tvaṃ pramādaṃ» nairṛt'|âdhipa.
uta dviṣo 'nuśoceyur viplave, kim u bāndhavāḥ.

You should have the king of the demons perfumed with the two pure fine scents. The priest should place his garlanded form pointing eastwards on a buckskin.

He should arrange the sacrificial utensils on his limbs according to rule, he should offer the oblation into the fire, and the *saman* singers should sing the Sama Veda."

Then they went to the city of Lanka and did everything as instructed, and near to the final oblation they tearfully called to Vibhíshana:

"All has been done as directed, O great king. You should 19.15
endeavor to perform the rite of fire and water with all your own kinsfolk.

You should not bear it like a fool, you should cultivate unshakeable firmness, you should abide by the duties of your kinsmen, you should give up the darkness that arises from grief.

It is inconceivable that you also should become despondent in the midst of sufferings: a wise man should not be deluded like an ordinary man.

Where you stand no other of Rávana's could stand; the great would censure it if you were to sink down in despair.

It is amazing that we should be giving you advice here. Is it not plain that you could teach Brihas·pati himself in difficulties?

It is the people's wish that you should abandon this mad- 19.20
ness, O king of the demons. In such a calamity even the enemy grieve, let alone the relatives.

sa bhavān bhrātṛvad rakṣed yathāvad akhilaṃ janam
na bhavān saṃpramuhyec ced āśvasyuś ca niśā|carāḥ.»

tataḥ sa gatavān kartuṃ bhrātur agni|jala|kriyām.
proktavān kṛta|kartavyaṃ vaco Rāmo 'tha rākṣasam,
ambhāṃsi rukma|kumbhena siñcan mūrdhi, samādhimān:
«tvaṃ rājā rakṣasāṃ Laṅkām avekṣethā Vibhīṣaṇa.

kruddhān anunayeḥ samyag, dhanair lubdhān upārjayeḥ,
mānino mānayeḥ kāle, trastān Paulastya, sāntvayeḥ.

19.25 icchā me param" ānandeḥ* kathaṃ tvaṃ Vṛtraśatruvat,
icchedd* hi suhṛdaṃ sarvo vṛddhi|saṃsthaṃ yataḥ suhṛt.

vardhiṣīṣṭāḥ sva|jāteṣu, vadhyās* tvaṃ ripu|saṃhatīḥ,
bhūyās tvaṃ guṇināṃ mānyas teṣāṃ stheyā vyavasthitau.

dheyās tvaṃ suhṛdāṃ prītiṃ, vandiṣīṣṭhā div'|âukasaḥ,
somaṃ peyāś ca, heyāś ca hiṃsrā hāni|karīḥ kriyāḥ.

avaseyāś* ca kāryāṇi dharmeṇa pura|vāsinām,
anurāgaṃ kriyā rājan, sadā sarva|gataṃ jane.

ghāniṣīṣṭa tvayā manyur, grāhiṣīṣṭa samunnatiḥ,
rakṣobhir darśiṣīṣṭhās tvaṃ drakṣīran bhavatā ca te.

Your honor should protect the entire population properly as your brother did. If your honor is not completely confounded then we nightstalkers can recover ourselves."

Then he went to perform the funeral rites for his brother. Rama spoke these words to the demon who had done his duty, sprinkling water on his head with a golden pitcher and absorbed in concentration: "May you as king of the demons oversee Lanka, O Vibhíshana.

You must properly conciliate those who are angry, win over the covetous with money, opportunely flatter the proud and calm the fearful, O Vibhíshana.

It is my supreme desire that you should rejoice like Indra 19.25
the enemy of Vrítra: for every friend wants his friend established in prosperity.

You should grow more prosperous within your own tribe, you should kill the hordes of your enemies, you should win respect among the virtuous and you should remain steady in their law.

You should bestow affection on your friends, you should give more veneration to the gods, you should drink *soma*, you should give up harmful and loss-causing actions.

You should determine the duties of the citizens justly, you should always have an all-inclusive affection for the people, O king.

You should destroy grief and seize hold of progress, you should be visible to the demons and they should be seen by you.

19.30 manyuṃ vadhyā bhaṭa|vadha|kṛtaṃ
bāla|vṛddhasya rājan.
śāstr'|âbhijñāḥ sadasi su|dhiyaḥ
sannidhiṃ te kriyāsuḥ.
saṃraṃsīṣṭhāḥ sura|muni|gate
vartmani prājya|dharme.
saṃbhutsīṣṭhāḥ sunaya|nayanair
vidviṣām īhitāni.»

You should slay the grief of young and old which has been 19.30
caused by the death of the soldiers, O king. The wise,
learned in the scriptures, should be close to you in the assembly. You should take the very highest delight in the supremely righteous way traveled by the gods and the sages. With an eye to good policy you should have an excellent understanding of the aspirations of your enemies.

CANTO 20
THE REJECTION OF SITA

20.1 SAMUPETYA TATAḤ Sītām uktavān pavan'|ātmajaḥ
«diṣṭyā vardhasva, Vaidehi, hatas trailokya|kaṇṭakaḥ.*

anujānīhi hanyantāṃ may" âitāḥ kṣudra|mānasāḥ
rakṣikās tava rākṣasyo, gṛhāṇ' âitāsu matsaram.

tṛṇahāni dur|ācārā ghora|rūp'|āśaya|kriyāḥ.
hiṃsrā bhavatu te buddhir, etāsu kuru niṣṭhuram.

paścimaṃ karavām' âitat priyaṃ devi, vayaṃ tava.»
tataḥ proktavatī Sītā vānaraṃ karuṇ'|āśayā:

20.5 «upaśāmyatu te buddhiḥ piṇḍa|nirveśa|kāriṣu
laghu|sattveṣu. doṣo 'yaṃ yat|kṛto nihato 'sakau.

na hi ‹preṣya|vadhaṃ ghoraṃ karavāṇy› astu* te matiḥ,
edhi,* kārya|karas tvaṃ me, gatvā pravada Rāghavam.

‹didṛkṣur Maithilī Rāma, paśyatu tv" â|vilambitam?› »
«tath"» êti sa pratijñāya gatvā Rāghavam uktavān.›

«utsuk" ānīyatāṃ devī Kākutstha|kula|nandana.»
kṣmāṃ likhitvā viniśvasya svar ālokya Vibhīṣaṇam
uktavān Rāghavaḥ «Sītām ānay' âlaṃ|kṛtām» iti.
gatvā praṇamya ten' ôktā Maithilī madhuraṃ vacaḥ:

20.10 «jahīhi* śokaṃ Vaidehi, prītaye dhehi mānasam,
Rāvaṇe jahihi dveṣāṃ, jahāhi pramadā|vanam.

THE SON OF the wind then approached Sita and said, 20.1
"Sita, thrive with good fortune, the thorn in the three worlds is slain.

Allow me to kill these mean-hearted demoness guards of yours, accept my hostility towards them.

May I crush these of evil conduct whose bodies, thoughts and deeds are horrible. May your mind be cruel: treat them harshly.

Let us do this final favor for you, O queen." Then with a merciful heart Sita addressed the monkey:

"Let your mind relent towards these minor beings who take 20.5
delight in sacrificial morsels. He by whom the wrong was done is dead.

Your intention should not be, 'Let me slaughter his minions horribly!' Come, you are dutiful to me, go and say to Rama:

'Sita wishes to see you, O Rama, may she see you immediately?'" "As you wish," he assented and went and spoke to Rama.

"The queen is anxious that she be brought here, O joy of the house of Kakútstha." Touching the ground, sighing and looking to heaven, Rama said to Vibhíshana, "Bring Sita here when she has been adorned." He went and bowing to Sita spoke sweet words to her:

"Shun your grief, Sita, prepare your heart for delight, shun 20.10
enmity towards Rávana, shun the pleasure grove.

snāhy, anulimpa, dhūpāya,* nivassv' āvidhya ca srajam,
ratnāny āmuñca,* saṃdīpte havir juhudhi pāvake,
addhi tvaṃ pañca|gavyaṃ ca cchindhi saṃrodha|jaṃ tamaḥ,
āroha śibikāṃ haimīṃ dviṣāṃ jahi* mano|rathān.

tṛṇeḍhu tvad|viyog'|ôtthāṃ rājanyānāṃ patiḥ śucam.
bhavatād* adhiyuktā tvam ata ūrdhvaṃ sva|veśmani.

dīkṣasva saha Rāmeṇa tvaritaṃ turag'|âdhvare.
dṛśyasva patyā prītena, prītyā prekṣasva Rāghavam.

20.15 ayaṃ niyogaḥ patyus te, kāryā n' âtra vicāraṇā:
bhūṣay' âṅgaṃ, pramāṇaṃ ced, Rāmaṃ gantuṃ yatasva ca.

mudā saṃyuhi Kākutsthaṃ, svayaṃ c' āpnūhi sampadam.
upehy ūrdhvaṃ muhūrtāt tvaṃ devi Rāghava|sannidhim.

ūrdhvaṃ muhūrtād ahno 'ṅga svāminī sma bhava* kṣiteḥ.
rāja|patnī|niyoga|stham anuśādhi* purī|janam.

uttiṣṭhasva* mate patyur,
yatasv' âlaṃ|kṛtau tathā,
pratiṣṭhasva* ca taṃ draṣṭuṃ
draṣṭavyaṃ* tvaṃ mahī|patim.»

anuṣṭhāya yath"|ādiṣṭaṃ niyogaṃ Janak'|ātmajā,
samārūḍhavatī yānaṃ, paṭṭ'|âṃśuka|vṛt'|ānanā.

20.20 lajj"|ānatā visaṃyoga|duḥkha|smaraṇa|vihvalā,
s'|âsrā gatv" ântikaṃ patyur dīnā ruditavaty asau.

Bathe, anoint yourself, burn incense, dress and prepare a garland, put on your jewels, make an offering into the blazing fire, and then eat the five products of the cow,* cut through the darkness born of confinement, mount the golden palanquin and scotch the dreams of your enemies.

May the lord of royalty crush the grief born of separation from you. May you be united hereafter in your own home.

Be consecrated with Rama soon in the horse sacrifice. May your joyful husband look upon you, may you behold Rama with joy.

This is your lord's instruction, there should be no disputing 20.15
this: ornament your body, and if this be authority for you, strive to reach to Rama.

Unite Rama with joy and gain your own good fortune. Reach Rama's presence within the hour, O queen.

In just one hour of the day be mistress of the earth, O queen. Govern the people of the city who abide by the command of the king's consort.

Rise according to your husband's wish, be meticulous in your costume, go forth to see the lord of the earth who is worthy to be seen."

The daughter of Jánaka, complying with the order as directed, mounted her conveyance, her face covered by a silk veil.

Bowing in her modesty, disturbed by the memory of the 20.20
pain of separation, tearfully she went to her husband's side, pitiful and weeping.

prāpta|cāritrya|sandehas tatas tām uktavān nṛpaḥ
«icchā me n' ādadai* Sīte tvām ahaṃ, gamyatām ataḥ.

Rāvaṇ'|âṅka|pariśliṣṭā tvaṃ hṛl|lekha|karī* mama:
matiṃ badhāna Sugrīve rākṣas'|êndraṃ gṛhāṇa vā.

aśāna Bharatād bhogān, Lakṣmaṇaṃ pravṛṇīṣva vā,
kāmād vā yāhi, mucyantām āśā Rāma|nibandhanāḥ.

kva ca khyāto Raghor vaṃśaḥ, kva tvaṃ para|gṛh'|ôṣitā.
anyasmai hṛdayaṃ dehi, n' ân|abhīṣṭe ghaṭāmahe.

20.25 yath"|êṣṭaṃ cara Vaidehi, panthānaḥ santu te śivāḥ,
kāmās te 'nyatra tāyantāṃ, viśaṅkāṃ tyaja mad|gatām.»

tataḥ pragaditā vākyaṃ Maithil'|âbhijanā nṛpam:
«strī|sāmānyena sambhūtā śaṅkā mayi vimucyatām.

daivād bibhīhi Kākutstha, jihrīhi tvaṃ tathā janāt,
mithyā mām abhisaṃkrudhyann a|vaśāṃ śatruṇā hṛtām.

cetasas tvayi vṛttir me, śarīraṃ rakṣasā hṛtam,
vidāṃ kurvantu samyañco devāḥ satyam idaṃ vacaḥ.

tvaṃ punīhi punīh' îti punan vāyo, jagat|trayam,*
caran deheṣu bhūtānāṃ, viddhi me buddhi|viplavam.*

Then the king who had doubts about her conduct said to her, "It is my wish that I should not take you back Sita, therefore be gone.

By being clasped about the waist by Rávana you have made a scar on my heart: fix your mind on Sugríva or accept Vibhíshana, lord of the demons.

Eat food from Bharata's house,* or choose Lákshmana, or as may be your pleasure depart, but give up your hopes with regard to Rama.

How can the celebrated house of Raghu be compatible with you who have dwelt in another's house? Give your heart to another, let us not exert ourselves for what is not wanted.

Do as you wish, Sita, may your paths be auspicious, do not 20.25
allow your desires to spread elsewhere, abandon any doubt with regard to me."

Then Sita whose family was of Míthila addressed words to the king: "Let go this doubt about me which derives from the commonality of women.

Fear fate, thus also feel shame before the people, Rama, for being wrongly angry at me who was snatched helpless by the enemy.

My mind is devoted to you but my body was snatched by the demon. May the united gods make it known that this speech is true.

You purify and purify, O Vayu, purifying the trio of worlds, moving in the bodies of creatures. Find out if my mind has been violated.

20.30 kham aṭa, dyām aṭ', âṭ' ôrvīm ity aṭantyo* 'tipāvanāḥ
yūyam āpo, vijānīta mano|vṛttiṃ śubhāṃ mama.

jaganti dhatsva, dhatsv' êti dadhatī* tvaṃ vasundhare,
avehi mama cāritraṃ naktaṃ|divam a|vicyutam.

rasān saṃhara, dīpyasva, dhvāntaṃ jahi, nabho bhrama,*
it' īhamānas* tigm'|âṃśo, vṛttaṃ jñātuṃ ghaṭasva me.

svarge vidyasva, bhuvy āsva, bhujaṅga|nilaye bhava,
evaṃ vasan* mam' ākāśa saṃbudhyasva kṛt'|âkṛtam.

citāṃ kuru ca Saumitre vyasanasy' âsya bheṣajam,
Rāmas tuṣyatu me v" âdya pāpāṃ pluṣṇātu v" ânalaḥ.»

20.35 Rāghavasya maten' âtha Lakṣmaṇen' ācitāṃ citām
dṛṣṭvā, pradakṣiṇī|kṛtya, Rāmaṃ pragaditā vacaḥ:

«pravapāṇi vapur vahnau Rām', âhaṃ śāṅkitā tvayā.
sarve vidantu śṛṇvantu bhavantaḥ sa|plavaṅgamāḥ.

māṃ duṣṭāṃ jvalita|vapuḥ pluṣāṇa vahne,
saṃrakṣa kṣata|malināṃ suhṛd yathā vā,
eṣ" âhaṃ kratuṣu Vasor yath" ājya|dhārā
tvāṃ prāptā vidhivad udīrṇa|dīpti|mālam.»

O most purifying, wandering waters, wandering the sky, 20.30
wandering heaven, wandering the earth, make known the
pure conduct of my heart.

O supporting earth, always supporting the worlds, understand that my conduct has not deviated day or night.

O sharp-rayed sun, drawing up moisture, shining, destroying darkness, wandering the sky, exerting yourself, try to understand my conduct.

O ether, you are found in heaven, you rest on earth, you exist in the nether lair of the snakes; dwelling thus, understand what I have done and not done.

And Lákshmana, prepare a pyre as a remedy for this distress: may Rama this day be satisfied with me or may the fire burn me as a sinner."

Then when she saw the pyre piled up by Lákshmana with 20.35
Rama's approval, she positioned herself to the right and
spoke to Rama:

"May I cast my body into the fire, O Rama, since you have doubted me. May you all, including the monkeys, know it and hear it.

O fire, with your flaming form, burn me as guilty, or as a friend protect me whose impurities are destroyed. Here am I like a stream of ghee in the rites of Vasu, come lawfully to you who have raised up your garland of flame."

CANTO 21
THE ORDEAL OF SITA

21.1 SAMUTKṢIPYA TATO vahnir
Maithilīṃ Rāmam uktavān:
«Kākutstha, dayitāṃ sādhvīṃ
tvam āśaṅkiṣyathāḥ katham?*

n' âbhaviṣyad iyaṃ śuddhā yady apāsyam ahaṃ tataḥ:
na c' âināṃ pakṣapāto me dharmād anyatra* Rāghava.

api tatra ripuḥ Sītāṃ n' ârthayiṣyata dur|matiḥ,
krūraṃ jātv avadiṣyac ca jātv astoṣyac chriyaṃ svakām.

saṅkalpaṃ n' âkariṣyac ca tatr' êyaṃ śuddha|mānasā?
saty'|âmarṣam avāpsyas tvaṃ Rāma* Sītā|nibandhanam?

21.5 tvay" âdrakṣyata kiṃ n' âsyāḥ śīlaṃ saṃvasatā ciram?
adarśiṣyanta vā ceṣṭāḥ kālena bahunā na kim?

yāvaj|jīvam aśociṣyo, n' âhāsyaś ced idaṃ tamaḥ:
bhānur apy apatiṣyat kṣmām akṣobhiṣyata ced iyam.

samapatsyata rājendra, straiṇaṃ yady atra cāpalam,
loka|pālā ih' āyāsyaṃs tato n' âmī kali|druhaḥ.

āścaryaṃ yacca yatra strī kṛcchre 'vartsyan mate tava:
trāsād asyāṃ vinaṣṭāyāṃ kiṃ kim ālapsyathāḥ phalam?

yatra yacc' âmariṣyat strī sādhvasād doṣa|varjitā,
tad asūyā|ratau loke tasyā vācy'|āspadaṃ mṛṣā.

21.10 amaṃsyata bhavān yadvat tath" âiva ca pitā tava
n' āgamiṣyad vimāna|sthaḥ sākṣād Daśaratho nṛpaḥ?

THEN THE FIRE lifting up Sita spoke to Rama: "O Kákut- 21.1
stha, how could you have doubted your good wife?

If she had not been pure then I would not have protected her: my partiality towards her is not other than righteous, O Rama.

Were the enemy not ill-intentioned he would not have solicited Sita, spoken cruelly and lauded his own glory.

Being pure of heart, would she not have been resolute? How could you, Rama, have become truly ireful towards Sita?

Could you, living so long together, not have perceived her 21.5
character? Or could her conduct have been unobserved af-
ter so long?

If you do not remove this darkness, you will grieve as long as you live: even the sun would fall to earth if she were troubled.

If this was a case of feminine fickleness, O great king, then the world guardians who are hostile to discord would not have come here.

It is a wonder how and where a woman might live in torture according to your wish: when she had been destroyed by fear whatever fruit would you have gained?

Were a virtuous woman to die of fear in whatever circumstances, that would be an occasion for her to be spoken of falsely in this world that so delights in calumny.

Surely your father king Dasha·ratha would not have thought 21.10
the same as you had he come in person standing in his car?

n' âkalpsyat sannidhiṃ Sthāṇuḥ śūlī vṛṣabha|vāhanaḥ
anvabhāviṣyat' ânyena Maithilī cet pati|vratā.

ānandayiṣyad āgamya kathaṃ tvām aravinda|sat
rājendra, viśva|sūr dhātā cāritrye Sītayā kṣate?»

praṇaman Brahmaṇā prokto rājak'|âdhipatis tataḥ:
«n' âśotsyan Maithilī loke, n' ācariṣyad idaṃ yadi.

n' âmokṣyāma vayaṃ śaṅkām ih' âdhāsyan na ced bhavān.
kiṃ vā citram idaṃ yuktaṃ bhavān yad akariṣyata?

21.15 prāvartiṣyanta ceṣṭāś ced a|yāthātathyavat tava
anuśāsye tvayā loke Rām' âvartsyaṃstarāṃ* tataḥ.»

praṇamantam tato Rāmam uktavān iti Śaṅkaraḥ:
«kiṃ Nārāyaṇam ātmānaṃ n' âbhotsyata bhavān a|jam?

ko 'nyo 'kartsyad iha prāṇān dṛptānāṃ ca sura|dviṣām?
ko vā viśva|janīneṣu karmasu prāghaṭiṣyata?

daitya|kṣaye mahā|rāja, yacca yatr' âghaṭiṣyathāḥ,
samāptiṃ jātu tatr' âpi kiṃ n' âneṣyas tvam īhitam?»*

tātaṃ prasādya Kaikeyyā Bharatāya prapīḍitam,
Sahasracakṣuṣaṃ Rāmo ninaṃsuḥ paridṛṣṭavān.

Shiva borne on a bull, bearing a trident would not have manifested himself here if Sita, whose vow is to her lord, had been enjoyed by someone else.

O great king, how would the lotus-throned, all-generating creator have come here and made you blissful if Sita had tarnished her virtue?"

Then Brahma addressed the lord of the princely castes as he bowed down: "If Sita had not conducted herself in this way, she would not have been pure in the eyes of the world.

If you had not put her in this situation, we would not have lost our doubts; is it so strange that what you did was proper?

If your business were not carried out properly then so still 21.15
more, O Rama, would it not be carried out in the world which you should be teaching."

Then Shiva spoke to Rama as he made obeisance: "Did you not become aware that you are the unborn Naráyana?

Who else would have excised the life breath of the proud enemies of the gods? And who would have striven in their actions for the benefit of all people?

O great king, however and wherever you may have exerted yourself in the destruction of the demons, why did you not also bring it to the desired conclusion?"

Now that he had pleased his father who had been harassed by Kékayi for the sake of her son Bharata, Rama who wished to pay obeisance had an audience with thousand-eyed Indra.

21.20 pretā vareṇa Śakrasya prāṇantaḥ kapayas tataḥ
saṃjātāḥ phalin'|ānamra|rociṣṇu|druma|sadravaḥ.

bhramara|kul'|ākul'|ôlba-ṇa|sugandhi|sapuṣpa|tarus,*
taruṇa|madhūka|sambha-va|piśaṅgita|tuṅga|śikhaḥ,
śikhara|śil"|ântarāla|parikḷpta|jal'|âvasaraḥ,
sa|rasa|phala|śriyaṃ sa vitatāna Suvela|giriḥ.

saṃvādbhiḥ sa|kusuma|reṇubhiḥ samīrair,
ānamrair bahu|phala|dhāribhir van'|ântaiḥ,
ścyotadbhir madhu|paṭalaiś ca, vānarāṇām
āpyāno ripu|vadha|sambhavaḥ pramodaḥ.

āyāntyaḥ sva|phala|bhareṇa bhaṅguratvaṃ
bhṛṅg'|ālī|nicaya|citā latās tarūṇām
s'|āmodāḥ, kṣiti|tala|saṃsthit'|âvalopyā,
bhoktṝṇāṃ śramam udayaṃ na nītavatyaḥ.

Then the dead monkeys came alive through Indra's boon 21.20
and became denizens of well-laden and colorful fruit trees.

Mount Suvéla stretched out with its very fragrant flowering trees enveloped by swarms of bees, its high peaks made golden by the tender *madhúka* blossom, its waterfalls forming in the gaps in the cliffs of its buttresses, luxuriant with sweet fruit.

The wafting breezes full of flower pollen and the forest edges with their trees bowed with abundant fruit and with their dripping honeycombs increased the monkeys' delight at the slaying of their enemies.

The branches of the trees brought to breaking point by their burden of fruit, piled with masses of bees, fragrant, to be plucked by one standing on the ground, brought no rising fatigue to their enjoyers.

CANTO 22
THE RETURN TO AYÓDHYA

22.1 Tato Rāmo Hanūmantam uktavān hṛṣṭa|mānasam
«Ayodhyāṃ śvaḥ prayāt" âsi kape Bharata|pālitām.*

gādhitā se nabho bhūyaḥ sphuṭan|megha|ghaṭ'|āvali,
īkṣitā se 'mbhasāṃ patyuḥ payaḥ śiśira|śīkaram.

sevitā se plavaṅga tvaṃ Mahendr'|âdrer adhityakāḥ
vyutkrānta|vartmano bhānoḥ saha|jyotsnā|kumudvatīḥ.

candana|druma|saṃcchannā nirākṛta|hima|śrathāḥ
darśitāras tvayā tāś ca Malay'|ôpatyakāḥ śubhāḥ.

22.5 pratanvyaḥ komalā Vindhye sahitāraḥ syadaṃ na te
latāḥ stabaka|śālinyo madhu|lehi|kul'|ākulāḥ.

draṣṭ" âsi prītimān ārāt sakhibhiḥ saha sevitām
sa|pakṣapātaṃ Kiṣkindhāṃ pūrva|krīḍāṃ smaran muhuḥ.

tvayā sandarśitārau te Mālyavad|Daṇḍakā|vane,
upadrutaś ciraṃ dvandvair yayoḥ kliśitavān aham.

āptārau bhavatā ramyāv āśramau hariṇ'|ākulau
puṇy'|ôdaka|dvij'|ākīrṇau Sutīkṣṇa|Śarabhaṅgayoḥ.

atikrāntā tvayā ramyaṃ duḥkham Atres tapo|vanam,
pavitra|Citrakūṭe 'drau tvaṃ sthāt" âsi kutūhalāt.

THEN RAMA SPOKE to Hánuman whose heart was 22.1
thrilled, "Tomorrow, O monkey, you shall go to Ayódhya which Bharata governs.

Once again you will set out through the sky with its lines of shining heaped-up clouds, you will see the waters of the water lord as cool rain.

O monkey, you will encounter the moon-lit and lotus-covered upper slopes of Mount Mahéndra obstructing the path of the sun.

You will see the lovely foothills of the Málaya range covered in sandalwood trees concealing the snowmelt.

In the Vindhya range the very delicate and tender vines full 22.5
of blossom and thronged with swarms of bees will not be able to bear your impetus.

Remembering fondly how you often played there before, you will see with pleasure nearby Kishkíndha where your friends resorted.

You will see the Dándaka and Mályavat forests in which I suffered so long assailed by the pairs of opposites.

You will reach those two lovely hermitages of Sutíkshna and Shara·bhanga thronged with deer and filled with holy water and the twice-born.

Sadly you will overpass Atri's delightful penance grove but from curiosity you will stop on the purifying Mount Chitra·kuta.

22.10 tataḥ paraṃ Bharadvājo bhavatā darśitā muniḥ,
draṣṭāraś* ca janāḥ punyā Yāmun'|âmbu|kṣat'|âṃhasaḥ.*

syantvā syantvā divaḥ Śambhor
mūrdhni skantvā bhuvaṃ gatām
gāhitā se 'tha puṇyasya
Gaṅgāṃ mūrtim iva drutām.

Tamasāyā mahā|nīla|pāṣāṇa|sadṛśa|tviṣaḥ
van'|ântān bahu mantā se nāgar'|ākrīḍa|sākṣinaḥ.*

nagara|strī|stana|nyasta|dhauta|kuṅkuma|piñjarām
vilokya Sarayūṃ ramyāṃ gant" Âyodhyā tvayā purī.

ānanditāras tvāṃ dṛṣṭvā praṣṭāraś c' âvayoḥ śivam
mātaraḥ saha Maithilyā, toṣṭā ca Bharataḥ param.

22.15 ākhyāt" âsi hataṃ śatrum, abhiṣiktaṃ Vibhīṣaṇam,
Sugrīvaṃ c' ârjitaṃ mitraṃ, sarvāṃś c' āgāmukān drutam.

gantāraḥ paramāṃ prītiṃ paurāḥ ṣrutvā vacas tava,
jñātv" âitat sammukhīnaś ca sametā Bharato dhruvam.

gate tvayi path" ânena vayam apy aṃhitā smahe,
labdhā he* 'haṃ dhṛtiṃ prāpte bhūyo bhavati sammukhe.»

gate tasmin gṛhīt' ârthe Rāmaḥ Sugrīva|rākṣasau
uktavān «śvo 'bhigantā stho yuvāṃ saha mayā puram.

Then finally you will see the sage Bharad·vaja and the virtu- 22.10
ous people who have washed away their sins in the waters
of the Yamuná.

Then you will plunge into the Ganges which ever flows through the sky landing in the world on top of Shiva's head like the flowing embodiment of merit.

You will much admire the forest regions of the Támasa river which shines as if with great sapphires and bears witness to the sportiveness of the city dwellers.

When you see the lovely Sárayu river ochre with the washed-away saffron which had been spread on the breasts of the city women, you will have reached the city of Ayódhya.

Our mothers seeing you will be delighted and will ask after the welfare of both us and of Sita, and Bharata will be supremely happy.

You will relate that the enemy has been killed, Vibhíshana 22.15
has been coronated, Sugríva has become a friend, and that
all are due to arrive soon.

The citizens will gain the highest delight at hearing your words and knowing this Bharata in the forefront will certainly meet you.

When you have gone we also shall go by that path. When you are once again in front of me I will be happy."

When he had gone and his object had been achieved, Rama spoke to Sugríva and the demon Vibhíshana: "You two will go to the city with me tomorrow.

draṣṭā sthas tatra tisro me mātṝs tuṣṭ'|ântar'|ātmanaḥ
ātyantīnaṃ sakhitvaṃ ca prāptā stho Bharat'|āśrayam.

22.20 n' âivaṃ viraha|duḥkhena vayaṃ vyāghānitā smahe,
śramo nubhavitā n' âivaṃ bhavadbhyāṃ ca viyoga|jaḥ.

evaṃ yuvāṃ mama prītyai kalptā sthaḥ kapi|rākṣasau,
gantuṃ prayatitā sāthe prātaḥ saha mayā yadi.»

uktavantau tato Rāmaṃ vacaḥ Paulastya|vānarau
«anugraho 'yaṃ Kākutstha, gantā svo yat tvayā saha.

anumantā svahe n' āvāṃ bhavantaṃ virahaṃ tvayā
api prāpya surendratvaṃ, kiṃ nu prattaṃ tvay" āspadam?»

tataḥ kathābhiḥ samatītya doṣām
  āruhya sainyaiḥ saha Puṣpakaṃ te
samprasthitā vega|vaśād a|gādhaṃ
  prakṣobhayantaḥ salilaṃ payo|dheḥ.

22.25 setuṃ, Mahendraṃ, Malayaṃ sa|Vindhyaṃ,
  sa|Mālyavantaṃ girim Ṛṣyamūkam,
sa Daṇḍak"|âraṇyavatīṃ ca Pampāṃ
  Rāmaḥ priyāyāḥ kathayan jagāma.

«ete te muni|jana|maṇḍitā dig|antāḥ;
  śailo 'yaṃ lulita|vanaḥ sa Citrakūṭaḥ;
Gaṅg" êyaṃ su|tanu, viśāla|tīra|ramyā.»
  Maithilyā Raghu|tanayo diśan nananda.

«śiñjāna|bhramara|kul'|ākul'|âgra|puṣpāḥ
  śīt'|âmbhaḥ|pravilaya|samplav'|âbhilīnāḥ
ete te sutanu, purī|jan'|ôpabhogyā
  dṛśyante nayana|manoramā van'|ântāḥ.

There you will see my three mothers whose inner souls are content and you will obtain the limitless friendship which is Bharata's refuge.

Thus we will not be wounded by the pain of separation and 22.20
you will not suffer the distress that comes of parting.

O monkey and demon, you will thus facilitate my joy if you will set out early with me."

Then Vibhíshana and the monkey said to Rama, "It is a privilege, O Rama, that we shall go with you.

Even after we had gained the status of the lord of gods we would not agree to being separated from you; what then when you have given us rank?"

Then after passing the night with stories they mounted the Púshpaka car with their armies. They set out disturbing the deep waters of the ocean with the force of their speed.

As Rama went he spoke to his beloved of the bridge, of 22.25
Mount Mahéndra, the Málaya range along with the Vin-
dhya, Mount Rishya·muka along with Mályavat and Lake
Pampa along with the Dándaka forest.

"These are the extremities of the quarters adorned with a population of sages; this mountain is Chitra·kuta with its swaying forests; this, O slender Sita, is the Ganges beautiful because of her broad banks." As Rama pointed them out to Sita he rejoiced.

"Here you can see the forest regions so charming to the eye which the citizens enjoy, O slender Sita, their flower tips are thronged with swarms of buzzing bees, they are run through with flowing streams of cool water.

sthānaṃ naḥ pūrva|jānām
iyam adhikam asau preyasī pūr Ayodhyā,
dūrād ālokyate yā
huta|vividha|haviḥ|prīṇit'|âśeṣa|devā.
so 'yaṃ deśo, rudantaṃ
pura|janam akhilaṃ yatra hitvā prayātāv
āvāṃ Sīte, van'|ântaṃ
saha dhṛta|dhṛtinā Lakṣmaṇena kṣap"|ânte.»

tūryāṇām atha niḥsvanena sakalaṃ
lokaṃ samāpūrayan,
vikrāntaiḥ kariṇāṃ gir'|îndra|sadṛśāṃ
kṣmāṃ kampayan sarvataḥ,
s'|ānand'|âśru|vilocanaḥ prakṛtibhiḥ
sārdhaṃ sah'|ântaḥ|puraḥ,
samprāpto Bharataḥ sa|Mārutir alaṃ
namraḥ samaṃ mātṛbhiḥ.

22.30 atha sa|sambhrama|paura|jan'|āvṛto,
Bharata|pāṇi|dhṛt'|ôjjvala|cāmaraḥ,
guru|jana|dvija|bandy|abhinanditaḥ,
praviśati sma puraṃ Raghunandanaḥ.

pravidhāya dhṛtiṃ parāṃ janānāṃ,
yuva|rājaṃ Bharataṃ tato 'bhiṣicya,
jaghaṭe turag'|âdhvareṇa yaṣṭuṃ
kṛta|sambhāra|vidhiḥ patiḥ prajānām.

idam *adhigatam ukti|mārga|citraṃ**
vivadiṣatāṃ vadatāṃ ca san|nibandhāt
janayati vijayaṃ sadā janānāṃ
yudhi su|samāhitam aiśvaraṃ yath" âstram.

The city of Ayódhya is a most favored place for our forbears, which can from afar be seen, where the gods are delighted by the various oblations offered. It was there that we left all the weeping populace and went at the end of the night, O Sita, to the forest region with Lákshmana, firm of resolution."

Then filling the entire world with the sound of trumpets, shaking the ground all over with the steps of the monkeys resembling great mountains, Bharata with tears of joy in his eyes, with his subjects and the ladies of the harem, Hánuman and the mothers, received them with full reverence.

Then surrounded by townsfolk bustling about, with a wav- 22.30
ing chowrie held over him in Bharata's hand, lauded by elders, brahmins and bards, Rama entered the city.

Then when he had inspired the greatest contentment in the people and anointed Bharata crown prince, when he had made the necessary preparations, the king undertook the performance of the horse sacrifice.

This poem, *when studied, marvelous in its paths of expression because of its composition*, always produces victory for people who seek dispute and who debate, like a well-aimed powerful weapon which because properly assembled produces victory for people in war, *marvelous when its ways of discharging have been learned*.

dīpa|tulyaḥ prabandho 'yaṃ śabda|lakṣaṇa|cakṣuṣām
hast'|ādarśa* iv' ândhānāṃ bhaved vyākaraṇād ṛte.

vyākhyā|gamyam idaṃ kāvyam utsavaḥ su|dhiyām alam;
hatā dur|medhasaś c' âsmin vidvat|priyatayā mayā.

22.35 kāvyam idaṃ vihitaṃ mayā Valabhyāṃ
Śrīdhara|sūnu*|Narendra|pālitāyām,
kīrtir ato bhavatān* nṛpasya tasya,
prema|karaḥ kṣiti|po yataḥ prajānām.

This composition is like a lamp to those who perceive the meaning of words and like a hand mirror for a blind man to those without grammar.

This poem which is to be understood by means of a commentary, is a joy to those sufficiently learned: through my fondness for the scholar I have here slighted the dullard.

I composed this poem in Válabhi which is protected by 22.35
Naréndra, son of Shri·dhara, hence may the fame of that king increase, since the king causes joy among his subjects.

NOTES

Bold *references are to the English text;* ***bold italic*** *references are to the Sanskrit text. An asterisk (*) in the body of the text marks the word or passage being annotated.*

1.2 ***sa/mūla/ghātam***: *ṇamul* by Pā. 3.4.36.

1.2 **The six inner foes** (*ṣaḍ/vargam*): lust, anger, greed, infatuation, pride and jealousy. See *Arthaśāstra* 1.6.1.

1.9 The three **studies** (*vidyā*) to which the wives are compared are the three ends of human life: pleasure (*kāma*), wealth (*artha*) and virtue (*dharma*).

1.9 **Approached sexually at the right time** (*'dhigatāsu kāle*): see *Manusmṛti* 3.46–7: "The natural season of women according to tradition, consists of sixteen nights, together with the other four days proscribed by good people. Of these nights the first four as well as the eleventh and the thirteenth are disapproved; the remaining ten nights are recommended."

1.10 **The wise and esteemed sage Rishya·shringa**: his story is given in the "Maha·bhárata," Critical Edition (CE), III.110–113.

1.16 ***adhyagāyi***: in the aorist √*gā* is optionally substituted for √*i* by Pā. 2.4.50.

1.20 ***ahaṃyunā … śubhaṃyuḥ***: Pā. 5.2.140.

1.25 **Lákshmana of three mothers** (*traimāturaḥ*): so called because the other two wives of Dasha·ratha gave the remainder of their shares of the food from the sacrifice to his mother in order that he should be born.

2.4 The **night lotuses** close up at daybreak and therefore the tree laments them.

2.7 **The calls of the restless geese**: the geese migrate in fall and their cries at this time are suggestive of romance and the hunter's separation from his beloved and hence distract him from his murderous intent. There is a neat parallel here between the innocent and unsuspecting deer absorbed in the beauties of nature listening to the bee and the cruel hunter hearing the geese and becoming similarly harmless.

2.10 ***vān*** here is pres. pt. nom. s. masc. of √*vā*, "to blow." The *vān* of *vyatiṣaṅgavān* is the possessive suffix *-vant*. Hence there is a *yamaka*.

2.10 ***su/gandhaḥ***: see Pā. 5.4.135 and *vārttika* for discussion of meaning.

2.11 ***anupātam***, ***avaskandam*** and ***upaveśam*** are all *ṇamul* by Pā. 3.4.56.

2.12 A similar trope is used in the *Jātakamālā* of Arya·shura (14.3): *ath' êndra/nīla/prakar'/âbhinīlaṃ sūry'/âṃśu/tāpād iva khaṃ vilīnam, samantato 'ntarhita/tīra/lekham a/gādham ambho/nidhi/madhyam īyuḥ.* "So they reached the center of the bottomless sea, / colored blue by heaps of sapphires, / like a sky melted by the sun's burning rays, / its coastline invisible on all sides" ("Garland of Past Lives, " volume 1, trans. Justin Meiland, New York: New York University Press & JJC Foundation, 2009).

2.14 **Paid their ordained tax**: for taxation see *Manusmṛti* 7.130–132.

2.16 **The dance of the cowherd girls...**: Mall. comments that the dance (*nṛtya*) is figurative (*rūpaka*) because of the superimposition of dancing upon the movements of the limbs; that is *svabhāvokti/saṃkīrṇa* "mixed with natural description."

2.17 ***ārāt***: may be taken in the sense of "near" (Jay.) or "far" (Mall.).

2.18 *Svabhāvokti* but also, according to Mall., *saṃdeha* (doubt) suggesting *sāmānya* (identity).

2.26 ***viṣṭara***: in the sense of tree or seat: Pā. 8.3.93 *vṛkṣāsanayor viṣṭaraḥ*, otherwise it would be *vistara*.

2.27 ***avoḍham***: 2nd du. P. root aor., Pā. 6.3.111–112.

2.29 ***yajñiya*** and ***ārtvijīna***: Pā. 5.1.71.

2.29 ***dakṣiṇya***: Pā. 5.1.69.

2.30 ***śirasya***: Pā. 4.3.53–55.

2.30 ***śirāla***: *la* is used in the sense of *matup* (possessive suffix *-mant*) after a part of the body by Pā. 5.2.96.

2.30 ***daghna***: has the sense of "measure" by Pā. 5.2.37.

2.30 ***prāvṛṣeṇya***: Pā. 4.3.17.

2.32 ***māyā/caṇam astra/cuñcuḥ*** by Pā. 5.2.26 *caṇa* and *cuñcu* have the sense of "famed through."

2.33 ***ātmaṃ/bhariḥ*** and ***phale/grahīn***: Pā. 3.1.26.

2.35 ***vyatiste***: 3rd s. Ā. *vy-aty√as* has the sense of exchange of action by Pā. 1.3.12–14.

2.35 *pra-ṇi√han* takes genitive object by Pā. 2.3.56.

2.36 ***tṛṇāya matvā***: by Pā. 2.3.17 the dative is optionally employed when contempt is to be shown.

2.37 ***varṣukā*** by Pā. 3.2.154 it has the sense of "the agent having such a habit." See also *sthāyuka* in 2.22 above.

2.38 ***mahīyyamānā*** and ***hriṇīyate***: by Pā. 3.1.27.

2.38 ***ghasmara***: Pā. 3.2.160, 163.

2.39 The verse refers to some of the avatars of Vishnu: namely Vámana the dwarf who conquered Bali; the tortoise who churned the oceans; in feminine form as Móhini snatching the nectar; and as the Great Boar lifting the earth on its tusks.

2.40 ***nijighṛkṣayiṣyan***: fut. pt. P. of caus. of desid. of *ni√grah* "being on the point of causing him to desire to overpower the fame of (other) kings." The desiderative of the causative would be *nijigrāhayiṣāmi*, of which the future would be *nijigrāhayiṣiṣyāmi*.

2.41 Reading ***itaḥ***: 3rd du. pres. P. √*i*, with *sma* for past sense, following Mall., in preference to Jay.'s *etau*.

2.42 TURNER prefers Mall.'s reading of ***daityapuraḥ*** acc. pl. in the sense of *Tripura* quoting Pā. 5.4.74, relying on *anuvṛtti* of *vibhāṣā* from 5.4.72. Jay. has *daityapuram*: in which case 5.4.68 would apply.

2.45 ***baṃhiṣṭha/kīrtir*** em. : *baṃhiṣṭha/kīrtiṃ*

2.46 ***tri/varga/pāriṇam***: by Pā. 5.2.11 *pāra* has the sense of "about to go."

2.46 ***dṛśva***: has a sense of past time by Pā. 3.2.94.

2.46 ***agāt***: Pā. 2.4.45, 77.

2.47 ***hiraṇmayī***: irregularly formed by Pā. 6.4.174.

2.48 ***viśva/janīna***: meaning "for the good of all" by Pā. 5.1.5, 9.

2.48 ***udavoḍha***: 3rd s. aor. *ud√vah* by Pā. 6.3.112.

2.48 ***Raghu/vargya***: "members of the house of Raghu:" *vargya* has the sense of "who stays there" by Pā. 4.3.64.

2.50 **Rama Jámadagnya**: this is Rama the son of Jamad·agni who is the sixth avatar of Vishnu. Rama Dásharathi—he of the "Ramáyana"—is the seventh.

2.52 *saṃkṣipya*: 2nd s. imp. P. *saṃ√kṣip*: MW gives this root as class IV only here in the *Bhaṭṭikāvya*. The *Dhātupāṭha* gives it in classes IV and VI.

2.53 *ajīgaṇat*: 3rd s. reduplicating aor. *√gaṇ*. The reduplicative vowel *ī* is optional by Pā. 7.4.97.

2.53 In the "Ramáyana" (1.75.6–16) Rama gives his adversary the option of having either his motion taken away or those worlds which he has won with his penance.

2.55 ***nedayat*** and ***davayat***: pres. pt. nom. s. neut. from a denominative verb. Pā. 5.3.63.

3.5 ***ukṣāṃ pracakrur*** em. Mall. : *ukṣān pracakrur*. Mall.'s interpretation of Pā. 3.1.40 allows an *upasarga* in the formation of the periphrastic perfect. See also note on 14.59.

3.17 ***kav'|ôṣṇam***: Pā. 6.3.107.

3.40 ***âśanāyāḥ*** em. : *âśanāyaḥ*

3.42 ***pari | nirvivapsoḥ***: retroflexion avoided here because *pari* is technically a *pada*.

3.50 ***prattam***: Pā. 7.4.47.

4.7 ***kṛśānusād bhūte***: "completely burned up" by Pā. 5.4.52.

4.9 ***devasāt kṛtvā***: Pā. 5.4.55.

4.21 **You whose fair body has not seen the sun**: the idea is that she has lived so secluded in a harem that even the sun has not seen her.

4.26 ***yenaupanīvikaḥ*** em. : *yenopanīvikaḥ*

5.1 ***nirākariṣṇū vartiṣṇū vardhiṣṇū, utpatiṣṇū, sahiṣṇū***: all governed by Pā. 3.2.136 where *-iṣṇu* follows the root in the sense of the agent having such a nature, duty or ability.

Canto 5 5.1–96 miscellaneous rules; 5.97–104 Pā. 3.2.16–23; 5.105–108 Pā. 3.1.35–39.

5.2 *āyudha/cchāyam*: neuter by Pā. 2.4.22.

5.3 *Yamasāc cakratuḥ*: Pā. 5.4.54.

5.4 Reading ***gatim*** with Mall. rather than *patim* with Jay.

5.5 ***rākṣasa/sabhaṃ***: *sabhā* is neuter at the end of a *tatpuruṣa* compound when preceeded by a word denoting "king" or "nonhuman" by Pā. 2.4.23.

5.10 *khaṭv"/ārūḍhaḥ*: Pā. 2.1.26.

5.14 ***aśnuvate diśaḥ***: "eat the quarters," eat nothing but empty space.

5.15 *anukāmīnatām*: Pā. 5.2.11.

5.15 *paramparīṇāṃ / putrapautrīṇatām*: Pā. 5.2.10.

5.17 *lakṣmīḥ*: nom. s. fem. Pā. 6.1.68 does not apply as the *ī* final is not *ṅī* but from the *Uṇādi sūtra* 448 *lakṣer mut ca* details in SHARMA (vol. 2, p. 501).

5.26 The **Airávata elephant** is Indra's elephant and is considered the prototype of the elephant race and the supporter of the eastern quarter.

5.33 **Rama vanquished the world-famous killer of Karta·virya**: he went after Párashu·rama, killer of the thousand-armed Árjuna Karta·virya ("Ramáyana" 7.33).

5.39 *bhītaṃ/kāram*: making out that he was a coward, Pā. 3.4.25.

5.46 *abhyamitryaḥ*: Pā. 5.2.17.

5.47 *abhyamitrīṇaḥ*: Pā. 5.2.17.

5.48 *yathā/mukhīnaḥ*: Jay. comments *Sītāyā agrato yathāmukhīnaḥ pratibimb'/āśraya iva bhūtvā pupluve bhramati sma. iva/śabda/ lopo draṣṭavyaḥ.* "Like a mirror (*yathāmukhīnaḥ*) in front of Sita, he moved around (*pupluve*). The missing word *iva* needs to be supplied." See Pā. 5.2.6.

5.52 *marmā/vid*: by Pā. 6.3.116 the final *a* of *marma* is lengthened. *Samprasāraṇa* of √*vyadh* to √*vidh* is by Pā. 6.1.16.

5.60 *mṛṣodyam*: Pā. 3.1.114.

5.61 *jañjapūkaḥ*: Pā. 7.4.86, 3.2.166.

5.61 *mṛd/alābunaḥ*: Pā. 4.1.66 (*vārttika*).

5.62 Mall. comments: *kamaṇḍalur eva kapālam karparaṃ jīrṇa/ kamaṇḍalur ity arthaḥ.* Jay. comments: *kamaṇḍalunā kapālena ca. «jātir a/prāṇinām»* (Pā. 2.4.6) *iti dvandv'/âikavad bhāvaḥ.* Mall.'s explanation that it is an appositional compound is more convincing especially as Jay.'s citation of Pā. 2.4.6 would mean that the two objects he was carrying were categories (*jāti*) when here the verse describes a person carrying particular things.

5.68 *priya/kārī*: Pā. 3.2.44.

5.68 *rahasi* em. : *harasi*

5.69 *pari pary udadhe*: Pā. 1.4.88, 2.3.10, 8.1.5.

5.75 *āmiṣa* can also mean "meat," hence "you similar to a tempting bit of (sacrificial) meat." Sita is spoken of as a gift given to a learned teacher or to a sacrificial priest.

5.85 Cake-hero (*piṇḍī/śūra*): one valorous only at eating.

5.96 *rārasyamānām*: pres. pt. intens. √*ras*, given in WR as *rārāsya-*.

5.96 *Jaṭāyuḥ*: there are two forms of this name: *Jaṭāyu* or *Jaṭāyus*. The name occurs in 5.96 and 7.81 as *Jaṭāyuḥ* nominative (which could be either from the *-u* or the *-us* form) and in 6.41 and 7.86 as *Jaṭāyuṃ* accusative (which can only be from the *-u* version). Thus it seems that Bhatti preferred the form *Jaṭāyu*. We therefore call him *Jatáyu* throughout the translation.

5.97–100 This section illustrates Pā. 3.2.17–23 treating of the affix *Ṭa*.

5.97 Pā. 3.2.17–19.

5.98 Pā. 3.2.20.

5.99 Pā. 3.2.21–22.

5.100 Pā. 3.2.21, 23.

5.104–107 This section treats of the suffix *ām* in the periphrastic perfect illustrating Pā. 3.1.35–40.

5.104 Pā. 3.1.35, 40.

5.105 Pā. 3.1.35.

5.106 Pā. 3.1.36–37.

6.1–4 Periphrastic formations based on Pā. 3.1.35–3.1.41 continue.

6.1 Pā. 3.1.35, 38.

6.2 Pā. 3.1.39.

6.3 Pā. 3.1.40.

6.4 Pā. 3.1.41.

6.8–10 Double accusatives based on Pā. 1.4.51.

6.16–34 Aorists using *sĪC* substitutes for the affix *CLI* exemplified in 6.16–34 according to Pā. 3.1.43–66.

6.16 Pā. 3.1.45–46.

6.17 Pā. 3.1.48, 57–58. Jay. comments: *vāmā mat|pratikūla|vartinī*, "behaving unpleasantly towards me."

6.18 Pā. 3.1.49.

6.19 Pā. 3.1.49, 52.

6.21 Pā. 3.1.53.

6.22 Pā. 3.1.47, 53.

6.26 Pā. 3.1.55.

6.27 Pā. 3.1.56.

6.28 Pā. 3.1.57.

6.30 Pā. 3.1.58.

6.31 Pā. 3.1.60.

6.32 Pā. 3.1.61.

6.33 Pā. 3.1.62.

6.34 ***samaruddh' êva vikramaḥ***: Pā. 3.1.87.

6.34 Pā. 3.1.63–66.

6.35–39 The affix *ŚnaM* given by Pā. 3.1.78 for the present tense system of class 7 verbs.

6.44 **A fearsome ravenous long-armed demon**: this is the demon Kabándha who tells his story in "Ramáyana" 3.67.

6.46–67 The future passive participles or gerundives and related forms formed from the *kṛtya* affixes *tavya*, *tavyaT*, *anīyaR*, *yaT*, *Kyap*, and *ṆyaT*, Pā. 3.1.96–132.

6.46 Pā. 3.1.96–97.

6.47 Pā. 3.1.98–100.

6.48 Pā. 3.1.100.

6.49 Pā. 3.1.100.

6.50 Pā. 3.1.101.

6.51 Pā. 3.1.102–103.

6.53 Pā. 3.1.105.

6.54 Pā. 3.1.106–108.

6.55 Pā. 3.1.109.

6.56 Pā. 3.1.111–113.

6.57 Pā. 3.1.114.

6.58 Pā. 3.1.114.

6.59 Pā. 3.1.114–116.

6.59 **Bhidya** and **Uddhya** are names of rivers but also mean "undercutting its banks" and "overflowing its banks." **Sidhya** is also a name for the auspicious *nakṣatra* better known as Pushya at 3°20′–16°40′ Cancer.

6.60 Pā. 3.1.117.

6.61 Pā. 3.1.118–119. The word ***pragríhya*** (*pragṛhya*) occurs in the rule *īd/ūd/ed/dvivacanaṃ pragṛhyam* (Pā. 1.1.11): "A dual termination ending in *ī*, *ū* or *e* is termed *pragṛhya* (exempt from sandhi)." Bhatti could have used the word in its etymological sense "acceptable" in this context. Rather than accuse him of monstrous artificiality, we can credit him with a sense of humor here for providing such an absurd simile which not only illustrates the point of grammar under discussion but also uses the example which is given by the commentators and which is also quoted direct from the *Aṣṭādhyāyī*.

6.62 Pā. 3.1.120–121.

6.63 Pā. 3.1.122, 124.

6.64 Pā. 3.1.125–126.

6.65 Pā. 3.1.126–127.

6.66 Pā. 3.1.128–129.

6.67 Pā. 3.1.130–132.

6.68–70 Miscellaneous forms.

6.71–86 Words formed with *nirupapada kṛt* affixes *ṆvuL*, *tṛC*, *Lyu*, *ṆinI*, *aC*, *Ka*, *Śa*, *Ṇa*, *ṢvuN*, *thakaN*, *ṆyuṬ* and *vuN* according to Pā. 3.1.133–150.

6.71 Pā. 3.1.133–134.

6.72 Pā. 3.1.134.

6.73 Pā. 3.1.134.

6.76 Pā. 3.1.136.

6.77 Pā. 3.1.137.

6.78 Pā. 3.1.138.

6.79 Pā. 3.1.138–141.

6.80 Pā. 3.1.141.

6.81 Pā. 3.1.141.

6.82 Pā. 3.1.141–142.

6.83 Pā. 3.1.143–144.

6.84 Pā. 3.1.145–146.

6.85 Pā. 3.1.148–149.

6.86 Pā. 3.1.150.

6.87–93 Words formed with *sopapada kṛt* affixes *aṆ*, *Ka*, *ṬaK*, *aC* according to Pā. 3.2.1–15.

6.87 Pā. 3.2.1.

6.88 Pā. 3.2.3–5.

6.89 Pā. 3.2.6–7.

6.90 Pā. 3.2.8.

6.91 Pā. 3.2.9–12.

6.92 Pā. 3.2.13–14.

6.93 Pā. 3.2.15.

6.94–108 Words formed with affixes *KHaŚ* and *KhaC* according to Pā. 3.2.28–47.

6.94 Pā. 3.2.28–30.

6.95 Pā. 3.2.31.

6.96 Pā. 3.2.32, 34.

6.97 Pā. 3.2.34.

6.98 The separate feminine instrumental ***mūrtyā*** can be taken to apply to the demon's body. Hence we may translate: "By trickery a demon with a form never seen in sunlight who wounds most painfully took my beloved from the forest; we are hunting for her."

6.98 Pā. 3.2.35–36.

6.99 Pā. 3.2.36.

6.100 Pā. 3.2.37–38.

6.101 Pā. 3.2.38–39.

6.102 Pā. 3.2.40–41.

6.103 Pā. 3.2.42.

6.104 Pā. 3.2.43.

6.105 Pā. 3.2.44.

6.106 Pā. 3.2.45.

6.107 ***kapir viśvaṃ/bhar'/âdhipam*** em. : *kapi/viśvaṃ/bhar'/âdhipam*

6.108–111 Words formed with the affix *Ḍa*, Pā. 3.2.48–50.

6.109 Pā. 3.2.48.

6.110 Pā. 3.2.49–50.

6.111 Pā. 3.2.50.

6.112–143 Words formed with *kṛt* affixes, Pā. 3.2.51–116.

6.112 Pā. 3.2.51–52.

6.112 **Husband-killer**: in Sanskrit poetry the goddess Śrī (Fortune) is personified as the wife of the king.

6.113 Pā. 3.2.53–55.

6.114 Pā. 3.2.56.

6.115 Pā. 3.2.57.

6.116 Pā. 3.2.58.

6.117 Pā. 3.2.59.

6.119 Pā. 3.2.60.

6.120 Pā. 3.2.61.

6.121 Pā. 3.2.61.

6.122 Pā. 3.2.62, 68.

6.123 Pā. 3.2.78–79.

6.124 Pā. 3.2.86.

6.125 Pā. 3.2.83.

6.126 Pā. 3.2.86–87.

6.127 Pā. 3.2.89.

6.128 Pā. 3.2.90–92.

6.129 Pā. 3.2.93–95.

6.130 Pā. 3.2.95–96.

6.131 Pā. 3.2.97, 101.

6.135 Pā. 3.2.59–108.

6.136 Pā. 3.2.109.

6.139 Pā. 3.2.12–114.

6.140 Pā. 3.2.116.

6.143 ***anvag/bhāvam***: Pā. 3.4.64.

7.1–25 *kṛt* (*tācchīlaka*) affixes *tṛN*, *iṣṇuC*, *Ksnu*, *Knu*, *GHinUṆ*, *vuÑ*, *yuC*, *ukaÑ*, *ṢākaN*, *inI*, *luC*, *KmaraC*, *GhuraC*, *KuraC*, *KvaraP*, *ūka*, *ra*, *u*, *najIṄ*, *āru*, *Kru*, *KlukaN*, *varaC* and *KvIP* according to Pā. 3.2.134–175.

7.1 Pā. 3.2.135.

7.2 Pā. 3.2.136.

7.3 Pā. 3.2.136.

7.4 Pā. 3.2.136–140.

7.5 Pā. 3.2.141.

7.6 Pā. 3.2.142.

7.7 Pā. 3.2.142.

7.8 Pā. 3.2.142.

7.9 ***an/apacāriṇam***: for *an/apakāriṇam*, ref. TRIVEDI (notes p 101).

7.9 Pā. 3.2.142.

7.10 Pā. 3.2.142.

7.11 Pā. 3.2.143.

7.12 Pā. 3.2.144–146.

7.13 Pā. 3.2.146–147.

7.14 Pā. 3.2.149.

7.16 Pā. 3.2.150.

7.18 Pā. 3.2.154.

7.19 Pā. 3.2.157.

7.20 Pā. 3.2.157.

7.21 Pā. 3.2.158–159.

7.22 Pā. 3.2.160–164.

7.23 Pā. 3.2.165–167.

7.24 Pā. 3.2.167–169.

7.25 Pā. 3.2.172–175.

7.28–34 *niradhikāra kṛt* affixes according to Pā. 3.3.1–21.

7.28 Pā. 3.3.1.

7.29 ***kārakā mitra/kāryāṇi***: accusative instead of genitive by Pā. 2.3.70.

7.29 Pā. 3.3.11.

7.30 Pā. 3.3.12.

7.31 Pā. 3.3.13.

7.32 Pā. 3.3.13, 16.

7.33 Pā. 3.3.17.

7.34–85 The affix *GhaÑ* according to Pā. 3.3.18–85.

7.34 Pā. 3.3.19–21.

7.35 Pā. 3.3.22–23.

7.36 Pā. 3.3.24–25.

7.37 Pā. 3.3.26–28.

7.38 Pā. 3.3.29–30.

7.39 Pā. 3.3.31–32.

7.40 Pā. 3.3.33–36.

7.41 Pā. 3.3.37–39.

7.42 Pā. 3.3.40–42.

7.43 Pā. 3.3.44–45.

7.44 Pā. 3.3.46.

7.45 ***māsatamād*** em. : *māsamatād*

7.45 Pā. 3.3.47.

7.46 Pā. 3.3.48–49.

7.47 Pā. 3.3.50.

7.48 Pā. 3.3.51.

7.49 Pā. 3.3.52.

7.50 Pā. 3.3.53, 58.

7.52 Pā. 3.3.53.

7.53 Pā. 3.3.54.

7.54 Pā. 3.3.55.

7.55 Pā. 3.3.56–57.

7.56 Pā. 3.3.59–61.

7.57 Pā. 3.3.62–64.

7.58 Pā. 3.3.65–67.

7.59 Pā. 3.3.68–69.

7.60 Pā. 3.3.71–74.

7.61 Pā. 3.3.75–78.

7.62 Pā. 3.3.78–81.

7.63 Pā. 3.3.82–84.

7.64 Pā. 3.3.85–86.

7.65 Pā. 3.3.90–91.

7.66 Pā. 3.3.93–94.

7.67 Pā. 3.3.93–94.

7.68 Pā. 3.3.95.

7.69 Pā. 3.3.97.

7.71 Pā. 3.3.103–104.

7.74 Pā. 3.3.108–109.

7.75 Pā. 3.3.100, 110.

7.76 Pā. 3.3.111.

7.77 Pā. 3.3.112.

7.79 Pā. 3.3.113–116.

7.80 Pā. 3.3.117–119.

7.82 Pā. 3.3.120–122.

7.83 Pā. 3.3.123–126.

7.84 Pā. 3.3.127.

7.85 Pā. 3.3.128.

7.90 *Kauśalyāyani*: Pā. 4.1.155.

7.91 Pā. 1.2.1.

7.92 Pā. 1.2.2.

7.93 Pā. 1.2.3–4.

7.94 Pā. 1.2.5.

7.95 Pā. 1.2.6–7, 18.

7.97 Pā. 1.2.8.

7.98 Pā. 1.2.8.

7.99 Pā. 1.2.9.

7.100 ***bhuddhvam***: 2nd pl. aor. injunctive, see WHITNEY (1924: §579) and Pā. 8.2.37; also 8.2.26 and 8.4.53.

7.100 Pā. 1.2.10–11.

7.101 ***samagadhvam … upāyaṃsta***: aorists of hoping, Pā. 3.3.132. See also 15.103.

7.101 Pā. 1.2.15–16.

7.102 Pā. 1.2.17.

7.103 Pā. 1.2.18–19.

7.104 Pā. 1.2.20–21.

7.105 Pā. 1.2.23.

7.106 Pā. 1.2.24–25.

7.107 Pā. 1.2.26.

8.1 Pā. 1.3.12.

8.2 Pā. 1.3.13.

8.3 Pā. 1.3.14–15.

8.6 Pā. 1.3.16.

8.7 Pā. 1.3.17.

8.8 Pā. 1.3.18.

8.9 Pā. 1.3.19.

8.10 Pā. 1.3.20–21.

8.11 Pā. 1.3.22.

8.12 Pā. 1.3.23–24.

8.13 Pā. 1.3.25.

8.14 Pā. 1.3.26–27.

8.15 Pā. 1.3.28.

8.16 Pā. 1.3.29.

8.17 Pā. 1.3.30.

8.18 Pā. 1.3.31–32.

8.20 Pā. 1.3.33–34.

8.21 Pā. 1.3.35–36.

8.22 Pā. 1.3.37–39.

8.23 Pā. 1.3.40.

8.24 Pā. 1.3.41.

8.25 Pā. 1.3.42–43.

8.26 Pā. 1.3.44–46.

8.27 Pā. 1.3.47.

8.28 Pā. 1.3.48.

8.29 Pā. 1.3.49.

8.30 Pā. 1.3.50–51.

8.31 Pā. 1.3.52–53.

8.32 Pā. 1.3.54–55.

8.33 Pā. 1.3.56–57.

8.34 Pā. 1.3.57.

8.35 Pā. 1.3.58.

8.36 Pā. 1.3.59–60.

8.37 Pā. 1.3.61.

8.38 Pā. 1.3.62–63.

8.39 Pā. 1.3.64.

8.40 Pā. 1.3.65–66.

8.41 Pā. 1.3.67.

8.42 Pā. 1.3.67–68.

8.43 Pā. 1.3.69.

8.44 Pā. 1.3.70–71.

8.45 Pā. 1.3.72–73.

8.46 Pā. 1.3.74–75.

8.47 Pā. 1.3.76.

8.49 Pā. 1.3.77–78.

8.50 Pā. 1.3.79.

8.51 Pā. 1.3.80.

8.52 Pā. 1.3.81–82.

8.53 Pā. 1.3.83.

8.54 Pā. 1.3.85.

8.55 Pā. 1.3.85.

8.56 Pā. 1.3.74, 86, 88.

8.59 Pā. 1.3.86.

8.60 Pā. 1.3.88.

8.61 Pā. 1.3.87, 89.

8.62 Pā. 1.3.89.

8.63 Pā. 1.3.89.

8.64 Pā. 1.3.89.

8.65 Pā. 1.3.90.

8.66 Pā. 1.3.91.

8.67 Pā. 1.3.92.

8.68 Pā. 1.3.92.

8.69 Pā. 1.3.92–93.

8.70–84 Use of the cases as detailed in Pā. 1.4.24–54 under the *adhikāra* "*kārake.*"

8.70 Pā. 1.4.24–25.

8.71 Pā. 1.4.26–31.

8.73 Pā. 1.4.32–34.

8.74 Pā. 1.4.35.

8.75 Pā. 1.4.36–37.

8.76 Pā. 1.4.38–39.

8.77 Pā. 1.4.40–41.

8.78 Pā. 1.4.42–44.

8.79 Pā. 1.4.45–47.

8.80 Pā. 1.4.47–48.

8.81 Pā. 1.4.49–50.

8.82 Pā. 1.4.51–52.

8.85–93 *karmapravacanīya* as detailed in Pā. 1.4.83–98.

8.85 Pā. 1.4.84–85.

8.86 Pā. 1.4.86–87.

8.87 Pā. 1.4.87–88.

8.88 Pā. 1.4.89–90.

8.89 Pā. 1.4.91–92.

8.90 Pā. 1.4.93–95.

8.91 Pā. 1.4.96.

8.94–130 *vibhakti* as detailed in Pā. 2.3.1–73.

8.94 Pā. 2.3.4–5.

8.95 Pā. 2.3.6–7.

8.96 Pā. 2.3.12.

8.97 Pā. 2.3.14–16.

8.98 Pā. 2.3.16.

8.99 Pā. 2.3.18.

8.100 *tanuḥ*: the feminine termination is optional in this case by Pā. 4.1.44.

8.100 Pā. 2.3.21.

8.101 Pā. 2.3.20.

8.102 Pā. 2.3.22–23.

8.103 Pā. 2.3.24–26.

8.104 Pā. 2.3.27, 29.

8.105 Pā. 2.3.29.

8.106 Pā. 2.3.29.

8.108 Pā. 2.3.31.

8.109 Pā. 2.3.32.

8.110 Pā. 2.3.33.

8.111 Pā. 2.3.34–36.

8.112 Pā. 2.3.37.

8.113 Pā. 2.3.38.

8.114 Pā. 2.3.39.

8.115 Pā. 2.3.40.

8.116 Pā. 2.3.41–42.

8.117 Pā. 2.3.44–46.

8.118 Pā. 2.3.47, 52.

8.119 Pā. 2.3.52–53.

8.120 Pā. 2.3.54–56.

8.121 Pā. 2.3.57.

8.122 Pā. 2.3.52, 58, 59, 64.

8.123 Pā. 2.3.65.

8.124 Pā. 2.3.66, 67, 69.

8.125 Pā. 2.3.68.

8.126 Pā. 2.3.65, 69.

8.128 Pā. 2.3.70.

8.129 Pā. 2.3.71–72.

8.129 **Nándana** is Indra's garden paradise.

8.131 ***citra*** em. metri causa : *vicitra*

8.131 ***nādita*** em. metri causa : *nādi*

9.8–11 The suffix *sIC* and *vṛddhi* of the P. aor., Pā. 7.2.1–7.

9.8 Pā. 7.2.2–3, 7.

9.9 Pā. 7.2.4–5.

9.10 Pā. 7.2.5–6.

9.11 Pā. 7.2.3–4, 7.

9.12–22 Prohibition of *iṬ*, Pā. 7.2.8–30.

9.12 Pā. 7.2.8–10.

9.13 Pā. 7.2.9–12.

9.14 Pā. 7.2.12.

9.15 Pā. 7.2.13.

9.16 ***minnān*** Mall. em. : *mitrān* Jay. Mall.'s reading is more in keeping with the sequence of *sūtra*s being illustrated.

9.16 Pā. 7.2.16.

9.17 Pā. 7.2.17–18.

9.18 Pā. 7.2.19–27.

9.20 Pā. 7.2.27–28.

9.21 Pā. 7.2.28.

9.22 Pā. 7.2.29–30.

9.23–57 The use of *iṬ*, Pā. 7.2.35–78.

9.23 Pā. 7.2.36–37.

9.24 ***varitum*** could be from √*vṛ* "to choose" or √*vṛ* "to cover;" the commentators differ on this. Hence we could translate: "the grove which rose up as if to cover the sky and to entice the birds."

9.25 Pā. 7.2.38–40.

9.26 ***a/kṣamyam***: can be taken with *akṣam* or *kapim*, Jay. does not commit himself on this point but Mall. takes it with *kapim*.

9.26–37 These verses illustrate the desiderative.

9.26 Pā. 7.2.41.

9.27 Pā. 7.2.42–44.

9.28 Pā. 7.2.44.

9.29 Pā. 7.2.44–45.

9.30 Pā. 7.2.46–47.

9.31 Pā. 7.2.48.

9.32 Pā. 7.2.49.

9.33 Pā. 7.2.49.

9.34 Pā. 7.2.49.

9.35 Pā. 7.2.49.

9.36 Pā. 7.2.49.

9.37 Pā. 7.2.49.

9.38 Pā. 7.2.50.

9.39 ***bhūyas***: this word would seem to apply to all the verbal forms in the second half of the verse.

9.39 Pā. 7.2.51–54.

9.41 Pā. 7.2.55.

9.42 Pā. 7.2.56–57.

9.43 Pā. 7.2.58–59.

9.44 Pā. 7.2.60.

9.45 Pā. 7.2.60.

9.47 Pā. 7.2.61–63.

9.48 Pā. 7.2.65–67.

9.49 Pā. 7.2.70–72.

9.50 Pā. 7.2.73.

9.51 Pā. 7.2.73.

9.53 Pā. 7.2.74.

9.54 Pā. 7.2.75.

9.55 Pā. 7.2.76.

9.57 Pā. 7.2.76–78.

9.58–66 *visarga* sandhi in compounds: Pā. 8.3.34–48.

9.58 Pā. 8.3.34–36.

9.59 Pā. 8.3.37–39.

9.60 Pā. 8.3.39–40.

9.61 Pā. 8.3.41.

9.62 Pā. 8.3.42–43.

9.63 Pā. 8.3.43–44.

9.64 Pā. 8.3.45.

9.65 Pā. 8.3.46.

9.66 Pā. 8.3.47–48.

9.67–91 Retroflexion of *s*: Pā. 8.3.55–118.

9.67 Pā. 8.3.56–59.

9.68 ***proṣita/trāsa/karkaśaḥ***: Jay. interprets this as meaning "fierce with fear of the absent (Rama)." We could also take it as a *dvaṃdva*: "fearless and fierce."

9.68 Pā. 8.3.59–60.

9.69 Pā. 8.3.61–62: desideratives and desideratives of causatives.

9.70 Pā. 8.3.64–65.

9.72 Pā. 8.3.65–69.

9.73 Pā. 8.3.71–72.

9.74 Pā. 8.3.72–73.

9.75 Pā. 8.3.74–75.

9.76 Pā. 8.3.77.

9.77 Pā. 8.3.77.

9.78 Pā. 8.3.80–81.

9.79 Pā. 8.3.82–83.

9.80 ***mātṛ|ṣvaseyyāḥ***: Pā. 4.1.134.

9.80 Pā. 8.3.84–85.

9.81 Pā. 8.3.87–88.

9.82 Pā. 8.3.89.

9.83 Pā. 8.3.90–91.

9.83 **Kapi·shthala** is an obscure Vedic sage. He is only mentioned here because he is the topic of Pā. 8.3.91.

9.84 Pā. 8.3.92–93, 95–97.

9.85 Pā. 8.3.98, 101–102, 111.

9.87 Pā. 8.3.112.

9.88 Pā. 8.3.113.

9.89 Pā. 8.3.115–116.

9.90 Pā. 8.3.117.

9.91 Pā. 8.3.118.

9.92–109 Retroflexion of *n*: Pā. 8.4.1–39.

9.92 Pā. 8.4.1.

9.93 Pā. 8.4.2–6.

9.95 Pā. 8.4.7–9.

9.96 Pā. 8.4.10–12.

9.97 Pā. 8.4.13–15.

9.98 Pā. 8.4.16.

9.99 Pā. 8.4.17.

9.99 **Vibhíshana** was Rávana's brother and as a result of his austerities was granted a boon by Brahma. He chose that he would not, even in extremis, stoop to a low action and hence he makes an objection.

9.100 Pā. 8.4.18.

9.101 Pā. 8.4.19–21.

9.102 Pā. 8.4.23.

9.103 Pā. 8.4.24–25, 29.

9.104 Pā. 8.4.30.

9.105 Pā. 8.4.31.

9.106 Pā. 8.4.32–33.

9.107 Pā. 8.4.34.

9.108 Pā. 8.4.35–36.

9.109 Pā. 8.4.39.

9.110–137 Miscellaneous forms.

9.135 This verse alludes to the story of Rávana's fight with Valin as told at "Ramáyana" 7.34.

10.1 *Anuprāsa* or alliteration.

10.2–22 ***Yamaka***: this figure is defined by Gerow as "A figure in which a part of a verse, specified either as to length or position or both, is repeated within the confines of the same verse, usually in such a way that the meaning of the two readings is different." Nāṭ. 16.59–86; KB 2.9–20; KD 3.1–72; KV 4.1.1–7; Ag. 343.12–17; KR 3.1–59; KM 10.117–118.

10.2 ***Yukpādayamaka*** or *vikrāntayamaka*: Nāṭ. 16.70–71; Ag. 343. 16.

10.3 ***Pādāntayamaka***: KB 2.9–10; KD 3.1–2; KV 4.1.2; Ag. 343. 15. According to Mall. this is also an example of *nidarśanālaṃkāra*: KB 3.32–33; KD 2.348–350; KV 4.3.20; KM 10.150.

10.3 **The Triple City** is a demon city that was destroyed by Shiva.

10.4 ***sa|kalaiḥ sakalaiḥ***: Brough notes: "The commentary gives *sakalaiḥ samastaiḥ sa-kalaiḥ sāṃśaiḥ*, i.e., taking it from *kalā*, 'part.' But this is after all the literal sense of the first *sakalaiḥ*, and it seems preferable to take the second from *kala*, 'indistinct noise;' though admittedly this is usually used for soft, pleasant sounds, such as the buzzing of bees."

10.4 ***Padādiyamaka***: KB 2.9–11; KD 3.1–4; KV 4.1.2; Ag. 343.15.

10.5 ***Pādamadhyayamaka***: KB 2.9; KD 3.1–2; KV 4.1.1–2; Ag. 343.15.

10.6 Although called *cakravālayamaka* by the commentators, this verse does not correspond exactly to the types described in the *alaṃkāra* texts: ref. Gerow p. 229 and Söhnen (1995: 503–04, 507).

10.7 *Samudgayamaka*: the whole half verse is repeated. Nāṭ. 16.68; KB 2.10; KD 3.53; Ag. 343.16; KR 3.16.

10.8 *hvalatā janena* em. : *halatā janena*

10.8 Called by the commentators *kāñcīyamaka* but they are confused by the example in Nāṭ. with *cakravālayamaka* in verse 10.6 (see note): Nāṭ. 16.72; Ag. 343.16.

10.9 Translated here according to Jay.'s commentary. BROUGH, partially following Mall., reads and interprets as follows: *na gajā naga|jā dayitā dayitā, vi|gataṃ vigataṃ, calitaṃ calitam, pramad" â|pra|madā, mahatā mahatām a|raṇaṃ maraṇaṃ samayāt samayāt.* "The beloved mountain-born elephants were not tended, the flight of birds ceased, activity came to an end, lovely woman was without delight, and death not in battle arrived at the fated time for heroes, by reason of the great (fire)." He further notes: "*valitaṃ valitam* is so interpreted by Mall., '*valitaṃ prāṇi-ceṣṭitaṃ ca valitaṃ vigataṃ.*' But it seems doubtful whether *valitam* could really mean 'ended,' and it is tempting to suggest that both in the text and commentary it should be corrected to *calitaṃ calitam*, the meaning remaining the same. A number of mss. read *lalitaṃ lalitam*, 'dalliance was shaken': Jay., '*lalitaṃ yad īpsitaṃ vastu tad lalitaṃ pīḍitam.*'" The same problem of a forced meaning applies to this reading of Jay.

10.9 *Yamakāvalī*: KB 2.9 but see SÖHNEN (1995: 506.)

10.10 *Ayugmapādayamaka*: not separately described but related to *yukpādayamaka* in verse 10.2 and *samudgayamaka* in verse 10.7.

10.11 *Pādādyantayamaka* according to the commentaries but closely related to the examples in 10.6 and 10.9.

10.12 *Mithunayamaka*.

10.13 *Vṛntayamaka* or *pādādiyamaka*: Nāṭ. 16.77.

10.14 ***viviktamālam***: Jay. comments, *viviktāḥ śucayo mālāḥ srajo yasmin tad vivikta-mālam*, so "pure lines;" similarly Mall. comments, *yasmiṃs tad vivikta-mālam asaṅkīrṇa-paṅkti*; ignoring these comments, TURNER translates, "from which the flowering sprays had been removed."

10.14 *Puṣpayamaka* or *pādāntayamaka* compare with verse 10.3: Nāṭ. 16.63.

10.15 BROUGH notes: "The sense of 'water' for *vana* in *vanaja* as understood by Mallinātha is doubtless a misunderstanding arising from the use of *vana* for a bed of lotuses, e.g. *kumudavana*; c.f. KB 6.60: *yathaitac chyāmam ābhūti vanaṃ vanajalocane.*"

10.15 ***Pādādimadhyayamaka***: KR 3.52; see also SÖHNEN (1995: 502).

10.16 ***sahamānā***: Mall. reads *asahamānā duḥkhaṃ* in the first half line: "unable to bear the pain."

10.16 ***Āvṛtiyamaka*** or *vipathayamaka*: KR 3.3; KM 10.118C.

10.17 ***Madhyāntayamaka***: KB 2.12; KD 3.43; KR 3.52.

10.18 In *pāda c* ***rucita/mun natimat*** could also be read as *rucitam unnatimat*: "shining, elevated."

10.18 *Garbhayamaka*: KR 3.7.

10.19 The commentators have a merry time making diverse interpretations of this verse. Two further interpretations could be: *babhau Marutvān vikṛtaḥ sa/mud/raḥ*, "Indra, once defeated, was glad in the company of the giver of joy (Hánuman);" *babhau Marutvān vikṛtaḥ sa/mudraḥ*, "The joyful wind god showed himself altered (gentle)."

10.19 *Sarvayamaka* or *Mahāyamaka*: KD 3.70.

10.20 *Mahāyamaka* or *ślokābhyāsayamaka*: KD 3.67; KR 3.16.

10.21 TURNER notes: "*Abhiyā* as instrumental and *atāvaram* as 'obstructing the wind' seems far fetched. Perhaps *abhiyātā* is instrumental, then *varam*, *tuṅgam*, *ruciram* and *karkaśam* would go with *bhūbhṛtam* (mountain) leaving *dhāma* (space) *sasattvaṃ puṣkare* as the subject of *prathitam*. It is hard to understand *karkaśam* as an epithet to *dhāma*." See commentaries for other interpretations.

10.22 ***Mumuhur muhuḥ***: KEITH (1928: 124) observes that Magha must be later than "Bhatti whose *mumuhur muhuḥ* he trumps with his *kim u mumuhur muhur gatabhartṛkāḥ*."

10.22 Although called *ādyantayamaka* by the commentators this does not correspond to the types described in the *alaṃkāra* texts.

10.23–25 ***Dīpaka*** "lamp" or "zeugma," defined by GEROW as "a construction wherein several parallel phrases are each completed by a single (unrepeated) word or phrase," rather as a lamp left in a doorway will illuminate what is on both sides. Nāṭ 16.40, 53–55; KB 2.25–29; KD 2.97–115; KV 4.3.18–19; KU 1.14; KR 7.64–71; KM 10.156–157. None of the examples in the *Bhaṭṭikāvya* correspond to this. Although Bharata does not employ the "first-middle-last" classification, he does insist that one word is used to complete the meaning of the two sentences. It may well be that Bhaṭṭi never intended his examples to illustrate this, and was working from a definition in a text now lost.

10.23 Called *ādidīpaka* by Jay.: KB 2.25; KD 2.102; KV 4.3.19; KU 1.14; KR 7.65. As *gacchan* can only (tenuously) be sustained as *dīpaka* for the first two *pāda*s, this is a weak example. It is probably for this reason that Mall. calls this *kāraṇamālā*, "a garland of causes:" KR 7.84; KM 10.186.

10.24 Again, although called *antadīpaka* by Jay., it does not fit the later definitions as one word is not used to support two syntactic structures. Mall. calls this *kāvyaliṅga*; according to GEROW, "a figure in which a metaphorical relation of cause and effect is expressed conventionally either as intention or rationale," KM 10.174.

10.25 Jay. calls this *madhyadīpaka* but Mall. calls it *kāvyaliṅga* (see note on 10.24) and *saṃkara*, a compound figure: KB 3.48–51; KD 2.363 (*saṃkīrṇa* 2.359); KV 4.3.30–33; KU 6.5; KM 10.207.

10.26–30 ***Rūpaka***, "metaphorical identification," defined by GEROW as "a figure in which the subject of comparison is identified with its object by a specific process of grammatical subordination." Bhatti's examples are complex and often illustrate several types of *rūpaka* in one verse. Nāṭ 16.56–58; KB 2.21–24; KD 2.66–96; KV 4.3.6; KU 1.11–13; KR 8.38–56; KM 10.139–145.

10.29 **Ángada** is the son of Vālin who is Sugrīva's brother.

10.30–35 ***Upamā***: Nāṭ 16.40–52; KB 2.30–33; KD 2.14–65; KV 4.2.1–21; KU 1.15–21; Ag. 344.6–21; KR 8.4–31; KM 10.125–134. Again, the examples have little relation to the definitions and examples given by other writers, but this series of verses using particles and suffixes of comparison seems to be the inspiration for Bhámaha's classification.

10.32 ***Pari/viral'/âṅguli/nirgat'/âlpa/dīpti***: a more literal translation would be "its faint light escaping through his fingers with their surrounding gaps."

10.33 ***Rucir'/ônnata/ratna/gauravaḥ***: hardly Bhatti's best moment!

10.33 Not an *upamā* at all unless we stretch it to translate "Rama saw the jewel as his life's hope."

10.36 The wind will fan the spark into a conflagration.

10.37 *Arthāntaranyāsa*, "apodoxis," defined by GEROW as "a figure in which a proposition or remark is justified or substantiated by the adjunction of a relevant moral or rationale." KB 2.71–74; KD 2.169–179; KV 4.3.21; KU 2.4; Ag. 344.24; KR 8.79–84; KM 10.165.

10.38 *Ākṣepa*, "objection," defined by GEROW as "a figure in which is expressed an objection to or denial of some state of affairs, either real or imagined, either past, present, or future; contradiction." Bhámaha and Dandin call this figure *pratiṣedhokti*. KB 2.66–70; KD 2.120–168; KU 2.2–3; Ag. 345.14–15; KR 8.89–91; KM 10.161.

10.40 *Vyatireka*, "distinction," defined by GEROW as "a figure wherein two notoriously similar things are said to be subject to a point of difference; usually the subject of comparison is stated to excel the object, surpassing the norm of its own comparability; hence, an inverted simile." KB 2.75; KD 2.180–198; KV 4.3.22; KU 2.6; KR 7.86–89; KM 10.159.

10.41 *Vibhāvanā*, "manifesting," defined by GEROW as "a figure in which an effect is realized in the absence of its normal or conventional cause, thus implying another, unusual cause." KB 2.77–78; KD 2.199–204; KV 4.3.13; KU 2.9; Ag. 344.27; KR 9.16, 21; KM 10.162. Mall. calls this example *kāvyaliṅga*.

10.42 *Samāsokti*, "concise speech," defined by GEROW as "a figure in which the descriptive qualifications of an explicit subject suggest an implicitly comparable object to which they likewise apply." KB 2.79–80; KD 2.205–213; KV 4.3.3; KU 2.10; Ag. 345.17; KR 8.67–68; KM 10.148. Mall. thinks it is a type of *atiśayokti*.

10.43 Mall. calls this figure *svabhāvokti*, "natural description." Defined by GEROW as "a figure in which a natural or typical individual is characterized." KB 1.30; KD 2.8–13; KU 3.5; KR 7.30; KM 10.168. HOOYKAAS (p. 359) speculates that this may be *sūkṣma*, "subtlety" defined by GEROW as "a figure in which an intention or idea is said to be conveyed through a gesture, glance or means other than language:" KB 2.86; KD 2.235, 260–264; KM 10.189. He adds the caveat that this verse mentions gesture and posture so explicit that not much subtle is left.

10.44 *Yathāsaṃkhya*, "correspondence," defined by GEROW as "a figure consisting of ordered sequences of terms, such as nouns and adjectives or subjects and objects of comparison, so arranged that item one of the first sequence matches item two of the second, and so on." KB 2.89–90; KD 2.273–274; KV 4.3.17; KU 3.2; Ag. 346.21; KR 7.34, 36–37; KM 10.164.

10.45 *Utprekṣā*: a complex and variously defined figure but here perhaps exemplified as the metaphorical ascription of a motive or rationale.

10.46 *Vārtā*, "the mention of facts:" not counted as an independent figure by most rhetoricians but see KB 2.87.

10.47 *Preyas*, "more agreeable," defined by GEROW as "the expression of affection in an extraordinary way." KB 3.5; KD 2.275–276. Identified by Mall. as *atiśayokti*, exaggeration or hyperbole: KB 2.81–85; KD 2.214–220; KV 4.3.10; KU 2.11; Ag. 344.26; KM 10.153.

10.48 *Rasavat*, "expressing a mood," defined by GEROW as "a figure in which is clearly expressed a mood or rasa—usually *śṛṅgāra*, the amorous." KB 3.6; KD 2.275 280–292; KU 4.3–4; KM 10.66, 123c.

10.49 *Ūrjasvin*, "violent," defined by GEROW as "the expression of extraordinary self-assurance or arrogance." KB 3.7; KD 2.294; KU 4.5.

10.50 *Bhrāntimat*, "confusion," defined by GEROW as "a figure in which one thing, usually the object of comparison, is mistaken for another, usually the subject of comparison." KR 8.87–88; KM 10.200.

10.51–52 ***Svabhāvokti***, "natural description," defined by GEROW as "telling the nature (of a thing)." KB 1.30, 2.93; KD 2.8–13; KU 3.5; KR 7.30–33; KM 10.168.

10.53–54 ***Udāra*** or *udātta*, "lofty," defined by GEROW as "a figure in which a great accumulation of wealth or greatness of character (viz. self-denial) is described." KB 3.11–13; KD 2.300–303; KU 4.8; KM 10.176–177.

10.54 See also Mall. who proposes *atiśayokti* as well.

10.55 Mall. identifies this as *tulyayogitā*, defined by GEROW as "a figure in which several subjects sharing a property or mode of action, though in unequal degrees, are represented as equivalently endowed; the lesser subject is thus magnified." It may be significant that Bhámaha uses the image of the earth-bearing serpent in his example, indicating that he may have drawn on Bhatti for inspiration or that they also shared a common source: *śeṣo himagiris tvaṃ ca mahānto guravaḥ sthirāḥ yad a/laṅghita/maryādāś calantīṃ bibhṛtha kṣitim.* (KB 3.27) "The primeval serpent, the Himálaya and you, O king, are great, weighty and firm; since you (three), surpassing all limitation, support the unstable world." Note also the similar phrases *a/laṅghya/dhāmnaḥ* and *a/laṅghita/maryādāś* and the common use of the root √*bhṛ* and the words *guru* and *giri*.

10.56 *Śleṣa*, paronomasia, double-entendre or punning. The previous verse is also traditionally included under this heading. This series of verses do not conform to the core definition of *śleṣa* indicating again that Bhatti is using a system not easily reconcilable with later tradition.

10.57 *Śleṣa*, see note on 10.55.

10.58 ***Apahnuti***, "denial," variously defined by later rhetoricians and defined by GEROW as "a figure in which the object of comparison is affirmed in place of the subject of comparison," or "in which an essential property of the subject is denied and portrayed otherwise; irony of qualification," or "in which the subject of comparison is portrayed as possessing a quality which in nature belongs to the object of comparison:" KB 3.20–21; KD 2.304–309; KV 4.3.5; Ag. 345.18; KR 8.57–58; KM 10.146. The obvious problem is that there is no element of comparison in Bhatti's example, only denial. This may be an earlier, more primitive form of the figure.

10.59 ***Viśeṣokti***, "speaking of distinction," defined by GEROW as "a figure in which a deficiency (a negative attribute), either natural or occasional, is pointed out in such a way as to magnify or emphasize the capability of its subject." KB 3.22; KD 2.323.

10.60 *Atiśayokti* and *upamā*, for which see notes on 10.46 and 10.30.

10.61 *Utprekṣā*: where a property or mode of behavior is attributed to an object incapable of sustaining that property thus implying a simile: KB 2.91–92; KD 2.221–234; KV 4.3.9; KU 3.3–4; Ag. 344.24–25; KR 8.32–37, 9.11–15; KM 10.137. There is also ***rūpaka*** in the identification of mountains with breasts and the covering water with clothing. The king (Rama) is the husband of the earth so the figure suggests an erotic attraction between the earth itself and Rama.

10.62 *Tulyayogitā*: see note on 10.55.

10.63 ***Nidarśana***, "illustration:" a figure in which a general truth is illustrated by a particular situation: KB 3.32–33; KD 2.348–350; KV 4.3.20; KM 10.150.

10.64 ***Virodha***, "contradiction," defined by GEROW as "a figure in which contradictory properties are expressed of the same subject; the affirmation of the excluded middle:" KB 3.24–25; KD 2.333–339; KV 4.3.12; KU 5.6; Ag. 344.28; KR 9.30–34;

KM 10.166–167. The verse also illustrates *dīpaka* and *yathā-saṃkhya* for which see notes on 10.22 and 10.43.

10.65 ***Upameyopamā***, "mutual simile:" also called *anyonyopamā*, a simile in which the comparison is made reciprocal: KB 3.36–37; KD 2.18; KV 4.3.15; KU 5.14; KM 10.136.

10.66 ***Sahokti***, "accompaniment," defined by GEROW as "a figure in which two separate things or ideas are represented as conjoined or occurring at once:" KB 3.24–25; KD 2.351–354; KV 4.3.28; KU 5.15; Ag. 344.23; KR 7.13–18; KM 10.170.

10.67 ***Parivṛtti***, "exchange:" one thing exchanged for another: KB 3.40–41; KD 2.355–356; KV 4.3.16; KU 5.16; KR 7.77–78; KM 10.172.

10.68 ***Saṃdeha***, "doubt:" KB 3.42–43; KV 4.3.11; KU 6.2–3; KR 8.59–64; KM 10.138.

10.69 ***Ananvaya*** or ***ananvayopamā***, "lack of consequence" or "self comparison:" KB 3.44; KD 2.358; KV 4.3.14; KU 6.4; KR 8.11; KM 10.135.

10.70 ***Utprekṣāvayava***, "component parts of the ascription," defined by GEROW as "a type of metaphorical ascription (*utprekṣā*) in which further subordinate metaphors explicate and expand the principal ascription:" KB 3.46–47; KV 4.3.31, 33.

10.71 ***Saṃsṛṣṭi***, "composite:" a figure comprised of a mixture of other figures. In this case *upamā* and *virodha*, for which, see notes on 10.30 and 10.63.

10.72 ***Āśīs***, "benediction," but identified by Mall. as *kāvyaliṅga* (for which see note on 10.24): KB 3.55–57; KD 2.357.

10.73 ***Hetu***, "cause:" a figure describing cause and effect: KD 2.235–259; Ag. 344.29; KR 7.82–83; refuted at KB 2.86; KM 10.186.

Canto 11 This canto exhibits the quality of "sweetness" (*mādhurya*) which presents nothing disagreeable to the ear and is characterized by the use of alliteration (*anuprāsa*), shorter compounds, ingenuity of expression and the absence of *śleṣa* or paranomasia.

11.31 Their **limbs** are smeared to obscure bite marks and scratches, their lips concealed to hide the swelling consequent on being bitten and they try not to blink so as to conceal the tiredness of those who have been at play all night.

11.35 ***lakṣmīḥ***: nom. s. fem., see note on 5.17.

11.36 ***tṛṣṇāturaḥ*** em. : *tṛṇāturaḥ*

11.40 ***ūrdhvaśoṣam***: *ṇamul* by Pā. 3.4.44.

11.41 **Bees** come to gather ichor from the temples of rutting elephants.

12.2 ***amṛtavat***: Jay. comments: *yathā amṛtaṃ devānām ānandanaṃ viṣasya Kālakūṭa|nāmnaḥ sodarasya ekasmin samudr'|ôdare sthitatvāt jaganti prabādhmānasya praśāntiṃ kṛtavad api*, "Just like the *amṛta* giving bliss to the gods which effected the neutralization of the poison called Kālakūṭa its brother (because it had resided in the womb of the same ocean) which was afflicting the worlds."

12.30 ***āsrāvayet***: Mall.'s reading is preferable to Jay.'s *āśrāvayet* for which the meaning "suborn" is not supported in MW.

12.50 **Tara** is the wife of Sugríva's older brother whence she has some sway with him and her son is Ángada.

12.58 After defeating Indra, **Námuchi** let him go on the condition that he wouldn't kill him day or night, wet or dry. Indra killed him at twilight with foam which is apparently neither wet nor dry. See *Ṛgveda* 1.53.7.

12.59 The allusion is to Hiránya·káshipu who persecuted his son Prahláda for his piety and was killed by Vishnu in his incarnation as Nara·simha, the **man-lion.**

12.76 ***sphāvayan***: pres. pt. √*sphāy* by Pā. 7.3.41.

Canto 13 This canto is characterized by the simultaneous usage of Sanskrit and Prakrit. It can therefore be read in Sanskrit by someone with no knowledge of Prakrit. With minor exceptions the vocabulary and grammar are common to both languages. Where the grammar is not common the differences are disguised by sandhi. See Introduction, p. xxx, for more details.

13.4 ***ārīṇam***: Jay. comments: *rīṇam ity aprayogaḥ prākṛte Mahārāṣṭre tasy'|âprayogāt*, "*rīṇam* could not be used because it is not usage in Maharastri Prakrit."

13.7 ***salila|bhareṇa giri|mahī|maṇḍala|saṃvara|vāraṇam*** can also be translated "which stopped the circle of the mountains and earth from being covered by a load of water." Note the *yamaka* at the beginning and end of each half verse. Jay. describes the meter as *gaṇita|krama*, probably becase it is unidentifiable.

13.13 The story referred to here is not found in the "Ramáyana."

13.14 Turner takes ***vīra|ras'|ābandha|ruddha|bhaya|saṃbandham*** as adverbial to *gacchantu* but this though quite plausible is not supported by the commentators.

13.15 The first half of this verse is not Prakrit.

13.21 This verse is not Prakrit.

13.25 ***tīre girim ārūḍhā*** em. metri causa : *tīra|girim ārūḍhā*

13.26–28 These verses are not Prakrit.

13.27 ***Suvéla***: Mount Tri·kuta or Chitra·kuta.

13.41 The meter of the source text is irregular: the third quarter is long by one mora and the fourth quarter is short four morae. If we take a clue from Jay.'s commentary (*bahuvāriṇaḥ tena subharāḥ paripūrṇā gambhīrā guhā yasya*) we can assume that he reads *subharāḥ* as it is glossed by *paripūrṇāḥ*. SHASTRI's edition does adopt this reading. Also, Jay. dwells quite a bit on the size of the moonstones (*mahācandrakāntaḥ … maṇimahattayā vārimahattvāt gambhīraguhāpūraṇam*), so actually we can also read a *mahā* somewhere in the third *pāda*, changing the reading from *hariṇa/kalaṅka/maṇi/saṃbhava/bahu/vāri/bhara/sugambhīra/guham* to ***hariṇa/kalaṅka/mahā/maṇi/saṃbhava/bahu/vāri/subhara/gambhīra/guham.***

14.1 *prajighāya*: 3rd s. P. *pra√hi*, Pā. 7.3.56.

Canto 14 The perfect tense.

14.2 *nijaghnire*: 3rd pl. pass. *ni√han*, Pā. 7.3.55.

14.6 *turaṅgāḥ* em. : *turaṅgā*

14.9 *ādadire*: Pā. 1.3.20 allows *ātmanepada* of *ā√dā* when not in the sense of opening one's own mouth.

14.13 *gambhīra/vedinaḥ*: see also *Raghuvaṃśa* 4.39, *Śisupālavadha* 5.49.

14.15 *āñjihiṣāṃ cakre*: perfect of desiderative of *√aṃh*, Pā. 6.1.2–3, 7.4.70.

14.19 *ānaśire*: 3rd pl. Ā. *√aṃś* / *√aś* by Pā. 7.4.70, 7.4.72.

14.19 *redhuḥ*: 3rd pl. P. *√rādh* in the sense of harming by Pā. 6.4.123.

14.20 *goṣpadapram*: *ṇamul* meaning "filling the hoof print of a cow" by Pā. 3.4.32.

14.22 *śuśruvān*: nom. s. masc. perf. pt. *√śru* by Pā. 3.2.108.

14.22 *niṣedivān*: nom. s. masc. perf. pt. √*sad* by Pā. 3.2.108.

14.24 *vividhuḥ*: 3rd pl. P. √*vyadh*, *samprasāraṇa* by Pā. 6.1.16.

14.24 *cūrṇayāṃ cakruḥ*: by Pā. 3.1.25.

14.25 *vicakaruḥ*: 3rd pl. P. *vi*√*kṝ*, the root vowel is *guṇa* by Pā. 7.4.11.

14.27 *teruḥ*: 3rd pl. P. √*tṝ*, by Pā. 6.4.122.

14.31 *jīva/nāśam*: *ṇamul* by Pā. 3.4.43.

14.32 *uccakhnāte*: 3rd du. pass. *ut*√*khan*, contracted by Pā. 6.4.98.

14.36 *jighye*: 3rd s. Ā. √*hi*: *gh* replaces *h* by Pā. 7.3.56.

14.38 *ūcuḥ*: *samprasāraṇa* by Pā. 6.1.17.

14.38 *abhituṣṭāva*: retroflexion by Pā. 8.3.65.

14.40 *jakṣuḥ*: √*ghas* replaces √*ad* by Pā. 2.4.40.

14.41 *palāyāṃ cakrire*: Pā. 3.1.37, 8.2.19.

14.44 *ājuhāva*: *samprasāraṇa* by Pā. 6.1.33.

14.44 *ājuhuve*: the meaning "challenge" given by Pā. 1.3.33.

14.46 *ācicāya* and *ācikāya*: the option of gutturalization (*kutva*) given by Pā. 7.3.58.

14.46 *jigāya*: gutturalization by Pā. 7.3.57.

14.47 *ācikyāte*: 3rd du. pass. *ā*√*ci*.

14.47 The beginning of the third *pāda* is unmetrical: -⏑⏑⏑.

14.50 *vidāṃ cakāra*: periphrastic perfect by Pā. 3.1.38.

14.51 *ānaṃhe*: Pā. 7.4.70–71.

14.52 *upajugūha*: Pā. 6.4.89.

14.58 *aṇaka/bhāryā*: Pā. 2.1.54.

14.59 *jugupsām pracakre* em. Mall. : *jugupsān pracakre*. Mall.'s interpretation of Pā. 3.1.40 allows an *upasarga* in the formation of the periphrastic perfect. See also 3.5.

14.60 *prāṇa*: Pā. 7.4.70.

14.60 *vivyathe*: *samprasāraṇa* by Pā. 7.4.68.

14.61 *prajāgarāṃ cakrur*: Pā. 3.1.38.

14.61 Tríjata: Rávana's wife, also at 8.99.

14.62 *oṣāṃ cakre*: Pā. 3.1.38.

14.62 *samāpipye*: Pā. 3.1.29.

14.63 *ānarce*: Pā. 7.4.71.

14.66 *virejuḥ*: contraction optional by Pā. 6.4.125.

14.67 *śaṃśamāṃ cakruḥ*: intensive perfect, the *anusvāra* of the reduplicative syllable given by Pā. 7.4.85.

14.68 *bhrejire/babhrāje*: the option is given by Pā. 6.4.125.

14.69 *ācakhyau*: √*khyā* is the optional substitute for √*cakṣ* by Pā. 2.4.54.

14.70 *āśaśāsire* em. : *āśaśāśire*

14.74 *saṃvivyayuḥ*: Pā. 6.1.17, 46.

14.74 *adhiśiśyire*: Pā. 6.4.82. *vāhanāny adhiśiśyire*: *adhi*√*śi* takes accusative by Pā. 1.4.46.

14.74 *ānarjuḥ*: Pā. 7.4.70–71.

14.75 *adhyuvāsa*: takes accusative by Pā. 1.4.48.

14.76 *nililye*: Pā. 6.4.82.

14.78 *bibhayāṃ cakruḥ*: simultaneous reduplication and periphrasis is optional by Pā. 3.1.39.

14.78 *bhīṣayāṃ cakrire*: *ātmanepada* by Pā. 1.3.68.

14.79 *śiśviyuḥ / śuśuvuḥ*: optional forms by Pā. 6.1.30.

14.84 *ūyuḥ / ūvuḥ*: optional forms from *√ve / √vay* by Pā. 6.1.39.

14.85 *bhasmasāc cakāra*: *taddhita* affix *sāt* + *√kṛ* has the sense of *sam√pad* "to become, to reach the state of" by Pā. 5.4.52.

14.89 *niyemire* em. : *niryemire*

14.91 *jijñāsāṃ cakrire*: perfect of desiderative, *ātmanepada* by Pā. 1.3.57.

14.92 *mamārjuḥ / mamṛjuḥ*: optional by Pā. 3.1.113 and 7.2.114.

14.95 *mumuce*: other translators render this as "put on" etc. and use with this meaning of "put on" seems unique to Bhaṭṭi and is perhaps supported by similar use of *ā√muc* at vv. 17.6 and 20.11, but apart from MW's entry for the *ātmanepada* "to put on Bhaṭṭ. (sch.)" I can find no further evidence for this. Jay. doesn't comment and Mall. says *ath' ôṣṇīṣam śiras/trāṇaṃ vyāmumoca āmuktavān*, which suggests that he may have read *ath' ôṣṇīṣaṃ vyāmumoca* which in any case doesn't scan. It is simplest to understand *√muc* in its primary sense of "let go, leave" even in the *ātmanepada* and translate "he took off his turban" implying that he then put on his helmet.

14.96 *ājaghnuḥ*: Pā. 1.3.28 does not apply as this verb is transitive.

14.99 *ānañcuḥ*: Pā. 7.4.70.

14.106 *vijigye*: *ātmanepada* by Pā. 1.3.19 and *j>g* by 7.3.57.

15.1 *abhaiṣīt*: *vṛddhi* by Pā. 7.2.1.

15.1 *prātiṣṭhipat*: radical vowel becomes *i* by Pā. 7.4.5.

Canto 15 The aorist tense.

15.2 *abhyaguḥ*: √*gā* substituted for √*i* by Pā. 2.4.49, see also 2.4.77, 6.1.96.

15.3 *acikraman*: Pā. 7.4.79, 83. 7.4.94 does not apply because the reduplicative syllable is already *guru*.

15.3 *abhyaṣican*: retroflexion by Pā. 8.3.63.

15.4 *adāṅkṣuḥ*: Pā. 8.2.41.

15.5 *ajīgaṇat*: Pā. 7.4.97.

15.5 *abuddha*: the *s* marker of the aorist is elided by Pā. 8.2.26.

15.6 *vyalipat*: Pā. 3.1.53.

15.6 *apāt*: Pā. 2.4.77.

15.7 *prāvṛtat*: *parasmaipada* by Pā. 1.3.91, 3.1.55.

15.7 *draṣṭum*/*adrākṣīt*: Pā. 6.1.58 and *vṛddhi* in the aorist by Pā. 7.2.1.

15.9 *avādīt*: Pā. 7.2.3.

15.9 *āhvaḥ*: 2nd s. P. √*hve* Pā. 3.1.53.

15.9 *pratyavādi*: 3rd s. pass. Pā. 3.1.66, 6.4.104.

15.11 *mā ... na vadhīḥ*: double negative aorist injunctive.

15.15 *avavañcanta*: Pā. 1.3.69.

15.16 *ārpipaḥ*: Pā. 7.3.36, 1.1.59, 6.1.2–3.

15.17 *avyayīḥ*: 2nd s. P. √*vyay* (1st conj.), Pā. 7.2.5.

15.19 *ajugupsiṣṭhāḥ*: 2nd s. P. aorist of desiderative.

15.19 *aididhaḥ*: 2nd s. P. √*edh*.

15.21 *nyavīvṛtat*: Pā. 7.4.7.

15.21 *upāyaṃsta*: Pā. 1.3.75.

15.25 *anaṃsīt*: Pā. 7.2.73.

15.25 *aluṭhan*: Pā. 1.3.91.

15.25 *prādudruvan*: Pā. 3.1.48.

15.26 *avāsiṣuḥ*: Pā. 7.2.73.

15.27 *nyapaptan*: Pā. 7.4.19.

15.28 *āhvāsta*: Pā. 1.3.31, 3.1.54.

15.29 *adhāt/adhāsīt*: 3rd s. √*dhe* "to suck, drink," optional by Pā. 2.4.78.

15.30 *aśvatām*: 3rd du./*aśiśviyat*: 3rd s. √*śvi* by Pā. 3.2.58.

15.30 *aglucat/aglocīt*: Pā. 3.1.58.

15.31 *nyamāṅkṣuḥ*: 3rd pl. *ni*√*majj*, Pā. 7.1.60.

15.33 *pratyavāsthita*: 3rd s. Ā. *prati-ava*√*sthā*, *ātmanepada* by Pā. 1.3.22, 8.2.27.

15.34 *ayuddha*: 3rd s. Ā. √*yudh*, Pā. 8.2.26.

15.35 *ayutsata*: Pā. 1.2.10.

15.35 *nirāsthat*: 3rd s. *nir*√*as* "to throw," Pā. 3.1.52, 7.4.17.

15.36 *abibhīṣata*: Pā. 7.3.40.

15.37 *hastavartam*: *ṇamul* by Pā. 3.4.39, 46.

15.41 *vadhiṣṭa*: √*vadh* for √*han* by Pā. 2.4.43.

15.42 *vyarāsiṣuḥ*: Pā. 7.2.7.

15.42 *āhvanta*: Pā. 3.1.54.

15.42 *apiplavan*: Pā. 7.4.81.

15.42 *ababhāsan*: Pā. 7.4.3.

15.48 *atastarat*: Pā. 7.4.95.

15.50 *ajaran*: Pā. 3.1.58, 7.4.16.

15.50 *āhvan*: Pā. 3.1.53.

15.53 *prāpaptat*: Pā. 7.4.19.

15.53 *alāsīt*: 3rd s. P. √*lā*, Pā. 7.2.73.

15.56 *aloṭhiṣṭa*: Pā. 1.3.91.

15.56 *asusruvat*: Pā. 3.1.48.

15.57 *anvārat*: Pā. 3.1.56, 7.4.16.

15.57 *abodhi*: with an active sense by Pā. 3.1.61.

15.58 *peṣṭum ārambhi*: passive aorist with infinitive.

15.60 *atatvarat*: Pā. 7.4.95.

15.60 *aciceṣṭat*: Pā. 7.4.96.

15.61 *ārukṣan*: Pā. 3.1.45.

15.61 *adhāvīt*: √*dhū*, "to shake," Pā. 7.2.44.

15.62 *samāślikṣat*: Pā. 3.1.45.

15.63 *sveṣām apy adayiṣṭa na*: genitive by Pā. 2.3.52.

15.63 *agrahīt*: Pā. 7.2.5.

15.66 *prodayaṃsīt*: 3rd s. P. *pra-ud√yam*, Pā. 7.2.73.

15.67 *ādīpi*: optional by Pā. 3.1.61.

15.68 *aśīśatat*: causative of *√śad*, Pā. 7.3.42.

15.70 *astāviṣuḥ*: Pā. 7.2.72.

15.71 *aśiśriyat*: Pā. 3.1.48.

15.72 *apaprathat*: Pā. 7.4.95.

15.72 *acikīrttat* em. Pā. 7.4.6–7, 7.1.101 : *acikīrtat*

15.75 *niragātām*: 3rd du. Pā. 2.4.45.

15.79 *prādudruvan*: Pā. 3.1.48.

15.91 *āsthatām*: 3rd du. *√as*, Pā. 7.4.17, see also 6.19 and 15.35.

15.99 *apisphavat*: from *√sphāy* by Pā. 7.3.41.

15.103 *amṛṣmahi*: by Pā. 3.3.132 the aorist can be used in the sense of future hopes. See also 7.101.

15.111 *samanātsīt*: 3rd s. P. *sam√nah*, Pā. 8.2.34.

15.111 *amārjīt*/*amārkṣīt*: Pā. 7.2.114.

15.111 *ababhāsat*: Pā. 7.4.3.

15.112 We read *samanāddhām* with Mall. for *samanaddhām* as it is better grammar by Pā. 7.2.1.

15.114 *akokūyiṣṭa*: 3rd s. aorist intensive *√ku* (1st class).

15.116 ***abebhidiṣṭa***: 3rd s. aorist intensive, Pā. 6.4.48–49.

16.1 ***kariṣyāmi/kariṣyate***: Pā. 7.2.70.

Canto 16 The simple future.

16.2 ***hrepayiṣyati***: Pā. 7.3.36.

16.3 ***tokṣyati***: Pā. 7.2.41.

16.5 ***bhokṣyate***: *ātmanepada* by Pā. 1.3.66.

16.5 ***vakṣyati***: 3rd s. √*vah*, Pā. 8.2.31, 41.

16.7 ***vartiṣyate***: Pā. 7.2.59.

16.9–10 ***saṃdarśiṣye*** and ***drakṣye***: the option is provided by Pā. 6.4.62.

16.12 ***kalpiṣyate***: Pā. 1.3.93.

16.15 ***tāta***: Jay. takes this to mean "father" but Mall. takes this in the sense of "child" as a vocative for Kumbha·karna.

16.17 ***samucchokṣyati***: 3rd s. P. *sam-ut*√*śuṣ*, Pā. 7.2.59.

16.17 ***dhakṣyati***: Pā. 8.2.31, 37.

16.21 Pā. 3.3.144–146.

16.26 ***vinaṅkṣyati***: Pā. 7.1.60.

16.26 ***kṣipraṃ, tūrṇam***: Pā. 3.3.133.

16.28 ***pat/kāṣī***: Pā. 6.3.54.

16.29 ***saṃnatsyāmi***: Pā. 8.2.34.

16.36 By Pā. 3.2.112 the future is used for the past when reminiscing.

Canto 17 The imperfect tense.

17.3 **The flesh of the gods** (*sur'|āmiṣam*): possibly flesh intended for the gods at sacrifices, but if analysed as *sur''|āmiṣam* it could also mean "wine and flesh."

17.4 ***nyaśyan***: 3rd pl. impf. *ni√śo*, Pā. 7.3.71.

17.6 ***āmuñcat***: also found with this meaning at 20.11, but see note to 14.95.

17.15 ***atṛṇeṭ***: 3rd s. P. impf. *√tṛh* Pā. 7.3.92.

17.16 ***hatās ten' âvidur dviṣaḥ***: Mall. breaks the words differently to Jay., reading *hatās te n' avidur dvisaḥ*, "the enemy did not know they had been struck."

17.19 ***ājuhūṣat***: Pā. 6.1.33, impf. of desid.

17.19 ***vyaṣṭabhnāt***: Pā. 3.1.82, retroflexion persists in spite of the augment by Pā. 8.3.67.

17.21 ***m'' âparādhnot ... mā ... nigṛhṇāḥ***: *mā* is not permitted with augmented imperfect by Pā. 3.3.175 but is permitted with the unaugmented imperfect by 6.4.74. Jay. therefore reads *n' âparādhnot*.

17.22 ***khaḍga|kṛṣṭaḥ***: see *vārtika* on Pā. 3.2.102, *praharaṇ'|ârthebhyaḥ pare niṣṭhā|saptamyau bhavataḥ* which reverses the order of the compound.

17.32 **Meat intended for the gods** (*sur'|âmiṣaiḥ*): see note to 17.3.

17.33 His **hand is still wet** (*pāṇim ārdram*) from sharing food.

17.34 ***ājānāḥ***: 2nd s. P. impf. *ā√jñā* Pā. 7.3.79.

17.43 ***asphāvayatām***: 3rd du. caus. *√sphāy* Pā. 7.3.41.

17.43 ***akṣipyat / akṣipat***: *√kṣip* conjugated as class IV and class VI.

17.48 *arodīt/arodat*: 3rd s. P. √*rud* as class II and class I, Pā. 7.3.98–99.

17.49 *nyarundhan/āruṇat*: √*rudh* as 3rd pl. P. *ni*√*rudh* class 6 and as 3rd s. P. *ā*√*rudh* class VII.

17.61 *adviṣuḥ / adviṣan*: option given by Pā. 3.4.112.

17.71 *samaraut*: Pā. 7.3.89.

17.73 *samārāryanta*: 3rd pl. Ā. impf. of intensive *sam*√*ṛ*. Pā. 7.4.29–30.

17.74 *cela/knopam*: *ṇamul* by Pā. 3.4.33.

17.77 *aśīyata*: 3rd s. pass. √*śad* by Pā. 1.3.60.

17.82 *askunāt* here and *pratyaskunot* in the next verse: Pā. 3.1.82.

17.99 *dhuryān*: Pā. 4.4.77.

Canto 18 The perfect tense.

18.14 Rahu (*svar/bhānuḥ*): the lunar node, the demon who consumes the sun during an eclipse.

18.16 Pā. 3.3.142.

18.17 *bravīti*: present in the sense of the past by Pā. 3.2.121.

18.18 *tyajasi*: present in the sense of the past by Pā. 3.2.122.

18.22 *veda*: 1st s. P. present √*vid* "to know" by Pā. 3.4.82–83.

18.25 *cañcūryate*: intensive of √*car* by Pā. 3.1.24, 7.4.87 etc., to move contemptuously.

18.25 *bhūmayanti*: Pā. 6.4.158.

18.25 *kanayanti*: Pā. 5.3.64.

18.27 *ujjihīṣe*: 2nd s. Ā. *ud√hā*, Pā. 7.4.46.

18.29 *saṃvidrate*: 3rd pl. Ā. *sam√vid*, optional by Pā. 7.1.7.

Canto 19 The optative mood.

19.3 *devadryañcaḥ*: turned towards the divine, Pā. 6.3.92.

19.6 The optative is optional where there is an expression of disapproval and the word *katham* by Pā. 3.3.143.

19.7 *āmantrayeta*: for the use of the optative with *ā√mantr* see Pā. 3.3.161.

19.16 *tvam*: the commentators read *kim* for *tvam* and cite Pā. 3.3. 144.

19.17 *jātu*: with optative by Pā. 3.3.147; optative with expressions of incredulity by Pā. 3.3.145.

19.18 For *yacca* with an expression of censure see Pā. 3.3.149.

19.19 *yacca*: with an expression of wonder by Pā. 3.3.150.

19.19 *api ... praśiṣyāḥ*: optative with *api* implying certainty by Pā. 3.3.152.

19.20 *jahyās*: optative with an expression of desire by Pā. 3.3.153.

19.25 *icchā me param" ānandeḥ*: Pā. 3.3.157.

19.25 *icchet*: in the sense of the present tense by Pā. 3.3.160.

19.26 *vadhyāḥ*: Pā. 2.4.42.

19.28 *avaseyāḥ*: Pā. 6.4.67.

Canto 20 The imperative mood.

20.6 *na ... astu*: imperative by Pā. 3.3.173.

20.6 ***edhi***: 2nd s. imp. of √*i* by Pā. 6.4.119, 101 etc.

20.10 ***jahīhi*** / *jahihi* / *jahāhi*: options given by Pā. 6.4.116–117.

20.11 ***dhūpāya***: 2nd s. P. imp., the stem is given by Pā. 3.1.28.

20.11 ***āmuñca***: also found with this meaning at 17.6, but see note to 14.95.

20.12 ***jahi***: 3rd s. P. imp. √*han* by Pā. 6.4.36.

20.12 **The five products of the cow** (*pañca|gavyam*): milk, curds, butter, urine and dung.

20.13 ***bhavatāt***: provided benediction is intended, the 2nd s. P. imp. ending *hi* is optionally replaced by *tāt* by Pā. 7.1.35.

20.17 ***sma bhava***: imperative with *sma* by Pā. 3.3.165.

20.17 ***anuśādhi***: √*śā* for √*śās* by Pā. 6.4.35.

20.18 ***uttiṣṭhasva***: *ātmanepada* by Pā. 1.3.24.

20.18 ***pratiṣṭhasva***: *ātmanepada* by Pā. 1.3.22.

20.18 ***draṣṭavyam***: Pā. 3.3.169.

20.21 ***ādadai*** em. : *ādade*

20.22 ***hṛl|lekha|karī***: Pā. 6.3.50 and 3.3.20.

20.23 **Eat food from Bharata's house**: the Sanskrit *aśāna Bharatād bhogān* also implies taking sexual pleasure from Bharata.

20.29 ***tvaṃ punīhi punīh' îti punan vāyo, jagat|trayam***: Jay. comments: *punīhi punīh' îti jagat|trayam punaḥ punaḥ punāmi, bhṛśaṃ vā punām' îty abhiprāyaḥ*, "The meaning of *punīhi punīhi* is 'again and again I purify the trio of worlds' or 'I purify vigorously.'" By Pā. 3.4.2 the second person imperative is doubled to denote *kriyā/samabhihāra*, "repetition of the action." By Pā. 3.4.4 it is specified that a tag phrase should be in accordance with the verb used in the imperative, hence the repetition of the root √*pū* in the tag.

20.29–33 Verses 29–33 illustrate an interesting series of *sūtras* (Pa. 3.4.2–5) on the iterative use of the imperative.

20.30 ***kham aṭa, dyām aṭ', âṭ' ôrvīm ity aṭantyaḥ***: Pā. 3.4.3 applies optionally to a combination of actions.

20.31 ***jaganti dhatsva dhatsv' êti dadhatī***: Pā. 3.4.2 applies again.

20.32 ***jahi, nabho bhrama***: Brough takes this imperative to be compounded with *nabhaḥ* to read *jahi/nabho bhrama*, "wander in a strike-the-clouds fashion," which, though allowed by the grammarians, is not the interpretation supported by the commentators.

20.32 ***rasān saṃhara, dīpyasva, dhvāntaṃ jahi, nabho bhrama, it' īhamānaḥ***: Pā. 3.4.3 applied again to a combination of actions (see 20.30) but now by 3.4.5 we get a tag phrase *samānya/vacana*, "denoting a common action."

20.33 ***svarge vidyasva, bhuvy āsva, bhujaṅga/nilaye bhava, evaṃ vasan***: Pā. 3.4.3 and 3.4.5 apply as for 20.32.

Canto 21 The conditional mood.

21.2 ***pakṣapāto me dharmād anyatra***: Jay. comments *dharmād anyatra adharme na me pakṣapāto 'nurāgaḥ*, but this seems to be forcing it a bit: it seems better to take the whole of the second half of the verse as a separate clause from the first.

21.4 ***Rāma*** em. : *Rāmaḥ*

21.15 ***avartsyaṃstarām***: *avartsyan* (3rd pl. cond. √*vṛt*) plus superlative *tarām* by Pā. 5.3.57.

21.18 Pā. 3.3.145, 147.

21.21 ***sugandhi/sapuṣpa/tarus*** em. : *sugandhi/puṣpa/tarus*

Canto 22 The periphrastic future.

22.10 ***draṣṭāraḥ***: both KARANDIKAR & KARANDIKAR (1982) and LEONARDI (1972) translate this with *janāḥ* as the logical subject against the commentators and thus need to supply an object but it clearly shares *bhavatā* in the first line as the logical subject.

22.10 ***Yāmun'/âmbu/kṣat'/âṃhasaḥ***: Mall. reads *Yamun"/âmbu/kṣat'/âṃhasaḥ*.

22.12 We prefer to read ***sākṣinaḥ*** with the commentators rather than *śākhinaḥ*.

22.17 ***labdhā he***: 1st s. Ā. periphrastic future √*labh* by Pā. 7.4.52.

22.32 ***adhigatam ukti/mārga/citram*** needs to be divided thus *adhigata/mukti/mārga/citram* in order to get the second meaning "**marvelous when its ways of discharging have been learned.**"

22.33 ***hast'/ādarśa***: variants are *hast'/āmarṣa* and *hast'/āmarśa*.

22.35 ***Śrīdhara/sūnu*** em. : *Śrīdhara/sena*

22.35 ***bhavatāt***: provided benediction is intended, the 2nd s. P. imp. ending *hi* is optionally replaced by *tāt* by Pā. 7.1.35.

GLOSSARY OF NAMES AND EPITHETS

Airávata (*Airāvata*; synonym: *Airāvaṇa*) Indra's elephant, regarded as the prototype of the elephant race and the supporter of the eastern quarter.

Ángada (*Aṅgada*) A monkey, the son of Valin.

Atikáya (*Atikāya*, "of excessive body") Son of Rávana.

Bali (*Bali*) A demon.

Bharata (*Bharata*, synonym: *Rāmānuja*, "younger brother of Rama") Younger brother of Rama, son of Kékayi.

Brahma (*Brahmā*, synonym: *Svayambhū*, "the self-existent") The Creator.

Dasha·ratha (*Daśaratha*, "having ten chariots") The father of Rama.

Devántaka (*Devāntaka*, "killer of the gods") Son of Rávana.

Gáruda (*Garuḍa*, synonyms: *Suparṇa*, "having fine feathers;" *Tārkṣya; Vainateya*) a mythical bird, the vehicle of Vishnu.

Hánuman (*Hanumān*, synonyms: *Hanūmān; Anilātmaja, Marutsuta, Mārutātmaja, Māruti, Pavanaja, Pavanasuta, Pavanātmaja, Prābhañjani*, "son of the wind;" *Marutvat*) The monkey hero, son of the wind.

Indra (*Indra*, synonyms: *Balabhid*, "splitter of Bala;" *Baladvis*, "enemy of Bala;" *Devendra*, "lord of the gods;" *Duścyavana*, "who cannot be toppled;" *Hari; Maghavat; Puruhūta*, "much invoked;" *Pūtakratu*, "pure minded;" *Sahasracakṣus*, "thousand-eyed;" *Śakra; Saṃkrandana*, "roaring;" *Śatakratu*, "having one hundred rites;" *Śatamanyu*, "whose wrath is one-hundredfold;" *Tridaśendra*, "lord of the thirty or thirty-three gods;" *Vajrāyudha*, "whose weapon is the thuderbolt;" *Vṛtraśatru*, "enemy of Vritra") Chief of the gods.

Índrajit (*Indrajit*, "defeater of Indra;" synonyms: *Meghanāda*, "who thunders like a cloud;" *Puruhūtadvis*, "enemy of Indra;" *Rāvaṇi*, "son of Rávana;" *Śatrujit*, "conqueror of Indra") Eldest son of Rávana.

Jánaka (*Janaka*) Father of Sita.

Kákutstha (*Kākutstha*, "descendant of Kakútstha") Rama or his brothers.

Kaushálya (*Kauśalyā*) Mother of Rama.

Kékayi (*Kekayī*, synonym: *Kaikeyī*) Mother of Bharata.

Kishkíndha Name of a mountain (*Kiṣkindha*) and a district (*Kiṣkindhā*).

Kubéra (*Kubera*, synonym: *Dhanada*, "giver of wealth;" *Yakṣendra*, "lord of the *yakṣas*") The god of wealth.

Kumára (*Kumāra*) The god of war.

Kumbha (*Kumbha*, synonym: *Kaumbhakarṇi*) Son of Kumbha·karna.

Kumbha·karna (*Kumbhakarṇa*, "jug-ears") a giant demon.

Lákshmana (*Lakṣmaṇa*, synonyms: *Rāmānuja*, "younger brother of Rama;" *Saumitri*, "son of Sumítra") Brother of Rama, son of Sumítra.

Lakshmi (*Lakṣmī* "wealth, glory;" synonym: *Śrī*) The goddess of wealth and glory, the consort of Vishnu.

Marícha (*Mārīca*) Demon henchman of Rávana.

Mátali (*Mātali*) Indra's charioteer.

Narántaka (*Narāntaka*, "killer of men") Son of Rávana.

Nikúmbha (*Nikumbha*, synonym: *Kaumbhakarṇi*) Son of Kumbha·karna.

Párashu·rama (*Paraśurāma*, "Rama with the Axe;" synonym: *Jāmadagnya*, "the son of Jamad·agni") son of Jamad·agni and the sixth avatar of Vishnu.

Paulástya (*Paulastya*, "descendant of Pulásti or Pulástya") Name of Rávana and Vibhíshana.

Púshpaka (*Puṣpaka*) Name of Rávana's chariot stolen from Kubéra.

RAGHU (*Raghu*) Great-grandfather of Rama.

RAHU (*Rāhu*, synonym: *Svarbhānu*) The ecliptic demon.

RAMA (*Rāma*, synonyms: *Dāśarathi*, "son of Dasha·ratha;" *Kauśalyāyani*, "son of Kaushálya;" *Raghunandana*, "joy of Raghu;" *Raghūttama*, "best of Raghu's line;" *Rāghava*, "descendant of Raghu") Son of Dasha·ratha, incarnation of Vishnu. See also Párashu·rama.

RÁVANA (*Rāvaṇa*, synonyms: *Daśagrīva*, "ten-necked;" *Daśamukha; Daśavaktra; Daśavadana; Daśānana; Daśāsya*, "ten-faced;" *Kratudvis*, "hostile to sacrifice") King of the Demons.

RUDRA Name of a the god of the storm, the wind and the hunt.

SHATRÚGHNA (*Śatrughna*, synonym: *Rāmānuja*, "younger brother of Rama") Brother of Rama, son of Sumítra.

SHIVA (*Śiva* "the Auspicious One;" synonyms: *Hara*; *Pinākin*, "possessor of the Pináka bow;" *Śaṅkara; Śambhu; Sthāṇu*) Euphemistic name of the destroying deity.

SHURPA·NAKHA (*Śūrpaṇakhā*) A demoness, niece of Rávana.

SITA (*Sītā*, synonyms: *Janakātmajā, Jānakī*, "daughter of Jánaka;" *Maithilī*, "Princess of Míthila;" *Vaidehī*, princess of Vidéha) Daughter of Jánaka, Wife of Rama.

SUGRÍVA (*Sugrīva*: "with a beautiful neck") King of the Monkeys, brother of Valin.

SUMÁNTRA (*Sumantra*) Rama's charioteer.

SUMÍTRA (*Sumitrā*) Mother of Lákshmana.

TARÁ (*Tārā*) Mother of Ángada, sister-in-law to Sugríva.

TRI·JATA (*Trijaṭā*, "wearing three braids of hair") A demoness, friend to Sita.

TRI·SHIRAS (*Triśiras*, "three-headed") Son of Rávana.

VALIN (*Vālin*) Brother of Sugríva, ally of Rávana.

VASHÍSHTHA (*Vaśiṣṭha*) Name of a sage.

VASU (*Vasu*) Name of a god.

VIBHÍSHANA (*Vibhīṣaṇa*) Brother of Rávana, ally of Rama.

VISHNU (*Viṣṇu*, synonyms: *Baliṃdama*, "controller of Bali;" *Hari; Nārāyaṇa*) The supreme person.

VISHVA·MITRA (*Viśvāmitra*, synonym: *Gādheya*, "descendant of Gadhi") An ancient sage, counselor of Rama in his youth.

YAMA (Yama, synonyms: *Kṛtānta*, "the terminator") God of death.

THE CLAY SANSKRIT LIBRARY

Current Volumes

For further details please consult the CSL website.

1. The Emperor of the Sorcerers (*Bṛhatkathāślokasaṃgraha*) (vol. 1 of 2) by *Budhasvāmin*. Sir James Mallinson
2. Heavenly Exploits (*Divyāvadāna*) Joel Tatelman
3. Maha·bhárata III: The Forest (*Vanaparvan*) (vol. 4 of 4) William J. Johnson
4. Much Ado about Religion (*Āgamaḍambara*) by *Bhaṭṭa Jayanta*. Csaba Dezső
5. The Birth of Kumára (*Kumārasaṃbhava*) by *Kālidāsa*. David Smith
6. Ramáyana I: Boyhood (*Bālakāṇḍa*) by *Vālmīki*. Robert P. Goldman
7. The Epitome of Queen Lilávati (*Līlāvatīsāra*) (vol. 1 of 2) by *Jinaratna*. R.C.C. Fynes
8. Ramáyana II: Ayódhya (*Ayodhyākāṇḍa*) by *Vālmīki*. Sheldon I. Pollock
9. Love Lyrics (*Amaruśataka, Śatakatraya & Caurapañcāśikā*) by *Amaru, Bhartṛhari & Bilhaṇa*. Greg Bailey & Richard Gombrich
10. What Ten Young Men Did (*Daśakumāracarita*) by *Daṇḍin*. Isabelle Onians
11. Three Satires (*Kaliviḍambana, Kalāvilāsa & Bhallaṭaśataka*) by *Nīlakaṇṭha, Kṣemendra & Bhallaṭa* Somadeva Vasudeva
12. Ramáyana IV: Kishkíndha (*Kiṣkindhākāṇḍa*) by *Vālmīki*. Rosalind Lefeber
13. The Emperor of the Sorcerers (*Bṛhatkathāślokasaṃgraha*) (vol. 2 of 2) by *Budhasvāmin*. Sir James Mallinson
14. Maha·bhárata IX: Shalya (*Śalyaparvan*) (vol. 1 of 2) Justin Meiland

15. Rákshasa's Ring (*Mudrārākṣasa*)
by *Viśākhadatta*. Michael Coulson
16. Messenger Poems (*Meghadūta, Pavanadūta & Haṃsadūta*)
by *Kālidāsa, Dhoyī & Rūpa Gosvāmin*. Sir James Mallinson
17. Ramáyana III: The Forest (*Araṇyakāṇḍa*)
by *Vālmiki*. Sheldon I. Pollock
18. The Epitome of Queen Lilávati (*Līlāvatīsāra*) (vol. 2 of 2)
by *Jinaratna*. R.C.C. Fynes
19. Five Discourses on Worldly Wisdom (*Pañcatantra*)
by *Viṣṇuśarman*. Patrick Olivelle
20. Ramáyana V: Súndara (*Sundarakāṇḍa*) by *Vālmiki*.
Robert P. Goldman & Sally J. Sutherland Goldman
21. Maha·bhárata II: The Great Hall (*Sabhāparvan*)
Paul Wilmot
22. The Recognition of Shakúntala (*Abhijñānaśākuntala*) (Kashmir Recension) by *Kālidāsa*. Somadeva Vasudeva
23. Maha·bhárata VII: Drona (*Droṇaparvan*) (vol. 1 of 4)
Vaughan Pilikian
24. Rama Beyond Price (*Anargharāghava*)
by *Murāri*. Judit Törzsök
25. Maha·bhárata IV: Viráta (*Virāṭaparvan*)
Kathleen Garbutt
26. Maha·bhárata VIII: Karna (*Karṇaparvan*) (vol. 1 of 2)
Adam Bowles
27. "The Lady of the Jewel Necklace" & "The Lady who Shows her Love" (*Ratnāvalī & Priyadarśikā*) by *Harṣa*.
Wendy Doniger
28. The Ocean of the Rivers of Story (*Kathāsaritsāgara*) (vol. 1 of 7)
by *Somadeva*. Sir James Mallinson
29. Handsome Nanda (*Saundarananda*)
by *Aśvaghoṣa*. Linda Covill
30. Maha·bhárata IX: Shalya (*Śalyaparvan*) (vol. 2 of 2)
Justin Meiland
31. Rama's Last Act (*Uttararāmacarita*) by *Bhavabhūti*.
Sheldon Pollock. Foreword by Girish Karnad

32. "Friendly Advice" (*Hitopadeśa*) by *Nārāyaṇa* &
 "King Víkrama's Adventures" (*Vikramacarita*). Judit Törzsök
33. Life of the Buddha (*Buddhacarita*)
 by *Aśvaghoṣa*. Patrick Olivelle
34. Maha·bhárata V: Preparations for War (*Udyogaparvan*) (vol. 1 of 2)
 Kathleen Garbutt. Foreword by Gurcharan Das
35. Maha·bhárata VIII: Karna (*Karṇaparvan*) (vol. 2 of 2)
 Adam Bowles
36. Maha·bhárata V: Preparations for War (*Udyogaparvan*) (vol. 2 of 2)
 Kathleen Garbutt
37. Maha·bhárata VI: Bhishma (*Bhīṣmaparvan*) (vol. 1 of 2)
 Including the "Bhagavad Gita" in Context
 Alex Cherniak. Foreword by Ranajit Guha
38. The Ocean of the Rivers of Story (*Kathāsaritsāgara*) (vol. 2 of 7)
 by *Somadeva*. Sir James Mallinson
39. "How the Nagas were Pleased" (*Nāgānanda*) by *Harṣa* &
 "The Shattered Thighs" (*Ūrubhaṅga*) by *Bhāsa*.
 Andrew Skilton
40. Gita·govínda: Love Songs of Radha and Krishna (*Gītagovinda*)
 by *Jayadeva*. Lee Siegel. Foreword by Sudipta Kaviraj
41. "Bouquet of Rasa" & "River of Rasa" (*Rasamañjarī & Rasataraṅgiṇī*)
 by *Bhānudatta*. Sheldon Pollock
42 Garland of the Buddha's Past Lives (*Jātakamālā*) (vol. 1 of 2)
 by *Āryaśūra*. Justin Meiland
43. Maha·bhárata XII: Peace (*Śāntiparvan*) (vol. 3 of 5)
 "The Book of Liberation" (*Mokṣadharma*). Alexander Wynne
44. Little Clay Cart (*Mṛcchakaṭikā*) by *Śūdraka*.
 Diwakar Acharya. Foreword by Partha Chatterjee
45 Bhatti's Poem: The Death of Rávana (*Bhaṭṭikāvya*)
 by *Bhaṭṭi*. Oliver Fallon

To Appear in 2009

Garland of the Buddha's Past Lives (*Jātakamālā*) (vol. 2 of 2)
by *Āryaśūra*. Justin Meiland

How Úrvashi Was Won (*Vikramorvaśīya*) by *Kālidāsa*
Velcheru Narayana Rao & David Shulman

Maha·bhárata VI: Bhishma (*Bhīṣmaparvan*) (vol. 2 of 2)
Alex Cherniak

Maha·bhárata XIV: The Horse Sacrifice (*Āśvamedhikaparvan*)
Greg Bailey

On Self-Surrender, Compassion, and the Mission of a Goose:
Sanskrit Poetry from the South (*Ātmārpaṇastuti, Dayāśataka & Haṃsasaṃdeśa*) by *Appaya Dīkṣita* and *Vedāntadeśika*.
Yigal Bronner & David Shulman

Princess Kadámbari (*Kādambarī*) (vol. 1 of 3)
by *Bāṇa*. David Smith

The Quartet of Causeries (*Caturbhāṇī*)
by *Śūdraka, Śyāmilaka, Vararuci & Īśvaradatta*.
Csaba Dezső & Somadeva Vasudeva

Seven Hundred Elegant Verses (*Āryāsaptaśatī*)
by *Govardhana*. Friedhelm Hardy